T0320464

Disruptive Developments in Biomedical Applications

This book covers advancements and future challenges in biomedical application development using disruptive technologies like artificial intelligence (AI), the Internet of Things (IoT), and signal processing. The book is divided into four main sections, namely, medical image processing using AI; IoT and biomedical devices; biomedical signal processing; and electronic health records, including advances in biomedical systems. It includes different case studies of biomedical applications using different AI algorithms related to diabetes, skin cancer, breast cancer, cervical cancer, and osteoarthritis.

Features:

- Covers different technologies like AI, IoT, and signal processing in the context of biomedical applications.
- Reviews medical image analysis, disease detection, and prediction.
- Comprehends the advantage of recent technologies for medical record keeping through electronic health records (EHRs).
- Presents state-of-the-art research in the field of biomedical engineering using various physiological signals.
- Explores different bio sensors used in healthcare applications using IOT.

This book is aimed at graduate students and researchers in AI, medical imaging, biomedical engineering, and IoT.

Disruptive Developments in Biomedical Applications

Edited by Swati V. Shinde, Parikshit N. Mahalle, Varsha Bendre and Oscar Castillo

CRC Press
Taylor & Francis Group
Boca Raton London New York

CRC Press is an imprint of the
Taylor & Francis Group, an **informa** business

First edition published 2023
by CRC Press
6000 Broken Sound Parkway NW, Suite 300, Boca Raton, FL 33487–2742

and by CRC Press
4 Park Square, Milton Park, Abingdon, Oxon, OX14 4RN

CRC Press is an imprint of Taylor & Francis Group, LLC

ISBN: 978-1-032-22470-1 (hbk)
ISBN: 978-1-032-22471-8 (pbk)
ISBN: 978-1-003-27269-4 (ebk)

DOI: 10.1201/9781003272694

Typeset in Times
by Apex CoVantage, LLC

Contents

PART I   AI/ML for Biomedical Applications

PART II   IOT and Smart Healthcare

PART III   Bio-Signal Processing

PART IV   Electronic Health Records

PART V   *Recent Devlopement in Biomedical Applications*

Editor Biographies

Swati V. Shinde holds a PhD in computer science and engineering from Swami Ramanand Teerth Marathwada University, Nanded. She has a total of 22 years of teaching experience and currently is Professor of Computer Engineering and Dean—Research & Developments in Pimpri Chinchwad College of Engineering (PCCoE), Pune. She worked as a HOD-IT for seven years in PCCoE. Her research interests include machine learning, deep learning, soft computing, artificial neural network, and fuzzy logic. She has published 95+ research papers in reputed conferences and journals. Five of these are published in the prestigious SCI indexed journals. She has received the five Best Paper Awards at different IEEE Conferences. She has filed five research patents and received the DST grant of almost Rs. 36 lakhs for the research project. She also has received a research grant from SPPU University, Pune, the International FDP grant from SPPU, and also the conference grant from AICTE. She is a certified trainer and ambassador of NVDIA's Deep Learning Institute. She was conferred the "Dr. APJ Abdul Kalam Women Achievers Award" by IItechBanglore. She was awarded the Indo Global Engineering Excellence Award by Indo Global Chamber of Commerce Industries and agriculture. She has delivered 20+ research talks in various workshops, STTPs, etc. Currently she is a SPPU-approved PhD supervisor and is guiding four PhD research scholars.

Dr. Parikshit N. Mahalle is a senior member of IEEE and Professor and Head of the Department of Artificial Intelligence and Data Science at Vishwakarma Institute of Information Technology, Pune, India. He completed his PhD at Aalborg University, Denmark, and continued as Post-Doc Researcher at CMI, Copenhagen, Denmark. He has 22+ years of teaching and research experience. He is a member of the Board of Studies in Computer Engineering, Ex-Chairman Information Technology, SPPU, and various universities and autonomous colleges across India. He has nine patents, 200+ research publications (Google Scholar citations-2020 plus, H index-21, and Scopus Citations are 986 with H index -14) and has authored/edited 40+ books with Springer, CRC Press, Cambridge University Press, etc. He is editor in chief for IGI Global—*International Journal of Rough Sets and Data Analysis*; Associate Editor for IGI Global—*International Journal of Synthetic Emotions* and *Inter-science International Journal of Grid and Utility Computing*; member of the Editorial Review Board for IGI Global—*International Journal of Ambient Computing and Intelligence*. His research interests are machine learning, data science, algorithms, Internet of Things, identity management and security. He is a recognized PhD guide of SSPU, Pune, and s guiding seven PhD students in the area of IoT and machine learning. Recently, four students successfully defended their PhDs. He is also the recipient of "Best Faculty Award" from Sinhgad Institutes and Cognizant Technologies Solutions. He has delivered 200+ lectures at the national and international level.

Varsha Bendre received her bachelor's degree in electronics and telecommunication engineering from Saint Gadge Baba Amravati University, Amravati, and her ME degree from Savitribai Phule Pune University in 2000 and 2010 respectively. After her ME, she completed her PhD in the area of nanotechnology and low power VLSI at Savitribai Phule Pune University, Pune, and Maharashtra, India, in Jan 2020. The area of her research work is analog circuit design at a very deep submicron technology using carbon nanotube field effect transistors. She has published five research papers in various SCI/Scopus indexed journals and 30 research papers in peer-reviewed international conferences.

She has a total teaching experience of 18 years and is currently working as an associate professor at Pimpri Chinchwad College of Engineering, Pune. She has worked as a reviewer of various SCI listed journals such as *International Journal of Electronics and Letters* for the IEEE Transactions on Circuits and Systems II: Express Briefs. She also worked as a reviewer for various international conferences like the IEEE International Symposium on Circuits and Systems (ISCAS-2020), International Conference on Pervasive Computing 2020 (ICPC—2020), IEEE International Conference on Microelectronics, Computing and Communication (MicroCom2016), the 6th International Conference on Cloud Computing and Big Data Engineering (Confluence 2016), and the International Conference on Computing, Communication, Control and Automation (ICCUBEA 2015, 2016, 2017, 2018, 2019).

Oscar Castillo holds a doctor in science (Doctor Habilitatus) in computer science from the Polish Academy of Sciences (with the dissertation "Soft Computing and Fractal Theory for Intelligent and Manufacturing"). He is Professor of Computer Science in the Graduate Division, Tijuana Institute of Technology, Tijuana, Mexico. In addition, he is serving as Research Director of Computer Science and head of the research group on Hybrid Fuzzy Intelligent Systems. Currently, he is President of HAFSA (Hispanic American Fuzzy Systems Association) and Past President of IFSA (International Fuzzy Systems Association). Prof. Castillo is also Chair of the Mexican Chapter of the Computational Intelligence Society (IEEE). He also belongs to the Technical Committee on Fuzzy Systems of IEEE and the Task Force on "Extensions to Type-1 Fuzzy Systems". He is also a member of NAFIPS, IFSA, and IEEE. He belongs to the Mexican Research System (SNI Level 3). His research interests are in type-2 fuzzy logic, fuzzy control, neuro-fuzzy and genetic-fuzzy hybrid approaches. He has published over 300 journal papers, ten authored books, 50 edited books, 300 papers in conference proceedings, and more than 300 chapters in edited books, in total more than 1000 publications (according to Scopus) with h index of 82 and more than 23,000 citations according to Google Scholar. He has been Guest Editor of several successful Special Issues in the past, for instance in the following journals: Applied Soft Computing, Intelligent Systems, Information Sciences, Soft Computing, Non-Linear Studies, Fuzzy Sets and Systems, JAMRIS, and Engineering Letters. He is currently Associate Editor of the Information Sciences Journal, Journal of Engineering Applications on Artificial Intelligence, International Journal of Fuzzy Systems, Journal of Complex Intelligent Systems, Granular Computing Journal and Intelligent Systems Journal. He was Associate Editor of Journal of Applied Soft Computing and IEEE Transactions on Fuzzy Systems. He was elected IFSA Fellow in 2015 and MICAI Fellow in 2016. Finally, he recently received the Recognition as Highly Cited Researcher in 2017 and 2018 from Clarivate Analytics and Web of Science.

Contributors

Md. Irshad Alam
QC Strides Pharma Ltd
South Africa

Jayashri Vitthalrao Bagade
Department of Information Technology
Vishwakarma Institute of Information
    Technology

Santrupti M. Bagali
Department of ECE
BMSIT&M

Kalyana Chakravarthy Bairapareddy
College of Health Sciences
University of Sharjah
Sharjah, United Arab Emirates

Aparna Bannore
SIES Graduate School of Technology
Mumbai, India

Neha Baranwal
Montpellier University
France

Varsha Bendre
Department of E&TC
Pimpri Chinchwad College of
    Engineering
Pune, India

Anup Bhat
Department of Physiotherapy
Manipal College of Health Professions
Manipal Academy of Higher
    Education
Manipal, Karnataka, India

H. T. Bhavana
Department of Electronics and
    Communication

Nivedita Bhirud
Vishwakarma Institute of Information
    Technology
Pune, India

Pallavi Bhosle
Department of Pharmacology

Anjali C. Birajdar
Department of Electrical and Instrumentation
    Engineering
M. B. E. Society's College of Engineering
Ambajogai, Maharashtra, India

Mikkel Brydegaard
Department of Physics
Lund University
Sölvegatan 14, 22362 Lund, SWEDEN.

Neeta Hemant Chapatwala
Electronics and Communication Engineering
    Department
Sarvajanik College of Engineering and Technology
Surat, Gujarat, India

Santosh D. Chede
Department of Electronics and
    Telecommunication Engineering
D. Y. Patil College of Engineering and Technology
Kasaba Bawada, Kolhapur, India

Sanjana Dathathri
Department of ECE
BMSIT&M

Ketan Sanjay Desale
Pimpri Chinchwad College of Engineering
Pune, India

Pratiksha R. Deshmukh
Department of Computer Engineering and
    Information Technology
College of Engineering (COEP)
Pune, India

Preethi Doravari
Montpellier University
France

Ramesh R. Galigekere
Department of Biomedical Engineering
Manipal Institute of Technology
Manipal Academy of Higher Education (MAHE)
Manipal, India

J. G. Gujar
Department of Chemical Engineering
Sinhgad College of Engineering
Pune, India

Rohan Gupta
MantleLabs Pvt Ltd.
604, Senapati Bapat Road
Lower Parel, Mumbai 400013, INDIA.

Sujeet Kumar Gupta
Guangdong Macau Traditional Chinese Medicine
    Industrial Park Development Co Ltd.
Hengqin, Zhuhai, Guangdong, China

B. Harshitha
Department of Electronics and Communication

G. Harshith
B.M.S. College of Engineering
Bangalore

Ishan Bhan
Student at B. M. S. College of Engineering
Bengaluru, Karnataka, India

Swapnaja Hiray
Institute of Computer Technology
Pune

N. K. Jain
CDAC
New Delhi, India

Priyanka Jain
CDAC
New Delhi, India

Jithu Jerin James
Faculty of Pharmacy
MS Ramaiah University of Applied Sciences
Bangalore

Sagar V. Joshi
Department of ENTC
Nutan Maharashtra Institute of Engineering
    and Technology
Pune, MH, India

Renu Kachhoria
Lunkad Amazon
Viman Nagar, Pune, India

Sonali Kadam
Department of Computer Engineering
Bharati Vidyapeeth's College of Engineering
    for Women
Pune, Maharashtra, India

Deepti Khurge
Department of E&TC
Pimpri Chinchwad College of Engineering
Pune, India

Vinaya Kumar
Vishwakarma Institute of Information
    Technology
Pune, India

S. Lalitha
B.M.S. College of Engineering
Bangalore

Dr. Lenina SVB
Department of Electronics and Telecom
SGGS NANDED MH

Rahul Magazine
Department of Respiratory Medicine
Kasturba Medical College
Manipal Academy of Higher Education
    (MAHE)
Manipal – 576104, INDIA.

Pranoti P. Mane
E&TC
Modern Education Society's College of
    Engineering
Pune, India

Rohit Nayak
Division of Chemistry and Chemical
    Engineering
California Institute of Technology
    (Caltech)
1200 E. California Blvd., Pasadena, California
    91125, USA.

Niveditha
Department of Biomedical Engineering
Manipal Institute of Technology—Manipal
Manipal Academy of Higher Education
    (MAHE)
Manipal, India

Shweta Pandav
Department of Electronics and Telecom
SGGS NANDED MH

Hujeb Pathan
Department of Pharmacology

Rachana Y. Patil
Department of Computer Engineering
Pimpri Chinchwad College of Engineering
Pune, India

Ujwal D. Patil
University Institute of Chemical Technology
Kavayitri Bahinabai Chaudhari North
    Maharashtra University
Jalgaon, Maharashtra, India

Vaishnavi Patil
Pimpri Chinchwad College of Engineering
Pune

Yogesh H. Patil
IMEI, VBK Infrastructures
Pune, India

Chirag N. Paunwala
Electronics and Communication Engineering
    Department
Sarvajanik College of Engineering and
    Technology
Surat, Gujarat

Rashmi Phalnikar
School of CET, MIT WPU
Pune, India

Rutuja Pote
Vishwakarma Institute of Information Technology
Pune, India

R. Priyanka
Department of ECE
BMSIT&M

Supriya O. Rajankar
E&TC Department
Sinhgad College of Engineering

Manjiri A. Ranjanikar
Department of Computer Engineering
Pimpri Chinchwad College of Engineering
Pune, India

Vrushali Ganesh Raut
E&TC Department
Sinhgad College of Engineering

Bhramaramba Ravi
GITAM Institute of Technology

Deepa N. Reddy
Department of ECE
BMSIT&M

Sara Sadiya
Department of ECE
BMSIT&M

Purvi Sampat
Vishwakarma Institute of Information Technology
Pune, India

K. V. Sandhya
Department of Pharmaceutics
Faculty of Pharmacy
MS Ramaiah University of Applied Sciences
Bangalore

T. Sanjana
B.M.S. College of Engineering

Priya Makarand Shelke
Department of Information Technology
Vishwakarma Institute of Information
    Technology

Swati V. Shinde
Department of Computer Engineering
Pimpri Chinchwad College of Engineering
Pune, India

Parth Shrivastava
Pimpri Chinchwad College of Engineering
Pune

M. Anantha Sunil
Department of Electronics and Communication

Ganesh Tapadiya
Department of Pharmacognosy

Subhash Tatale
Vishwakarma Institute of Information
    Technology
Pune India

Vijaya R. Thool
Department of Instrumentation Engineering
Shri Guru Gobind Singhji Institute of
    Engineering & Technology
Nanded, Maharashtra, India

Jaishri M. Waghmare
Department of Computer Science & Engineering
Shri Guru Gobind Singhji Institute of
    Engineering and Technology
MH, India

Preface

Biomedical engineering is an interdisciplinary field of engineering that deals with application of engineering concepts to develop essential healthcare applications and devices. This book covers different aspects of recent technologies, such as AI/ML, medical IoT, biomedical signal processing, electronic health records, and other recent advancements. This book will be beneficial to researchers, industry persons, faculty, and students working in biomedical applications of computer science and electronic engineering. This book will also be useful for teaching courses on AI/ML, medical IoT, signal processing, biomedical engineering, medical image analysis, etc.

Part I of this book begins with the introductory chapter on AI for biomedical applications and future trends. This chapter is followed by the set of chapters that focuses on AI/ML applications, medical image analysis, and deep learning applications to different disease diagnoses; this part of the book ends with a detailed case study on oropharyngeal cancer prediction based on different image modalities.

Part II of this book has three chapters, beginning with the role of medical IOT in healthcare applications and future prospects. The next chapter in this part is on a web-cam–based belt-system for respiratory and chest measurements. This section of the book ends with a data analysis framework in smart city healthcare.

Part III has six chapters that focus on bio-signal processing. There are some diseases that are diagnosed based on body signals recorded by using different instruments. There are two main kinds of signals, namely ECG and EEG, which are signals of the heart and brain respectively. These signals are helpful in the diagnosis of heart diseases, epilepsy, arrhythmia, etc.

Electronic health records (EHR), which keep a patient's information and documents, have become an active research area, as it is important and contributes to effective and organized treatment of disease. Part IV of the book focuses on the need, challenges, and future scope of EHRs.

Part V has four chapters that focus on recent developments, including drug discovery, implants, organ donation, etc.

This book offers a nice coverage of most biomedical applications using trending technologies like AI/ML/DL, medical IOT, and biomedical signal processing.

Part I

AI/ML for Biomedical Applications

1 Recent Advances of Artificial Intelligence (AI) for Nanobiomedical Applications
Trends, Challenges, and Future Prospects

J. G. Gujar, Sonali Kadam, and Ujwal D. Patil

CONTENTS

1.1 INTRODUCTION

Nanotechnology is an advanced technical field that comprises specific materials and equipment able to employ the physicochemical properties of this apparatus at the atomic extent. Biotechnology refers to the practice of biological techniques and understanding to engineer

DOI: 10.1201/9781003272694-2

the inherent group of an atom and cellular functions to progress beneficial facilities and goods in a number of diverse sectors, from agronomy to fitness systems [1, 2]. Nanobiotechnology is an innovative fusion of nanotechnology and biotechnology through which standard micro-technology will be fused into a real group of atomic approaches. With this technology, a group of atoms or even atomic tools can be fabricated by integrating biological phenomena or blending small tools to convert into various attributes of living systems at the group of the atomic extent [3]. Therefore, nanobiotechnology can facilitate many pathways in the life sciences by integrating cutting-edge exploitation of nanotechnology and computer technology into current biological problems. This is a renowned technology with the potential to break down the borders between chemistry, physics, and biology to a certain extent and to develop our current thinking and concepts. Thus, over time, modern guidance and challenges related to investigation and diagnostics may emerge through the broad practice of nanobiotechnology, including in education, analysis, and medicine.

Artificial intelligence is a new area of research with a noticeable place in our lives. It exists in almost every type of machinery that handles an enormous amount of information through group actions and is used for systematic operations. AI has prognostic power that supports the feasibility of its data analysis and some levels of self-directed schooling, as its raw material is simply a huge amount of data. Informatics is concerned with collecting value from the evidence that, once insights are gained, offers essential commercial value.

AI has a variety of elementary uses across numerous and highly diverse areas and businesses. In recent decades, artificial intelligence has been used often in technology investigation. The conjunction of computing and technology will pave the way for various technological developments and expansion of disciplines. In this chapter, we reveal those innovative and dynamic advancements that use AI in different areas of nanobiotechnology. An AI approach based on nanobiotechnology could offer concrete solutions for social betterment, including effective responses in sudden and unexpected pandemics like COVID-19. This effort aims to provide a suitable platform for researchers to focus on advancement, challenges, and future prospects in the field of nanobiomedical applications.

1.2   LITERATURE SURVEY: NANOBIOTECHNOLOGY

Investigations into nanotechnology and biotechnology have been highly favorable approaches in the twenty-first century. Biotechnology covers the physiological and metabolic methods of existing entities, including about 4,444 types of microorganisms. Nanotechnology shows the uses and development of materials, the smallest functional units, in the range of 1 to 100 nm [4]. Blending these innovative technologies, namely nanobiotechnology, could play a surprising role in the execution and improvement of many valuable tools for studying genetic organisms. An existing investigation has revealed that plant extracts, microorganisms, and fungi could biologically synthesize nanoparticles [5]. They have unique characteristics that differ from larger molecules of like components. Their optical, electrical, and biochemical properties change from those seen in bulk mixtures to those seen in bulk or unpackaged materials owing to their larger surface-to-volume ratio [6]. In general, nanotechnology is concerned with emerging constituents, components, or other configurations that have a minimum scale of 1 to 100 nanometers. However, biotechnology focuses on the metabolic and physical procedures of biological issues with microorganisms. Nanobiotechnology can play a critical part in the development and application of many important perspectives in the research of human life.

The field of nanotechnology encompasses a wide range of subjects, ranging from traditional device physics extensions to wholly novel ways connected to molecular self-assembly and developing new nanoscale materials to establish if one may directly change things at the microscopic level. Organic chemistry, surface science, molecular biology, and semiconductor physics are among the scientific fields involved in micro fabrication, etc. The prefix "nano" means one-billionth of a meter or 10^{-9} in metric MKS unit dimensional terms or International

System Units (ISU); thus, one nanometer is one-billionth of a meter. The following examples illustrate nanoscale:

1. The thickness of human hair is about 80,000–100,000 nanometers.
2. The thickness of a sheet of paper is approximately 100,000 nanometers.
3. A particular golden atom has a diameter of roughly one-third of a nanometer.
4. One nanometer is roughly the length of a fingernail that grew in one second.
5. The diameter of a thread of human DNA is 2.5 nanometers.
6. One inch has 25,400,000 nanometers.

Three visual illustrations of the size and scale of nanotechnology are shown in Figure 1.1, demonstrating just how small objects are at the nanoscale. The capability to interpret and regulate specific atoms and particles is at the core of nanotechnology and nanoscience. Atoms are made entirely on earth and comprise the food we eat, the garments we wear, the buildings we live in, and our bodies. An atom cannot be seen through the human eye and is difficult to see through microscopes that are commonly used in science classes. It was only in the early 1980s that microscopes powerful enough to see matters at the nanoscale were developed.

The age of nanotechnology came into being once professionals acquired the instruments needed, for instance the Atomic Force Microscope (AFM) and the Scanning Tunneling Microscope (STM). Even though current nanoscience and nanotechnology are relatively innovative, tiny materials have been in use for millennia [3].

1.3   BIOTECHNOLOGY

Biotechnology is commonly defined as the application of biological organisms, systems, and processes to produce goods or offer facilities. Three groups of biotechnology are possible. First there is the practice of complete organisms in fermentation, like in brewing. The second generation helped improve microbiological understanding in the early twentieth century, which directed attention to the growth of culture and extraction techniques. The third generation, which began in the 1970s, is associated with the separation and use of restricted enzymes and monoclonal antibodies. The extensive history and extent of biotechnology with regard to events, technologies, and required fields make it impossible to provide accurate and worldwide meaning of its importance, although third-generation biotechnology is in a special situation regarding its use in the medicinal modernization process. Since the 1970s, recombinant DNA and monoclonal antibody related applications have been used, with genomics emerging as a subdivision of biotechnology in the 1990s and extensive improvements following genomics. Biotechnology arose in the last decades of the twentieth century as a point of fast development in science and technology, as well as a center of social and institutional reform. New approaches for researching, innovating, and rebuilding living things resulted in significant applications in medicine and farming, as well as considerable investment. Biotechnology has frequently been at the forefront of change in scientific organizations and methods in the field of research. Biotechnology, in general, was often seen as having "revolutionary" implications, which has sparked both tremendous curiosity and determined resistance.

1.4   BIONANOTECHNOLOGY

Nanobiotechnology and bionanotechnology are sometimes used interchangeably. However, whether or not a difference is recognized depends on if the emphasis is on the application of biological principles or the study of biology using nanotechnology. In general, bionanotechnology deals with the way the aims of nanotechnology can be directed by examining how biological technologies operate and adjusting particular biological principles to enhance existing nanotechnologies or build

FIGURE 1.1   The scale of things [2].

new nanotechnologies. However, nanobiotechnology considers how it is used for the development of equipment for studying biological systems. In other words, nanobiotechnology is a smaller kind of biotechnology, whereas bionanotechnology is a subset of nanotechnology. Because they operate with biomolecules at the nanoscale, DNA nanotechnology and cell engineering would be classified as bionanotechnology. Many new therapeutic technologies that employ nanoparticles as delivery systems or sensors, however, would be instances of nanobiotechnology since they include the use of nanotechnology to accomplish biological aims.

When distinguishing between nanobiotech and bionanotech in this chapter, the definitions just given are always applied. Given the practice of terminology in present English, specific technologies might need to be considered with regard to selecting which name is most suitable. As a result, it is preferable to address them simultaneously. The terms "nanobiotechnology," "bionanotechnology," and "nanobiology" all related to the convergence of nanotechnology and biology. Because of the topic's recent emergence, bionanotechnology and nanobiotechnology have become generic names for a range of related technologies. This aids in demonstrating the intersection of genetic study and the many aspects of nanotechnology.

Scientists can visualize and construct systems for biological research using this technical approach to biology. Bio-inspired nanotechnology is a type of nanotechnology that takes inspiration from biological systems to yield novel technologies. However, bionanotechnology, like nano and biotechnology, has a slew of possible ethical issues. The use of nanotools for relevant medico-biological problems and their further development are two of the most essential goals in nanobiology. Another significant goal for nanotechnology is the development of novel tools, such as peptide nanosheets, for medicinal and biological applications. The development of new nanotools is existence.

1.5 ARTIFICIAL INTELLIGENCE (AI)

To support the new AI regulation, the idea of artificial intelligence (AI) has existed in community discourse for about ten years and is frequently portrayed in scientific literature, as well as in movies that speculate on how smart technologies could conquer the world by condemning humanity to a submissive and secular existence. While this is a fairly comical portrayal of AI, the truth is that artificial intelligence is already here, and many of us deal with technology daily. AI application is the domain of future prospects, but it is also a critical constituent of many firms' profitable models and a critical planned component in the strategies of many branches of economics, medicine, and governments around the world. This revolutionary impact of AI has piqued academic attention, with new studies focusing on the implications and repercussions of technology rather than the effects of AI on performance, which had previously appeared to be the major focus of study for several years.

The literature shows several terms for AI, every one of which includes the fundamental ideas of automating non-human intellect to achieve certain work. Russell and Norvig (2016) [7] show artificial intelligence (AI) as structures that replicate intellectual capabilities commonly connected through human characteristics like knowledge, language, and problem undertaking. Kaplan and Haenlein (2019) [8] give a more extensive and maybe more nuanced characterization of AI from the perspective of AI's capability to autonomously comprehend and study outside contributions in order to accomplish specified objectives through a flexible version. The utilization of large data has enabled algorithms to excel at specialized jobs (robotic vehicles, games, autonomous planning, etc.). Thoughts and feelings, however, have yet to be adequately translated [7]. The throughline across these statements is the growing capacity of apparatuses to accomplish certain activities and duties that are currently performed by persons in the workplace and society as a whole.

The capability of AI to do a variety of human intellectual, inventive, and computation-extensive hurdles is spawning new utility domain names in training and advertising, healthcare, economics, and production, with consequent effects on yield and performance. AI-enabled structures in businesses have been quickly expanding, transforming enterprises and manufacturing, and expanding their reach to areas that were formerly believed to be entirely human [9]. The generation of synthetic intelligence structures has reached a degree in which independent vehicles, chatbots, independent making of plans and scheduling, games, translations, clinical diagnostics, and even antispam can all be completed via synthetic intelligence. Synthetic intelligence professionals, as observed in Müller and Bostrom [10], expect that synthetic intelligence structures will in all likelihood reach smarter human functionality through 2075; a few professionals consider that advances in synthetic intelligence closer to amazing intelligence will be terrible for humanity.

1.6 CHALLENGES

As the extent and significance of possible applications expand and the usage of AI becomes increasingly widespread, the adoption of AI technology may create significant issues for governments and organizations.

1.6.1 SOCIAL CHALLENGES

The application of AI technology may provide substantial challenges for administrations and society as the opportunity and intensity of capacity programs expand and the usage of AI becomes more common. The growing use of AI is likely to encounter social rules and function as a capacity obstacle across certain segments of the population. For instance, Xu et al. [11] emphasized the connections that AI would offer to healthcare from the perspective of an increase in communication and patient preparation. This might be used to regulate both the patient and the doctor. The study emphasized the need for doctors to learn how to use AI technology in healthcare systems, as well as for patient education to alleviate the anxiety of aging among a wide range of patient demographics [11]. Community trials have been identified as capacity constraints to additional AI technology implementation. Sun and Medaglia [12] depicted societal challenges associated with impractical prospects for AI's future and a lack of understanding of the values and benefits of AI technology. Several literature studies have also looked at the social implications of capacity work losses caused by AI technology. This issue has received extensive media coverage and has been debated in several forums. A study with the assistance of Risse [13] argued that AI generates difficult conditions for individuals, which might affect the character of labor and have an effect on personal popularity utilizing members of society. Employees may advance up the value chain to raise awareness about using human qualities to elucidate, design, and incorporate issues as a measure of a combined AI and personnel-specific workforce.

1.6.2 FINANCIAL CHALLENGES

The widespread use of AI technology may have a substantial potential influence on businesses and associations in terms of necessary assets and variations in operational techniques. Reza et al. [14] advocated for knowledge in the health sector, stating that AI is expected to need considerable economic assets. The investigation focused on pathology research facilities, where present economic challenges could be compounded by increased burdens to incorporate AI technology. Sun and Medaglia [12] recognized many healthcare-associated financial challenges, stating that the development of AI-based technology will have an effect on hospital profitability and, most likely, raise treatment costs for patients.

1.6.3 TECHNOLOGY IMPLEMENTATION CHALLENGES

Several studies have been conducted to study the non-boolean atmosphere of diagnostic responsibilities in healthcare, as well as the applications of using AI technology in the translation of statistics and imaging. Reza et al. [14] highlighted the reality that human beings practice careful language or descriptive terminology rather than simple binary language, while

AI-based structures generally are likely to be characterized as a dark field. These aspects were strengthened by Cleophas and Cleophas [15], whose investigations identified various hurdles in the use of AI for imaging and scientific diagnosis, consequently influencing clinician assurance inside the generation. Cheshire [16] discusses the limitations of scientific AI loop assumptions. The period loop assumption can be highlighted as a type of unconscious preference that no longer allows for an accurate overview of data or amendment of the continuing strategy of the act. As a result, AI has the potential to discredit particular human ethical standards. There are issues with the construction of AI structures and the necessity for fashionable systems to recognize human intellectual shifting, learning approaches, or even ethical traits [17, 18]. Sun and Medaglia [12] examined the technologically hard scenarios of the rule set opacity and lack of capability to investigate random statistics. Thrall et al. [19] examine the concept of a restricted researcher educated in radiology and AI. It can be addressed by hiring inventors who are experts in AI; however, they can be addressed by organizing university programmers in radiology [20]. According to Varga Szemes et al. [21], system-gaining knowledge of algorithms must be produced by the system-gaining knowledge of professionals with a relevant understanding of medicine and knowledge of viable results and repercussions. It is emphasized that AI structures currently have the spirit of social intelligence [22] but were unable to recognize circumstances. This barrier renders current AI systems susceptible to attack in a diversity of areas, mostly to hacker spasms dubbed "adverse instances." In case of occurrences, a hacker may make particular and dispersed adjustments to sound, image, or the textual content of documents, which will no longer have an influence on human cognition but may cause a programmer to commit possibly catastrophic mistakes due to the fact that programmers no longer identify the efforts they receive and the products they generate, opening up potential vulnerability to sudden mistakes and undetected attacks. Such issues can have an impact on domain names such as computer vision, scientific photo processing, speech reputation, and language processing [22].

1.6.4 CHALLENGES IN POLITICS AND POLICY

Gupta and Kumari [23] mentioned prison-demanding situations related to AI obligation as mistakes arise in the usage of AI structures. Another authorized undertaking of the usage of AI structures may be the problem of rights. Present legal structures desire important adjustments that allow you to guard effectively and incentivize human-produced tasks [24]. Wirtz et al. [25] concentrated on the difficulties of enforcing AI inside a government, calling for a fuller knowledge of the scope and influence of AI-based programmers, as well as accompanying obstacles. The study looked at the notion of AI regulation and norms for power control, which includes self-reliant intelligence structures, duty and responsibility, and confidentiality.

Several innovations have demonstrated the difficulties associated with integrating AI-based solutions in government and the community sector. Using a case study approach, Sun and Medaglia [12] investigated the challenges of incorporating AI in the Chinese community. The research surveyed three different clusters of stakeholders – hospital administrators/doctors, government officials, and executives from IT companies – to determine how they see the challenges of AI use in the community. The investigation shows the possibilities of the variations and their influence among countries in an environment of administrative and regulatory issues, in addition to domestic safety pressures posed by internationally retained enterprises.

1.6.5 MORAL CHALLENGES

Investigators have argued the moral aspects of AI as well as recommendations for better use of the technology. Individuals and organizations may voice doubt and worry regarding the ethical aspects of AI schemes and their usage of community data [12]. Because of the quick rate of change and growth of AI expertise, there is increasing anxiety that moral concerns will not be clearly discussed. It is uncertain how moral and authorized difficulties, mainly those associated with concern and investigation of AI-based system results, could be studied.

To avoid the abuse of AI, controllers should design and execute suitable instructions, laws, ethical principles, and legal frameworks [26]. Many of these ideas are reinforced by Gupta and Kumari [23], who stress the ethical problems associated with expanding AI use, data sharing issues, and system ineptitude. Artificial intelligence-based systems can discriminate even when no humans are engaged in the administrative development process, highlighting the need for openness in AI algorithms [27]. In the future, as application reach and degrees of automation increase, AI technology in all its manifestations is expected to gain traction within businesses. Research indicates that by 2030, 70% of businesses will have integrated some form of artificial intelligence technology into their commercial operations or production settings [28]. Several studies have proposed the profits of rising AI adoption rates in a range of fields, with industrial, healthcare, and arithmetical advertising receiving significant educational attention [29]. Future industries are expected to make extensive use of AI technology as manufacturing develops additional computerized components and the industry moves to smarter platforms utilizing AI and cyber-physical systems [17]. Researchers in healthcare studies have discussed novel prospects for the use of AI in health analysis and pathology, in which tedious activities may be computerized and offer better speed and precision [35]. AI arrangements are connected to sensors located above and around the human physique to monitor fitness and comfort [26]. AI is being employed in advertising and trade, with big data analytics is being utilized to generate individualized customer outlines and to anticipate their buying behaviors. Considering and anticipating consumer response through a cohesive source chain is more important than ever, and AI technology is undoubtedly a key component. AI-powered novelties like the simulated mirror and pictorial examination are positioned to strengthen client connections and bridge the gap between physical and simulated experiences.

Investigators have called for additional genuine forthcoming conversation in which the connection between AI and people in the loop is more likely to change to a collaborative human context than an industry-based human emergency [15]. Stead [27] highlights the necessity of establishing a relationship in which the AI machine calculates and/or forecasts while people discuss and agree on the required steps. People were more expected to pay attention to new value-added events that need design, examination, and clarification built on AI processing and outcomes [28].

1.7 APPLICATIONS OF AI IN THE COVID-19 EPIDEMIC

The health sector is considering innovative tools to display and manage the extent of the universal health disaster that is the COVID-19 (Coronavirus) epidemic. AI is a tool that may rapidly follow the spread of this disease, recognize more hazardous individuals, and support actual contamination management. It may assess the death hazard by systematically estimating a patient's past statistics. AI can support individuals in combating this virus through population screening, health support, announcements, and contamination control [29]. As a piece of an evidence-built health device, this technology has the potential to improve the COVID-19 patient's development, treatment, and informed products.

Figure 1.2 demonstrates a technique for AI and non-AI apps that could support common practitioners to recognize COVID-19 symptoms. This figure shows and contrasts the course of a minimum non-AI treatment to that of an AI-based treatment. It also explores the function of AI in key stages of therapy with remarkable precision, minimizing problems and time. The doctor is concerned not just with the patient's therapy, but also with sickness control utilizing the AI software. With the aid of AI, main indicators and trial examinations were accomplished with the highest precision feasible. During this global health calamity, the health business is seeking breakthrough technologies to show and manage the extent of the COVID-19 epidemic. AI is one of the

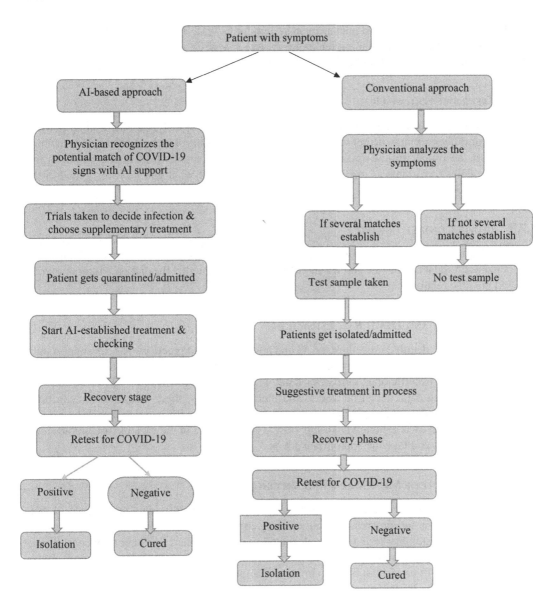

FIGURE 1.2   Procedure for AI and non-AI–focused uses that can support common doctors in identifying COVID-19 indications [36].

technologies that can swiftly track the distribution of this disease, identify severely ill patients, and aid in real-time monitoring of this sickness by properly examining previous patient data. You can also anticipate the danger of fatality by correctly reviewing past patient data. By scanning the population, giving medical care, reporting, and making infection control suggestions, AI can assist us in combating the epidemic [29]. This research, as an evidence-related health device, has the probability of improving COVID-19 patient forecasting, treatment, and reporting outcomes.

1.7.1   INITIAL CONTAMINATION DETECTION AND DIAGNOSIS

AI can swiftly assess erratic signals and other "red flags," warning patients and health officials [30]. It allows for speedy policymaking, which is beneficial. Through valuable algorithms, it aids in the growth of a new identification and management system for COVID-19 cases. AI can detect infected patients utilizing therapeutic imaging technologies like magnetic resonance imaging (MRI) and computed tomography (CT) of human body sections.

1.7.2 TREATMENT FOLLOW-UP

AI can provide a smarter phase for the programmed observation and assessment of the virus's level. A neural network may be constructed to extract the imaging structures of this virus, which will support the proper follow-up and treatment of affected persons [31]. It is capable of giving daily updates to patients as well as offering explanations of what will be investigated in the COVID19 pandemic.

1.7.3 PEOPLE CONTACT TRACING

AI can assist in determining the extent of contamination by this disease by categorizing and grouping "hot zones," and it can pursue and watch people. This could predict the disease's future progression and possible recurrence.

1.7.4 CASE STUDY AND DEATH RATE ESTIMATION

Figure 2.1 shows the detailed procedure for AI and non-AI–focused practices that can support public doctors in identifying COVID-19 indications. With the support of AI, spotting initial symptoms and performing test examinations were carried out with maximum precision.

Based on existing data, social networks, and media platforms, these investigations can track virus types for infection risk and potential spread. It can also predict the number of positive circumstances and deaths in each region. AI can support the classification of the various susceptible areas, persons, and nations and take the appropriate action.

1.7.5 DEVELOPMENT OF MEDICATIONS AND VACCINES

AI can be recommended for drug discovery by investigating particular data on COVID-19. It is suitable for the design and progress of drug delivery. It is practiced to speed up actual medicine analysis, whereas customary tests take an elongated period, and therefore help to encourage this practice considerably, which isn't possible for a human being [31]. It can help identify drugs suitable for treating COVID-19 patients. It has developed a dominant device for diagnostic testing and vaccine development [32, 33]. AI is helping to develop vaccines and therapeutics much more quickly than standard and is valuable for clinical research through vaccine development.

1.7.6 REDUCE HEALTH WORKLOAD

Owing to a rapid and considerable rise in the total number of patients for the duration of the COVID-19 pandemic, health workers have taken on an enormous amount of work. In this case, AI application can be utilized to decrease the extent of work performed by the medical workforce [34]. This could support primary detection and treatment through digital methods and assessment science and provide students and clinicians with the best possible training on this novel disease [35]. For disease inhibition with actual data examination, AI can provide the most up-to-date knowledge to support the inhibition of these kinds of illness. It may be applied to predict similar sources of infection, disease invasion, the necessity for beds, and the role of healthcare authorities for the duration of an emergency. AI can help avoid future infections and illnesses by leveraging previously stored data for data that prevails at various periods and work to determine the nature, source, and cause of the infection's transmission. It will be valuable expertise in the battle against other epidemics in the future. It can be applied as a defensive strategy along with the treatment for a variety of diverse disorders. AI will serve a significant role in illness prevention and avoidance of forthcoming epidemic situations.

1.8 ARTIFICIAL INTELLIGENCE IN HEALTHCARE DISEASE PREVENTION

AI can give up-to-date knowledge to assist in avoiding this condition by utilizing real-time data analytics. It may be used to forecast probable infection sources, viral propagation, bed requirements, and the involvement of health officials during this crisis. Because it uses previously recorded facts in common at various eras, AI is effective in averting future infections and illnesses through classifying the features, causes, and reasons for infection dissemination. It will be a critical asset in the fight against forthcoming plagues and pandemics. It can be used to both prevent and cure a variety of different ailments. AI will soon play a vital part in health inhibition and protection.

1.9 AI IN MEDICAL IMAGE ANALYSIS

In recent years, medical imaging has become an essential measure of medical care. Images have been extensively used for the discovery, confirmation, differential diagnosis, and treatment of illnesses and in recuperation. When AI algorithms were run, they produced significant results. X-ray, ultrasound (US), magnetic resonance imaging (MRI), computed tomography (CT), and positron emission tomography (PET) slides, as well as mammography, retinal photography, morphology, and histology, are all examined by doctors. Image reporting is a laborious assignment that is generally performed through the work of skilled radiologists and general practitioners. Image interpretation is prone to inaccuracy due to differences in pathology's visual presentation and techniques of image interpretation. The potential exhaustion of human specialists can similarly be responsible for improper diagnostic decisions; mammography examinations, for example, have been reported to have sensitivity and specificity of 77–87% and 89–97%, respectively [37].

1.10 APPLICATIONS FOR PATIENT APPOINTMENT AND OBSERVANCE

Patient commitment and loyalty have significantly been seen as the "last mile" trial in healthcare, the last barrier between bad and good health results. The better the application of outcomes, economic results, and participation capabilities, the more involved patients are in their comfort and precaution. These factors have gradually been highlighted by big data and artificial intelligence. Healthcare workforces and hospitals frequently use their medical information to improve a care plan that will increase the health of an acute or chronic patient; however, this often does not matter if the patient does not make the necessary behavior adjustments, e.g. lose weight, make a follow-up appointment, fill prescriptions, or monitor a diagnosis plan. Non-compliance, that is, when a patient does not monitor a particular treatment or does not take recommended medications as prescribed, is a major problem. In 300 science and health caretaker surveys, more than 70% of defendants stated that less than 50% of patients were very enthusiastic, and 42% of those surveyed had less than 25% of severe patients who showed they had a disability [38]. The use of business rule mechanisms and machine learning to enable fine-grained interactions during management is increasingly emphasized [39]. News alerts and relevant content that encourages action at critical moments are lucrative areas of research. Another emerging effort in healthcare is the actual design of "selective architectures" to better shape patient characteristics in practice. The program may tailor statements by matching patient statistics to additional active treatment options for comparable units with statistics given by EHR organizations, biosensors, wearables, cell phones, chat interfaces, and other resources. Approval can be communicated with medical personnel, patients, attendant, and customer service representative.

1.11   AI IN PERSONALIZED MEDICINE

Personalized medicine is a novel research area that focuses on disease inhibition and treatment. Individual inconsistencies in genes, environment, and lifestyle are all taken into account. In recent years, the health prototype has evolved [40]. The advancement of AI systems that could analyze massive amounts of genomic data to predict and avoid disease has accelerated the science of precision medicine. Precision medicine progresses personalized treatment regimens for subsets of patients, whereas traditional medicine provides uniform care to the entire population. Some elements may be more essential to one subgroup than others. This encourages medical researchers to investigate innovative techniques and encourages physicians and medical investigators to improve new approaches to identify and analyze subgroups. This is an effective approach for tailored treatment [41, 42]. The creative idea of *personalized* medicine comprises prevention and treatment approaches. These approaches take separate inconsistencies into account by assessing big data sets comprising patient facts, medical images, and genomic arrangements [43]. This methodology permits clinicians and investigators to predict suitable treatment and precautions.

1.12   CONCLUSION

Nanobiotechnology applications in therapeutic diagnosis and treatment need an appropriate assessment of the protection and risk factors of this technology. Investigators who disagree with nanotechnology in biological systems also concur that nanobiotechnology must constantly improve as it has great advantages, but in vivo investigations must be conducted to ensure the level of safety. Possibly, in the future, nano-pharmaceuticals will play an essential part in to fight against human diseases and will confirm usual human physiology. If nanotechnology continues to evolve, it will soon become a part of our daily lives, helping to save many lives. Artificial intelligence is a novel and beneficial device to identify early infection of COVID-19 and will help monitor the condition of infected patients. This could greatly increase the direction of treatment and policymaking through the progress of beneficial algorithms. AI is valuable for not only treating patients ill with COVID-19 but also appropriately handling the health of the patient. AI can identify the COVID-19 epidemic at various levels, such as through therapeutic, molecular, and epidemiological applications. This can be useful to assist the study of such diseases through investigating existing records. AI applications could be utilized to improve suitable cures, inhibition approaches, and medicine, as well as to aid in the creation of vaccines.

   This chapter looked at how AI is fighting the COVID-19 pandemic from a data science perspective. We proposed a time-step approach that describes current research studies, looks at how AI observes and affects society and the healthcare system, and informs different types of data. AI applications have so far only been investigated for small tasks like diagnosing images, but today's pandemic could reveal solutions that could benefit our society. However, there is still time for research development to improve overall AI support for the current pandemic. Taking into account the knowledge and restrictions of the various solutions offered in the research papers presented in this chapter, it is expected that the deliberations provided in this chapter will enable AI to advance the future contribution of healthcare systems and society.

   A nanobiotechnology-based AI methodology could provide concrete solutions for societal improvement in terms of affecting unforeseen epidemics like COVID-19. An attempt has been made to deliver a suitable platform for investigators with an emphasis on developments, challenges, and future prospects in the field of nanobiomedical applications.

REFERENCES

1. Stewart Jr., C. N. 2016. *Plant biotechnology and genetics: Principles, techniques, and applications.* Knoxville, TN: John Wiley & Sons. http://125.234.102.146:8080/dspace/handle/DNULIB_52011/8909.

2. Gartland, K. M., & Gartland, J. S. 2018. Opportunities in biotechnology. *Journal of Biotechnology*, *282*, 38–45. https://doi.org/10.1016/j.jbiotec.2018.06.303.

3. Thirumavalavan, M., Settu, K., & Lee, J. F. 2016. A short review on applications of nanomaterials in biotechnology and pharmacology. *Current Bionanotechnology*, *2*, 116–121. www.ingentaconnect.com/content/ben/cbnt/2016/00000002/00000002/art0001.

4. Courtney, J., Gao, X., Elmlund, L., Maniruzzaman, M., & Freitas, D. N. 2017. Advances in Nano Biotechnology. *Advances in Nano Biotechnology*, *276*.

5. Qamar, S. A., Asgher, M., Khalid, N., & Sadaf, M. 2019. Nanobiotechnology in health sciences: Current applications and future perspectives. *Biocatalysis and Agricultural Biotechnology*, *22*, 101388.

6. Roy, R., Pal, A., & Chaudhuri, A. N. 2015. Antimicrobial effect of silver nanoparticle on pathogenic organisms isolated from East Kolkata Wetland. *International Journal of Applied Research*, *1*, 745–752.

7. Russell, S. J., & Norvig, P. 2016. *Artificial intelligence: A modern approach*. Harlow, UK: Malaysia: Pearson Education Limited.

8. Kaplan, A., & Haenlein, M. 2019. Siri, Siri, in my hand: Who's the fairest in the land? On the interpretations, illustrations, and implications of artificial intelligence. *Business Horizons*, *62*(1), 15–25.

9. Wilson, J., & Daugherty, P. R. 2018. Collaborative intelligence humans and AI are joining forces. *Harvard Business Review*, *96*(4), 115–123.

10. Müller, V. C., & Bostrom, N. 2016. Future progress in artificial intelligence: A survey of expert opinion. In *Fundamental issues of artificial intelligence*. Cham: Springer, 555–572.

11. Xu, J., Yang, P., Xue, S., Sharma, B., Sanchez-Martin, M., Wang, F., & Parikh, B. 2019. Translating cancer genomics into precision medicine with artificial intelligence: Applications, challenges and future perspectives. *Human Genetics*, *138*(2), 109–124. http://doi.org/10.1007/s00439-019-01970-5.

12. Sun, T. Q., & Medaglia, R. 2019. Mapping the challenges of artificial intelligence in the public sector: Evidence from public healthcare. *Government Information Quarterly*, *36*(2), 368–383.

13. Risse, M. 2019. Human rights and artificial intelligence: An urgently needed agenda. *Human Rights Quarterly*, *41*(1), 1–16.

14. Reza Tizhoosh, H., & Pantanowitz, L. 2018. Artificial intelligence and digital pathology: Challenges and opportunities. *Journal of Pathology Informatics*, *9*(1).

15. Cleophas, T. J., & Cleophas, T. F. 2010. Artificial intelligence for diagnostic purposes: Principles, procedures, and limitations. *Clinical Chemistry and Laboratory Medicine*, *48*(2), 159–165.

16. Cheshire, W. P. 2017. Loopthink: A limitation of medical artificial intelligence. *Ethics and Medicine*, *33*(1), 7–12.

17. Baldassarre, G., Santucci, V. G., Cartoni, E., & Caligiore, D. 2017. The architecture challenge: Future artificial-intelligence systems will require sophisticated architectures, and knowledge of the brain might guide their construction. *The Behavioral and Brain Sciences*, *40*, e254.

18. Edwards, S. D. 2018. The Heart Math coherence model: Implications and challenges for artificial intelligence and robotics. *AI and Society*, 1–7. https://doi.org/10.1007/s00146-018-0834-8.

19. Thrall, J. H., Li, X., Li, Q., Cruz, C., Do, S., Dreyer, K., & Brink, J. 2018. Artificial intelligence and machine learning in radiology: Opportunities, challenges, pitfalls, and criteria for success. *Journal of the American College of Radiology*, *15*(3), 504–508.

20. Nguyen, G. K., & Shetty, A. S. 2018. Artificial intelligence and machine learning: Opportunities for radiologists in training. *Journal of the American College of Radiology*, *15*(9), 1320–1321.

21. Varga-Szemes, A., Jacobs, B. E., & Schoepf, U. J. 2018. The power and limitations of machine learning and artificial intelligence in cardiac CT. *Journal of Cardiovascular Computed Tomography*, *12*(3), 202–203.

22. Mitchell, M. 2019. Artificial intelligence hits the barrier of meaning. *Information (Switzerland)*, *10*(2). https://doi.org/10.3390/info10020051.

23. Gupta, R. K., & Kumari, R. 2017. Artificial intelligence in public health: Opportunities and challenges. *JK Science*, *19*(4), 191–192.

24. Zatarain, J. M. N. 2017. The role of automated technology in the creation of copyright works: The challenges of artificial intelligence. *International Review of Law, Computers and Technology*, *31*(1), 91–104.

25. Wirtz, B. W., Weyerer, J. C., & Geyer, C. 2019. Artificial intelligence and the public sector-applications and challenges. *International Journal of Public Administration*, *42*(7), 596–615.

26. Duan, Y., Edwards, J. S., & Dwivedi, Y. K. 2019. Artificial intelligence for decision making in the era of big data Evolution, challenges and research agenda. *International Journal of Information Management*, *48*, 63–71.

27. Stead, W. W. 2018. Clinical implications and challenges of artificial intelligence and deep learning. *JAMA—Journal of the American Medical Association, 320*(11), 1107–1108.

28. Dwivedi, Y. K., Hughes, L., Ismagilov, E., et al. 2021. Artificial Intelligence (AI): Multidisciplinary perspectives on emerging challenges, opportunities, and agenda for research, practice, and policy. *International Journal of Information Management, 57*, 1–47.

29. Hu, Z., Ge, Q., Jin, L., & Xiong, M. 2020. Artificial intelligence forecasting of COVID-19 in China. *arXiv preprint arXiv:2002.07112.*

30. Luo, H., Tang, Q. L., Shang, Y. X., Liang, S. B., Yang, M., Robinson, N., & Liu, J. P. 2019. Can Chinese medicine be used for prevention of coronavirus disease (COVID-19)? A review of historical classics, research evidence, and current prevention programs. *Chinese Journal of Integrative Medicine, 26*(4), 243–250. https://doi.org/10.1007/s11655-020-3192-6.

31. Haleem, A., Vaishya, R., Javaid, M., & Khan, I. H. 2019. Artificial Intelligence (AI) applications in orthopaedics: An innovative technology to embrace. *Journal of Clinical Orthopaedics and Trauma, 11*(Suppl 1), S80–S81. https://doi.org/10.1016/j.jcot.2019.06.012.

32. Sohrabi, C., Alsafi, Z., O'Neill, N., Khan, M., Kerwan, A., Al-Jabir, A., Iosifidis, C., & Agha, R. 2020. World Health Organization declares global emergency: A review of the 2019 novel coronavirus (COVID-19). *International Journal of Surgery, 71*–76. http://doi.org/10.1016/j.ijsu.2020.02.034.

33. Chen, S., Yang, J., Yang, W., Wang, C., & Barnighausen, T. 2002. COVID-19 control in China € during mass population movements at New Year. *Lancet, 395*(10226), 764–766. https://doi.org/10.1016/S0140-6736(20)30421-9.

34. Wan, K. H., Huang, S. S., Young, A., & Lam, D. S. 2020. Precautionary measures needed for ophthalmologists during pandemic of the coronavirus disease 2019 (COVID19). *Acta Ophthalmologica, 98*(3), 221–222.

35. Gupta, R., Ghosh, A., Singh, A. K., & Misra, A. 2020. Clinical considerations for patients with diabetes in times of COVID-19 epidemic. *Diabetes & Metabolic Syndrome: Clinical Research & Reviews, 14*(3), 211e2. https://doi.org/10.1016/j.dsx.2020.04.004.

36. Vaishya, R., Javaid, M., Khan, I. H., & Haleem, A. 2020. Artificial Intelligence (AI) applications for COVID-19 pandemic. *Diabetes & Metabolic Syndrome: Clinical Research & Reviews, 14*(4), 337–339.

37. Bae, M. S., Moon, W. K., Chang, J. M., Koo, H. R., Kim, W. H., Cho, N., Yi, A., Lyun, B., Lee, S. H., Kim, M. Y., et al. 2014. Breast cancer detected with screening us: Reasons for non-detection at mammography. *Radiology, 270*(2), 369–377.

38. Davenport, T. H., Hongsermeier, T., & Mc Cord, K. A. 2018. Using AI to improve electronic health records. *Harvard Business Review*. https://hbr.org/2018/12/using-ai-to-improve-electronic-health-records.

39. Volpp, K., & Mohta, S. 2016. Improved engagement leads to better outcomes, but better tools are needed. *Insights Report*. NEJM Catalyst. https://catalyst.nejm.org/patient-engagement-report-improved-engagement-leads-better-outcomes-better-tools-needed.

40. Collins, F. S., & Varmus, H. 2015. A new initiative on precision medicine. *The New England Journal of Medicine, 372*(9), 793–795.

41. Nezhad, M. Z., Zhu, D., Sadati, N., Yang, K., & Levi, P. 2017. Subic: A supervised bi-clustering approach for precision medicine. *2017 16th IEEE International conference on machine learning and applications ICMLA*, IEEE, 755–760.

42. Habuza, T., Navaz, A. N., Hashim, F., Alnajjar, F., Zaki, N., Serhani, M. A., Statsenko, Y. 2021. AI applications in robotics, precision medicine, and medical image analysis: An overview and future trends. *Informatics in Medicine, 24*, 100596.

43. Lee, J.-G., Jun, S., Cho, Y.-W., Lee, H., Kim, G. B., Seo, J. B., & Kim, N. 2017. Deep learning in medical imaging: General overview. *Korean Journal of Radiology, 18*(4), 570–584.

2 Medical Imaging Modalities and Different Image Processing Techniques
State of the Art Review

*S. Lalitha, T. Sanjana, H. T. Bhavana,
Ishan Bhan, and G. Harshith*

CONTENTS

DOI: 10.1201/9781003272694-3

2.1 INTRODUCTION TO MEDICAL IMAGING MODALITIES

Medical imaging processes are applied through various stages of treatment: screening, diagnosis, and evaluation and therapy. There are many types of imaging modalities, but they are mainly classified into three categories:

- Invasive
- Minimally invasive
- Non-invasive

Invasive imaging modalities require an incision for the introduction of the instrument for examination and assessment. On the contrary, non-invasive medical imaging techniques do not require breaking the skin or entering the body. Minimally invasive imaging modalities encompass smaller surgical incisions for shortening the healing time of the wound. Non-invasive imaging modalities, due to their safe and risk-free nature, are preferred over invasive and minimally invasive modalities. They also keep radioactive exposure to a minimum and have no need for incisions to provide a scanned image [1].

Non-invasive medical imaging modalities are vast in number, so for a better understanding of how these techniques work, we must familiarize ourselves with a few terminologies related to them.

- **Radiotracer and Radiopharmaceuticals:** Radiotracer is a substance that has a radioactive molecule tightly bonded with another molecule. It can be administered through injection or can be swallowed. Radiotracers work on the principle of radioactive labeling. It is the process where an atom in the radiotracer (chemical compound) is replaced by an isotope, also called a radioisotope.

  Radiopharmaceuticals, which are radiotracers, vary from modality to modality. For example, Technetium (99mTc) tilmanocept (tradename Lymphoseek) is used in SPECT scans and Tetrofosmin (Myoview) is used in PET scans [2].
- **Artifacts:** Artifacts refer to something that caught on an image but isn't present in reality. It is an error. They can be caused by resonant offsets, hardware limitations (radiofrequency non-uniformity) or motion (blood flow, respiration). An artifact is dependent on the type of imaging modality, but some common artifacts include clothing artifacts (jewels) and patient-based artifacts (motion artifacts).

The different types of medical imaging modalities discussed in this chapter are listed in Figure 2.1. These are broadly classified as invasive, minimally invasive, and non-invasive techniques.

2.1.1 INVASIVE IMAGING MODALITIES

Intravascular ultrasound (IVUS) is an invasive medical image modality that is a combination of echocardiography and cardiac catheterization. Echocardiography uses high-frequency waves known as ultrasound to produce live images of the heart; cardiac catheterization is the insertion of a catheter into the chamber of the heart. The catheter is connected to a transducer, which is guided through an artery and into the heart. The sound waves produced by the wall of the artery are captured by the transducer, and these echoes are then converted into images. The utilization of IVUS provides distinguishing proof of atherosclerosis for angiographically typical vessels, assessing halfway injuries, deciding the degree of heart allograft vasculopathy, and evaluating the aftereffect of percutaneous transluminal coronary angioplasty [3,4].

2.1.2 MINIMALLY INVASIVE MEDICAL IMAGING MODALITIES

An endoscopy is a procedure to look inside the body to examine any hollow cavity or organ. It is performed through an instrument endoscope. An endoscope is a long thin tubular instrument

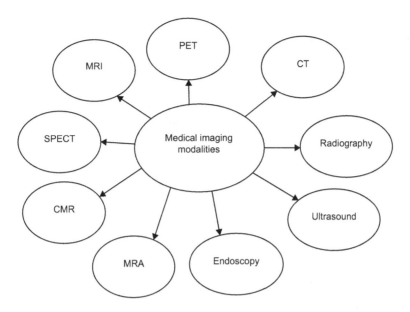

FIGURE 2.1   Different types of medical imaging modalities.

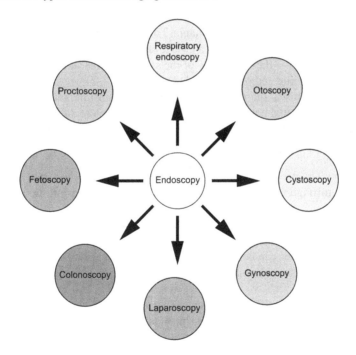

FIGURE 2.2   Different types of endoscopy.

coupled with a tiny camera and powerful light source for illumination. There are many types of endoscopies, as it is the procedure to review any part of the body. Different types of endoscopy are indicated in Figure 2.2.

The following shows the region of interest and the types of endoscopies concerning them:

- Respiratory tract:
  i. **Rhinoscopy:** This is the procedure for examination of the nose using an instrument called a rhinoscope. It is divided into anterior and posterior rhinoscopy.

  ii. **Laryngoscopy:** This is the endoscopy of the larynx. This procedure can be done using direct or indirect laryngoscopy.
  iii. **Bronchoscopy:** This is the endoscopy concerning the lower respiratory tract, predominantly areas like the bronchioles, trachea, and lung.
- Ear canal:
  i. **Otoscope:** This is the endoscopy of the ear used to diagnose otitis media (an inflammatory disease in the middle ear region) and otitis externa (inflammation of ear canal).
- Urinary tract:
  i. **Cystoscopy:** This is the endoscopy of the urinary tract and is used to diagnose conditions like hematuria, interstitial cystitis (also known as bladder pain syndrome), and other urinary tract infections.
- Female reproductive system:
  i. **Colposcopy:** This is the endoscopy of the cervix and is used to detect precancerous lesions, thus aiding in early detection of cervical cancer.
  ii. **Hysteroscopy:** This is the endoscopy of the uterus used for the diagnoses of Asherman's syndrome (intrauterine adhesions), adenomyosis, abnormal uterine bleeding (AUB), and removal of IUDs.
  iii. **Falloposcopy:** This is the endoscopy of fallopian tubes. It is used to assess and manage tubal infertility.
- Gastrointestinal tract:
  i. **Esophagogastroduodenoscopy:** This is the endoscopy of upper gastrointestinal tract, used to evaluate dysphagia, odynophagia, IBD (inflammatory bowel disease), and for the surveillance of ulcers and after a gastric surgery.
  ii. **Enteroscopy:** This is the endoscopy of the small intestine. It is used to diagnose gastrointestinal bleeding and other related conditions.
  iii. **Colonoscopy:** This is the endoscopy of the large intestine and is used to diagnose ulcers, gastrointestinal hemorrhage, and detection of colorectal cancers.
- **Proctoscopy:** This is the endoscopy of both rectum and anus and is used for the screening of colon cancer and diagnosis of the conditions such as bleeding and hemorrhoids.
- During pregnancy:
  i. **Fetoscopy:** The procedure that allows surgical access to the fetus. The endoscope is entered through a small incision and is placed into the amniotic sac through the uterus.
      The risk related to endoscopy are infections, tear of the stomach lining or the lining of the esophagus, over-sedation, and bleeding. If there should arise an occurrence of perforation, most causes can be treated with anti-infection agents and intravenous liquids. Minor bleeding may essentially stop without anyone interference or can be halted by cauterization.
  ii. **Virtopsy:** Virtopsy, as the term suggests, is a portmanteau of the words virtual and autopsy. The traditional method of postmortem is an invasive body-opening autopsy to which the best current alternative is virtopsy.

To conduct a virtopsy, the following photographic and medical tools are required:

- 3-D optical surface scanner
- CT scanner for postmortem CT (PMCT)
- MRI scanner for postmortem MRI (pm-MRI)

The virtopsy is performed as follows:

- A 3D surface scan is used to create a 3D color model of the body.
- The body is placed in a sealed bag and put through a CT scan. The sealed bags prevent contamination of the body from X-rays.

- The CT scan is used to render images of the body for examination.
- The filtered pictures give clear and itemized data on bullet paths, inner bleeding, and hidden fractures, which are elusive in a conventional postmortem [5,6].

The advantages of virtopsy method are:

- Preservation of body in virtual form.
- It is fast, detailed, and almost as accurate as a traditional autopsy.
- It provides information on difficult to access areas of the body (e.g. atlanto-occipital joints).
- It maintains the religious belief of the community about bodily integrity.

The main disadvantage of virtopsy is that it has a high equipment cost and is a relatively new field of study.

2.1.3 Non-Invasive Techniques

2.1.3.1 Radiography

Radiographic examinations are essential in the field of medicine to provide both physicians and surgeons with static and moving images of body structures for diagnosis and treatment planning. This medical imaging modality uses X-rays, gamma rays, and ionized or non-ionized radiations for viewing the internal structure of an organ. The images produced via this technique are also called roentgenograms or X-rays. Radiography is used for both diagnostic and therapeutic purposes in medicine. Medical ailments such as breast cancer, osteoporosis, pneumonia, kidney and bladder stones, arthritis, blood clots, peripheral artery disease (PAD), lung cancer, breast cancer, and colorectal cancer can be detected and screened using radiography. The merits and demerits of radiography include:

- Merits:
  i. It is a cheaper and simple technique.
  ii. It has lower radiation compared to a CT scan.
  iii. It can eliminate the requirement for surgery.
- Demerits:
  i. The image thus processed is available in a 2D format and hence less informative than a 3D image produced by other means.
  ii. It has limited abilities to detect finer cracks and is sensitive to defect orientation.

Radiography finds its uses in orthopedics, pulmonology, dentistry, and oncology.

2.1.3.2 Computed Tomography Scan (CT scan)

This is a medical imaging technique that uses an X-ray scanner to take cross-sectional images of the body. It uses energy beams to generate multiple detailed images of various organs and structures within the body, including bone, muscles, fat, and water. It produces 3D interactive reconstructions that are precise and give an idea of how organs function together as part of larger systems such as muscles or blood vessels. There are three major types of CT scans:

- **Spiral CT:** Spiral CT or helical CT checks involve the whole X-beam tube being rotated around the focal hub of the space being filtered. It produces detailed scans that may be better at finding small abnormal areas inside the body. These are the dominating scanners utilized in the clinical business since they offer a lower cost of creation and buy.
- **Electron Beam Tomography:** EBT is a type of computed tomography where an electron gun is used to scan for abnormalities. The upside of EBT machines is that because the

X-beam source-point is cleared electronically, not mechanically, it tends to be cleared with far greater speed. This upgrades the nature of the scan and works on the exactness of the output. EBT is explicitly utilized for imaging of moving organs, like the heart and arteries (coronary angiogram).

- **CT Perfusion Imaging:** CT perfusion imaging is the imaging technique that indicates the parts of brain supplied with sufficient blood and also information regarding flow of blood to the brain. It is better for stroke diagnosis than other CT types.

2.1.3.3   Magnetic Resonance Imaging (MRI)

MRI or nuclear MRI (NMRI) is a type of imaging that provides diagnostic images without the use of X-rays. It differs from radiography and CT scans in that it doesn't employ X-rays. It is the use of nuclear magnetic resonance in medicine (NMR). Because of its non-ionizing nature, MRI is widely employed. The images are formed by altering the sequence of radiofrequency (RF) pulses, and the contrast of the images is determined by two tissue-specific parameters:

- The longitudinal relaxation time (T1): This is the time constant, which regulates the rate at which energized protons return to equilibrium.
- The transverse relaxation time (T2): This is the time constant that controls the rate at which energized protons reach equilibrium.

By reconfiguring repetition time (TR) and time of echo (TE), MRI images are made to contrast different tissue types:

- **T1 Weighted MRI:** These images are produced by using short TR and TE times and has the following characteristics:
  i. Fat and meniscal tear appear white.
  ii. Muscle and ligaments are light gray or dark gray in color.
  iii. Air and conical bones appear dark.
- **T2 Weighted MRI:** These images are produced by using longer TR and TE times and have the following characteristics:
  i. Water and CSF appear bright white.
  ii. Fat, muscle, tendons, and ligaments appear light to dark gray.
  iii. Air and conical bones appear dark.

An example of T1 MRI image of the brain region of a healthy human is as shown in Figure 2.3. Some prominent medical applications include:

- **Neuroimaging:** Neuroimaging or brain imaging is a non-invasive technique to construct an image of the nervous system to study its structure and functions. It specifically deals with conditions like dementia, cerebrovascular disease, infectious diseases, and Alzheimer's disease.
- **Cardiovascular MRI (CMR):** CMR is the non-invasive imaging technique used for evaluating the structure and function of the heart. It is specifically used for the valuation of conditions like cardiomyopathies, vascular diseases, and congenital heart disease [2].
- **Magnetic Resonance Angiography (MRA):** MRA is the imaging technique used to image arteries. It is used for evaluation of stenosis (abnormal narrowing of blood vessels), occlusions (closing of blood vessels), aneurysms (vessel wall dilatations), congenital abnormalities in blood vessels (malformations in the heart due to congenital heart disease), and other abnormalities.

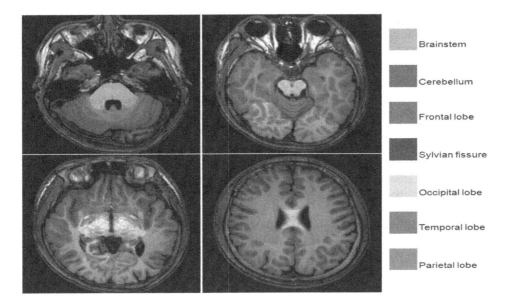

FIGURE 2.3   T1 MRI images of brain region [7].

Even though MRI does not use ionizing radiation, there are still dangers related to it. It is not advised for patients or individuals with steel implants or synthetic joints as the strong magnetic field used by the scanner may dislodge or heat them [8].

2.1.3.4   Ultrasound

Ultrasound is one of the most risk-free and cost-effective methods of medical imaging. It utilizes sound waves to deliver pictures of within the body. This technique uses a high-frequency transducer that sends sound waves traveling through the body. Once the waves get deflected to the transducer, they produce the image for prognosis. Ultrasound is a cost-effective and a mobile option of medical imaging, but it also has its demerits which include:

- It generates a low-quality image that needs skilled interpretation.
- It may be incapable of indicating whether a mass is malignant or not.

Since ultrasound is a non-ionizing type of medical imaging modality, it is considered pregnancy-friendly and is the best choice in case of pregnancies. It is mainly used in cardiology, gynecology and obstetrics, urology, and gastrology [9,10,11].

2.1.3.5   Single Photon Emission Computed Tomography (SPECT)

A SPECT scan is an imaging technique that uses gamma rays to render a 3D image of the scanned section/area generated from a large number of projection images captured from multiple angles. This technique incorporates the use of radiopharmaceuticals injected into to patient's body, which are then detected by the collimated radiation detectors. The data acquired is then reconstructed into a 3D format for interpretation [12]. Some widely used radiopharmaceuticals include:

- Technetium (99mTc) exametazime or Ceretec
- Technetium (99mTc) sestamibi or Cardiolite
- Technetium-99m-teboroxime or CardioTec
- Iobenguane i-131 or MIBG [2]

The most common use of SPECT is for tumor imaging, infection imaging, and bone scan or bone scintigraphy. Specific examples include:

- **Functional Brain Imaging:** It uses radiopharmaceuticals like Technetium (99mTc) exametazime, which detects the gamma rays emitted from the patient's body and produces an image of the malignant area or region for diagnosis. It is used to diagnose dementia, Alzheimer's disease, epilepsy, brain seizures, and so on.
- **Bone Scintigraphy:** Bone scintigraphy is the tomographic methodology that permits delivering a picture of an examined region/area, fundamentally for the analysis of bone-related issues. It is utilized to analyze conditions like joint inflammation (joint irritation), benign bone growths, Paget's sickness (thickening and mellowing of the bones and bending of the long bones), and avascular rot (death of bone tissue because of absence of blood supply to the bones).
- **Myocardial Perfusion Imaging (MPI):** Myocardial perfusion imaging is a medical imaging technique that involves scanning the condition of the heart muscle(myocardium) before and after a stress test. The stress test shows the physical stress on the blood flow through the coronary arteries and the heart muscle. It is used mainly for the diagnosis of heart diseases such as coronary artery disease (CAD) and for the detection of myocardial infarction (blockage of blood flow to the heart).

2.1.3.6   Positron Emission Tomography (PET)

Other imaging modalities capture the size and shape of the tumor, while PET is based on the metabolism of the body tissue. A PET scan works on the fact that cancer cells metabolize sugar (glucose) more rapidly than normal cells. The image produced thus has functional as well as biochemical changes and indicates the metabolic changes occurred, which with skillful interpretation and biochemical analysis is diagnosed. Since PET is a type of nuclear medicine, a certain number of radiopharmaceuticals, such as sodium fluoride, rubidium chloride, and fludeoxyglucose, are used for assisting in evaluation. The principle behind PET scans is that the radiopharmaceutical that is administered intravenously to the patient emits radiation, which is detected by the detectors positioned around the patient. The image is produced from the projection data collected by the PET's system computer. This projection data is then reconstructed into a 3D image of the region scanned.

Since PET is an emerging field in medical imaging, overtaking SPECT scanners, PET scans are mainly used for the diagnosis of conditions in the field of oncology, neurology, and cardiology [13,14].

The advantages of PET scan include:

- It provides a detailed medical image with good resolution and high sensitivity.
- It produces fewer artifacts than SPECT scans. Artifacts are features that appear in the scan but are not present in the original object.
- It generates less attenuation than SPECT scans. Attenuation is the process of removal of soft-tissue artifacts from medical images [15].

PET scans provide better results both in terms of image quality and detail, but they also cost more. For comparison, a PET scanner costs more than a SPECT scanner. Also, the radiotracers or radiopharmaceutical production for PET scans cost a lot more than its production for SPECT.

2.1.3.7   Functional Near-Infrared Spectroscopy (fNIRS)

fNIRS is a new field in neuroimaging, providing a more detailed and accurate analysis of the outer cortex of the brain [16,17]. It relies on the hemodynamic response, which is also known as the blood-oxygen-level-dependent (BOLD) response that evaluates the changes in deoxygenated and oxygenated hemoglobin concentrations of the cortex. fNIRS is a medical imaging modality that is complementary to other imaging techniques like functional MRI (fMRI) and electroencephalogram (EEG) [18]. fMRIs are based on the assessment of the changes in blood flow of the brain. EEG is a medical test based on the evaluation of the electrical activity of the brain [19]. The advantages of fNIRS are:

- It is relatively inexpensive, portable, and easily accessible.
- It has a high temporal resolution. Temporal resolution refers to the time required for the retrieval of a single frame in a dynamic image. fNIRS provides a temporal resolution of 0.01 seconds.
- It also is immune to motion artifacts and invulnerable to the electromagnetic environment.
- It is non-invasive and non-ionizing (concerning fMRI).
- It is highly compatible with other neuroimaging modalities [20].

Cerebral oximetry, diffuse optical tomography, and hyperscanning are just a few of the uses for fNIRS.

2.1.3.8 Photoacoustic Imaging

Photoacoustic imaging is a bioimaging modality that works on the photoacoustic effect. The formation of a soundwave by absorption of light by a material is called the photoacoustic effect. The soundwaves (ultrasound) are picked up by a detector and rendered as images. It is a hybrid modality combining optical imaging with ultrasound detection.

Photoacoustic imaging differs from other modalities because it renders an image based on the contrast of optical absorption of the tissue rather than their mechanical and elastic property. It has the following merits over other imaging modalities:

- It uses non-ionizing radiation and has near real-time imaging capabilities.
- It offers high-resolution multispectral images with high penetration depth.
- It offers minimal acoustic noise.
- It has a low cost of operation and it is a mobile unit.

Its limitations include:

- It is not applicable for cellular imaging.
- It shows weak absorption at short wavelengths.
- It is temperature-dependent.

2.2 MACHINE LEARNING AND IMAGE PROCESSING TECHNIQUES

To learn from data, machine learning algorithms use a specific pipeline or sequence of stages. ML algorithms require a large amount of high-quality data from which to learn and predict extremely accurate results. As a result, we must ensure that the photos have been appropriately processed, tagged, and are machine learning image processing generic. This is where computer vision comes in; this is a field concerned with machines' ability to comprehend image data. We can process, load, modify, and alter images using computer vision to provide an optimal dataset for the machine learning algorithm.

Let's imagine we want to create an algorithm that can predict whether a given image contains a dog or a cat. Because the data we acquire or produce is largely undeveloped, it should not be used directly in applications for a variety of reasons. As a result, we must first assess it, then use computer vision to perform the appropriate preprocessing, and finally apply it. The following are the steps in the preprocessing process:

- Converting all of the photographs to the same format and resizing them to the correct dimensions.
- Cropping photos to remove superfluous areas.
- Transformation into numbers so that algorithms can learn from them (array of numbers).

Each image is represented as a matrix of pixel values, or an array of pixels. Pixel values in a gray image range from 0 to 255, representing the intensity of the pixel. A 20 × 20-pixel image, for example, will be represented by a 20 × 20 matrix (total value of 400 pixels). There will be three channels when working with a colored image—red, green, and blue (RGB). As a result, one image will have three such matrices.

The processed data is then used in the next phase, which involves selecting and developing a machine-learning method for categorizing unknown feature vectors from a large database of feature vectors with known classifications. To accomplish so, we must first select an ideal algorithm. Patterns are learned by algorithms based on training data with certain parameters. However, the trained model can always be fine-tuned based on its performance metrics. Finally, we may utilize the trained model to make new predictions based on previously unknown data [21].

2.2.1 Deep Learning and Image Processing Techniques

Deep learning uses neural networks to develop effective feature presentations from data. You can use a pretrained neural network to recognize and remove noise from photos, for example. Natural imagery is made up of a variety of items with various structures. This enables the neural network to learn sophisticated and varied filters, particularly in the deeper layers.

As previously said, supervised learning is a method of learning that necessitates the use of a known dataset. This dataset includes both the right inputs and outputs for the algorithm. The algorithm is prompted to construct a model that can predict the proper output using the dataset as an example. The predictions must now be confirmed against another known dataset that is not part of the training set. The approach can only be regarded as reliable and used on unknown data if the validation phase is successful.

- **Selection of the Algorithm:** The first step is to select the algorithm to be utilized. The algorithm chosen will be determined by the task as well as the type and quantity of data available. Support vector machine (SVM), decision tree, artificial neural network, and deep learning are some of the techniques that can be applied.
- **Training:** This is the most crucial stage because the final results are determined by the predictive model created. A well-known dataset is chosen to illustrate the problem at hand. Using a dataset that isn't broad enough can lead to overfitting and poor results. For each input listed in this training dataset, an output (label) must be provided. The chosen dataset is used to train the algorithm. The goal is to create a model that can accurately anticipate each input.
- **Validation:** During this phase, the prediction model's performance is evaluated. Another well-known dataset, dubbed the test dataset, is being created. This dataset should offer correct input and output for each example and be as separate from the training dataset as possible. Using the input, the model created in the previous phase is utilized to predict the test set's output data. The algorithm predicts and stores the outcome using only the input. The distinction between training and validation is that in validation, the output label is used to evaluate the model's performance rather than improving its accuracy of prediction. The projected outcomes are confirmed.

2.2.2 Image Recognition

Image recognition is a subfield of computer vision and AI that encompasses a collection of technologies for identifying and analyzing images in order to automate a certain job. It's a technology that can recognize places, people, objects, and a variety of other things in a photograph and form conclusions from them after analyzing them. Depending on the sort of information or notion to be recognized, photo or video identification can be done with varying degrees of accuracy. A model or algorithm may detect a specific constituent just as easily as it can assign an image to a broad category. As a result, picture recognition may execute a variety of tasks, which include:

- **Classification:** This is the process of determining the "class" of an image, i.e. the category to which it belongs. A single class can be assigned to an image.
- **Tagging:** This is similar to classification, but with a higher level of precision. It can detect the existence of several concepts or objects in a single image. As a result, a specific image might be allocated one or more tags.
- **Detection:** This is required when trying to locate an object in a photograph. Once the object has been located, a bounding box is drawn around it.
- **Segmentation:** It is a detection task as well. A component on a picture can be located to the nearest pixel via segmentation. In other circumstances, such as in the case of self-driving automobiles, high precision is required [22]. The flow chart depicting the steps followed to apply image processing techniques after acquiring image from different imaging modalities is shown in Figure 2.4.

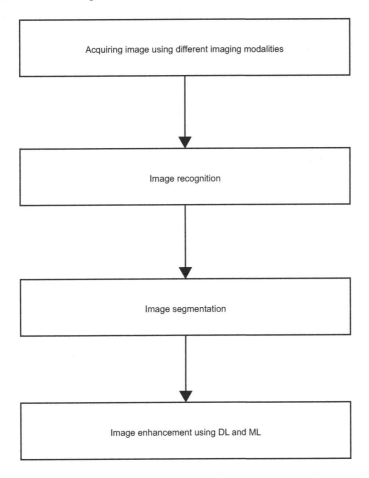

FIGURE 2.4 Flowchart indicating steps for imaging modalities and processing for better diagnosis.

2.2.3 DL-Based Medical Image Processing

CNN and RNN are popularly used for image processing as both use number of layers for performing various operations on the image. These DL techniques can be used for image segmentation and enhancement. Deep learning techniques used for image processing can be easily implemented using TensorFlow [23], PyTorch [24], Theano, Webgazer [25], and OpenCV. They support high speed processing of images as they support hardware accelerators such as GPU.

2.2.4 Image Enhancement

In medical image processing there is a need to localize certain subregions of the image. The segmented part of the image is processed to remove noise using filters. Filtering is also used for edge detection and sharpening for image enhancement [26]. In order to obtain exact information and evaluate the information with clarity, image enhancement is necessary. Image segmentation extracts and emphasizes useful information. Image enhancement will simplify the task to be achieved by emphasizing the required information from the original image. However, evaluating the performance of image enhancement is quite subjective.

2.2.5 Image Segmentation

Image segmentation means dividing the image into subregions based on the application. It is an important part of image processing as it is essential for further operations such as feature extraction and classification in case of deep neural network. Autonomous segmentation is an emerging area of research in computer vision that involves live image processing. The amount of correlation between a pixel and neighboring pixel plays an essential role in image segmentation.

The required relationship of a pixel with its neighboring pixels and other pixels in the image for segmentation is addressed in one of two ways:

- **Edge Methods:** The identification of edges or boundaries between different regions is the foundation of this technique. As a result, it's used for pixel groupings with sharp differences.
- **Region-Based Methods:** In these methods, pixels of a region is decided based on how similar they are to one other.

2.2.6 Growing and Splitting Regions

In a region-growing segmentation technique, pixels are grouped based on similarity index. It is not only necessary to define similarity criteria for grouping of pixels but also spatial relationship among pixels need to be given prominence. Similarity criteria is defined based on intensity or color. The following are some instances of similarity criteria:

- The difference in intensity between the seed pixel (randomly dispersed pixel in the image) and candidate pixel should be within a defined range.
- The difference between average intensity of growing region and absolute intensity of candidate pixel should be within a certain range.
- The difference in intensity measured over a specified region in the neighborhood of candidate pixel that should or should not surpass a certain threshold—this is frequently a basic requirement.

Region splitting follows a similar principle to region expansion but takes the opposite strategy. In this scenario, the process of segmentation begins with treating the entire image as one region, which is gradually broken down into smaller regions until the differences between adjacent regions fall below a predetermined threshold [26].

2.3 APPLICATION OF MACHINE LEARNING TO PET SCAN IMAGES AND APPLICATION OF AI FOR DIAGNOSIS OF BRAIN PATHOLOGY—CASE STUDIES

There are several current issues in medical imaging that can be addressed using ML and DL. Some of the concerns include dealing with standard formats of medical images, acquisition of images, obtaining high-resolution images, handling large volumes of data generated, and protecting privacy of the data. ML and DL techniques such as CNN, unsupervised learning, and generative adversarial network are used to handle images obtained from PET, CT, and MRI. These algorithms help in accelerating acquisition of images, image reconstruction, and improving signal to noise ratio by reducing noise and reducing artifacts. Privacy protection is also possible by federated learning. ML techniques are very much helpful in critical analysis of data with minimal human intervention and thus reduce time for diagnosis of disease. Availability of high computing power and storage devices have encouraged the use of ML and DL on large amounts of medical data. ML/DL techniques combined with domain expertise can bring in tremendous improvements in medical image processing, quick diagnosis, and treatment of diseases.

PET/MR (magnetic resonance) images can be used for diagnosing and analyzing oncology and Alzheimer's disease. In practice, there are several factors that can degrade image quality of PET images. Thus, in order to obtain accurate attenuation maps, machine learning algorithms can be used. There are several works carried out in literature where different ML techniques are implemented to improve classification, image reconstruction, and early diagnosis. For example, the Dixon-Volumetric Interpolated Breath-Hold Examination algorithm was developed in [27], which generated accurate correction from PET/MR data. A CNN-based approach was proposed in [28] to generate accurate attenuation maps from PET scan images of the entire body and identify bone. Bradshaw et al. developed a 3D CNN approach to detect cervical cancer from PET/MR data with fewer errors. A convolutional encoder–decoder network was proposed in [29], which generated good quality images during image reconstruction. Artificial neural networks (ANN) are used to improve resolution of images after obtaining reconstructed images from conventional methods such as maximum a posteriori (MAP) and iterative expectation maximization algorithm. Convolutional autoencoder and generative adversarial network are popularly used to generate spatially normalized PET images. ANN, CNN, and other ML algorithms are used to improve the quality of low-dosage PET so much that it is comparable with that of full-dose PET images. Prediction of Alzheimer's disease (AD) and corresponding diagnosis is possible with the help of AI and big data. CNN, DNN, and unsupervised learning approaches have been reported to be used for prediction, detection, and early diagnosis of AD. Classification of AD is possible with the help of CNN and RNN using segmentation and analysis of PET images. Tumor delineation and segmentation can be automated using CNN, supervised, and unsupervised learning techniques [30]. However, a challenge in applying ML algorithms for PET images is the availability of datasets.

Powerful tools used for brain disease detection include AI, data analytics, and robotics. One cannot solely depend on the decisions of the AI model since the decision-making is not clear and they appear to be a black box. Through transfer learning with the knowledge of trained professionals, the complexity of the problem can be reduced to apply ML algorithms. Misclassifications during diagnosis are not tolerable. There are two important cases that need to be addressed, namely, brain tumor analysis and diagnosis of brain injury. There is also a need to extract meaningful information from the MRI images. Brain image segmentation, soft-tissue segmentation, classification, and diagnosis can be achieved using CNN and ML algorithms. CNN is a good candidate for feature extraction. Feature extraction from raw MRI images is possible with the help of actor-critique (AC) ML architectures [31]. Partial classification and multiple decision paths, arranging them hierarchically helps in the final classification. AI techniques can be easily incorporated in the work flow followed by radiologists.

2.4   FUTURE SCOPE AND RECENT ADVANCEMENTS IN THE FIELD OF MEDICAL IMAGING

Previous sections discussed different medical imaging modalities, their diagnosis, their working, and the different frameworks and libraries used to build such modalities. In this section, focus is on the recent developments in this field and its future scope.

Medical imaging saves millions of lives every year. Over the last 25 years, this industry has revolutionized the health care sector itself. It has gone from the usage of analog to digital devices; invasive to non-invasive techniques; and from a pixelated 2D representation to a colored 3D representation, greatly enhance imaging capabilities and performance and thus aiding the detection and diagnosis of conditions and disease.

Lot of research and investments are done in the field of medical imaging modalities and its processing techniques as they play a very important role in the healthcare industry by aiding doctors in precise detection and diagnosis of various diseases. In recent years, AI and data analytics have revolutionized the field of medical imaging. With the help of these technologies, it is possible to make critical analysis of medical data and make quick decisions. Some of the recent breakthroughs include Google's DeepMind in the field of ophthalmology, ProFound AI in the field of cancer detection, and Siemens Healthineers & Intel in the field of cardiac-related disease diagnosis. There are a few other technologies like virtual reality, augmented reality, and 3D imaging that have aided surgeons in carrying out complicated operations in a planned and effective manner. Nuclear imaging is another important field that has improved diagnosis of many diseases such as cancer, Alzheimer's, thyroid problems, etc. Diagnosis is also improved by means of wearables such as a Portable MEG Brain Scanner and MRI Glove as they provide improved imaging.

Innovations that can revolutionize the future include mobile imaging, which provides the ability to provide remote monitoring, mobility, and sharing of the images. Portable ultrasound devices and their manufacturing have also transformed the healthcare industry. In addition to devices, it is also necessary to interpret large volumes of diverse data. Thus, there is a lot of scope in the field of imaging informatics. Fusion of different medical modalities such as SPECT and CT, PET and CT, PET and MRI etc., is called hybrid imaging. Some of the hybrid imaging techniques are still under research and development and thus can be explored further.

2.4.1   HYBRID MODALITIES

We are now familiar with different kinds of medical imaging modalities, such as MRI, PET, CT, and SPECT, which play a crucial role in diagnosis and other applications. Hybrid modalities, or multimodality imaging, is the combination of two or more individual modalities for better assessment and diagnosis. The purpose behind these hybrid modalities is that they should save time and provide more conclusive results than individual modalities. Modalities like SPECT/CT, PET/CT, and PET/MR are a few examples of hybrid modalities.

- **SPECT/CT:** This hybrid modality is designed to have a camera that includes one SPECT scanner and one CT scanner so that the image generated has detailed information from both scans (co-registered image). It has the following merits:
  i.   It provides clarity where other diagnostic modalities turn out to be inconclusive.
  ii. Its detection capabilities are better than other modalities.
  iii. It is time-saving. SPECT/CT has a minimum time duration of 30–45 minutes.

This hybrid modality is showing huge developments due to recent advancements in technology. Some of them are:

i. **Theranostics:** This is a new approach in which diagnosis and therapy are combined to achieve a personalized treatment for the specific patient. In relation to SPECT/CT, it coordinates nuclear medicine with standard radiation oncology, setting a model for personalized molecular oncology and precision medicine.
ii. **Minimizing Radiation:** A common trend moving forward in radiology is to reduce radiation exposure to patients.
iii. **Full Body SPECT/CT:** Unlike planar scans, a whole-body scan provides more detailed and structured features. It has better capabilities for the detection of bone metastasis and other conditions.

- **PET/CT:** Just like SPECT/CT, PET/CT is a hybrid modality that has a camera that combines a PET and a CT scanner to generate an image that the combination of the two scans (co-registered image). It revolutionized medical diagnosis by rendering images that show acute anatomical localization, which was not a part of pure PET imaging. PET/CT differs from SPECT/CT in its functionality and also the radiotracer or radiopharmaceutical used. SPECT employs a single photon emitter while PET uses a positron emitter that produces two photons in opposite directions.
- **PET/MR:** This is a multimodality that renders an image based on characteristics of PET (morphological imaging) and MRI (functional imaging). It is regarded as a better choice than PET/CT because MRI renders images based on tissue contrast (T1 and T2 weighted MRIs), which provide better features than an image taken by PET/CT. Other advantages include:
  i. It offers more accurate diagnostic capabilities (about 50% more) than PET/CT.
  ii. It offers less radiation exposure than PET/CT as MRI offers non-ionizing radiation.
  iii. It offers improved soft-tissue contrast over PET/CT [32].

The major drawback of PET/MRIs is their cost and numbers as they are greatly more expensive compared to PET/CT machines and very few exist.

2.4.2 VIRTUAL REALITY AND 3D IMAGING

Virtual reality (VR) has more uses than just video games and other recreational purposes. Currently, our scanners and modalities can produce more than 2D images; they are capable of producing various vibrant and informative scans using multimodalities. In upcoming decades, we aim to shift to virtually 3D rendered scans that may show all the intricate and necessary information that cannot be seen in 2D images or reconstructed 3D images. The power of virtual reality coupled with 3D printing can be used to enhance the accuracy of the diagnosis and limit guesswork. 3D printing can be used to print the region of interest, and this can be used for diagnosis and even educational purposes.

2.4.3 ARTIFICIAL INTELLIGENCE

AI is not just a branch of technology that impacts the future of medical imaging; rather, its main strength lies in the unification of different sectors of technology, thus revolutionizing all these sectors. With essential research and investment, AI can transform the healthcare industry. Major trends include:

- Brain–computer interfaces
- Innovation of next-generation imaging and radiological tools

- Accessibility and expansion to remote areas
- Aiding in the improvement of accuracy and analytics for pathology
- Development of smart machines
- Monitoring health via compact and small wearables
- Transforming smartphones into diagnostic tools
- Shifting from EHR (electronic health record) to more AI-maintained and automated processes
- Identification of ailment patterns and incorporating personalized diagnostics

There have recent advancements in AI-based technology. A few examples include:

- **Google's DeepMind:** It can assess 50 distinguished ophthalmic conditions with near 100% accuracy.
- **ProFound AI:** It was developed by iCAD and is used in the diagnosis of breast cancer.
- **Siemens Healthineers & Intel:** They teamed up to explore improvements that can revolutionize cardiac MRI diagnostics.

The urgent need for human-aware AI systems and the need to transform the healthcare industry will exponentially expand the AI healthcare market and ensure its future development and delivery of promising services. According to Data Bridge Market Research, global artificial intelligence in the healthcare market is expected to reach US$123.14 billion by 2028.

2.4.4 INTRAOPERATIVE IMAGING

Intraoperative means a procedure that happens during the duration of surgery. Thus, we explain intraoperative imaging as imaging techniques that are performed (and aid) during surgery so that it is a clean and precise operation. The evolution of imaging modalities has made it an important commodity, and in this scenario, it is used for verifying surgical accuracy. It is used in all surgeries ranging from neurology to spine surgeries. Fluoroscopy, cone beam CT, and fan beam CT are a few examples of intraoperative imaging.

2.4.5 WEARABLE TECHNOLOGY

Wearables have become popular in the last decade. They can be distinguished in two main categories:

- General-purpose wearables
- Medical-specific wearables

General-purpose wearables include devices that are used for collecting general medical information such as heart rate, steps, and calories burned. This is more of a feature provided rather than a full medical-based application. The devices and applications used are:

Devices:
- Fitbit
- Mi Smart Band
- Apple Watch
- Garmin

Apps:
- StepSetGo
- Google Fit

Medical-specific wearables are designed to monitor and assess a particular condition or ailment. In patients, these devices are used to monitor vitals and report in case of any disturbance. A few notable wearables include:

- **MEG Brain Scanner:** A magnetoencephalography (MEG) portable brain scanner manufactured by companies RICOH-USA helps to provide a precise mapping of brain activity and monitor the electromagnetic activity of the brain. The scanner detects absolute neuron activity and thus has an edge over fMRI and EEG.
- **MRI Glove:** This device provides clear and consistent images of moving tendons and joints, hence giving insight into the anatomy of the hand.

2.4.6 BIG DATA IN HEALTHCARE AND IMAGING INFORMATICS

Big data is a systematic method to analyze datasets that are too large, diverse, and complex. In the healthcare sector, the recent method of dataset collection is by:

- Electronic health records (EHR)
- Medical imaging
- Pharmaceutical research
- Wearables
- Medical devices
- Health examinations
- Genetic databases

Big data helps to dismantle and explore datasets generated by such methods to uncover hidden insights that improve patient care. Some renowned big data platforms include Hadoop and NoSQL.

Imaging informatics provides efficient, accurate, and trustworthy medical imaging services. We know of computer-aided diagnostic imaging techniques, and imaging informatics helps in evolving it to computer-only diagnosis.

2.4.7 AUGMENTED INTELLIGENCE AND REALITY

Augmented intelligence is similar to artificial intelligence. AI is real-time emulation of human behavior, whereas augmented intelligence allows human input and interaction with the augmented environment. Even though this is a relatively new research area, major advancements have been made [33]. Its application includes:

- As a medical education platform, AR provides an interactive and user-friendly environment of learning and education. AR can create models of the structure understudying and they can also be printed via a 3D printer. The particular applications include training nurses and anatomy.
- Preparations of crowns and caps in dentistry.
- Location of vein on patients using AccuVein.
- Projection of anatomical parts by 3D holography introduced by SentiAR.
- Improvements in aids for visually impaired (VA-ST's SmartSpecs).
- Evolving remote surgery is an act of performing surgery, even though the surgeon and the patient aren't at the same location. The AR simulates the whole process with the help of an expert who leads it and is performed in real-time by other fellow surgeons.

Advances in app development have provided great accessibility to AR apps from the PlayStore (Android) and Apple Store. A few examples include:

- **EyeDecide:** This allows the visualization and learning of anatomical features of the eye and educates us about various eye defects, such as cataract and muscular degeneration.
- **DoctorMole:** This is used for the analysis of melanoma, which in rare cases happens due to the growth of mole.
- **Medic AR:** This is based on the Google Glass app for surgeons and aids in the alignment of incision points.
- **MEVIS Surgery App:** A real-time 3D image rendering app.
- **Anatomy 4D:** An educational app.

2.5   THE ROAD AHEAD

Medical imaging in the healthcare sector is evolving at a great pace, but ensuring innovations and changing ideas into reality pose a greater challenge. Moving forward, we need to focus on the cost-effectiveness and accessibility of such modalities and innovation of new hybrid modalities, transforming computer-aided techniques to solely computer-performed techniques, developments in fully integrated medical systems and inter-system communication, improving and enhancing the role of AR and VR, automating the workstream, and much more. Successful implementation of the ideas mentioned would tremendously boost the development of the healthcare sector, taking us closer to a future of endless possibilities.

REFERENCES

[1] Zhang, X., Smith, N., & Webb, A. (2008). Medical imaging. *Biomedical Information Technology.* Academic Press, pp. 3–27. ISBN 9780123735836. https://doi.org/10.1016/B978-012373583-6.50005-0.

[2] Sogbein, O. O., Pelletier-Galarneau, M., Schindler, T. H., Wei, L., Wells, R. G., & Ruddy, T. D. (2014). New SPECT and PET radiopharmaceuticals for imaging cardiovascular disease. *BioMed Research International*, 2014, 942960. https://doi.org/10.1155/2014/942960

[3] Mantziari, A., Ziakas, A., Stavropoulos, G., & Styliadis, I. H. (2011). Clinical applications of intra-vascular ultrasound (IVUS): Experience from an academic high-volume center of Northern Greece. *Hippokratia*, 15(1), 60–63.

[4] Bourantas, C. V., Garg, S., Naka, K. K., et al. (2011). Focus on the research utility of intravascular ultrasound—comparison with other invasive modalities. *Cardiovasc Ultrasound*, 9(2). https://doi.org/10.1186/1476-7120-9-2

[5] Badam, R. K., Sownetha, T., Babu, D., Waghray, S., Reddy, L., Garlapati, K., & Chavva, S. (2017). Virtopsy: Touch-free autopsy. *Journal of Forensic Dental Sciences*, 9(1), 42. https://doi.org/10.4103/jfo.jfds_7_16

[6] Thali, M. J. (2006). VIRTOPSY: Minimally invasive, imaging-guided virtual autopsy. *RadioGraphics*, 26, 1305–1333. http://doi.org/10.1148/rg.265065001

[7] Zhao, H., Wang, J., Lu, Z., Wu, Q., L, H., Liu, H., & Gong, X. (2015). Superficial siderosis of the central nervous system induced by a single episode of traumatic subarachnoid hemorrhage: A study using MRI-enhanced gradient echo T2 star-weighted angiography. *PLoS ONE*, 10(2), e0116632. ISSN 1932–6203. http://doi.org/10.1371/journal.pone.0116632

[8] Kim, Y. H., Choi, M., & Kim, J. W. (2019). Are titanium implants safe for magnetic resonance imaging examinations? *Archives of Plastic Surgery*, 46(1), 96–97. https://doi.org/10.5999/aps.2018.01466

[9] ter Haar, G. (2007). Therapeutic applications of ultrasound. *Progress in Biophysics and Molecular Biology*, 93(1–3), 111–129. ISSN 0079–6107. https://doi.org/10.1016/j.pbiomolbio.2006.07.005

[10] Eber, J., & Villaseñor, C. (1991). Ultrasound: Advantages, disadvantages, and controversies. *Nurse Practitioner Forum*, 2(4), 239–242.

[11] Carovac, A., Smajlovic, F., & Junuzovic, D. (2011). Application of ultrasound in medicine. *Acta Informatica Medica: AIM: Journal of the Society for Medical Informatics of Bosnia & Herzegovina: Casopis Drustva za medicinsku Informatiku BiH*, 19(3), 168–171. https://doi.org/10.5455/aim.2011.19.168-171

[12] Naqvi, S. A. R., & Imran, M. B. (2020). Single-photon emission computed tomography (SPECT) radiopharmaceuticals, medical isotopes. *IntechOpen*. ISBN: 978-1-83880-629-3. http://doi.org/10.5772/intechopen.93449

[13] Anand, S. S., Singh, H., & Dash, A. K. (2009). Clinical applications of PET and PET-CT. *Medical Journal, Armed Forces India*, 65(4), 353–358. https://doi.org/10.1016/S0377-1237(09)80099-3

[14] Yeh, R., Miloushev, V. Z., & Ichise, M. (2016). Chapter 33—Positron emission tomography (PET) and single photon emission computed tomography (SPECT) imaging. Editor(s): Herbert B. Newton, *Handbook of Neuro-Oncology Neuroimaging* (Second Edition). Academic Press, pp. 359–370. ISBN 9780128009451. https://doi.org/10.1016/B978-0-12-800945-1.00033-1.

[15] Vassaux, G., & Groot-Wassink, T. (2003). In vivo noninvasive imaging for gene therapy. *Journal of Biomedicine & Biotechnology*, 92–101. http://doi.org/10.1155/S1110724303209050

[16] Irani, F., Platek, S. M., Bunce, S., Ruocco, A. C., & Chute, D. (2007). Functional near-infrared spectroscopy (fNIRS): An emerging neuroimaging technology with important applications for the study of brain disorders. *The Clinical Neuropsychologist*, 21(1), 9–37. https://doi.org/10.1080/13854040600910018

[17] Ayaz, H., Izzetoglu, M., Izzetoglu, K., & Onaral, B. (2019). Chapter 3—The use of functional near-infrared spectroscopy in neuroergonomics. Editor(s): Hasan Ayaz, Frédéric Dehais, *Neuroergonomics*. Academic Press, pp. 17–25. ISBN:9780128119266. https://doi.org/10.1016/B978-0-12-811926-6.00003-8.

[18] Bunce, S. C., Izzetoglu, M., Izzetoglu, K., Onaral, B., & Pourrezaei, K. (2006). Functional near-infrared spectroscopy. *IEEE Engineering in Medicine and Biology Magazine*, 25(4), 54–62. http://doi.org/10.1109/MEMB.2006.1657788

[19] Irani, F., Platek, S. M., Bunce, S., Ruocco, A. C., & Chute, D. (2007). Functional near-infrared spectroscopy (fNIRS): An emerging neuroimaging technology with important applications for the study of brain disorders. *The Clinical Neuropsychologist*, 21(1), 9–37. https://doi.org/10.1080/13854040600910018

[20] Wilcox, T., & Biondi, M. (2015). fNIRS in the developmental sciences. Wiley interdisciplinary reviews. *Cognitive Science*, 6(3), 263–283. https://doi.org/10.1002/wcs.1343

[21] https://nanonets.com/blog/machine-learning-image-processing/ (Accessed on 30–09–2021).

[22] deepomatic.com/en/what-is-image-recognition (Accessed on 30–09–2021).

[23] Abadi, M., et al. (2016). Tensorflow: A system for large-scale machine learning. *12th USENIX Symposium on Operating Systems Design and Implementation (OSDI 16)*. USENIX Association, ISBN 978-1-931971-33-1.

[24] Paszke, A., Gross, S., Massa, F., Lerer, A., Bradbury, J., Chanan, G., . . . & Chintala, S. (2019). Pytorch: An imperative style, high-performance deep learning library. *Advances in Neural Information Processing Systems*, 32, 8026–8037.

[25] Papoutsaki, A., Sangkloy, P., Laskey, J., Daskalova, N., Huang, J., & Hays, J. (2016). *WebGazer: Scalable Webcam Eye Tracking Using User Interactions*. IJCAI.

[26] Solomon, C., & Breckon, T. (2010). *Fundamentals of Digital Image Processing: A Practical Approach with Examples in Matlab*. Wiley Blackwell, 344 pages. ISBN: 978-0-470-84472-4.

[27] Torrado-Carvajal, A., Vera-Olmos, J., Izquierdo-Garcia, D., Catalano, O. A., Morales, M. A., Margolin, J., Soricelli, A., Salvatore, M., Malpica, N., & Catana, C. (2019). Dixon-VIBE deep learning (DIVIDE) Pseudo-CT synthesis for pelvis PET/MR attenuation correction. *The Journal of Nuclear Medicine*, 60(3), 429–435. http://doi.org/10.2967/jnumed.118.209288. Epub 2018 Aug 30. Erratum in: *The Journal of Nuclear Medicine*. 2020 Jan, 61(1), 161. PMID: 30166357; PMCID: PMC6910626.

[28] Hwang, D., Kang, S. K., Kim, K. Y., et al. (2019). Generation of PET attenuation map for whole-body time-of-flight 18F-FDG PET/MRI using a deep neural network trained with simultaneously reconstructed activity and attenuation maps. *The Journal of Nuclear Medicine*, 60(8), 1183–1189. http://doi.org/10.2967/jnumed.118.219493

[29] Häggström, I., Schmidtlein, C. R., Campanella, G., & Fuchs, T. J. (2019). DeepPET: A deep encoder-decoder network for directly solving the PET image reconstruction inverse problem. *Medical Image Analysis*, 54, 253–262. http://doi.org/10.1016/j.media.2019.03.013

[30] Duffy, I. R., Boyle, A. J., & Vasdev, N. (2019). Improving PET imaging acquisition and analysis with machine learning: A narrative review with a focus on Alzheimer's disease and oncology. *Molecular Imaging*, 18, 1536012119869070. http://doi.org/10.1177/1536012119869070

[31] Cenek, M., Hu, M., York, G., & Dahl, S. (2018). Survey of image processing techniques for brain pathology diagnosis: Challenges and opportunities. *Front Robot AI*, 5, 120. PMID: 33500999; PMCID: PMC7805910. http://doi.org/10.3389/frobt.2018.00120

[32] Ehman, E. C., et al. (2017). PET/MRI: Where might it replace PET/CT? *Journal of Magnetic Resonance Imaging: JMRI*, 46(5), 1247–1262. http://doi.org/10.1002/jmri.25711

[33] www.oreilly.com/library/view/visual-computing-for/9780124158733/xhtml/CHP023.html (Accessed on 01–10–2021).

3 Prognosis and Diagnosis of Disease Using AI/ML Techniques

K. V. Sandhya and Jithu Jerin James

CONTENTS

3.1   INTRODUCTION

Health is certainly one of the most important factors in life. In terms of the use of prediction and analysis in healthcare, the healthcare industry is making significant progress. According to the WHO, 58.39 million people died in 2019, and 2020 claimed around 59.23 million lives. Cardiovascular, respiratory, and neonatal disorders are some reasons for global death rates. The development of information technology has culminated in a substantial number of databases and enormous amounts of data in different fields. In addition, a method for storing and manipulating data for future decision-making has been derived from various databases. It is critical to extract meaningful knowledge from massive datasets and provide decision-making results for disease diagnosis and treatment. By analyzing and predicting diseases, data mining could be used to extract knowledge.

Developments in ML and AI have improved healthcare systems and delivery. Machine learning employs statistical approaches to enable computers to learn from data; in effect, data is used to construct an algorithm. Modern developments in computationally intensive methodologies, such as deep learning (DL) and artificial intelligence (AI), have resulted in noteworthy applications in healthcare due to notable advances in computing capacity. AI refers to systems or technologies that resemble human intellect and may develop themselves over time based on the data they collect.

Many applications exist that provide a prediction score based on patient information, genetic screening, etc., which can aid in the diagnosis of possible diseases, and faster and more accurate

DOI: 10.1201/9781003272694-4

37

explanations of different images like X-ray reports, among others. Remote patient monitoring can also help with getting vital patient data that can predict hospital visits, admissions, and emergencies because a lot of patient data is available, even from wearables (proactive care). It is now feasible to more accurately predict therapeutic side effects and complications. The world is seeing a global shift towards AI in the healthcare industry. Part of this stems from the healthcare industry's transition towards a cloud environment for data management; with the cloud, data is now available on a real-time scale for further analysis. As AI's capabilities increase, everything from internal operations to medical records benefits from integrating predictive modeling, automatic report generation, and other artificial intelligence features.

Prediction utilizing AI and ML techniques can aid in the analysis of data related to side effects and the development of insights, correlations, and patterns that can aid in the prediction of better results, allowing practitioners to build the best treatments to treat illnesses. It can predict health hazards such as the likelihood of death during surgery based on a patient's medical history and current conditions. Large datasets, such as cohort data, can be handled via predictive analytics employing AI and ML. It is feasible to determine a community's overall health using predictive analysis. This chapter highlights various clinical studies performed by researchers and clinician across the globe for prognosis and diagnosis of various types of diseases, with special emphasis on cancers, central nervous system (CNS) diseases, cardiovascular system (CVS) diseases, and other metabolic disorders. Most of the data used are directly from the patient during clinical studies, i.e., the primary data. The secondary data is obtained from various databases of important predictors specific to a particular disease. Further, the algorithms used to predict the outcome of the study using the data have also been explained.

3.2 ALGORITHMS POPULARLY USED IN ML/AI

Machine learning advances have led to development of powerful, adaptive learning algorithms that can outperform humans in specific domains. To effectively teach an algorithm, labeled data, including outcome data, is required. Several algorithms and techniques are being used for knowledge discovery from databases. Some of the prevalent algorithms that are used are listed next.

3.2.1 DECISION TREES/RANDOM FOREST (DT/RF)

A graph or model that looks like an inverted tree (Figure 3.1) is a decision tree (DT). The benefit of using a DT is that it is meaningful and easy to understand and deduce relations. The focus is on generating a classification model that can predict the value of a target attribute given various input values. One dataset for Alzheimer's considers age, gender, socioeconomic status, mini mental status examination, clinical dementia rating, estimated total intracranial blood volume, normalized whole brain volume, and atlas scaling factor as the nine predictors, and the target attribute dependent on the predictors is the "Group," which could be demented, non-demented, or converted. Each of the input attributes correlates to one of the tree's internal nodes. The number of potential input attribute values is the same as the number of edges on a hypothetical inner node. Recursive partitioning is used to generate decision trees. Recursive partitioning refers to separating data based on attribute values multiple times. The recursion ends in general when all of the instances have the same label value, i.e., when the subset is pure. If the majority of the samples have the same label value, the recursion may come to an end. There could be additional conditions that could also cause a halt. Pruning is a strategy for removing leaf nodes that do not contribute to the discriminative capabilities of a decision tree. This is done to improve the prediction potential of an over-specific or over-fitted tree on unknown datasets by converting it to a more general form. Pre-pruning is a sort of pruning that takes place concurrently, while post-pruning takes place after the tree has been created.

This strategy could be used for training trees, classification, and regression, and to overcome the problem of overfitting. RF is used to predict illness and analyze ECG and MRI data, etc., based on a patient's medical history.

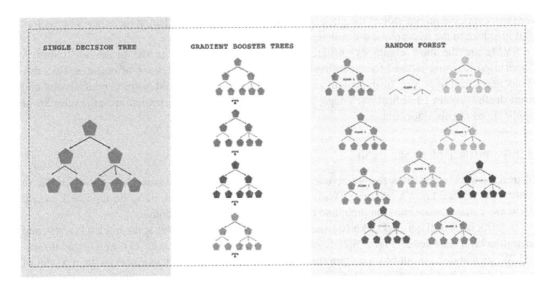

FIGURE 3.1   Decision tree (inverted tree)—single tree, gradient-booster and random forest architecture.

3.2.2   k-Nearest Neighborhood (KNN)

The KNN technique analogy base is where a test sample is compared with the training set. There are no attributes that describe the training examples. A KNN algorithm looks for the pattern that is most similar to the unknown sample. These k training examples are the unknown example's k "nearest neighbors." Euclidean distance is used to define "closeness." k is a positive integer, typically small. If k = 1, the instance is simply allocated to the nearest neighbor's class. In regression, the same technique can be used. Two phases make up the basic KNN algorithm, which includes primarily to find the k training examples that are the most similar to the unseen instance. The second phase is to take the most common classification for each of the k samples.

3.2.3   Naïve Bayes (NB)

The NB classifier is a simple probabilistic classifier that employs Bayes' theorem with strong independence assumptions. The underlying probability model would be better described as an "independent feature model." NB classifier assumes that the presence (or absence) of one feature of a class (i.e., attribute) has no effect on the presence (or absence) of any other feature. It is widely used in the healthcare industry for medical data clarity and disease prediction. When it comes to data mining, classification is sometimes referred to as data analysis, and it is frequently used to generate models that describe data classes. The Bayes classifier can produce an optimal outcome because the probability distribution is high.

3.2.4   Support Vector Machine (SVM)

SVM splits data into two groups as effectively as possible by producing an N-dimensional hyperplane. The similarities between SVM models and neural networks are striking. In fact, a two-layer feed-forward neural network and a sigmoid kernel function SVM model are the same. The process of determining the best-suited representation is known as feature selection. A vector is a set of attributes that characterizes a specific case (e.g., a row of predictor values). The goal of the SVM model is to find the best hyperplane for dividing vector clusters, with cases belonging to one category of the target variable on one side of the plane and cases belonging to the other on the other. The vectors that are close to the hyperplane are called support vectors.

SVMs are the most commonly utilized standard ML algorithm in the healthcare industry. Supervised learning is used for classification, regression, and identification of outlines. Recently it has been used to predict heart patient medication adherence and avoid hospital readmission and even death. Protein classification, image segregation, and text categorization are all examples of applications of this algorithm.

3.2.5 NEURAL NETWORK (NN)

Neural network algorithms recognize underlying correlations in data using a method similar to that of the human brain's operation. Without requiring the output criteria to be modified, neural networks can adapt to changing input and deliver the best possible outcome.

In artificial neural networks (ANNs), there is an input layer (first node), some hidden layer(s), and an output layer (last node) (Figure 3.2). Each node or artificial neuron has its own weight and threshold. When a node's output hits a certain threshold, it is activated, and data is sent to the next tier of the network. The applications include diagnosis from pathological reports, biochemical analysis, etc. It could be classified into convolutional neural networks (CNN) and a recurrent neural network (RNN). CNN helps alert doctors to the presence of a disease even before symptoms appear using various imaging methods like mammograms, colonoscopy, etc. RNN is useful in medical time-series data analysis when used for pattern recognition.

3.2.6 LOGISTIC REGRESSION (LR)

When the target variable is categorical, such as has disease/doesn't have disease, lives/die, buys product/doesn't buy, and so on, LR is utilized. Logistic regression is a form of prediction model that is similar to nonlinear regression in that it fits a polynomial to a set of data values, but it does so without using decision trees. LR is used to classify and predict the occurrence of a disease and its

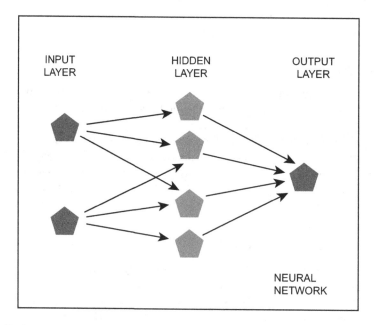

FIGURE 3.2 Basic components of neural network—input layer, one or two hidden layers, and an output layer.

management by physicians to make proper medical decisions. It also assists medical institutions in identifying patients who are at higher risk and helps patients with behavioral problems.

3.2.7 Discriminant Analysis

It is a ML method for classifying and allocating an object to one or more groups. It can be used for blood vessel imaging, understanding mental health status, diabetic peripheral neuropathy detection, and management of e-health records.

3.3 PROGNOSIS OF DISEASE USING AI/ML

The impact that different diseases have or may have varies from one to another. This state would refer to the present moment, but it is the basis that allows us to try to predict how the health of the person or patient in question will evolve. Such a prediction of the most likely course an illness or injury can take and the chances of overcoming it is known as the prognosis. This prognosis is derived from the available dataset on the patient's current status, history, environment, and the disease or injury in question.

Prognosis can be defined as

> the determination of the predicted optimal level of improvement in function and the amount of time needed to reach that level and may also include a prediction of levels of improvement that may be reached at various intervals during the course of therapy.

The prognosis itself does not necessarily have to be related to the disorder the subject presents, but rather to the expectation that is held in each specific case. Thus, for example, two patients with the same type of cancer may have different prognoses. There could be a favorable or good prognosis when the existing evidence suggests that the course of the disease the patient is suffering from leads to recovery or moderate to intermediate prognosis when the patient's state of health is not extremely positive, but there are not many indications that the possibility of death in the near future due to functional limitations or even some type of disability. Severe prognosis, or poor prognosis, refers to the conditions of a given patient leading one to believe that there is a severe risk for his death or for the existence of severe limitations in his life. The last type is the reserved prognosis, in which the doctors and professionals in charge of a patient are unable to determine the possible evolution or expectation of the outcome of the patient's condition; this is typical of moments when there is not enough information to be able to speculate on the future of the patient or when there is a risk of complications. An example of this is a patient who has suffered a traffic accident and is unconscious and with a head injury, but whose degree of affectation is not yet known.

A prognosis study was performed by Sepehri et al. (2021) on a cohort of 138 patients suffering from non-small cell lung cancer (NCLC). In stage II–III NCLC, radiomics data from ^{18}F-FDG-PET/CT scans was utilized to predict outcome. SVM, RF, and LR were used. It was observed that radiomic-based models outperformed the standard clinical staging in median overall survival and survival shorter than six months, and an accuracy of 58% and 53% respectively was obtained.

Wang et al. (2019) developed a two-stage ML model for analysis of colorectal cancer data from the SEER database. The first stage classified advanced-stage cancer patients' survivability using a tree-based imbalanced ensemble classification technique. The second stage attempted predicting survival time using a selective ensemble regression technique. Studies suggested a two-stage model was more accurate than the one-stage regression model at predicting colorectal cancer. The method's precision, sensitivity, and specificity were determined to be 0.9554, 0.0111, and 0.9954, respectively. The prognosis on different types of cancers, the algorithm used, and the outcome of the study are listed in Table 3.1.

Prognosis of CVS/CNS/metabolic disorders has also been studied using ML/AI methods. Table 3.2 lists some of the studies carried out on multiple sclerosis, rheumatoid arthritis, etc.

TABLE 3.1

Prognosis of Different Types of Cancer Using ML/AI Methods

Sl. No	Author and Year	Disease	Data Source	Algorithms Used	Performance Metrics
1	Karadaghy O A et al. (2019)	Oral squamous cell carcinoma	Using 33065 patients identified in the NCDB.	A prediction model built using the TNM clinical and pathologic stages was compared to a two-class decision forest architecture.	The model had 71% accuracy, 71% precision, and 68% recall, and treatment types predicted overall survival over a five-year period.
2	Hasnain Z et al. (2019)	Urinary bladder cancer	3503 patients with bladder cancer were used to develop prediction models.	Mutual information (MI) and machine learning techniques (SVM, KNN, AdaBoost, RF, and GBT).	With a sensitivity and specificity of more than 70%, patient recurrence and survival one, three, and five years after cystectomy could be predicted.
3	Lu T P et al. (2019)	Ovarian cancer	Cancer Cell Line Encyclopedia was used to construct a model composed of ten selected genes for chemo-response.	SVM algorithm, which was then validated in the TCGA and GSE9891 datasets. The expression of the ten predicted genes chosen by GA from 575 genes was studied.	The SVM predictive model correctly classified the cell lines into three groups with various efficacies with 100% accuracy.
4	Sun D et al. (2018)	Breast cancer	The METABRIC dataset of 1,980 valid breast cancer subjects.	MDNNMD was proposed as a method for predicting human breast cancer survival time. The algorithms employed were SVM, RF, and LR.	The precision value of the proposed technique was 0.749 and the matching sensitivity value of MDNNMD was 0.450 when specificity was 95.0%. MDNNMD.
5	Acharya U R et al. (2018)	Ovarian cancer	The proposed approach was tested on 469 patients (non-suspicious: 238, suspicious: 231).	The fuzzy forest-based ensemble classifier was used, which analyzed ultrasonography images.	Accuracy (80.60%), sensitivity (81.40%), and specificity (76.30 %) were found with non-suspect and suspicious patients, respectively.
6	Bychkov D et al. (2018)	Colorectal cancer	420 colorectal cancer patients' digitized H&E-stained tumor TMA samples with clinicopathological and outcome data were examined.	Convolutional and recurrent architectures (ANNs) using small sections of tumor tissue images as input (CRC).	The methods findings were as follows: hazard ratio 2.3; and AUC 0.69.
7	Lynch C M et al. (2017)	Lung cancer	SEER database (10,442 instances).	Supervised learning techniques like linear regression, DT, GBM, SVM.	With an RMSE of 15.32, GBM was the most accurate model, whereas SVM underperformed but produced a distinct output.
8	Zhang S et al. (2017)	Prostate cancer	The Cancer Genome Atlas.	Atypical genetic markers to create an effective prognostic prediction model (SVM).	The prediction accuracy was found to be 66%.

TABLE 3.1
(Continued)

Sl. No	Author and Year	Disease	Data Source	Algorithms Used	Performance Metrics
9	Abbod M F et al. (2006)	Urinary bladder cancer	The study looked at 67 bladder neoplasms and eight normal bladder specimens in total.	NFM and ANN were used. Gene expression profiling by DNA microarrays. With similar or greater accuracy than traditional LR, the AI techniques could predict the occurrence and timing of tumor relapse.	The approach was 100% accurate in predicting tumor progression and predicting the occurrence and timing of tumor relapse.

National Cancer Database—NCDB; tumor, node, metastasis—TNM; adaptive boosted trees—AdaBoost; random forest—RF; gradient boosting machine—GBM; gradient boosted trees—GBT; neuro-fuzzy modeling—NFM; The Cancer Genome Atlas—TCGA; The Surveillance, Epidemiology, and End Results—SEER; colorectal cancer—CRC; confidence interval—CI; tissue microarray—TMA; area under the ROC curve—AUC/AROC; root mean square error—RMSE.

TABLE 3.2
Prognosis of CVS/CNS/Metabolic Disorders Using ML/AI Methods

Sl. No	Author and Year	Disease	Data Source	Algorithms Used	Performance Metrics
1	Golas S B et al. (2018)	Heart failure (HF)	The model was trained using data from 11,510 individuals who had 27,334 hospitalizations and 6369 30-day readmissions. After data processing, the final model has 3512 variables.	Deep unified networks (DUNs), LR, gradient boosting, and maxout networks.	For LR, gradient boosting, maxout networks, and DUNs, the AUCs were 0.664 ± 0.015, 0.650 ± 0.011, 0.695 ± 0.016, and 0.705 ± 0.015, respectively. The DUNs model had a classification threshold accuracy of 76.4%, which corresponded to the hospital's greatest cost savings.
2.	Vasudevan P et al. (2018)	Glioblastoma	A GBM dataset with a suitable cohort, an aggressive adult brain tumor, was chosen, and 215 patients' miRNA expression (12042 genes) was studied.	Clustering using the max-flow/min-cut method was employed. Finally, a prognosis-enhanced NN classifier is developed for classification.	Accuracy of the method was 88.93%. The accuracy rate of the proposed prognosis-enhanced NN classifier algorithm was 89.2%.
3.	Zhao Y et al. (2017)	Multiple sclerosis	Following a period of time, up to five years after their initial visit, 1693 CLIMB, MS Center study patients were classed as having an elevated Expanded Disability Status Scores (EDSS) ≥ 1.5 (worsening) or not (non-worsening).	To predict EDSS at five years, SVM was utilized to develop the classifier, which was then compared to LR using demographic, clinical, and MRI data collected at years one and two.	In most cases, LR performed more poorly than SVM. Overall SVM sensitivity and specificity were 62% and 65% respectively in the first year. One year of additional MRI data boosted sensitivity (71%) and specificity (68%).

(Continued)

TABLE 3.2
(Continued)

Sl. No	Author and Year	Disease	Data Source	Algorithms Used	Performance Metrics
4.	Andreu-Perez J et al. (2017)	Rheu-matoid arthritis	There were 30 participants in the study: 10 RA patients and 20 healthy controls. Developed a method for creating fine-grained actigraphies to record the impact of the disease on patients' regular activities.	ML method dichotomous mapped forest (DMF) was employed. Several alternative ML methods, such as radial basis-SVM (RB-SVM), RF, convolutional deep belief networks (CDBN), and continuous hidden Markov models (HMMs), were used and compared the performance results.	Accuracy was found to be 95% and F-Score 81%.

Heart failure—HF; electronic medical record—EMR; CLIMB-Comprehensive Longitudinal Investigation of MS at the Brigham and Women's Hospital.

Krittanawong C et al. (2020) developed a meta-analytic approach in ML using CNN, SVM, boosting algorithm, and custom-built algorithm to predict coronary artery disease; CNN, SVM, boosting algorithm, decision tree, custom-built algorithm, and random forest to predict stroke; and CNN, LR, SVM, boosting algorithm, in-house algorithm, and RF to predict heart failure and for the prediction of cardiac arrhythmias. MEDLINE, Embase, and Scopus databases were used. There were 103 cohorts in all, with a total of 3,377,318 patients in the research. Twelve cohorts examined cardiac arrhythmias (3,144,799 patients), 45 cohorts assessed coronary artery disease (117,200 patients), 34 cohorts assessed stroke (5,577 patients), and 12 cohorts tested heart failure (109,742 patients). For coronary artery disease (CAD) prediction, boosting algorithms and custom-built algorithms had a pooled AUC of 0.88 and 0.93 at 95% confidence interval respectively. For stroke prediction, SVM, boosting, and CNN algorithms had a pooled AUC of 0.92, 0.91, and 0.90 at 95% confidence interval respectively. This study clearly demonstrates the efficacy of various algorithms in the prognosis of coronary artery disease.

3.4 DIAGNOSIS OF DISEASE USING AI/ML

There is immense population pressure on doctors, and hence providing proper medical attention is not an easy approach. AI/ML could aid doctors in swift diagnosis and save consultancy time and brain work and enable quick and accurate diagnosis. AI/ML is being used in natural language processing for symptoms and disease expectancy, diagnosing different types of cancers, in diabetes, etc. Image processing techniques like MRI, CT scan, X-ray, ultrasound, and other techniques are popular source of data. The algorithms are trained with thousands of images of confirmed and susceptible cases and hence are able to predict the condition with new image data. SkinVision and MelaFind for detecting skin cancers and EyeArt for diabetic retinopathy are some of the AI medical diagnostics. OneRemission and youper are some chatbots using AI to offer lifestyle advice like diet and exercise, and some are used for navigation to the nearest medical facility.

Nilashi M et al. (2017) analyzed the Wisconsin Diagnostic Breast Cancer (WDBC) datasets containing a total of 569 instances, of which 357 instances were benign while 212 were malignant.

Also, mammographic mass contained data of 830 patients. The methodology adopted included clustering (EM), noise removal (PCA), and classification algorithms (fuzzy rule-based reasoning approaches were generated using CART). The method's accuracies for the WDBC and mammographic datasets were 0.932 and 0.941 respectively. Table 3.3 lists diagnosis of various types of cancers using suitable algorithms carried out by various researchers.

TABLE 3.3

Diagnosis of Different Types of Cancer Using ML/AI Methods

Sr. No	Author and Year	Disease	Data Source	Algorithms Used	Performance Metrics
1.	Prakash P et al. (2019)	Breast cancer	The dataset was obtained from the UCI machine learning repository.	On a binary classification task, supervised ML algorithms (SVM, CART, KNN, and NB) were compared for various metrics.	SVM method was most suited for breast cancer prediction, having the highest specificity (94.7%) and the lowest rate of misclassification (19.5%).
2	Esteva A et al. (2017)	Skin cancer	To differentiate skin cancer, a total of 129,450 clinical images were used in the study.	CNN and the predictors include Keratinocyte carcinomas versus benign seborrheic keratosis and malignant melanomas versus benign nevi.	CNN achieved 72.1 ± 0.9% three-way accuracy and 55.4 ± 1.7% nine-way accuracy. The competency level was comparable to dermatologists.
3	Bejnordi B E et al. (2017)	Breast cancer metastasis	A training set of 110 whole-slide images with metastases and 160 without metastases was used. A total of 129 whole-slide images were used as a test set (49 with and 80 without metastases). (Primary).	In a simulated time-constrained diagnosis environment, seven deep learning algorithms out of 32 outperformed a panel of 11 pathologists.	AUC 0.994—best algorithm versus 0.884—best pathologist.
4	Asri H et al. (2016)	Breast cancer	Wisconsin Diagnostic Breast Cancer (699 instances—benign: 458; malignant: 241) from the UCI ML Repository.	A performance comparison was conducted among different ML algorithms: SVM, DT (C4.5), NB, and KNN. (WEKA data mining tool.)	SVM has the best accuracy (97.13%) and the lowest error rate.
5	Miranda G H and Felipe J C (2015)	Breast cancer	40 images of nodules and 36 images regarding calcifications were obtained from Digital Database for screening mammography (DDSM).	Developed a computer-aided diagnosis tool using fuzzy logic for classification as per BI-RADS. Fuzzy Omega algorithm was used.	The accuracy was 76.67% for nodules and 83.34% for calcifications when the findings were compared.
6	Kim S et al. (2014)	Liver cancer	Used sensor arrays with a large number of sensing points to diagnose liver cancer from 314 healthy people and 81 patients.	NN and FNN.	An accuracy of 99.19% for NN and 98.19% for FNN.

fuzzy neural network—FNN; classification and regression tree—CART; breast imaging reporting and data system—BI-RADS; area under the ROC curve—AUC.

Hannun et al. (2019) used 91,232 single-lead ECGs from 53,549 individuals. A deep neural network (DNN) was developed to categorize 12 rhythm classes, and to detect arrhythmias a convolutional DNN that accepted raw ECG data was used as input. DNN outperformed average cardiologists (AROC-0.780) with an AROC of 0.97 and an average F1 score of 0.837. Table 3.4 lists the various CVS-related studies.

Lu D et al. (2018) worked on the Alzheimer's Disease Neuroimaging Initiative (ADNI) database. The participants in this study were ADNI individuals (N=1242) who received both an MRI scan and an FDG-PET image. The MMDNN (Multimodal and Multiscale Deep Neural Network) was used to discriminate individuals with Alzheimer's disease. The method showed great accuracy in identifying patients with MCI who would convert to Alzheimer's disease. Table 3.5 lists a few studies carried out in CNS related disorders.

Hamidi S H et al. (2021) suggested theoretically that pirfenidone could be used as an effective medicine for suppressing inflammatory response during COVID-19. Son L H et al. (2018) suggested Dental Diagnosis System (DDS). It was developed using real dental images, which included 87 dental images of five common diseases, namely root fracture, missing teeth, decay, and periodontal

TABLE 3.4
Diagnosis of CVS Disorders Using ML/AI Methods

Sl. No	Author and Year	Disease	Data Source	Algorithms Used	Performance Metrics
1	Isinkaye F O et al. (2017)	Cardiovascular Disease (CVD)	MySQL, PHP, JAVA (Android), and XML (Android Studio) were used, with tools like XAMPP, PhpStorm, and Android O/S assisting in the integration of these techniques.	Designed a mobile neuro-fuzzy system that diagnoses and suggests possible therapies for CVD through interactivity with the user, combining the intelligence approach of ANN with the human-like reasoning style of fuzzy logic.	Diagnosis of common heart-related issues was possible. It could be utilized on mobile devices to provide rapid aid to patients who do not have immediate access to medical professionals.
2	Rubin J et al. (2017)	Cardiac auscultation	2016 PhysioNet Computing in Cardiology challenge (48 teams who submitted 348 entries).	Developed an algorithm that takes PCG waveforms as input and classifies them as normal or abnormal using a deep CNN architecture.	The final specificity, sensitivity, and overall scores for the challenge entry were 0.95, 0.73, and 0.84, respectively.
3	Acharya U R et al. (2013)	CAD	400 each normal cases and CAD patients.	Many supervised classifiers (DT, FS, GMM, RBPNN, KNN, NB) were tested utilizing a variety of combinations of relevant attributes in order to discover the best combination. In addition, a novel, highly discriminative HeartIndex was established.	For CAD identification, the GMM classifier using a feature subset of nine significant characteristics had the highest accuracy, sensitivity, specificity, and positive predictive value of 100%. If the HeartIndex value is greater than 2.6, the individual is diagnosed with CAD; otherwise, the subject is considered normal.

Gaussian Mixture Model—GMM; fuzzy sugeno—FS; radial basis probabilistic neural network—RBPNN; phonocardiogram—PCG.

TABLE 3.5

Diagnosis of CNS Disorders Using ML/AI Method

Sr. No	Author and Year	Disease	Data Source	Algorithms Used	Performance Metrics
1	Arbabshirani M R et al. (2018)	Intracranial hemorrhage (ICH)	A total of 46,583 CT scans of the head were used in the study (almost 2 million images). Before being tested on 9499 unknown research, a deep CNN was trained on 37,074 trials.	Deep CNN could analyze head CTs automatically, prioritize radiology worklists, and shorten the time it takes to diagnose ICH.	The AROC for the model was 0.846 (0.837–0.856).
2	Liu M et al. (2018)	Alzheimer's disease (AD)	The approach was tested on FDG-PET images from 339 individuals in the ADNI database, including 93 Alzheimer's patients, 146 MCI patients, and 100 healthy controls.	A mixture of 2D CNN and RNNs was produced after decomposing a 3D PET picture into a sequence of 2D slices. For classification, it learns intra-slice and inter-slice features.	The method's AUC for AD vs. NC (normal control) classification was 95.3%, and for MCI (mild cognitive impairment) vs. NC classification was 83.9%, demonstrating promising outcomes for AD and MCI classifications.
3	Ma C et al. (2014)	Parkinson's disease (PD)	ML repository at the University of California, Irvine (UCI). The PD dataset contains voice measurements from 31 subjects, 23 of whom have been diagnosed with PD. The dataset contains 195 instances, 48 of which are healthy and 147 of which are PD cases.	A two-stage hybrid method called SCFW-KELM was compared with KELM, SVM, KNN, and ELM.	The method resulted in 99.49% classification accuracy, 100% sensitivity, 99.39% specificity, 99.69% AUC; 0.9964 was the f—measure value and 0.9867 the kappa value.
4	Salvatore C et al. (2014)	Parkinson's disease (PD) and progressive supranuclear palsy (PSP)	The researchers employed morphological T1-weighted magnetic resonance images (MRIs) of 28 PD, PSP, and healthy control participants.	To analyze MRIs, researchers employed a combination of principal component analysis (PCA) as a feature extraction approach and SVM as a classification tool.	Individual diagnosis was achieved with accuracy, specificity, and sensitivity > 90% using this approach. It helped in obtaining PD and PSP morphological biomarkers based on voxels.

Computed tomography—CT; fluorodeoxyglucose-positron emission tomography—FDG-*PET;* subtractive clustering features weighting—SCFW; kernel-based extreme learning machine—KELM.

bone resorption. It was based on the hybrid approach of segmentation using semi-supervised fuzzy clustering, classification based on graph-based clustering algorithm-affinity propagation clustering (APC), APC+, and decision-making. The suggested DDS approach was validated and compared to other relevant algorithms. The DDS accuracy was superior to other methods. Table 3.6 lists the diagnosis of various metabolic disorders using ML/AI methods. AI/ML technology can thus help improve diagnosis of various diseases.

TABLE 3.6

Diagnosis of Metabolic Disorders Using ML/AI Methods

Sr. No	Author and Year	Disease	Data Source	Algorithms Used	Performance Metrics
1	Gulati V et al. (2021)	Kidney disease	Patient records were downloaded from UCI Repository.	Following ML algorithms were used for comparative analysis—SVM, DT, NB, RF, RNN.	SVM accuracy was 96.7% with 14 features, and MLP accuracy was 99.5% with 24 attributes. RNN had the best result with 95.6% accuracy for all metabolite features.
2	Stidham R W et al. (2019)	Ulcerative colitis	The four-level Mayo subscore was used to grade endoscopic pictures retrospectively. The investigation included a total of 16514 images from 3082 patients.	A 159-layer CNN was used to create a deep learning model.	With an AUROC of 0.966 (95% CI, 0.967–0.972) and a PPV of 0.87, the CNN was effective in making the distinction between endoscopic remission and moderate-to-severe disease.
3	Ahmad W et al. (2018)	Thyroid disease	ML repository at the University of California, Irvin (UCI). The dataset includes 3163 records with 25 attributes, containing 152 disease samples and 3011 healthy samples.	A hybrid decision support system was developed using linear discriminant analysis (LDA), KNN weighted preprocessing, and adaptive neuro-fuzzy inference system (ANFIS).	The accuracy, sensitivity, and specificity of this approach computed classification analysis were 98.5, 94.7, and 99.7%, respectively.
4	Ibrahim R et al. (2018)	Hepatitis	On a dataset (Carnegie Mellon University database) with 155 instances and 20 attributes, the system was constructed using MATHLAB, a technical computing language.	Adaptive neuro-fuzzy inference system (ANFIS) that combines fuzzy logic's knowledge base and reasoning aspects with an ANN's self-learning capability.	The method gave an accuracy of 90.2%.
5	Bhargava N et al. (2017)	Arthritis	The patient dataset was generated using data obtained by data from Koch & Edwards from a double-blind clinical experiment. The study takes into account five attributes.	Simple CART (classification and regression tree) algorithm was used to analyze the improvement using WEKA.	Measured the accuracy of class like TP rate, FP rate, precision, and recall.
6	Charleonnan A et al. (2016)	Kidney disease	The prediction models were built using the Indians Chronic Kidney Disease (CKD) dataset, which consisted of 400 cases and 24 attributes with two classes and was downloaded from the UCI machine learning repository.	KNN, SVM, LR, and DT classifiers were four machine learning approaches investigated.	SVM classifier had the highest accuracy (98.3%). SVM has the highest sensitivity (0.99). Hence, SVM classifier was suitable for predicting chronic renal disease.
7	Sinha P et al. (2015)	Kidney disease	The kidney function test (KFT) dataset containing 400 instances and 25 attributes are used in this comparative study.	SVM and KNN classifiers were compared.	KNN (accuracy=0.7875, precision=0.8571) classifier was better than SVM (accuracy = 0.7375, precision = 0.5000).
8	Lukmanto R B et al. (2015)	Diabetes mellitus (DM)	Indonesia's eastern Jakarta hospital laboratories (311 relevant data).	Computational intelligence was used to construct a fuzzy hierarchical model capable of early identification of DM.	87.46% of the 311 pertinent data matched the statement of the medical doctor.

Positive predictive value—PPV.

3.5 MATHEMATICAL MODELS FOR PREDICTING INFECTIOUS DISEASES

There are many mathematical models that could be could be used to predict the transmission of infectious diseases. Some popular ones include SEIR (susceptible, exposed, infected, and removed), SIR (susceptible, infected, and recovered), GLEaM (global epidemic and mobility model), TRANSIMS (transportation analysis simulation system), IBM (individual based model), etc Mohamadou Y et al (2020). SIR and IBM are used to study the infection rate of the disease. GLEaM simulates global transmission and TRANSIMS models the physical contact patterns due to global travel. Some of these models were popularly used in the prediction of the spread of COVID-19.

3.6 CONCLUSIONS

The impact of AI in healthcare will be critical to improve the efficiency and precision in the diagnosis and prognosis of several diseases, including cancer, diabetes, Alzheimer's, etc. Karadaghy O A et al., Hasnain Z et al., Lu T P et al., Sun D et al., and many other scientists working on various types of cancers, including breast cancer, ovarian cancer, etc., evidently proved the prognosis of cancers could be predicted with greater than 70% accuracy. Similar results were obtained in the prognosis of metabolic disorders like stroke, rheumatoid arthritis, etc.

Application of AI/ML also showed promising results in the diagnosis of cancers like breast cancer, liver cancer, and lung cancer and CVS disorders like CAD, cardiac auscultation, and other CVS diseases that were reviewed. Arbabshirani M R et al., Liu M et al., and Ma C et al. have reported the diagnosis of Alzheimer's and Parkinson's disease with greater than 80% accuracy. This method proved helpful in the diagnosis of diabetes (Lukmanto R B et al.), thyroid disease (Ahmad W et al.) and other metabolic disorders with greater than 90% accuracy.

Early detection as well as successful diagnosis and prognosis could thus drastically reduce the mortality rate and continue improving human health. Currently its drawbacks are its inability to diagnose rarer diseases with scarce datasets effectively; however with increasing datasets over time, it is safe to say that this will be a temporary setback. With the huge amount of data being added on a daily basis and advances in the field of informatics, the future of AI in healthcare seems bright.

3.7 AUTHORSHIP CONTRIBUTION STATEMENT

K. V. Sandhya: Resources, conceptualization, supervision, writing—original draft, writing—review and editing, validation. Jithu Jerin James: Resources, writing—review and editing, visualization.

3.8 DECLARATION OF COMPETING INTEREST

The authors declare that they have no known competing financial interests or personal relationships that could have appeared to influence the work reported in this chapter.

ACKNOWLEDGMENTS

The authors are grateful to Dr. S. Bharath, Dean, Faculty of Pharmacy, M S Ramaiah University of Applied Sciences, Bengaluru, and the Management of MS Ramaiah University of Applied Sciences, Bengaluru, for providing the necessary support for the study.

REFERENCES

Abbod, M. F., Catto, J. W. F., Linkens, P. J., et al. 2006. Artificial intelligence technique for gene expression profiling of urinary bladder cancer. In: *3rd International IEEE Conference Intelligent Systems*, IEEE: 646–651.

Acharya, U. R., Rajendra, A., Akter, P. C., et al. 2018. Use of nonlinear features for automated characterization of suspicious ovarian tumors using ultrasound images in Fuzzy Forest Framework. *Int J Fuzzy Syst* 20, no. 4: 1385–1402.

Acharya, U. R., Vinitha, S. S., Muthu, M. R. K., et al. 2013. Automated classification of patients with coronary artery disease using grayscale features from left ventricle echocardiographic images. *Comput Methods Programs Biomed* 112, no. 3: 624–632.

Ahmad, W., Ayaz, A., Chuncheng, L., Barkat, A. K., and Lican, H. 2018. A novel hybrid decision support system for thyroid disease forecasting. *Soft Comput* 22, no. 16: 5377–5383.

Andreu-Perez, J., Garcia-Gancedo, L., Jonathan, M., et al. 2017. Developing fine-grained actigraphies for rheumatoid arthritis patients from a single accelerometer using machine learning. *Sensors* 17, no. 9: 1–22.

Arbabshirani, M. R., Brandon, K. F., Gino, J. M., et al. 2018. Advanced machine learning in action: identification of intracranial hemorrhage on computed tomography scans of the head with clinical workflow integration. *NPJ Digit Med* 1, no. 9.

Asri, H., Hajar, M., Hassan, A. M., and Thomas, N. 2016. Using machine learning algorithms for breast cancer risk prediction and diagnosis. *Procedia Comput Sci* 83: 1064–1069.

Bejnordi, B. E., Mitko, V., Paul, J. V. D., et al. 2017. Diagnostic assessment of deep learning algorithms for detection of lymph node metastases in women with breast cancer. *J Am Med Assoc* 318, no. 22: 2199–2210.

Bhargava, N., Purohit, R., Sharma, S., and Kumar, A. 2017. Prediction of arthritis using classification and regression tree algorithm. *Proceedings of the 2nd International Conference on Communication and Electronics Systems*, ICCES: 606–610.

Bychkov, D., Nina, L., Riku, T., et al. 2018. Deep learning-based tissue analysis predicts outcome in colorectal cancer. *Sci Rep* 8, no. 1: 1–11.

Charleonnan, A., Thipwan, F., Tippawan, N., Wandee, C., Sathit, S., and Nitat, N. 2016. Predictive analytics for chronic kidney disease using machine learning techniques. *2016 Management and Innovation Technology International Conference, MITiCON*, MIT: 80–83.

Esteva, A., Brett, K., Roberto, A., et al. 2017. Dermatologist-level classification of skin cancer with deep neural networks. *Nature* 542, no. 7639: 115–118.

Golas, S. B., Takuma, S., Stephen, A., et al. 2018. A machine learning model to predict the risk of 30-day readmissions in patients with heart failure: a retrospective analysis of electronic medical records data. *BMC Med Inform Decis Mak* 18, no. 1.

Gulati, V., and Neeraj, R. 2021. Comparative analysis of machine learning techniques based on chronic kidney disease dataset. *IOP Conference Series: Materials Science and Engineering* 1131, no. 1.

Hamidi, S. H., Sandhya, K. V., and Hamidi, S. H. 2021. Role of pirfenidone in TGF-β pathways and other inflammatory pathways in acute respiratory syndrome coronavirus 2 (SARS-Cov-2) infection: a theoretical perspective. *Pharmacol Rep* 73, no. 3: 712–727.

Hannun, A. Y., Rajpurkar, P., Haghpanahi, M., et al. 2019. Cardiologist-level arrhythmia detection and classification in ambulatory electrocardiograms using a deep neural network. *Nat Med* 25, no. 1: 65–69.

Hasnain, Z., Mason, J., Gill, K., et al. 2019. Machine learning models for predicting post-cystectomy recurrence and survival in bladder cancer patients. *PLoS ONE* 14, no. 2: 1–15.

Ibrahim, R., Omotosho, O., and Kasali, F. 2018. Diagnosis of hepatitis using Adaptive Neuro-Fuzzy Inference System (ANFIS). *Int J Comput Appl* 180, no. 38: 45–53.

Isinkaye, F. O., Soyemi, J., and Oluwafemi, O. P. 2017. A mobile-based Neuro-Fuzzy system for diagnosing and treating cardiovascular diseases. *Int J Inform Eng Electron Bus* 6: 19–26.

Karadaghy, O. A., Shew, M., New, J., and Bur, A. M. 2019. Development and assessment of a machine learning model to help predict survival among patients with oral squamous cell carcinoma. *JAMA Otolaryngol Head Neck Surg* 145, no. 12: 1115–1120.

Kim, S., Jung, S., Park, Y., Lee, J., and Park, J. 2014. Effective liver cancer diagnosis method based on machine learning algorithm. *Proceedings—7th International Conference on BioMedical Engineering and Informatics*, IEEE: 714–718.

Krittanawong, C., Hafeez, U. H. V., Sripal, B., et al. 2020. Machine learning prediction in cardiovascular diseases: a Meta-analysis. *Sci Rep* 10, no. 1: 1–11.

Liu, M., Danni, C., and Weiwu, Y. 2018. Classification of Alzheimer's disease by combination of convolutional and recurrent neural networks using FDG-PET images. *Front Neuroinform* 12: 1–12.

Lu, D., Karteek, P., Gavin, W. D., et al. 2018. Multimodal and multiscale deep neural networks for the early diagnosis of Alzheimer's disease using structural MR and FDG-PET images. *Sci Rep* 8, no. 1: 1–13.

Lu, T. P., Kuan, T. K., Ching, H. C., et al. 2019. Developing a prognostic gene panel of epithelial ovarian cancer patients by a machine learning model. *Cancers* 11, no. 2: 1–13.

Lukmanto, R. B., and Irwansyah, E. 2015. The early detection of diabetes mellitus (DM) using Fuzzy hierarchical model. *Procedia Comput Sci* 59: 312–319.

Lynch, C. M., Behnaz, A., Joshua, D. F., et al. 2017. Prediction of lung cancer patient survival via supervised machine learning classification techniques. *Int J Med Inform* 108: 1–8.

Ma, C., Jihong, O., Hui, L. C., and Xue, H. Z. 2014. An efficient diagnosis system for Parkinson's Disease using kernel-based extreme learning machine with subtractive clustering features weighting approach. *Comput Math Methods Med.* Article ID: 985789. https://doi.org/10.1155/2014/985789

Miranda, G. H., and Felipe, J. C. 2015. Computer-aided diagnosis system based on Fuzzy Logic for breast cancer categorization. *Comput Biol Med* 64: 334–346.

Mohamadou, Y., Halidou, A., and Kapen, P. T. 2020. A review of mathematical modeling, artificial intelligence and datasets used in the study, prediction and management of COVID-19. *Appl Intell* 50: 3913–3925.

Nilashi, M., Othman, I., Hossein, A., and Leila, S. 2017. A knowledge-based system for breast cancer classification using Fuzzy Logic method. *Telemat Inform* 34, no. 4: 133–144.

Prakash, P., Nidhi, E., and Manjit, J. 2019. A reckoning analysis and assessment of different supervised machine learning algorithm for breast cancer prediction. *Int J Comput Sci Eng* 7, no. 3: 83–88.

Rubin, J., Rui, A., Anurag, G., Saigopal, N., Ion, M., and Kumar, S. 2017. Recognizing abnormal heart sounds using deep learning. *CEUR Workshop Proc* 1891: 13–19.

Salvatore, C., Cerasa, A., Castiglioni, I., et al. 2014. Machine learning on brain MRI data for differential diagnosis of Parkinson's Disease and Progressive Supranuclear Palsy. *J Neurosci Methods* 222: 230–237.

Sepehri, S., Olena, T., Taman, U., Dimitris, V., Mathieu, H., and Catherine, C. L. R. 2021. Comparison and fusion of machine learning algorithms for prospective validation of PET/CT radiomic features prognostic value in stage II-III non-small cell lung cancer. *Diagnostics* 11, no. 4: 1–10.

Sinha, P., and Poonam, S. 2015. Comparative study of chronic kidney disease prediction using KNN and SVM. *Int J Eng Res Technol* 4, no. 12: 608–612.

Son, L. H., Tuan, T. M., Fujita, H., et al. 2018. Dental diagnosis from X-Ray images: An expert system based on Fuzzy Computing. *Biomed Signal Process Control* 39: 64–73.

Stidham, R. W., Wenshuo, L., Shrinivas, B., et al. 2019. Performance of a deep learning model vs human reviewers in grading endoscopic disease severity of patients with ulcerative colitis. *JAMA Netw Open* 2, no. 5: 1–10.

Sun, D., Wang, M., and Li, A. 2018. A multimodal deep neural network for human breast cancer prognosis prediction by integrating multi-dimensional data. *IEEE/ACM Trans Comput Biol Bioinform* 16, no. 3: 841–850.

Vasudevan, P., and Thangamani, M. 2018. Cancer subtype discovery using prognosis-enhanced neural network classifier in multigenomic data. *Technol Cancer Res Treat* 17: 1–13.

Wang, Y., Dujuan, W., Xin, Y., et al. 2019. A tree ensemble-based two-stage model for advanced-stage colorectal cancer survival prediction. *Inf Sci* 474: 106–124.

Zhang, S., Yafei, X., Xinjie, H., et al. 2017. Improvement in prediction of prostate cancer prognosis with somatic mutational signatures. *Journal of Cancer* 8, no. 16: 3261–3267.

Zhao, Y., Brian, C. H., Dalia, R., et al. 2017. Exploration of machine learning techniques in predicting multiple sclerosis disease course. *PLoS ONE* 12, no. 4: 1–13.

4 AI-Based Approach for Brain Tumor Detection and Classification

Shweta Pandav and Dr. Lenina SVB

CONTENTS

4.1 INTRODUCTION

Cancer is a dangerous disease. It is the second leading cause of death between ages 15 and 41 [25]. The rate of brain tumor and cancer related to neurons was 6.4 among 1000000 humans. The rate of death was 4.4 among the same database provided earlier [22]. As per the standard, throughout the complete life period of the total population, nearly 0.6% will be found to have brain or other types of tumors. According to the National Cancer Institute, the number of new cases expected in 2021 is 24,530, with the percentage of new cancer cases 1.3%, while estimated deaths in 2021 are 18,600 and the percentage of all cancer deaths 3.1%.

One of the leading cause of deaths in humans of age older than 65 is brain tumor. A tumor is an abnormal growth of tissues. Tumors are checked by performing a computer tomography (CT) scan or magnetic resonance imaging (MRI) of the affected body parts [12]. Other histopathology methods can also detect tumors, such as blood tests and biopsy of tumor parts.

Tumors are mainly divided into two types: benign (non-cancerous) and malignant (cancerous). Malignant tumors spread within the body in a small amount of time and are dangerous for the survival of humans. Brain tumor segmentation is a challenging task. A tumor may be of any shape or size and may appear, with differing intensities, in any location of the brain. Early tumor detection increases the chance of patient recovery. Timely diagnosing of a tumor is helpful in terms of removing it completely. Radiologists mark the tumor region manually in MRI images. Researchers are working on engineering methods for finding the area of affected regions in brain tumors.

The proposed method uses support vector machine along with featured extraction techniques to find tumors in brain images. The second technique used is an artificial intelligence algorithm based on convolution neural networks (CNN) to classify cancerous and non-cancerous images. The first method results in more mistakenly classified images, while the second method with Softmax classifier corrected all of the incorrectly classified images. CNN is a very innovative technique in brain tumor segmentation and provides increased network accuracy.

The chapter is arranged as follows. Section 4.2 describes the current state of the art in the field of brain tumor segmentation, Section 4.3 explains the proposed methods used and Section 4.4 provides methodology details. Section 4.5 gives the experimental setup and Section 4.6 highlights the results, while Section 4.7 offers a conclusion, Section 4.8 delineates limitations, and Section 4.9 describes the future scope.

4.2 CURRENT STATE OF THE ART RELATED TO BRAIN TUMOR SEGMENTATION

The structure of brain imaging, different tumor types, and a detailed literature survey are explained in this section.

4.2.1 MRI ANATOMY OF THE BRAIN

Figure 4.1 shows the MRI anatomy of the brain. Primary brain tumors are those that originate in the brain [24].

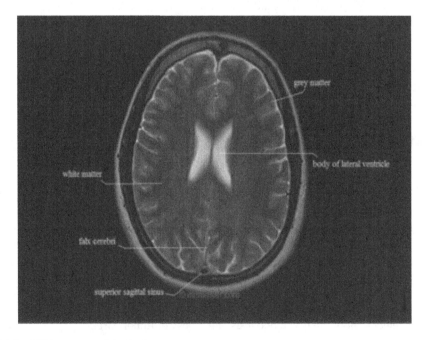

FIGURE 4.1   MRI anatomy of the brain.

Figure 4.1shows MRI anatomy of the brain. It consists of different parts of brain such as grey matter, white matter, flax cerebra etc.

These primary tumors can circulate within the brain but do not affect other body parts. Generally, brain tumorsdo not directly originate in the brain ; they start somewhere else in the body and then affect the brain. These are called metastatic brain tumors.

4.2.2 LITERATURE SURVEY

Various researchers are working on the segmentation of tumor images. A brief review of all segmentation methods is shown in Table 4.1.

TABLE 4.1
Current State of the Art of Brain TumorSegmentation Methods

Sr No.	Author	Dataset	Methods Used	Conclusion
1	S. Hondre and D. Kokare	Random MRI images	Edge detection and watershed segmentation	Basic method and gives good result [1]
2	M.R. Mahmud et al.	100 MRI images	K-means and bisecting K-means algorithm	K-means gives accuracy as 78.81% in 1.672 seconds [2]
3	J. Sachdeva et al.	428 real-time MRI images	Genetic algorithm with SVM	Identified five different classifiers and get accuracy as 91.7% [3]
4	B. Shrinivas and G. S. Roy	Publicly available dataset	K-means and fuzzy C-means clustering algorithm	FCM gives better results [4]
5	S. E. I. El Kaitouni, H. Tairi	BRATS-2019 Dataset	Automatic LBP K-means with hidden Markov techniques and deep learning with U net	K-means accuracy as 97.17% as compared to U net [5]
6	D. Haritha	Random images	K-means LBP, morphological operation, edge detection, and its combination	K-means with LBP and edge detection gives satisfactory results [6]
7	S. Pavlov, A. Aremov et al.	BRATS-2018	Machine learning with Resnet	Number of pixel-wise segmentation gets reduced in it [7]
8	F. Gargouri, I. N. A. Ben Hamida, and K. Chtourou	21 MRI brain images	Mean square error, mean error and Otsu's multilevel threshold and iterative closest point matching (ICP)	Checked with half symmetry divided and is tested against MSE with ICP and gives better results [8]
9	M. Shukla, K. Kumar Sharma	Kaggle dataset	Computer-based cropping segmentation with anisotropic filter and post processing with median filter	Erosion followed by dilation and get highest accuracy with it [9]
10	P. Su et al.	Random MRI images	SVM active learning algorithm for automated glioblastoma disease segmentation	With this method accuracy is 77.7% but accuracy increases to 88.4% with knowledge-based algorithms [10]
11	A. Bougacha et al.	50 different real-time images	K-means with watershed and genetic algorithm as well as optimized FCM clustering with genetic algorithm	Comparing all concluded last methods gives best results [11]

(Continued)

TABLE 4.1
(Continued)

Sr No.	Author	Dataset	Methods Used	Conclusion
12	H. Mzoughi et al.	BRATS-15	Histogram-based equalization techniques such as AHE, CLAHE, AIR-AHE, and BPDHE	Performance measure as PSNR and entropy, out of which adaptive histogram equalization technique gives better results [13]
13	N. Gupta et al.	100 images from CT Scan Centre	Selective block approach with local binary pattern	Accuracy of 99.67% [14]
14	M. T. El-Melegy et al.	BRATS-16	Deep learning with WEKA algorithm in which 20 different classifiers used. Dice method is used for accuracy check	Random forest classifier is obtained as best classifier [15]
15	H. Tulsani et al.	Random MRI image	Morphological watershed segmentation-means and FCM methods	K-means does segmentation in 0.6416 seconds [16]
16	S. Lu et al.	BRATS-2015	Supervised and unsupervised classification methods	ANN with GMM gives accurate results [17]
17	N. Iriawan, A. A. Pravitasari	Real-time MRI images	K-means cluster, FCM, Gaussian mixture model, Fernandez Steel Skew Normal (FSSN) methods for brain tumor segmentation and noise reduction	FCM is used for Gaussian noise reduction and GMM is proved effective for salt and pepper noise reduction. FSSN is efficient for both noise reductions [18]
18	N. Afshan et al.	Standard dataset	Histogram thresholding, K-means clustering, FCM and combination to detect the tumor	FCM with K-means clustering illustrates the best outcome [19]
19	M. Siar and M. Teshnehlab	153 MRI Images	CNN with feature extraction method	Accuracy at 98.6% with two misclassified images [20]
20	F. Gargouri et al.	19 MRI brain images	Otsu's threshold and entropy-based segmentation	Harvada gives good result [21]

4.3   PROPOSED METHOD

This chapter includes two new approaches to detect tumors in a given dataset. The first method contains SVM along with HOG as a feature to detect tumors in brain MRI images; thesecond method highlights detection using artificial intelligence methods such as CNN with Alexnet. The following section provides algorithms of both proposed methods and a detailed explanation.

4.3.1   METHOD 1 ALGORITHM FOR SVM WITH HOG

For Training:

1) Read the dataset and put it into variables.
2) Read different images used for loop.
3) Extract the HOG as a feature from each image.
4) Add the labels based on features.
5) Store the training data in separate folder.

For Testing:

1) Load the classifier.
2) Choose the image to be tested.
3) Extract HOG feature of test image.
4) Compare this feature with trained classifier.
5) Label the data by comparing.
6) Display the label.

4.3.2 Method 2 Algorithm for CNN Using Alexnet

For Training:

1) Read the image dataset and include the subfolders.
2) Label the data and calculate number of classes.
3) Use Alexnet function for classification.
4) Store the result in one folder.
5) Let max epoch be 50 and mini batch size be 300.
6) Train the network using SGDM and the above values.
7) Store trained data in separate file.

For Testing:

1) Choose the image to be tested.
2) Resize the image as per Alexnet standard.
3) Classify image by comparing with trained data.
4) Label the data and display.

4.4 METHODOLOGY

The methods used in this chapter are SVM and CNN. These are explained in the following subsections.

4.4.1 Support Vector Machine

The most difficult task in machine learning is classifying an object. Let us say we have a data item that belongs to one of the two classes. The SVM decides to which class the data item belongs. The SVM is a trained algorithm used in classification of images. The SVM algorithm plots each data item as a point in n-dimensional space (where n is the number of features used) in which feature value is the same as the value of a particular coordinate. Then, with the help of the mainplane, the two classes are clearly distinguished. SVM produces a clear margin to separate the classes. In high dimensional spaces, it produces good results.

Figure 4.2 shows the graph of the main plane and two distinguished classes. In this, the M3 plane separates two classes correctly.

Figure 4.2 shows the SVM graph of the main plane and two distinguished classes. In this, the M3 plane separates two classes correctly.

This gives accurate results when the number of sample points is smaller than the number of dimensions. It requires less memory because it uses a small set of training points in support vectors.

Let us say we have a dataset of m points:

$$(Xi, Yi), \ldots \ldots (Xm, Ym),$$

where Yi has values (1,−1)

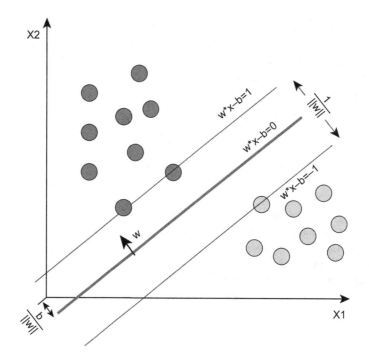

FIGURE 4.2 SVM graph.

Then the main plane can be defined as set of point x satisfying

$$W^T X - b = 0,$$

where the vector to the main plane is W.

The margins are divided into two types: hard margin and soft margin.

4.4.1.1 Hard Margin

If the training dataset contains the data points that are separated by a straight line, then we select two parallel main planes to separate two classes so the distance between them is large enough. The region under these planes is called a margin. The main planes are given by the following equations:

$$\left(W^T X - b\right) = 1 \tag{1}$$

$$\left(W^T X - b\right) = -1. \tag{2}$$

The space formed by the main plane is shown by $\frac{2}{\|W\|}$:

$$(W^T X_i - b) \geq 1 \, if \, Y_i = 1; \tag{3}$$

or

$$(W^T X_i - b) \leq -1 \, if \, Y_i = -1. \tag{4}$$

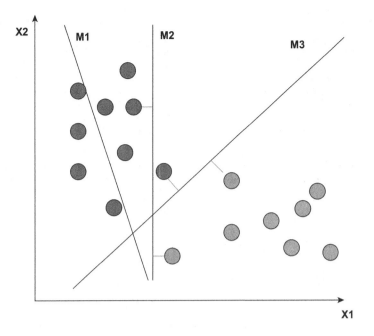

FIGURE 4.3 SVM graph with main plane.

From this equation, we summarize that the margin's right side contains data points.

This can be concluded as

$$Y_i\left(W^T X_i - b\right) \geq 1, \text{ for all } 1 \leq i \leq n. \tag{5}$$

We will get an optimization problem as follows:

Minimize ‖W‖ subject to Y_i (W^{T-b}) ≥ 1 for i = 1 . . . . . . n.

W and b determine the outer classifier.

Figure 4.3 shows the SVM graph with main plane.

Figure 4.3 shows SVM graph with main plane. It has 3 planes i.e. M1, M2 and M3 which separates two classes.

4.4.1.2 Soft Margin

To separate the data points that are not distinguished easily, the following function is used:

$$\max\left(0, 1 - Y_i\left(W^T X_i - b\right)\right), \tag{6}$$

where y_i = (1,–1), and the output is given by $W^T X_{i-b}$.

For data on the incorrect side of the margin, Equation (6) is comparative to the distance from the margin.

The purpose of Equation (6) is to make small value:

$$\left[\frac{1}{n}\sum_{i=1}^{n}\max(0, 1 - Y_i(W^T X_i - b)\right] + \lambda \, \| W \|^2, \tag{7}$$

where λ destermines the exchange value between the growing size of margin and clinching that the X_i Present on the true side of the margin. So, for small values of λ, the second term in Equation (6) is very little and neglected, so it performs like a hard margin of SVM.

The proposed method uses HOG as a feature vector to extract it from brain MRI images. The dataset is trained with an SVM classifier. The test images are checked against their own HOG feature with classifiers labeled and then classified correctly.

4.4.2 CONVOLUTION NEURAL NETWORK

Deep learning is used as an efficient technique to analyze data that is large in size. It requires the help of complex algorithms and artificial neural networks to train the system or computer to divide or classify the big data into proper classes.

One of the special deep learning networks is CNN. This is mostly inspired by human brain architecture. It has an input layer, hidden layer, and output layer. Similarly, CNN consists of a multi-layer structure that includes convolution layers, pooling layers, and fully connected layers. CNN can recognize patterns in an image very easily.

1) **Convolution Layer:** The network's computational weight age is taken by this layer. In this layer, multiplication between two matrices is performed, where the kernel is known as a matrix with known parameters, and the other matrix contains the limited value of the receptive field. If the three red, green, blue channels form one image, the kernel height and width will be dimensionally small, but the depth increases to three channels.
2) **Pooling Layer:** This layer is added to reduce the number of repeated layers to one. It decreases the structural size of the representation. The required quantity of computation and weight is reduced with this layer. Every slice of the image is checked one by one by the pooling method.
3) **Fully Connected Layer:** Every neuron in this layer is completely connected with all neurons in the previous and upcoming layers. The result is obtained with matrix multiplication. The FC layer gives the connection between input and output.

Figure 4.4 shows a block diagram of CNN.

Figure 4.4 shows a block diagram of CNN. It mainly consists of 6 blocks, first is input layer second is convolution + ReLu layer third is pooling layer fourth is convolution + ReLu layer followed by pooling layer and finally Softmax layer as output layer.

4.4.3 ALEXNET

Alexnet was first invented in 2012 by Alex Krizhevsky and his colleagues. It is pretrained model in terms of computer vision area. It has eight layers and consists of two max pooling layers followed

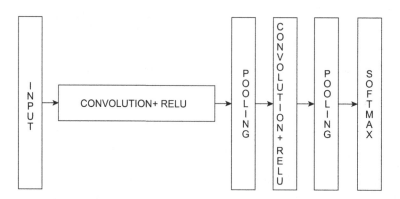

FIGURE 4.4 Block diagram of CNN.

TABLE 4.2
Alexnet Architecture with Filters and Activation Function

Layer	Filter/Neuron	Filter Size	Stride	Padding	Size of Feature Map	Activation Function
Input	Nil	Nil	Nil	Nil	$227 \times 227 \times 3$	Nil
Conv1	96	11×11	4	Nil	$55 \times 55 \times 96$	ReLU
Max pool1	Nil	3×3	2		$27 \times 27 \times 96$	Nil
Conv2	256	5×5	1	2	$27 \times 27 \times 256$	ReLU
Max pool2	Nil	3×3	2	Nil	$13 \times 13 \times 256$	Nil
Conv 3	384	3×3	1	1	$13 \times 13 \times 384$	ReLU
Conv 4	384	3×3	1	1	$13 \times 13 \times 384$	ReLU
Conv 5	256	3×3	1	1	$13 \times 13 \times 256$	ReLU
Max pool3	Nil	3×3	2	Nil	$6 \times 6 \times 256$	Nil
Dropout1	Rate = 0.5	Nil	Nil	Nil	$6 \times 6 \times 256$	Nil

TABLE 4.3
Fully Connected and Dropout Layer Details

Layer	#Filters/ Neurons	Filter Size	Stride	Padding	Size of Feature Map	Activation Function
–	–	–	–	–	–	–
–	–	–	–	–	–	–
–	–	–	–	–	–	–
Dropout 1	Rate = 0.5	–	–	–	$6 \times 6 \times 256$	–
Fully connected1	–	–	–	–	4096	ReLU
Dropout 2	Rate = 0.5	–	–	–	4096	–
Fully connected2	–	–	–	–	4096	ReLU
Fully connected3	–	–	–	–	1000	Softmax

by three fully connected layers. It uses ReLU as an activation function, which increases the training speed by six times. This model is prevented from over-fitting by using dropout layers [23].

Alexnet architecture is shown in Table 4.2.

Fully connected and dropout layers are shown in Table 4.3.

4.5 EXPERIMENTAL SETUP

The experimental setup consists of details in upcoming sections of the image dataset, the simulation techniques, and the performance measures.

4.5.1 DATASET

The dataset used in this chapter includes brain MRI images of 253 patients, including normal and tumorous patients who went to MRI centers. After examination, 155 patients are found to have cancerous images and 97 images are of healthy patients without cancer.

4.5.2 SIMULATION

The brain MRI images are observed and tested with Matlab 2021 software. Seventy percent of data is used for training and 30% is for testing purposes. The two algorithms checked in this chapter are, first, SVM, and second, CNN with Alexnet. For training purposes, 177 images are used, and for testing, 74 images. In SVM, the HOG features are extracted from trained images and tested against labeled data.

In CNN, Alexnet is used. The images used in it are of size $227 \times 227 \times 3$. It has five convolution layers and three fully connected layers. The activation function used is ReLU. Softmax is the activation used in the output layer of Alexnet. It has a total of 62.3 million neurons. All the results are tested based on accuracy, sensitivity, specificity, and precision.

4.5.3 PERFORMANCE MEASURES

The performance measure criteria used in both methods are formulated in the following for accuracy, sensitivity, specificity, and precision.

$$Acuraccy = \frac{(True\,Positive + True\,Negative)}{All\,Images}, \tag{8}$$

$$Sensitivity = \frac{True\,Positive}{(True\,Positive + False\,Negative)}, \tag{9}$$

$$Specificity = \frac{True\,negative}{(True\,Negative + False\,Positive)}, \tag{10}$$

$$Precision = \frac{True\,Positive}{(True\,Positive + False\,Positive)}. \tag{11}$$

4.6 RESULTS

The results are tested on a total 253 patients with cancerous and non-cancerous brain MRI images from standard datasets available on theKaggle website. For training, 177 images are used, while 76 images are used for testing. Two algorithms are used to detect tumors and classify the images into normal and abnormal images. The SVM with HOG feature extraction is used.

According to SVM, we get an accuracy of 87.83%, sensitivity of 93.13%, and specificity of 82.75%. With CNN and Alexnet, we get increased accuracy of 98.67%, sensitivity of 100%, and specificity of 96.55%. As per the obtained results, CNN with Softmax layer gives the best classification accuracy at 98.67%. We have used a maximum epoch size of 50 and a mini batch size of 300, and have used a fully connected layer in Matlab. Table 4.4 explains the performance measures of two methods and shows the results obtained on test data brain images.

Figure 4.5 shows misclassified images with SVM.

Figure 4.5 shows misclassified images with SVM. Out of 253 images only nine images are misclassified with SVM.

With CNN, only one image is incorrectly classified, as shown in Figure 4.6.

TABLE 4.4

Results Obtained on Test Data Brain Images

Methods	Accuracy	Sensitivity	Specificity	Precision	False
SVM (Proposed)	87.83%	93.18%	82.75%	89.13%	9
CNN + SoftMax (Proposed)	98.68%	100%	96.55%	97.82%	1
CNN + SoftMax (19)	98.67%	100%	94.64%	98.26%	2

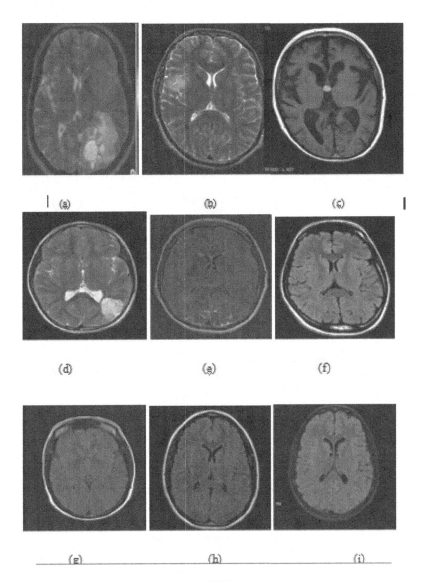

FIGURE 4.5 Brain MRI images misclassified with SVM.

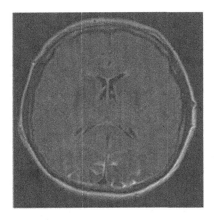

FIGURE 4.6 Brain MRI images misclassified with CNN.

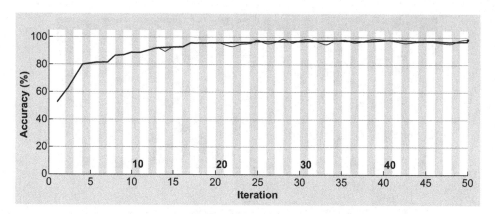

FIGURE 4.7 Testing network accuracy graph with CNN.

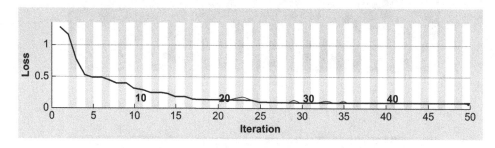

FIGURE 4.8 Testing network loss graph with CNN.

Figure 4.6 shows one brain MRI image misclassified with CNN.
The network accuracy graph is shown in Figure 4.7, and the loss is shown in Figure 4.8.
Figure 4.7 shows the testing network accuracy graph with CNN.
Figure 4.8 shows the testing network loss graph with CNN.

4.7   CONCLUSION

In this chapter, two new approaches are proposed to identify and classify brain cancer images. The SVM with feature extraction gives accuracy of 87.83%, and a total nine images are misclassified. With the new artificial intelligence algorithm, CNN and Softmax in combination give 98.68% accuracy, and only one image is misclassified. The existing CNN method gives two misclassified images, whereas the proposed method gives only one misclassified image. The comparison between the two proposed methods shows that CNN gives the best results and accuracy because it has a strong classifier with multi-layered hyperplanes. As CNN with Alexnet is very simple and a less time-consuming method, it is preferred in this chapter. From the given dataset of 253 patients, 155 images are classified as tumorous images and 97 as non-tumorous; only one is misclassified with a second method.

Different performance measures are tested, such as accuracy, sensitivity, specificity, and precision. From the obtained results, CNN with Softmax proves to be an efficient method to classify tumor images, while SVM with HOG is also a new approach for classifying the two types of images.

4.8 LIMITATIONS

1) Only two methods, SVM with HOG feature extraction and CNN with Alexnet, are compared.
2) Different datasets are not used to check the results.
3) The tumor is not extracted from the original image with given methods.
4) The area of the tumorous part is not calculated.

4.9 FUTURE SCOPE

This chapter focuses on two methods: SVM with HOG feature and CNN with Alexnet. It provides a limited approach. In the future, continuous monitoring of a patient's data and applying other methods, such as Resnet, U net, etc., will be helpful in detecting and curing the tumor. This adds accuracy for detection and can save a patient's life with proper treatment. Different datasets with more images could be used and tested against different methods in the future to get better results.

REFERENCES

1. S. Handore, D. Kokare: Performance Analysis of Various Methods of Tumor Detection Published in *International Conference on Pervasive Computing (ICPC)* (2015).
2. M. Mahmud, M. Mamun, M. Hussain: Comparative Analysis of K-Means and Bisecting K-Means Algorithms for Brain Tumor Detection published in *International Conference on Computer, Communication, Chemical, Material and Electronic Engineering (IC4ME2)* (2018).
3. J. Sachdeva, V. Kumar, I. Gupta, N. Khandelwal, C. K. Ahuja: Multiclass Brain Tumor Classification Using GA-SVM published in *Developments in E-systems Engineering*, pp. 182–187 (2011).
4. B. Srinivas, G. S. Rao: Unsupervised Learning Algorithms for MRI Brain Tumor Seg-Mentation published in *Conference on Signal Processing and Communication Engineering Systems (SPACES)*, pp. 181–184 (2018).
5. S. E. I. El Kaitouni, H. Tairi: Segmentation of Medical Images for the Extraction of Brain Tumors: A Comparative Study Between the Hidden Markov and Deep Learning Approaches published in *International Conference on Intelligent Systems and Computer Vision (ISCV)* (2020).
6. D. Haritha: Comparative Study on Brain Tumor Detection Techniques published in *International Conference on Signal Processing, Communication, Power and Embedded System (SCOPES)*, pp. 1387–1391 (2016).
7. S. Pavlov, A. Artemov, M. Sharaev, A. Bernstein, E. Burnaev: Weakly Supervised Fine Tuning Approach for Brain Tumor Segmentation Problem published in *18th IEEE International Conference on Machine Learning and Applications (ICMLA)* (2019).
8. F. Gargouri, I. N. A. Ben Hamida, K. Chtourou: Automatic Localization Methodology Dedicated to Brain Tumors Based on ICP Matching by Using Axial MRI Symmetry published in *1st International Conference on Advanced Technologies for Signal and Image Processing (ATSIP)*, pp. 209–212 (2014).
9. M. Shukla, K. Kumar, A. Sharma: Comparative Study to Detect Tumor in Brain MRI Images using Clustering Algorithms published in *2nd International Conference on Innovative Mechanisms for Industry Applications (ICIMIA)*, pp. 773–777 (2020).
10. P. Su, Z. Xue, L. Chi, J. Yang, S. T. Wong: Support Vector Machine (SVM) Active Learning for Automated Glioblastoma Segmentation published in *9th IEEE International Symposium on Biomedical Imaging (ISBI)*, pp. 468–473 (2012).
11. Bougacha, J. Boughariou, M. Ben Slima, A. Ben Hamida, K. Ben Mahfoudh, O. Kammoun, C. Mhiri, et al.: Efficient Segmentation Methods for Tumor Detection in MRI Images published in *4th International Conference on Advanced Technologies for Signal and Image Processing (ATSIP)* (2018).
12. K. K. Gupta, N. Dhanda, U. Kumar: A Comparative Study of Medical Image Seg-mentation Techniques for Brain Tumor Detection published in *4th International Conference on Computing Communication and Automation (ICCCA)*, pp. 1–4 (2018).
13. H. Mzoughi, I. Njeh, M. Ben Slima, A. Ben Hamida: Histogram Equalization-based Techniques for Contrast Enhancement of MRI Brain Glioma Tumor Images: Comparative Study published in *4th International Conference on Advanced Technologies for Signal and Image Processing (ATSIP)* (2018).

14. N. Gupta, A. Seal, P. Bhatele, P. Khanna: Selective Block Based Approach for Neoplasm Detection from T2-Weighted Brain MRIs published in *International Conference on Signal and Image Processing* (ICSIP), pp. 151–155 (2016).
15. M. T. El-Melegy, K. M. A. El-Magd, S. A. Ali, K. F. Hussain, Y. B. Mahdy: A Comparative Study of Classification Methods for Automatic Multimodal Brain Tumor Seg-Mentation published in *International Conference on Innovative Trends in Computer Engineering (ITCE)*, pp. 36–40 (2018).
16. H. Tulsani, S. Saxena, M. Bharadwaj: Comparative Study of Techniques for Brain Tumor Segmentation published in *IMPACT*, pp. 118–112 (2013).
17. S. Lu, X. Guo, T. Ma, C. Yang, T. Wang, P. Zhou: Comparative Study of Supervised and Unsupervised Classification Methods: Application to Automatic MRI Glioma Brain Tumors Segmentation published in *International Conference on Medical Imaging Physics and Engineering (ICMIPE)* (2019).
18. N. Iriawan, A. A. Pravitasari, K. Fithriasari, Irhamah, S. W. Purnami, W. Ferriastuti: Comparative Study of Brain Tumor Segmentation using Different Segmentation Techniques in Handling Noise published in *International Conference on Computer Engineering, Network and Intelligent Multimedia (CENIM)*, pp. 289–292 (2018).
19. N. Afshan, S. Qureshi, S. M. Hussain: Comparative Study of Tumour Detection Algorithms published in *International Conference on Medical Imaging, m-Health and Emerging Communication Systems (MedCom)*, pp. 251–255 (2014).
20. M. Siar, M. Teshnehlab: Brain Tumor Detection Using Deep Neural Network published in *9th International Conference on Computer and Knowledge Engineering (ICCKE)*, pp. 363–368 (2019).
21. F. Gargouri, S. Jayaswal, A. Khunteta: A Comparative Study of Otsu and Entropy Based Segmentation Approaches for Tumour Extraction from MRI published in *2nd International Conference on Advances in Computing, Communication, & Automation (ICACCA) (Fall)* (2016).
22. https://seer.cancer.gov/statfacts/html/brain.html_6-sept-2021
23. www.analyticsvidhya.com/blog/2021/03/Introduction-to-The-Architecture-of Alexnet/_6-sept-2021
24. Mrimaster.com/index.5.html_6-sept-2021
25. R. B. Dubey, M. Hanmandlu, S. Vasikarla: Evaluation of Three Methods for MRI Brain Tumour Segmentation published in *8th International Conference on Information Technology: New Generations* (2011).

5 Prediction and Classification of Alzheimer's Disease Using Machine Learning Models

Santrupti M. Bagali, S. Sanjana, Priyanka. R,
Sara Sadiya, and Deepa N. Reddy

CONTENTS

5.1 INTRODUCTION

An artificial intelligence subset known as machine learning includes algorithms or methods for creating models from data. Computers can learn and act like humans by being fed datasets and information without having to be explicitly programmed [1][2]. A machine learning system learns from experience, unlike a machine that performs a task by following clear-cut rules [3][4]. A rule-based system will perform a task the same way every time, whereas the performance of a machine learning system can be made better through training and testing by exposing the algorithm to more data. The machine learning model can be broadly classified into three categories: supervised machine learning models, unsupervised machine learning models, and semi-supervised machine learning models.

DOI: 10.1201/9781003272694-6

5.2 LITERATURE SURVEY

Muhammad Shahbaz [5] obtained an accuracy of 74.65% using a Gaussian naïve Bayes machine learning model. In this research, a subset of the TADPOLE dataset was used. The examination records of 530 participants were selected. The dataset of 3091 was divided into 70% (2164) training data and the rest of the data (927) into testing data. Their results also revealed that using different machine learning algorithms like KNN, decision trees, and more can be successfully used in healthcare and medicine for the early detection and diagnosis of Alzheimer's. Profound accuracies of 73.10% and 76.43% were obtained for algorithms like KNN and decision trees. The accuracies for random forest and XGBoost were found to be 80% and 77% respectively. J. Neelaveni and M. S. G. Devasana [6] used different machine learning algorithms, such as support vector machines and decision trees to predict the disease, with different accuracies. Each algorithm was trained with 70% training dataset and tested with 30% test dataset. In [7], they obtained their best diagnostic model, which significantly distinguished the probable AD group from the healthy elderly group with a better area under the receiving operating characteristics curve (AUC) using the support vector machines (SVM).

5.3 METHODOLOGY

5.3.1 GATHERING DATA

Alzheimer's illness data would be the initial step in developing the machine learning model. Once the data collection is complete, the machine learning process is in place. An inefficient model may result from picking features inappropriately or using a small number of distinct classifications for the dataset. Collecting data is vital since mistakes here will only make things worse later.

5.3.2 FILLING UP THE NULL VALUES (PREPARING THE DATA)

After collecting data on the characteristics, the next step would be to prepare data for use in the processes that follow. The primary goal in this stage is to identify and eliminate any bias and null values from the datasets. Using this additional information would help identify and correct any bias in the model, as it would show that the model performs well with one condition but does poorly with the other. Improved model efficiency can be realized by including well-prepared data. Increased accuracy in predictions is possible since the model's blind spots are reduced. As a result, it makes sense to analyze and reexamine the datasets to ensure their effectiveness.

5.3.3 DATASET DIVISION

The data utilized is often divided into two categories: training data and test data. It is expected that the training set comprises a known output, and the model learns from this data so that it may be applied to new data later on. With the test dataset (or subset), the accuracy of the model's prediction on this subset of data is evaluated.

5.3.4 TRAINING THE DATA

Machine learning is focused on training models. This is a critical milestone. As a result, most of the "learning" has already been done. A willingness to try and an abundance of patience are both essential for training. It is also important to possess specialist knowledge of the field in which the model will be implemented. If the model learns to do well in the relevant profession, training can be quite rewarding.

5.3.5 TESTING THE DATA

After training, the model must be tested to see if it will perform well in the actual world. The prepared data is used to determine the model's competence to function. Evaluation becomes considerably more crucial in commercial applications. To evaluate whether or not the goals they established have been reached, data scientists can employ evaluation. Accuracy is also calculated.

5.4 ANALYSIS AND DISCUSSION

The machine learning algorithms implemented are: random forest, support vector machine with linear kernel, decision tree, and logistic regression. Model training, validation, and testing were done using nested stratified cross-validation with iterations. Feature selection was done within train sets using the variance threshold method. Hyper-parameter optimization was performed, with the following hyper-parameters tuned: for random forest, the minimum number of samples required at a leaf node and the number of trees in the forest; for support vector machine, regularization strength; for decision tree, the maximum depth of the tree; for logistic regression, the inverse of regularization strength. In logistic regression, L2 regularization was used. Lastly, generalizability of model performance was assessed on the test sets. The model performance metrics measured in the test set are: the area under the receiver operating characteristic curve (ROC), sensitivity, and specificity. As a whole, the dataset contains a wide range of variables, but only those that can be used to accurately predict disease progression were included. They predicted the disease with varying degrees of accuracy using machine learning algorithms like support vector machines and decision trees. Seventy percent of the datasets are used to train the algorithms, and 30% of the datasets are used to test them. Algorithms are judged based on how accurate they are. The dataset is then partitioned based on that ratio, and the best algorithm is selected and used for the next stage of prediction, which is the next step in the process.

5.4.1 RANDOM FOREST

Random forest is a model made of many decision trees using random subset, bootstrapping, and average voting to make predictions. The word "forest" suggests that it will contain a lot of trees. Random forests are used because of their adaptability. They can be used for both regression and classification tasks, and the relative importance it assigns to the input features is easily visible. Random forest is a meta estimator that fits several decision tree classifiers on various subsamples of the dataset; the number of trees are set, i.e., n-estimators as 100, and the RandomForestClassifier parameter was used in our code instead of GridSearchCV, which is more generally used. The criterion was set to "entropy," which by default is "Gini." This model gave us an accuracy of 86.6.7%, which was comparatively much better than the literature survey result, which was 80% [8]. The random forest model was only trained on time series with at least four points, which was determined during training. The ideal number of trees was 60, and the minimum number of leaf data points was 5.

5.4.2 XGBOOST

XGBoost is a decision-tree–based machine learning algorithm that uses a gradient boosting framework. This algorithm was chosen as it has recently been dominating applied machine learning and Kaggle competitions for structured or tabular data. XGBoost is an implementation of gradient-boosted decision trees designed for speed and performance. XGBoost stands for extreme gradient boosting. This algorithm has become famous for two main reasons: XGBoost is really fast when compared to other implementations of gradient boosting, and it offers excellent model performance. According to the literature survey, an accuracy of 77% [9] was obtained, but through our model the accuracy was improved. The paper proposed a novel protein subcellular localization method by integrating the CNN and the XGBoost as a new model for possible application in the pathogens verification of Alzheimer's disease.

5.4.3 SUPPORT VECTOR MACHINES (SVM)

Regression and classification tasks can be handled by support vector machines, which is better known by its abbreviation, SVM. However, classification objectives frequently use it. This algorithm uses a support vector machine to find a hyperplane in N-dimensional space (N is the number of features) that classifies the data points. There are many different types of linear support vector classifiers (SVC), but the most common type is the linear SVC. Following the hyperplane, we then feed some features into the classifier to see what the "predicted" class is. Using SVM is a good strategy for dealing with large datasets. It has a wide range of kernel functions that can be used for the decision function, making it flexible. Default kernels are provided, but custom kernels can also be specified.

5.4.4 DECISION TREE ALGORITHM

The decision tree algorithm is a predictive modeling technique commonly used for classification in data mining, statistics, and machine learning applications. It classifies the dataset by computing the information gain values for all attributes of a dataset. A decision tree is a flowchart-like tree structure in which each leaf node represents the outcome, with the internal nodes representing features (or attributes). The root node is the node at the top of a decision tree. Attribute-based partitioning is learned by it. It partitions the tree in recursively manner called recursive partitioning. This flowchart-like structure helps in decision making. Its visualization is like a flowchart diagram that easily mimics human-level thinking. This is why decision trees are easy to understand and interpret. The result determines whether it descends to the left or right child branch. Generally, the most important features are located near the root. This model gave an accuracy of 80.35%.

5.4.5 GAUSSIAN NAÏVE BAYES

A collection of Bayes' theorem-based Bayes classifiers are referred to as naïve Bayes classifiers. Each feature pair is classified independently of the other, so it's not a single algorithm but rather a family of algorithms with a common principle. Gaussian normal distribution and continuous data are supported by naïve Bayes. This model gave an accuracy of 73.21%. Gaussian naïve Bayes is simple and easy to implement. It doesn't require as much training data. Mainly, Gaussian naïve Bayes is fast and can be used to make real-time classification and predictions.

5.4.6 GRADIENT BOOSTING (GB)

Models are constructed sequentially, and the GB algorithm allows for the optimization of loss functions that can be differentiated. Boosting classifiers use AdaBoosting and weighted minimization to recalculate classifiers and weighted inputs. Loss, or the difference between the training example's actual class value and its predicted class value, is a primary goal of gradient boosting classifiers. The accuracy of this model is high, which is 83.9%.

TABLE 5.1

Comparison of Literature Survey and Simulation Results

Models	Literature Survey	Simulation Results
Random forest	80.00% [7]	86.607%
SVM	70.09% [6]	77.678%
Decision tree	76.43% [5]	80.357%
XGBoost	77% [8]	83.035%
Gradient boosting	–	84.821%
Gaussian naïve Bayes	74.65% [5]	73.214%
LightGBM	—	85.714%
K-nearest neighbors	73.10% [1]	79.464%

5.4.7 LightGBM

Tree-based learning algorithms are used in this gradient boosting framework, which is regarded as one of the most powerful algorithms for computation. In terms of speed, it's a popular algorithm. Instead of using a level-wise approach to produce more accurate trees, it uses a leaf-wise split approach to create much more complex trees. The number of boosted trees to fit was set to 220 and the default value of minimum tree leaves and maximum tree depth tuned the algorithm to provide an accuracy of 85.71%.

5.4.8 K-Nearest Neighbors (KNN)

The K-nearest neighbor algorithm is a simple data mining technique used for both classification and regression problems. The KNN algorithm assumes the similarity between the new case/data and available cases and puts the new case into the category that is most similar to the available categories. The positive value of k gives the number of neighbors to be considered. The model produced an accuracy of 79.46% with the value of k at 5. Along with the value of k, other parameters that impacted the accuracy were the Minkowski metric and the distance system of weights. KNN provides for quick calculation and is also a simple algorithm that provides higher accuracy. This model does not require tuning of several parameters or making additional assumptions. The accuracy comparison between the evaluated eight machine learning models is as illustrated in Table 5.1. It can be seen that the random forest classifier outperforms the other training models in AD prediction with an accuracy of 86.607%. The performance of the classifiers is evaluated using the unseen test dataset. The classification accuracy of the classifiers during the test period is illustrated in Table 5.1. The table provides the results seen during the literature survey along with the simulation results obtained.

5.5 DATASET

- This collection includes 150 subjects ranging in age from 60 to 96. A total of 373 imaging sessions were performed on each subject, with at least one year between each scan.
- The subjects are all right-handed and include both men and women.
- Seventy-two of the subjects were characterized as nondemented throughout the study.
- Sixty-four of the included subjects were characterized as demented.
- Another 14 subjects were characterized as nondemented at the time of their initial visit and were subsequently characterized as demented at a later visit.

5.5.1 CLINICAL INFORMATION

- **MMSE (Mini-Mental State Examination score):** Cognitive impairment can be assessed with this 30-item questionnaire, which is widely used in clinical and research settings. As a diagnostic tool, it can also be used to estimate the severity of cognitive impairment and to track changes in an individual's cognitive abilities over time. A score of at least 24 points (out of a possible 30) indicates a normal mental state and below 9 points can indicate severe cognitive impairment.
- **SES (Socioeconomic Examination):** This is based on 1–5 points, with 1 being the lowest point and 5 highest. People with low socioeconomic status (SES) have been found to have a higher prevalence of dementia, which has been linked to an increased risk of developing dementia.
- **Education:** Dementia is less common the more education one has. Since a person's ability to conserve and maintain cognitive function is enhanced by higher education, this remains the case.
- **CDR (Clinical Dementia Rating):** To diagnose Alzheimer's disease and related dementias, the CDR utilizes a 5-point scale to assess six different aspects of cognitive and functional functioning: memory and orientation, judgment and problem-solving skills, and social engagement, as well as personal care. Patients and a trustworthy informant or collateral source provide the information required to make these ratings in a semi-structured interview (e.g., family member). Although the Clinical Dementia Rating (CDR) has demonstrated high validity and reliability for this purpose, its use requires extensive data collection from both the patient and an informant, which can be time consuming.
- **Whole-Brain Volume:** Structural imaging takes into account the total volume of the brain and considers the total amount of grey and white matter in the brain as well. One of its main benefits is that it measures the degree of interconnection between different brain regions. We are looking for any volume loss in the brain by measuring the volume of the brain. That is a sign of brain cell degeneration. This is known as brain atrophy, and it affects the ability to communicate.
- **Atlas Scaling Factor:** This transforms the matrix space of the brain and skull into a transform matrix determinant. However, this matrix is not used in its original form when measuring; instead, it is adjusted for the brain's intracranial volume. People's heads are measured differently in structured imaging, which is why this is done. A specific structure's intracranial volume and scaling factor are the only variables of concern here.

5.6 RESULTS

As explained earlier, the use of eight different machine learning models for the prediction and classification of Alzheimer's disease has provided a range of significant results. The eight different models are random forest, SVC, decision tree, XGBoost, LightGBM, gradient boosting, Gaussian naïve Bayes, and KNN. Accuracies obtained by individual models along with their comparison with other models are as seen in Figure 5.1. From the graph, it is evident that the four models that provided the highest accuracies are random forest, XGBoost, LightGBM, and gradient boosting. Among these four, random forest is the highest with an accuracy of 86.67%. It is also seen that there are five models that gave accuracies above 80% and three models in the range 70–80%. The least accuracy obtained is 73.21%, which was obtained from Gaussian naïve Bayes. The two new models implemented provided significant accuracies and belong to the category of models giving accuracies of more than 80%.

Figure 5.1 provides the graph on the accuracy levels achieved with different models.

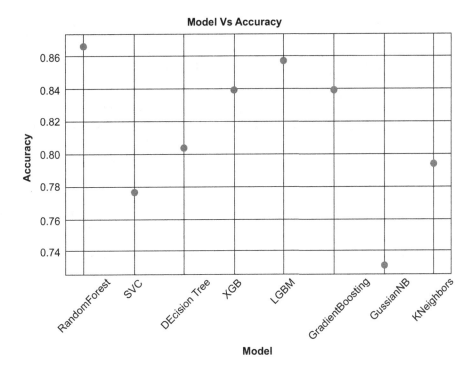

FIGURE 5.1 Accuracy vs. model.

5.7 CONCLUSION AND FUTURE SCOPE

Machine learning and data mining techniques are very helpful in medicine and healthcare studies for early detection and diagnosis of several diseases. A machine learning approach to predict Alzheimer's disease using machine learning algorithms is successfully implemented and gives greater prediction accuracy results. The model predicts the disease in the patient and also distinguishes between cognitive impairment. In this chapter, machine learning algorithms were used along with data preprocessing, principal component analysis (PCA), and feature selection techniques to classify patients with AD using datasets obtained from the Oasis organization. The CNN algorithm has been employed to carry out the predictions. Compared with traditional methods, the proposed method has achieved improvement on classification accuracy, suggesting that neural networks are a powerful tool for the diagnosis of neurological diseases. Future work can combine both brain MRI scans and psychological parameters to predict the disease with higher accuracy using machine learning algorithms. When they are combined, the disease could be predicted with a higher accuracy in the earlier stages. Based on our work, the same or similar methods can be used to diagnose other neurological diseases, providing intelligent healthcare systems. Potential future work includes evaluating the proposed method on larger datasets and applying it to the diagnosis of other neurological diseases.

REFERENCES

[1] Nithya, B., and V. Ilango. "Predictive analytics in health care using machine learning tools and techniques." In *2017 International Conference on Intelligent Computing and Control Systems (ICICCS)*, pp. 492–499. IEEE, 2017.

[2] Sharmila, S. Leoni, C. Dharuman, and Perumal Venkatesan. "Disease classification using machine learning algorithms-a comparative study." *International Journal of Pure and Applied Mathematics* 114, no. 6 (2017): 1–10.

[3] Das, Kajaree, and Rabi Narayan Behera. "A survey on machine learning: concept, algorithms and applications." *International Journal of Innovative Research in Computer and Communication Engineering* 5, no. 2 (2017): 1301–1309.

[4] Kaur, Sunpreet, and Sonika Jindal. "A survey on machine learning algorithms." *International Journal of Innovative Research in Advanced Engineering (IJIRAE)* 3, no. 11 (2016): 2349–2763.

[5] Shahbaz M., Ali S., Guergachi A., Niazi A., and Umer A. Classification of Alzheimer's disease using machine learning techniques. In *Data* 2019, pp. 296–303. https://doi.org/10.5220/0007949902960303

[6] Neelaveni J., Devasana M. G. Alzheimer disease prediction using machine learning algorithms. In *6th International Conference on Advanced Computing and Communication Systems (ICACCS)*, March 6, 2020, pp. 101–104. https://doi.org/10.1109/ICACCS48705.2020.9074248 .

[7] Orimaye, Sylvester O., Jojo S. M. Wong, Karen J. Golden, Chee P. Wong, and Ireneous N. Soyiri. "Predicting probable Alzheimer's disease using linguistic deficits and biomarkers." *BMC Bioinformatics* 18, no. 1 (2017): 1–13.

[8] Moore, P. J., T. J. Lyons, John Gallacher, and Alzheimer's Disease Neuroimaging Initiative. "Random forest prediction of Alzheimer's disease using pairwise selection from time series data." *PLoS ONE* 14, no. 2 (2019): e0211558.

[9] Pang, Long, Junjie Wang, Lingling Zhao, Chunyu Wang, and Hui Zhan. "A novel protein subcellular localization method with CNN-XGBoost model for Alzheimer's disease." *Frontiers in Genetics* 9 (2019): 751.

6 Classification of Histopathology Images of Lung Cancer Using Convolutional Neural Network (CNN)

Neha Baranwal, Preethi Doravari, and Renu Kachhoria

CONTENTS

6.1   INTRODUCTION

Cancer is the uncontrollable cell division of abnormal cells inside the human body, which can spread to other body organs. The process of the transformation of normal cells into cancerous cells due to genetic alteration is known as carcinogenesis, as shown in Figure 6.1. The process of carcinogenesis occurs in three phases. The first is the initiation phase, where any alterations that occur in the normal cell due to gene mutation can cause a change in gene expression and even deletion of a part of deoxyribonucleic acid (DNA) sometimes. If these changes skip the repair mechanism during the cell cycle, then the cell with altered genes remains as it is. In the promotion phase, which is the second phase, the altered cell starts proliferation. In the final stage, the progressive phase, the cells start proliferating aggressively by number and size and form primary tumors. In this stage, the cells become invasive and metastatic. Phases of carcinogenesis are shown in Figure 6.2 (Chegg.com, 2021).

The name for a cancer type is given based on the body organ or the cell type from which cancer originates. So far, more than 100 types of cancer have been found. There are various types of cancer, such as breast, brain, lung, colon cancer, etc. Cancer is one of the non-communicable diseases (NCDs), which account for 71% of total deaths worldwide (World Health Organization, 2019). Lung cancer is the second most diagnosed cancer after female breast cancer (Abdel-Zaher and Eldeib, 2016). According to GLOBOCAN 2018, 2.09 million new lung cancer cases are reported and account for 1.76 million deaths globally, resulting in the highest mortality rate in both men

DOI: 10.1201/9781003272694-7

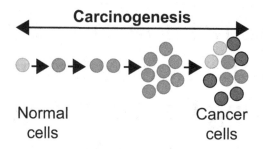

FIGURE 6.1 Process of carcinogenesis.

Source: Chegg.com (2021)

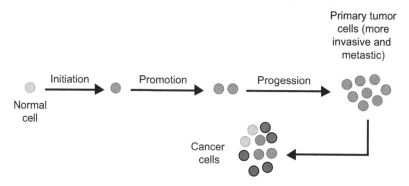

FIGURE 6.2 Three phases of carcinogenesis.

Source: Chegg.com (2021)

and women when compared to other cancer types (Bray et al., 2018; Ferlay, Jacques et al., 2021). The incidence of lung cancer is higher among young women compared to young men in the United States (Jemal et al., 2018). Approximately 63,000 lung cancer cases are recorded each year in India (Noronha et al., 2012). The cancer survival rate of lung cancer is only 19% (Siegel et al., 2019).

Lung cancer is divided into two major types based on histology, biological behavior, prognosis, and treatment. These are non-small cell lung cancer (NSCLC) and small cell lung cancer (SCLC). NSCLC is the most common cancer type, accounting for 85%, and the remaining 15% is SCLC. NSCLC is again sub-divided into adenocarcinoma, squamous cell carcinoma, and large cell carcinoma. As shown in Figure 6.3, adenocarcinoma is the most common cancer type and is formed in epithelial cells that secrete mucus or fluids. In squamous cell carcinoma, cancer originates in the squamous cells that line many organs such as the lung, bladder, kidney, intestines, and stomach (Pêgo-Fernandes et al., 2021; Cancer.gov, 2007).

There are various methods for the diagnosis of lung cancer, such as X-rays, CT scan, PET-CT scan, bronchoscopy, and biopsy. However, to know the subtype of lung cancer based on the tissue type, H and E staining is widely used, where the staining is done on the tissue aspirated from a biopsy. Hematoxylin (H) has a deep purple color and stains nucleic acids in the cells, while Eosin (E) has a pink color and stains proteins. (Fischer et al., 2008). Studies have reported that the type of histology is associated with prognosis and treatment in lung cancer (Hirsch et al., 2008; Itaya et al., 2007; Weiss et al., 2007). Recent advances in genomic studies have paved the way to personalized medicine for lung cancer patients (Travis et al., 2021; Galli and Rossi, 2020).

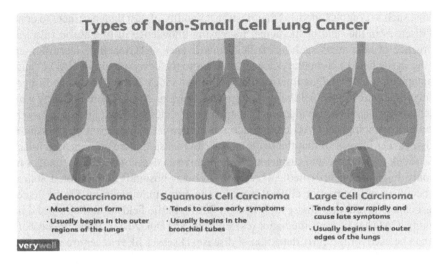

FIGURE 6.3   Types of non-small cell lung cancer (NSCLC).

Source: Lynne Eldridge (2021)

Therefore, early and accurate detection of lung cancer histology is an urgent need, and as treatment is dependent on the type of histology, molecular profile, and stage of the disease, it is essential to analyze histopathology images of lung cancer. However, manual analysis of histopathology reports is time consuming and subjective. With the advent of personalized medicine, pathologists are finding it difficult to manage the workload of dealing with a histopathologic cancer diagnosis. Hence, to speed up the vital process of diagnosis of lung cancer and reduce the burden on pathologists, deep learning techniques (Baranwal et al., 2017; Singh et al., 2020) are used. These techniques have shown improved efficacy in the analysis of histopathology slides of cancer (Litjens et al., 2016).

6.2   ANALYSIS OF PREVIOUS RESEARCH

In the next few decades, cancer is expected to be the leading cause of death and one of the biggest threats to human life (Tang et al., 2009). To improve the efficiency and speed of cancer diagnostics, computer-aided diagnosis (CAD) was applied to the analysis of clinical data. There has been vast development in the field of CAD, and many machine learning techniques are developed for the purpose of diagnosis. Among all machine learning techniques, neural networks have shown increased performance in the detection of medical images. In the classification of lung cancer images, different CNN algorithms are used to improve the accuracy of the prediction and classification. Such accurate predictions aid doctors by reducing the workload and preventing human errors in the process of diagnosis.

a) **Computer-Aided Diagnosis in Medicine:** CAD is cutting-edge technology in the field of medicine that interfaces computer science and medicine. CAD systems imitate the skilled human expert to make diagnostic decisions with the help of diagnostic rules. The performance of CAD systems can improve over time, and advanced CAD can infer new knowledge by analyzing the clinical data. To learn such capability, the system must have a feedback mechanism where the learning happens by successes and failures. During the last century, there has been a dramatic improvement in human expertise and examination tools, such as X-ray, MRI, CT, and ultrasound. With the discovery and study of new diseases and their progression, diagnosis has become difficult and more complex. Various factors, such as complex medical diagnosis, availability of vast data pertinent to conditions and diseases in the field of medicine, increasing knowledge of diagnostic rules, and the emergence of new areas such as artificial intelligence (AI), machine learning, and data mining in the field of computer science, have led to the development of CAD (Yanase and Triantaphyllou, 2019a). Quantitative analysis of pathology images has gained importance among researchers in the field of pathology and image analysis. There is clearly a need for quantitative image-based evaluation of pathological slides, as the diagnosis is based on the opinion of pathologists. CAD can reduce the burden on pathologists by filtering out the benign cancer images so that the pathologists can focus on more complicated images that are difficult to diagnose and suspicious. Quantitative analysis of pathology images helps in not only diagnosis but also medical research. At many hospitals in the United States, CAD has become a part of routine clinical work for screening mammograms for the detection of breast cancer (Freer and Ulissey, 2001; Doi, 2007). In the fields of radiology and medical imaging, CAD has become the major research subject (Doi, 2007). These are cost effective and can be used for the early detection of disease. Diseases like cancer are very aggressive when detected at later or advanced stages, and hence screening and detection of such disease can avoid unnecessary invasive procedures for the treatment of the disease. Moreover, these models can eliminate human errors, such as the detection of microcalcifications, and help to improve the workflow of diagnostic screening procedures (Nishikawa et al., 2012; Yanase and Triantaphyllou, 2019a).

b) **CNN and Cancer Image Detection:** In the field of medicine, to improve the quality of patient care, machine learning–based approaches are used. These approaches are used to analyze and evaluate the complex data. The applications of AI can speed up support delivery, be cost effective, and, at the same time, reduce medical errors (Jia et al., 2016). Recent studies revealed that advances in AI have exceeded human performance in various fields and domains (Fogel and Kvedar, 2018), such as human–robot interaction (Baranwal and Nandi, 2017a; Singh et al., 2020), face recognition (Baranwal and Nandi, 2017b; Baranwal et al., 2014), etc. Several studies reported the importance of CNN in the classification of histopathological pictures of various cancer types, such as brain, skin, breast, lung, and colorectal cancer (Garg and Garg, 2021; Mobadersany et al., 2018). Convolution neural networks have exceeded even human performance on the ImageNet large-scale visual recognition challenge (ILSVRC) and performed well in classification with a second-best error rate (Lundervold and Lundervold, 2019). Deep convolutional neural network (DCNN) models for the classification of lung cancer images showed increased accuracy and reduced model overfitting by using various data augmentation techniques (Teramoto et al., 2017). A study that used LC25000 and colorectal adenocarcinoma gland (CRAG) datasets to train and classify the histopathology images reported the highest sensitivity using ResNet-50 (96.77%), followed by ResNet-30 and ResNet-18 with 95.74% and 94.79% sensitivity, respectively (Bukhari et al., 2020). Another study used low dose computed tomography (LDCT) images for the detection of early lung cancer, where they reported 97.5% sensitivity where the support vector machines (SVM) model was used for classification where VGG19 was used for feature extraction. As the image dataset was small, they used transfer learning methods to obtain better prediction results (Elnakib et al., 2020). Satvik Garg and Somya Garg developed eight pre-trained CNN models that include various feature extraction tools such as VGG16, InceptionV3, ResNet50, etc., for the classification of lung and colon cancer images and achieved accuracies ranging from 96% to 100%. To boost the performance of the model for a better augmentation technique, an imaging library was used (Garg and Garg, 2021). A homology-based image processing (HI) model for the multicategory classification of lung cancer images achieved better accuracy when compared to conventional texture analysis (TA). For feature extraction in the HI model, Betti numbers are the important metrics (Nishio et al., 2021). A convolution neural network model with cross-entropy as a loss function achieved training and validation accuracy of 96.11% and 97.2% for the classification of lung cancer images. The combination of deep learning and digital image processing for the classification of lung and colon cancer histopathology images obtained a maximum accuracy of 96.33% (Masud et al., 2021). In the classification of histopathological images of colorectal cancer ResNet-50 along with transfer, learning reported an accuracy of 97.7%, which is so far the best when compared to all previous results in the literature. In the classification of histopathology images of breast cancer, Inception_ResNet_V2 has proved to be the best deep learning architecture.

Hence, there is a need to explore different techniques to improve the model performance other than increasing parameters. In the classification of images of cancer, there should be immense effort to differentiate cancer images from non-cancer images. The accuracy of the model needs to be high in such cases and the model should be able to detect both intra-class diversity and inter-class similarity. To consider such factors and guide the model accordingly, FaceNet introduced triplet loss (Schroff et al., 2015).

TABLE 6.1
Summary of Classification of Various Cancer Types Using Machine Learning Techniques

Cancer Type	Contribution	Technique Used
Lymphoma data, SRBCT, liver cancer, different tumor types	Finding the smallest set of genes	Gene importance ranking, SVMs (Wang et al., 2007)
Leukemia, colon, and lymphoma	Cancer classification	Ensemble of neural networks (Cho and Won, 2007)
Ovarian cancer	Ovarian cancer diagnosis	Fuzzy neural network (Tan et al., 2008)
Prostate cancer, lymphoma, breast cancer	Gene prioritization and sample classification	Rule-based machine learning (Glaab et al., 2012)
Microarray data of six cancer types (leukemia, lymphoma, prostate, colon, breast, CNS embryonal tumor)	Gene selection and classification	Recursive feature addition, supervised learning (Liu et al., 2011)
Microarray data of multiple cancer types	Cancer classification	Particle swarm optimization, Decision tree classifier (Chen et al., 2014)
Multiple cancer types	Cancer classification	Ensemble-based classifiers (Margoosian and Abouei, 2013)
Leukemia	Cancer classification	Artificial neural network (ANN) (Dwivedi, 2018)
Gene expression data from multiple cancer types	Molecular cancer classification	Transfer learning, deep neural networks (Sevakula et al., 2018)
Breast cancer	Breast cancer classification	Convolutional neural network (Ting et al., 2019)
Cervical cancer	Cervical cancer classification	Convolutional neural networks and extreme learning machines (Ghoneim et al., 2020)
Melanoma	Automated melanoma recognition	Deep residual networks (Yu et al., 2016)
Breast cancer	Breast cancer detection	Deep learning from crowds for mitosis (Albarqouni et al., 2016)
Cervical cancer	Classification of cervical pap smear images	Mean-shift clustering algorithm and mathematical morphology (Wang et al., 2019)
Cervical cancer	Cervical cell classification	Deep convolutional networks (Zhang et al., 2017)

Source: Sharma and Rani (2021)

6.3   PROPOSED RESEARCH WORK

To classify lung cancer images, the dataset is obtained from the LC25000 lung and colon histo-pathological image dataset, which is already augmented data, with 5000 images in each class of lung cancer image set comprising three classes. This dataset is pre-processed using python tools and features are extracted by CNN techniques; later, the model is created and evaluated. Various CNN techniques are used to compare and classify the images. The complete flow of the proposed method is shown in Figure 6.4.

6.3.1   DATASET DESCRIPTION

Data is drawn from the LC25000 lung and colon histopathological image dataset, which consists of 5000 images each in three classes of benign (normal cells), adenocarcinoma, and squamous carcinoma cells (the latter two are both are cancerous cells). The dataset is HIPAA compliant and validated (Borkowski et al., 2019). The original images obtained are only 750 images in total and the size of the images is 1024 × 768 pixels, where each category gets 250 each. These images are cropped to 768 × 768 pixels using python and expanded using the augmenter software package.

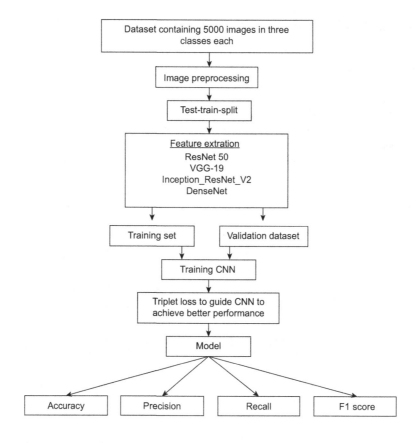

FIGURE 6.4   Proposed methodology.

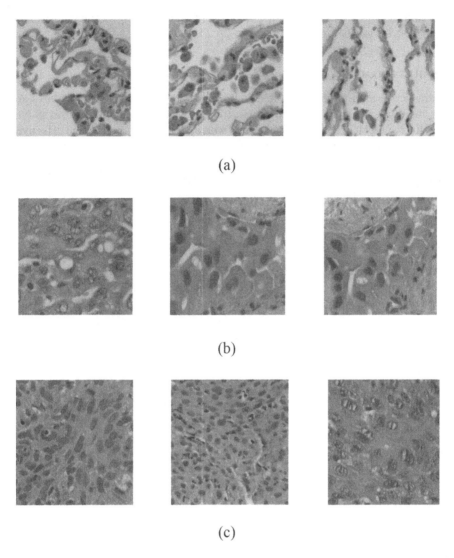

FIGURE 6.5 Sample images of three classes present in the dataset: (a) lung_n (lung normal cells), (b) lung_
aca (lung adenocarcinoma cells), and (c) lung_scc (lung squamous cell carcinoma).

Thus, the expanded dataset contains 5000 images in each category. Augmentation is done by horizontal and vertical flips and by left and right rotations (Borkowski et al., 2019). The sample images
for each category are shown in Figure 6.5.

6.3.2 DATA PRE-PROCESSING

Data pre-processing is an essential step, which helps in improving the quality of the images;
it includes data preparation, data normalization, data cleaning, and data formatting. Data
preparation aids in the transformation of data by modifying it into the appropriate format. While data normalization makes a different image format into a regular format where
all the images are uniform, in data transformation, the data is compressed (Zubi and Saad,
2011). As the images are already augmented, Image Data Generator is imported from Keras.

A total of 15000 images are used for the train–test split, in which 80% of the images are used for training and 20% for validating the data.

6.3.3 FEATURE EXTRACTION

Feature extraction is used to decrease the model complexity where important features are recognized from the images. For the knowledge extraction from images, not all features provide interesting rules for the problem. This is a major step where model performance and effectiveness are dependent. To extract such features as color, texture, and structure, image processing techniques are used. This can be achieved by localizing the extraction to small regions and ensuring all areas of the image are captured (Zubi and Saad, 2011). For feature extraction, ResNet 50 (He et al., 2016), VGG19 (Munir et al., 2019), Inception_ResNet_V2 (Xie et al., 2019; Kensert et al., 2019), and DenseNet121(Huang et al., 2017; Chen et al., 2021) are used.

6.3.4 LOSS FUNCTION

For a machine learning model to fit better while training the neural networks, loss function acts as a major key for adjusting the weights of the network. During the back propagation while training, loss function penalizes the model if there is any deviation between the label predicted by model and the actual target label (https://ieeexplore.ieee.org/abstract/document/8943952). Hence, the use of loss function is critical to achieve better model performance. Triplet loss is used as the loss function in this study.

6.3.4.1 Triplet Loss

Triplet loss was first developed for face recognition by Schroff et al., 2015 by mapping Euclidean distance to find the similarities in the face images. Although the images are blurred, with the help of the distances between faces of similar and different identities this method can be used (Schroff et al., 2015). To increase the inter-cluster similarity and intra-cluster diversity, triplet loss is used as a cost function to guide the learning of convolutional neural networks. It can increase the inter-class distance and decrease the intra-class, aiding the classification process of the model. In Equation (1), a and p are the vectors that belong to the same category, whereas n is a vector that belongs to another category.

$$L_t = \left(d\left(a, p \right) - d\left(a, n \right) + margin, 0 \right). \tag{1}$$

From this formula, we can say that the triplet loss guides the model to shorten the distance between images of the same category and increase the distance between images that belong to different categories (Zhang et al., 2020). It has been reported that the use of triplet loss has shown improved accuracy in binary classification when compared to using the base model (Agarwal et al., 2018).

6.3.5 MODEL AND EVALUATION METRICS

A CNN is created using a stack of layers for image recognition and classification. Before passing through the fully connected layer, the training and testing data is passed through parameters such as max-pooling and kernel filters. Activation function ReLU is used in all three hidden layers and a softmax function is applied to classify the images.

In order to evaluate the performance of the model, the following metrics are measured:

- **Accuracy:** Over the total number of data instances, accuracy represents the correctly classified data. Equation (2) represents the formula to calculate accuracy. However, accuracy alone may not be a good measure to decide the performance of the model.

- **Precision:** This is used to measure the positive predictive observations. It represents the correctly predicted positive observations of total predicted positive observations. Equation (3) is the formula to calculate the precision. High precision relates to a low false-positive rate.
- **Recall (Sensitivity):** Recall represents the correctly predicted positive observations of total actual positive observations. The formula to calculate recall is given in Equation (4). It is also known as sensitivity or true positive rate.
- **F1 Score:** Ideally, a good evaluation should consider both precision and recall to seek balance. A weighted average of precision and recall is the F1 score. Equation (5) is the formula to calculate the F1 score. For uneven class distribution, the F1 score is more useful to evaluate the model.

$$\text{Accuracy} = (TP + TN)/((TP + FP + FN + TN)) \tag{2}$$
$$\text{Precision} = TP/((TP + FP)) \tag{3}$$
$$\text{Recall} = TP/((TP+FN)) \tag{4}$$
$$\text{F1 Score} = (2* (\text{Recall} * \text{Precision}))/((\text{Recall} + \text{Precision})) \tag{5}$$

6.4   RESULT AND ANALYSIS

All four CNN architecture models have been trained using specific and fine-tuned parameters to achieve better model performance. Initially, pre-trained CNN architecture is used to classify the lung cancer cells. In these models, cross-entropy is used as loss function. The VGG19 model is trained by adding two hidden layers with embeddings 256 and 128, with ReLU as an activation function, and for the final output layer, softmax is used as the activation function. For this model, cross-entropy is used to calculate the loss over an 18 batch size. When the model is trained with 30 epochs with Adam as an optimizer (in default setting), it showed a validation loss of 0.196. The performance of the model has shown accuracy of 92.1%, precision of 92.5%, recall of 92.1%, and F1 score of 92.04% on the validation dataset. Similarly, ResNet50 model is trained using the same number of hidden layers as VGG19. All the parameters are same for both the models, and when the model is trained for 30 epochs, the validation loss showed by the model is 0.03. Among all, ResNet has shown improved performance when compared to the VGG19 model. This model showed accuracy, precision, recall, and F1 score of 99%. Inception-ResNetv2 is trained using two layers, in which one is global average pooling and the other one is dense layer with 1024 embeddings. The activation layer used for the hidden layer is ReLU and for the output layer is softmax. When the model is trained for 30 epochs with Adam as optimizer in default, the validation loss of the model is 0.008. The performance of this model is much better than other models, where test accuracy, precision, recall, and F1 score is 99.7%. Lastly, the DenseNet121 model, which is trained with two hidden layers of 1024 and 500 embeddings with Adam in default setting as optimizer, has shown validation loss of 0.01. After evaluation of this model on test data, the accuracy, precision, recall, and F1 score is 99.4%. These evaluation metrics are shown in Table 6.2 for comparison. All four

TABLE 6.2
Evaluation Metrics for All Four CNN Architectures

Evaluation metrics	VGG19	ResNet50	Inception-ResNetv2	DenseNet121
Accuracy	92.1%	99	99.7	99.4
Specificity	92.5%	99	99.7	99.4
Recall	92.1%	99	99.7	99.4
F1 score	92.4%	99	99.7	99.4

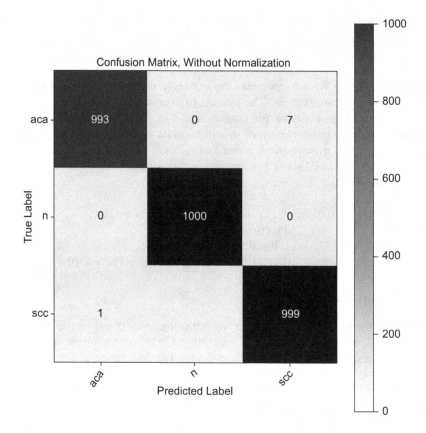

FIGURE 6.6   Confusion matrix of test data of Inception-ResNetv2ple images.

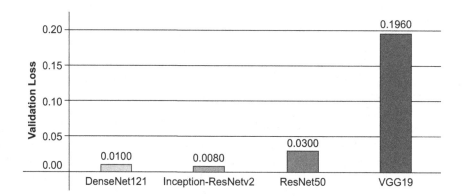

FIGURE 6.7   Validation loss obtained after training four CNN architectures.

CNN architecture Inception-ResNetv2 models have shown improved performance and classified benign tissue images from cancer images without any misclassifications. The only misclassification happened between the subclasses of lung cancer images, as shown in Figure 6.6. Even validation loss is also very minimum for this model, as shown in Figure 6.7.

   To compare the pre-trained model with triplet neural network, again the four CNN architectures are trained using triplet neural network. In these models, after the train–test split, the data

TABLE 6.3

Fine-Tuning of Learning Rate for Different CNN Models

Model	Adam Learning Rate Used
VGG19	0.00001
ResNet50	0.0001
Inception-ResNetv1	0.00001
DenseNet121	0.0001

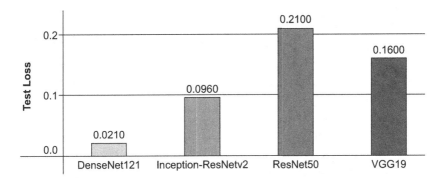

FIGURE 6.8   Validation loss of four CNN architectures trained on triplet neural network.

is divided into three images; the first is the anchor, second is the positive image, which has the same class label as the anchor, and the third is the negative image, where the class label of this is different from the anchor. For such triplet selection, the loss function is introduced such that the distance between anchor and positive image should be always less than the distance between anchor and negative image. For such triplet loss function, margin/alpha is added to calculate the distance. In these models, this margin is set to 0.4, as from analysis, the model did not perform better at higher or lower margin than 0.4. The batch size of input image is set to 16 and data type of each input is changed to float16 because of GPU memory constraints. After training the four models with introducing triplet selected, the learning rate of the Adam is also finely tuned to fit the model, as shown in Table 5.2. For all the models, global average pooling layer and L2 normalization are used.

All four models are trained for ten epochs using 150 steps in each epoch and validation steps of 50. Validation loss of all four models is mentioned in Figure 6.8.

Evaluation of the triplet model is done by using a KNN approach, where the model embeddings from training dataset are taken and trained using nearest neighbors. Later, the nearest neighbor for test data embeddings is predicted using the trained model. Using this class label of the predicted test data is considered for evaluating the model.

It is observed that DenseNet121 has shown least validation loss of all four networks. After the evaluation of all models, the highest accuracy is reported by DenseNet121 and the least by ResNet50. The evaluation metrics of the models are given in Table 6.4. As shown in Figure 6.9, when the test data embeddings are plotted, the DenseNet121 model showed defined clusters when compared to other models.

TABLE 6.4

Evaluation Metrics for All Four CNN Architectures

Evaluation Metrics	VGG19	ResNet50	Inception-ResNetv2	DenseNet121
Accuracy	97.69	96.2	97.04	99.08
Specificity	97.7	96.2	97.03	99.09
Recall	97.69	96.2	97.04	99.08
F1 score	97.69	96.1	97.04	99.08

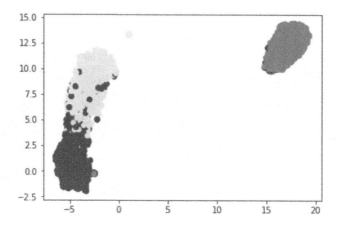

FIGURE 6.9 Clusters obtained when test embeddings are plotted. (2D array of embeddings are plotted along x and y axis.)

6.5 CONCLUSION

CNN models have been shown to increase accuracy with fine-tuning of hyperparameters. Various CNN architectures are compared in the study to get better accuracy and to compare which architecture gives a better performance for this dataset. Model performance of all four CNN models, such as VGG19, ResNet50, Inception-ResNetv2, and DenseNet121, have shown increased accuracy. Although the pre-trained models are available, fine-tuning of these models is necessary to obtain desired results. In this study, Inception-ResNetv2 has shown a very high test accuracy rate of 99.7% when compared to other models, where the accuracy of VGG19, ResNet50, and DenseNet121 are 92%, 99%, and 99.4%, respectively. When the triplet neural network model is trained on these four pre-trained models, DenseNet121 achieved a test accuracy of 99.08%, which is the highest of all four. Test accuracies of the other three models are 97.69%, 96.2%, and 97.04% for VGG19, ResNet50, and Inception-ResNetv2 respectively. The obtained model with high accuracy has significantly classified cancer images from non-cancerous images, which is a crucial step in cancer diagnosis. There were no misclassifications among cancer and non-cancer images. Only very few misclassifications happened among the two lung cancer subtypes, that is, adenocarcinoma and squamous cell carcinoma. Although the image aspect ratio of image-trained triplet neural networks is low, that is, $128 \times 128 \times 3$ and batch size is 16 due to GPU constraints, the triplet network model has shown better performance.

REFERENCES

Abdel-Zaher, A.M., & Eldeib, A.M. (2016). Breast cancer classification using deep belief networks. *Expert Systems with Applications*, 46, 139–144.

Agarwal, N., Balasubramanian, V.N., & Jawahar, C.V. (2018). Improving multiclass classification by deep networks using DAGSVM and Triplet Loss. *Pattern Recognition Letters*, 112, 184–190.

Albarqouni, S., Baur, C., Achilles, F., Belagiannis, V., Demirci, S., & Navab, N. (2016). Aggnet: Deep learning from crowds for mitosis detection in breast cancer histology images. *IEEE Transactions on Medical Imaging*, 35(5), 1313–1321.

Baranwal, N., Jaiswal, G., & Nandi, G.C. (2014). A speech recognition technique using MFCC with dwt in isolated Hindi words. In: *Intelligent Computing, Networking, and Informatics*, pp. 697–703. Springer. Conflict Resolution in Human-robot Interaction 5.

Baranwal, Neha, Gora Chand Nandi, and Avinash Kumar Singh. "Real-Time Gesture–Based Communication Using Possibility Theory–Based Hidden Markov Model." *Computational Intelligence,* 33.4(2017): 843–862.

Baranwal, N., & Nandi, G.C. (2017a). A mathematical framework for possibility theory-based hidden Markov model. *International Journal of Bio-Inspired Computation*, 10(4), 239–247.

Baranwal, N., & Nandi, G.C. (2017b). An efficient gesture based humanoid learning using wavelet descriptor and MFCC techniques. *International Journal of Machine Learning and Cybernetics*, 8(4), 1369–1388.

Borkowski, A.A., Bui, M.M., Thomas, L.B., Wilson, C.P., DeLand, L.A., & Mastorides, S.M. (2019). Lung and colon cancer histopathological image dataset (LC25000). *arXiv [eess.IV]*. Available at: http://arxiv.org/abs/1912.12142 [Accessed 17 June 2021].

Bray, F., Ferlay, J., Soerjomataram, I., Siegel, R.L., Torre, L.A., & Jemal, A. (2018). Global cancer statistics 2018: GLOBOCAN estimates of incidence and mortality worldwide for 36 cancers in 185 countries. *CA: A Cancer Journal for Clinicians*, 686, 394–424.

Bukhari, S.U.K., Syed, A., Bokhari, S.K.A., Hussain, S.S., Armaghan, S.U., & Shah, S.S.H. (2020). The histological diagnosis of colonic adenocarcinoma by applying partial self supervised learning. *bioRxiv*, p. 2020.08.15.20175760.

Cancer.gov (2007). *What Is Cancer?* [online]. Available at: www.cancer.gov/about-cancer/understanding/what-is-cancer [Accessed 10 June 2021].

Chegg.com (2021). *Learn about Carcinogenesis* [online]. Available at: www.chegg.com/learn/biology/introduction-to-biology/carcinogenesis-in-introduction-to-biology [Accessed 16 June 2021].

Chen, B., Zhao, T., Liu, J., & Lin, L. (2021). Multipath feature recalibration DenseNet for image classification. *International Journal of Machine Learning and Cybernetics*, 12(3), 651–660.

Chen, K.H., Wang, K.J., Wang, K.M., & Angelia, M.A. (2014). Applying particle swarm optimization-based decision tree classifier for cancer classification on gene expression data. *Applied Soft Computing*, 24, 773–780.

Cho, S.B., & Won, H.H. (2007). Cancer classification using ensemble of neural networks with multiple significant gene subsets. *Applied Intelligence*, 26(3), 243–250.

Doi, K. (2007). Computer-aided diagnosis in medical imaging: Historical review, current status and future potential. *Computerized Medical Imaging and Graphics: The Official Journal of the Computerized Medical Imaging Society*, 31(4–5), 198–211.

Dwivedi, A.K. (2018). Artificial neural network model for effective cancer classification using microarray gene expression data. *Neural Computing and Applications*, 29(12), 1545–1554.

Elnakib, A., Amer, H., & EZ Abou-Chadi, F. (2020). Early lung cancer detection using deep learning optimization. *International Journal of Online and Biomedical Engineering (iJOE)*, 1606, 82.

Ferlay, Jacques et al. (2021). Cancer statistics for the year 2020: An overview. *International Journal of Cancer*, 149(4), 778–789.

Fischer, A.H., Jacobson, K.A., Rose, J., & Zeller, R. (2008). Hematoxylin and eosin staining of tissue and cell sections. *CSH Protocols*, 20086, db.prot4986.

Fogel, A.L., & Kvedar, J.C. (2018). Artificial intelligence powers digital medicine. *NPJ Digital Medicine*, 11, 5.

Freer, T.W., & Ulissey, M.J. (2001). Screening mammography with computer-aided detection: Prospective study of 12,860 patients in a community breast center. *Radiology*, 220(3), 781–786.

Galli, G., & Rossi, G. (2020). Lung cancer histology-driven strategic therapeutic approaches. *Shanghai Chest*, 40, 29.

Garg, S., & Garg, S. (2021). Prediction of lung and colon cancer through analysis of histopathological images by utilizing Pre-trained CNN models with visualization of class activation and saliency maps. *arXiv* [cs.CV].

Ghoneim, A., Muhammad, G., & Hossain, M.S. (2020). Cervical cancer classification using convolutional neural networks and extreme learning machines. *Future Generation Computer Systems*, 102, 643–649.

Glaab, E., Bacardit, J., Garibaldi, J.M., & Krasnogor, N. (2012). Using rule-based machine learning for candidate disease gene prioritization and sample classification of cancer gene expression data. *PLoS ONE*, 7(7), e39932.

He, K., Zhang, X., Ren, S., & Sun, J. (2016). Deep residual learning for image recognition. In: *2016 IEEE Conference on Computer Vision and Pattern Recognition (CVPR)*, pp. 770–778.

Hirsch, F.R., Spreafico, A., Novello, S., Wood, M.D., Simms, L., & Papotti, M. (2008). The prognostic and predictive role of histology in advanced non-small cell lung cancer: A literature review. *Journal of Thoracic Oncology: Official Publication of the International Association for the Study of Lung Cancer*, 312, 1468–1481.

Huang, G., Liu, Z., Van Der Maaten, L., & Weinberger, K.Q. (2017). Densely connected convolutional networks. In: *2017 IEEE Conference on Computer Vision and Pattern Recognition (CVPR)*. IEEE.

Itaya, T., Yamaoto, N., Ando, M., Ebisawa, M., Nakamura, Y., Murakami, H., Asai, G., Endo, M., & Takahashi, T. (2007). Influence of histological type, smoking history and chemotherapy on survival after first-line therapy in patients with advanced non-small cell lung cancer. *Cancer Science*, 982, 226–230.

Jemal, A., Miller, K.D., Ma, J., Siegel, R.L., Fedewa, S.A., Islami, F., Devesa, S.S., & Thun, M.J. (2018). Higher lung cancer incidence in young women than young men in the United States. *The New England Journal of Medicine*, 37821, 1999–2009.

Jia, P., Zhang, L., Chen, J., Zhao, P., & Zhang, M. (2016). The effects of clinical decision support systems on medication safety: An overview. *PLoS ONE*, 1112, e0167683.

Kensert, A., Harrison, P.J., & Spjuth, O. (2019). Transfer learning with deep convolutional neural networks for classifying cellular morphological changes. *SLAS Discovery*, 244, 466–475.

Litjens, G., Sánchez, C.I., Timofeeva, N., Hermsen, M., Nagtegaal, I., Kovacs, I., Hulsbergen-van de Kaa, C., Bult, P., van Ginneken, B., & van der Laak, J. (2016). Deep learning as a tool for increased accuracy and efficiency of histopathological diagnosis. *Scientific Reports*, 61, 26286.

Liu, Q., Sung, A.H., Chen, Z., Liu, J., Chen, L., Qiao, M., Wang, Z., Huang, X., & Deng, Y. (2011). Gene selection and classification for cancer microarray data based on machine learning and similarity measures. *BMC Genomics*, 12(S5), S1.

Lundervold, A.S., & Lundervold, A. (2019). An overview of deep learning in medical imaging focusing on MRI. *Zeitschrift Für Medizinische Physik*, 29(2), 102–127.

Margoosian, A., & Abouei, J. (2013). Ensemble-based classifiers for cancer classification using human tumor microarray data. In: *2013 21st Iranian Conference on Electrical Engineering (ICEE)*. IEEE, pp. 1–6

Masud, M., Sikder, N., Nahid, A.-A., Bairagi, A.K., & AlZain, M.A. (2021). A machine learning approach to diagnosing lung and colon cancer using a Deep Learning-based classification framework. *Sensors (Basel, Switzerland)*, 213, 748.

Mobadersany, P., Yousefi, S., Amgad, M., Gutman, D.A., Barnholtz-Sloan, J.S., Velázquez Vega, J.E., Brat, D.J., & Cooper, L.A.D. (2018). Predicting cancer outcomes from histology and genomics using convolutional networks. *Proceedings of the National Academy of Sciences of the United States of America*, 11513, E2970–E2979.

Nishikawa, R.M., Schmidt, R.A., Linver, M.N., Edwards, A.V., Papaioannou, J., & Stull, M.A. (2012). Clinically missed cancer: How effectively can radiologists use computer-aided detection? *American Journal of Roentgenology*, 198(3), 708–716.

Nishio, M., Nishio, M., Jimbo, N., & Nakane, K. (2021). Homology-based image processing for automatic classification of histopathological images of lung tissue. *Cancers*, 136, 1192.

Noronha, V., Dikshit, R., Raut, N., Joshi, A., Pramesh, C.S., George, K., Agarwal, J.P., Munshi, A., & Prabhash, K. (2012). Epidemiology of lung cancer in India: Focus on the differences between non-smokers and smokers: a single-centre experience. *Indian Journal of Cancer*, 491, 74–81.

Pêgo-Fernandes, P.M., Haddad, F.J., Imaeda, C.J., & Sandrini, M. (2021). The role of the surgeon in treating patients with lung cancer. An updating article. *Sao Paulo Medical Journal*, 1393, 293–300.

Schroff, F., Kalenichenko, D., & Philbin, J. (2015). FaceNet: A unified embedding for face recognition and clustering. In: *2015 IEEE Conference on Computer Vision and Pattern Recognition (CVPR)*. IEEE, pp. 815–823.

Sevakula, R.K., Singh, V., Verma, N.K., Kumar, C., & Cui, Y. (2018). Transfer learning for molecular cancer classification using deep neural networks. *IEEE/ACM Transactions on Computational Biology and Bioinformatics*, 16(6), 2089–2100.

Sharma, A., & Rani, R. (2021). A systematic review of applications of machine learning in cancer prediction and diagnosis. *Archives of Computational Methods in Engineering*, 28(7), 4875–4896.

Siegel, R.L., Miller, K.D., & Jemal, A. (2019). Cancer statistics, 2019: Cancer statistics, 2019. *CA: A Cancer Journal for Clinicians*, 691, 7–34.

Singh, A.K., Baranwal, N., Richter, K.F., Hellström, T., & Bensch, S. (2020). Understandable collaborating robot teams. In: De La Prieta, F. et al. (Eds.), *Highlights in Practical Applications of Agents, Multi-Agent Systems, and Trust-Worthiness*. The PAAMS Collection. PAAMS 2020. Communications in Computer and Information Science, 1233. Springer.

Tan, T.Z., Quek, C., Ng, G.S., & Razvi, K. (2008). Ovarian cancer diagnosis with complementary learning fuzzy neural network. *Artificial Intelligence in Medicine*, 43(3), 207–222.

Tang, J., Rangayyan, R.M., Xu, J., El Naqa, I., & Yang, Y. (2009). Computer-aided detection and diagnosis of breast cancer with mammography: Recent advances. *Transactions on Information Technology in Biomedicine: A Publication of the IEEE Engineering in Medicine and Biology Society*, 13(2), 236–251.

Teramoto, A., Tsukamoto, T., Kiriyama, Y., & Fujita, H. (2017). Automated classification of lung cancer types from cytological images using deep convolutional neural networks. *BioMed Research International*, 2017, 4067832.

Ting, F.F., Tan, Y.J., & Sim, K.S. (2019). Convolutional neural network improvement for breast cancer classification. *Expert Systems with Applications*, 120, 103–115.

Travis, E.W., Brambilla, E., Konrad Müller-Hermelink, H., & Harris, C.C. (2021). *Tumours of the Lung, Pleura, Thymus and Heart* [online]. Patologi.com. Available at: https://patologi.com/who%20lunge.pdf [Accessed 17 June 2021].

Wang, L., Chu, F., & Xie, W. (2007). Accurate cancer classification using expressions of very few genes. *IEEE/ACM Transactions on Computational Biology and Bioinformatics*, 4(1), 40–53.

Wang, S., Yang, D.M., Rong, R., Zhan, X., Fujimoto, J., Liu, H., . . . & Xiao, G. (2019). Artificial intelligence in lung cancer pathology image analysis. *Cancers*, 11(11), 1673.

Weiss, G.J., Rosell, R., Fossella, F., Perry, M., Stahel, R., Barata, F., Nguyen, B., Paul, S., McAndrews, P., Hanna, N., Kelly, K., & Bunn, P.A., Jr. (2007). The impact of induction chemotherapy on the outcome of second-line therapy with pemetrexed or docetaxel in patients with advanced non-small-cell lung cancer. *Annals of Oncology*, 183, 453–460.

World Health Organization. (2019). *World Health Statistics 2019: Monitoring Health for the SDGs, Sustainable Development Goals*. Genève, Switzerland: World Health Organization.

Xie, J., Liu, R., Luttrell, J., & Zhang, C. (2019). Deep learning based analysis of histopathological images of breast cancer. *Frontiers in Genetics*, 10, 80.

Yanase, J., & Triantaphyllou, E. (2019a). A systematic survey of computer-aided diagnosis in medicine: Past and present developments. *Expert Systems with Applications*, 138(112821), 112821

Yanase, J., & Triantaphyllou, E. (2019b). The seven key challenges for the future of computer-aided diagnosis in medicine. *International Journal of Medical Informatics*, 129, 413–422.

Yu, L., Chen, H., Dou, Q., Qin, J., & Heng, P.A. (2016). Automated melanoma recognition in dermoscopy images via very deep residual networks. *IEEE Trans Med Imaging*, 36(4), 994–1004.

Zhang, J., Lu, C., Wang, J., Yue, X.-G., Lim, S.-J., Al-Makhadmeh, Z., & Tolba, A. (2020). Training convolutional neural networks with multi-size images and triplet loss for RemoteSensing scene classification. *Sensors (Basel, Switzerland)*, 204, 1188.

Zhang, L., Lu, L., Nogues, I., Summers, R.M., Liu, S., & Yao, J. (2017). DeepPap: Deep convolutional networks for cervical cell classification. *IEEE Journal of Biomedical and Health Informatics*, 21(6), 1633–1643.

Zubi, Z.S., & Saad, R.A. (2011). Using some data mining techniques for early diagnosis of lung cancer. In: *Proceedings of the 10th WSEAS International Conference on Artificial Intelligence, Knowledge Engineering and Data Bases*, pp. 32–37. Stevens Point, Wisconsin, USA: World Scientific and Engineering Academy and Society (WSEAS).

7 Case Study on Oropharyngeal Cancer Prediction and Diagnosis and Management Based upon MRI, CT Scan Imaging Techniques

Pallavi Bhosle, Hujeb Pathan, Ganesh Tapadiya, and Md. Irshad Alam

CONTENTS

DOI: 10.1201/9781003272694-8

7.1 INTRODUCTION

"Cancer is characterized as any unlimited proliferation of cells that occupy and originate the disability nearer tissue". Just beyond your mouth lies the oropharynx, and then the portion of your throat that is in the middle (pharynx). The base of your tongue, tonsils, soft palate (rear portion of the roof of your mouth), and the sides and walls of your throat make up the oropharynx. The oropharynx produces saliva, keeps your mouth and throat wet, and begins to improve digestion (Figure 7.1). Oropharyngeal cancer (OPC) is related to the throat, soft palate, and tonsils, which make up the oropharynx cavity. Other official names are tonsil cancer and oropharyngeal squamous cell carcinoma (OPSCC). Patients suffer serious health risks from this disease.[1,2,3,4,5]

7.1.1 HISTOPATHOLOGY OF OROPHARYNGEAL CANCER

Although small salivary tumors, primarily lymphoid tumors and undifferentiated tumors, occur in the oropharynx, various sarcomas also occur and account for the majority of the primary stages of oropharyngeal cancer (OPC). Invasive oropharyngeal cancer has been being diagnosed and treated for decades. The histologic subtypes of head and neck OPC as well as their nomenclature and clinical consequences have sparked discussion. As more specific molecular markers and gene expression patterns are uncovered, genomics and proteomics are likely to change how we sub-classify many malignancies, including OPC of the head and neck.[6,7]

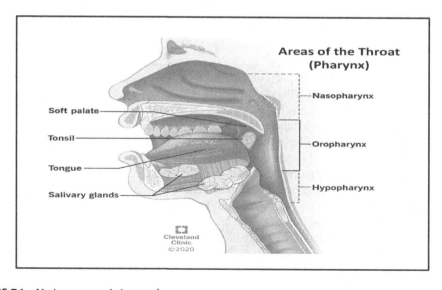

FIGURE 7.1 Various areas of pharynx.[5]

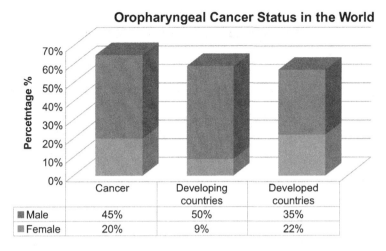

Oropharyngeal Cancer Status in the World

	Cancer	Developing countries	Developed countries
Male	45%	50%	35%
Female	20%	9%	22%

FIGURE 7.2   Status of oral cancer in the world.[8]

7.1.2 STATUS OF OROPHARYNGEAL CANCER IN THE WORLD

In developing countries, oropharyngeal cancer is the most epidemic type of cancer and the top 6th most typical cancer all over the world. This is one of the commonest types of cancer in India and is the most serious worry for community health. Around 52,000 deaths and 77,000 new cases are reported per year. Gender-based suffering data for oropharyngeal cancer is shown in Figure 7.2.

Approximately 60% of oropharyngeal cancers are moderately differentiated, 20% are well distinguished, and 20% are poorly differentiated, according to retrospective assessments across all anatomic sub-sites. As more specific molecular markers and gene expression patterns are uncovered, genomics and proteomics are likely to change how we sub-classify many malignancies, including OPC of the head and neck. Oropharyngeal cancer accounts for a significant portion of oral cancer, ranging from 84 to 97% of all cases. OPC is most usually caused by possible cancerous lesions or normal epithelial linings. OPC preclinical stage signs include leukoplakia, candidal leukoplakia, inflammatory oral submucosa, fibrosis, erythroplakia, and dyskeratosis congenital.[8,9,10]

7.1.3 FACTORS RESPONSIBLE FOR OROPHARYNGEAL CANCER[11,12,13]

- Use of chewing tobacco containing areca nut leaves, cinnamon, lime, and catechu is a major cause of oropharyngeal cancer, and is seen especially in developing nations.
- Many occurrences of oropharyngeal cancer are directly related to cigarette smoking and excessive alcohol consumption.
- Using alcohol along with tobacco and allied products produces a much higher risk of oropharyngeal cancer.
- Oropharyngeal cancer is considerably more likely when alcohol is combined with tobacco and its related products.
- A subgroup of oropharyngeal malignancies has been linked to the sexually transmitted human papillomavirus (HPV) infection.
- Oral cancer is more commonly found in those over the age of 40.
- Excessive exposure to sun rays is a factor responsible for lip cancer.
- Oropharyngeal cancer may be accelerated by foods that are low in nutrients such as fruit and nutritious vegetables (shown in Figure 7.3).

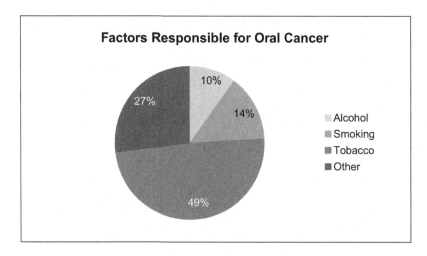

FIGURE 7.3   Factors responsible for oral cancer.[13]

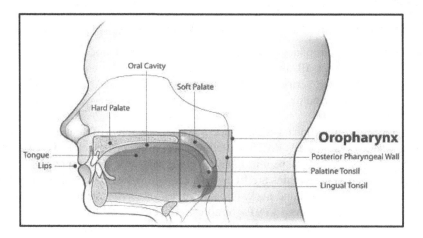

FIGURE 7.4   Oropharyngeal cancer and oral cavity.[3]

7.1.4   SIGNS AND SYMPTOMS OF OROPHARYNGEAL CANCER[14]

- Struggling for movements of the tongue and jaw.
- Artificial teeth don't fit well when the jaw is inflamed.
- A painful, irritating mass present in the throat, mouth, and/or lip.
- Struggling to chew or swallow anything.
- In the mouth, whitish red smears appear.
- A feeling of something present in the throat.
- Immobility of the tongue or immobility in other parts of the mouth.
- Feeling of pain without hearing loss in one ear.

7.1.5   OROPHARYNGEAL CANCER AND MOUTH CAVITY[15,16]

The most common and major cancers seen in Asia, specifically, in India are oropharyngeal and oral cavity cancers. Cancer that starts in the middle of the throat is known as oropharyngeal cancer.

As shown in Figure 7.4, these cancers start when cells in the oral cavity or oropharynx undergo dedifferentiation and irregular apoptosis and crowd out normal cells, forming a tumor.

While clinical examination can suggest cellular changes and visualization of disease, it is unable to assess the extent to which the sickness has spread. Cross-sectional imaging of the affected and adjacent areas becomes an important step prior to treatment in evaluation of these types of cancers because it gives precise information about the length, breadth, and depth of disease, which aids in determining the best management approach and determining prognosis.

7.1.6 EXAMINATION OF OROPHARYNGEAL CANCER[17,18,19]

- Early signs of cancer are detected in an oral cancer examination.
- The examination is simple and pain free, and it only takes a couple of minutes to complete.
- Between the examinations, the physician looks for signs of cancer in the facial area, neck region, lips, mouth, tongue, and back of the throat.

7.1.7 THE SPECIALIST WHO TREATS OROPHARYNGEAL CANCER[20,21,22,23,24,25,26]

Various types of physicians may be required depending on the stage and location of oropharyngeal cancer. These physicians may be involved:

- Oral and maxillofacial surgeons are involved in the treatment of illnesses of the mouth, teeth, and jaws.
- Plastic surgeons are involved in the therapy of repairing parts of the body.
- Medical oncologists are involved in cancer treatment with drugs such as chemotherapy, immunotherapy, or targeted therapy.
- Otolaryngologists (ENT doctors) are presents in the treatment of certain diseases of the head and neck.

7.2 LITERATURE SURVEY ON OROPHARYNGEAL CANCER PREDICTION AND DIAGNOSIS

It is critical to diagnose oropharyngeal cancer patients as soon as possible in sequence to lower the fatality rate. There is high demand for non-invasive, quick, and simple oropharyngeal cancer detection techniques. Oropharyngeal cancer is diagnosed by first checking for evidence of oral lesions in the mouth cavity, which must be properly examined by a physician. Following suspicious cancerous findings, the patient is referred to an oral or maxillofacial specialist, who conducts the specific tests. A dental physician plays an essential role in the early detection process of oropharyngeal cancer. Oral cancer is diagnosed using a variety of techniques (Table 7.1).[27,28,29,30]

TABLE 7.1
Techniques Used for Oral Cancer Diagnosis

Biomarker Detection	Biopsy	Imaging Technique	Spectroscopy
Enzyme assay	Incisional	CT scan	Diffuse reflectance
DNA/gene arrays	Liquid	Magnetic resonance imaging scan	Laser-induced auto fluorescence
Polymerase chain reactions	Brush	Positron emission tomography scan	Raman
Immunohistochemistry	Fine needle	Ultrasound scan	Elastic scattering
Immunoprecipitation	Endoscopic	Confocal scan	FTIR
Liquid chromatography	Exfoliative		Mass-MALDI

7.2.1   BENEFITS OF IMAGING TECHNIQUES IN PREDICTION AND DETECTION OF OROPHARYNGEAL CANCER[31,32]

In the management of oropharyngeal cancers, imaging is important. It clearly displays clinical data so that appropriate treatment can be planned. When surgery is being considered, it offers details about the surgery's output, resection extent, and repair. Information from imaging can also indicate management modules and treatment outcomes. The goal of this chapter is to explain oral squamous cell carcinoma/oropharyngeal cancer through a case study of a patient that explains the use of different imaging techniques for the progression, diagnosis, management, and outcome of the disease. MRI with dynamic sequences and diffusion-weighted, dental radiographs, single-photon emission CT, perfusion CT, panoramic radiographs, cone beam CT, ultrasound, and some other mixed methods are all imaging techniques that are used in dentistry. Imaging investigations provide reliable information for the treatment of certain cancers.

7.2.2   ROLE OF COMPUTED TOMOGRAPHY IN THE DETECTION OF OROPHARYNGEAL CANCER[33,34,35,36,37]

Computed tomography (CT) scan is one of the most reliable imaging processes and employs specialized X-ray equipment to produce detailed photographs, or scans, of internal body locations along with more detailed images of a wider range of tissue types. CT scanning is now widely performed with 16- or 64-slice multi-detector CT (MDCT) scanners in order to recognize recurring spots, identify the difference between surgical changes and persistent disease, and identify the location of a primary cancer that has yet to be diagnosed.

The benefits for using CT scans in cancer detection are:

- To contribute in the detection of a cancer.
- To convey information about the cancer's stage.
- To identify a specific region of a biopsy procedure.
- Certain local therapies like cryotherapy and radiofrequency ablation are guided by this information.
- To support the scheduling of surgery or external-beam radiation treatment.
- To find out if a cancer is responding to therapy.

Computer tomography (CT) is used for the diagnosis of atherosclerosis and heart, blood clots, and blood vessel–related aneurysms, as well as spinal cord–related issues, traumas to the head, kidney and bladder stones, inflammatory bowel illnesses, skeletal systems, and internal organs; these are all examples of circulatory system diseases and related conditions. In addition to cancer, CT scan imaging is also applied to diagnose irregular brain functioning syndromes.

7.2.2.1   Technical Aspects of CT Scan Imaging

CT scanners use an extremely narrow beam of X-rays to create a cross-sectional image of the patient. This beam strikes electronic detectors as it goes through the patient. The beam moves around the subject during the scan, taking several measurements. Computers process the data and rebuild digital images that are devoid of the superimposition of underlying features.

Most CT scanners on the doughnut-shaped gantry are multi-slice equipment, with numerous rows of detectors now available (ranging from 4 to 256). The patient is placed on the scanner table and led through the gantry, which spins constantly while recording data in each row. In a short length of time, a large amount of data may be acquired. There is a compromise between the resolution of the photos and the speed with which they are scanned. The average person can hold their breath for around 20 seconds, which is about the time it takes to visualize the thorax. If very thin slices are required for increased resolution, the scan will take longer.

Scanners reconstruct sets of images in the axial plane in routine clinical practice. Volume data collection allows for high-quality two- and three-dimensional reformations along numerous planes without further radiation exposure. The additional reconstructions help with diagnosis and surgical planning. Surface rendering is a three-dimensional (3D) imaging technique that is particularly useful for visualizing anatomical structural lumens such as those seen in the bronchial tree.

The X-ray beam attenuation of the tissues is depicted. On a CT scan, a voxel is a small amount of tissue that appears as a two-dimensional pixel. The pixel is given a Hounsfield unit (HU) value based on the density of the tissues it contains. The HU of water is 0, the HU of dense bone is 2000, and the HU of air is 1000. The HU values of the image's numerous pixels are then converted to greyscale. Windowing is a method of showing data to its fullest extent. For picture presentation reasons, no single window choice can adequately display all of the information offered on a chest CT scan. The CT picture is presented on the monitor according to the window width and level.

7.2.3   ROLE OF MAGNETIC RESONANCE IMAGING (MRI) IN THE DETECTION OF OROPHARYNGEAL CANCER[38,39,40,41,42,43,45]

The specifics of structures within the mouth cavity, as well as neighboring structures, may be obtained using an MRI. MRI's superior soft-tissue discrimination quickly identifies cancer invasion and dissemination to nearby tissues. The amount of locally enhanced and regional cancer dissemination, the depth of invasion, and the extent of lymphadenopathy are all assessed by MRI. The primary benefit of MRI over CT is that it gives superior soft-tissue details and does not expose patients to potentially harmful levels of radiation.

7.2.3.1   Technical Aspects of MRI Scan Imaging

To create images of the body's organs, MRI scanners use powerful magnetic fields, magnetic field gradients, and radio waves. MRI scans are different from CT and PET scans in that they do not use X-rays or ionizing radiation. MRI is a sort of nuclear magnetic resonance (NMR) imaging method that may also be used for NMR spectroscopy and other NMR applications.

In hospitals and clinics, MRIs are widely utilized for medical diagnosis, staging, and sickness follow-up. Soft-tissue MRI scans, such as those of the brain and abdomen, offer better contrast than CT pictures. Patients may find it less pleasant since the measurements are typically longer and noisier with the subject in a lengthy, constraining tube. Implants and other non-removable metal in the body can potentially pose a concern, prohibiting certain people from undergoing an MRI study.

7.2.3.2   Real-Time MRI

Real-time MRI is a technique for imaging moving objects (such as the heart) in real time. Two of the various approaches developed in the early 2000s include radial FLASH MRI and iterative reconstruction. Although balanced steady-state free precession (bSSFP) imaging provides greater image contrast between the blood pool and myocardium than FLASH MRI, it can result in significant banding abnormalities when B0 in homogeneity is high, resulting in a temporal resolution of 20–30 ms for pictures with an in-plane resolution of 1.5–2.0 mm. It is anticipated to provide more information on heart and joint problems, and it may also make MRI scans simpler and more comfortable for patients, particularly those who cannot hold their breath or have arrhythmia.

7.2.3.3   Interventional MRI

Because of its lack of negative effects on the patient and the operator, MRI is well suited for interventional radiology, where the images produced by an MRI scanner guide minimally invasive surgeries. In these operations, no ferromagnetic tools are employed.

Intraoperative MRI, in which an MRI is utilized during surgery, is a developing subgroup of interventional MRI. Some customized MRI systems allow imaging to take place while surgery is being performed. The surgical operation is usually momentarily halted so that an MRI may assess the surgery's success or guide following surgical treatment.

7.2.4 ROLE OF INTENSITY-MODULATED RADIATION THERAPY (IMRT) IN THE DETECTION OF OROPHARYNGEAL CANCER[46,47,48]

IMRT (intensity-modulated radiation therapy) is a cancer treatment method that uses sophisticated computer systems to calculate and administer radiation to cancer cells from a variety of angles. It allows cancer patients to receive higher, more effective radiation doses while minimizing injury to nearby healthy tissues and organs. This increases the likelihood of a cure while minimizing the danger of side effects. The following are the primary benefits of using the IMRT technology. IMRT allows the radiation dose to be tailored more precisely to the 3D structure of the tumor by dividing the radiation beam into many smaller beams. This enables a higher dose of radiation to be administered.

7.2.4.1 Technical Aspects of Intensity-Modulated Radiation Therapy (IMRT)

Radiation treatment, such as IMRT, damages cancer cells' DNA, preventing them from multiplying and growing, thereby slowing or stopping tumor development. Radiation treatment has the ability to eradicate all cancer cells in many cases, resulting in tumors shrinking or vanishing. Radiation treatment is sometimes used in combination with surgery (adjuvant radiation). In this case, radiation is utilized to target suspected microscopic illness following surgery.

IMRT is a high-precision radiotherapy technique that uses computer-controlled linear accelerators to deliver exact radiation doses to a malignant tumor or particular locations inside the tumor. By modulating—or controlling—the intensity of the radiation beam in many microscopic compartments, IMRT allows the radiation dose to adapt more accurately to the 3D structure of the tumor. Furthermore, IMRT enables higher doses of radiation to be targeted on the tumor, while doses to surrounding normal essential tissues are decreased.

Using 3D CT or MRI images of the patient and computerized dosage calculations, the dose intensity pattern that best fits to the tumor shape is determined. To optimize tumor exposure while reducing dosage to adjacent normal tissues, a customized radiation dose is often achieved by mixing several intensity-modulated fields from distinct beam directions.

Because the IMRT method minimizes the ratio of normal tissue to tumor exposure, greater and more effective radiation doses may be safely given to malignancies with fewer side effects than standard radiotherapy treatments. IMRT has the ability to reduce treatment toxicity even when doses are not increased. In comparison to traditional radiation, IMRT necessitates somewhat longer daily treatment periods, as well as extra planning and safety checks, before the patient may begin therapy.

A medical linear accelerator produces the photons, or X-rays, utilized in IMRT (LINAC). With a height of 10 feet and a length of 15 feet, the machine is nearly the size of a compact truck. Throughout the process, the patient must stay totally motionless. The power of each beam's radiation dosage is constantly modified depending on the treatment plan. The patient will not feel anything while the radiation is on, but they will hear noise from the machine, smell an odor from the electrical equipment, and see the warning light. Noises and odors from the machine are usual. The patient will be alone in the room throughout treatment, but radiation therapists will keep an eye on him or her from outside the room.

7.3 CLINICAL CASE STUDY OF OROPHARYNGEAL CANCER PATIENT

A 44-year-old male patient presented to an ENT specialist at Kamalnayan Bajaj Hospital, Aurangabad, Maharashtra, for a checkup on January 1, 2019, complaining of a painful lesion on the left side of his tongue that had been bothering him for approximately a month. The patient's history suggested that he had addictions to alcoholism, tobacco, and related products. Medical examination revealed a nonhealing homogeneously enhancing ulceration of the buccal mucosa. A traumatic ulcer in the mouth was detected by the ENT specialist, who administered triamcinolone in carmellose and chlorhexidine mouthwash. The ulceration did not healed, and the white patch grew nodular, and therefore the patient was advised to have a review after a week. Three days later, the discomfort on the left side of the tongue persisted, aggravated by spicy meals but unabated by empirical treatment, leaving the region with painful palpation. Treatments were obtained from the practitioner at the one-month follow-up visit. A 25 mm diameter white verrucous patch ran from the left lateral border of the tongue into the sublingual area, and it was painful to the touch. The patient was then referred for radiological CECT imaging to determine the extent of the illness and its progression. The tissue proximal to the lesion was erythematous and atrophic in appearance, and it was identified as an oropharyngeal tumor based on the reports. The lesion was biopsied to confirm the malignancy and differentiation of the cell mass, and histopathology revealed a well-differentiated squamous cell carcinoma of the mouth. The patient had surgery to remove the lesion and rebuild it using a split skin transplant. When surgery was contemplated, the information about the outputs of the surgery was drawn using imaging techniques CECT and MRI. The amount of resection and reconstruction information was also checked. CECT scanning was used to track the treatment's results at a one-year follow-up. It was observed that the patient remained disease-free.

7.4 METHODOLOGY AND RESULTS FOR MANAGEMENT OF OROPHARYNGEAL CANCER DISEASE

Oropharyngeal cancers can be diagnosed using a variety of imaging modalities. MRI, IMRT, CT, X-ray, and other modalities are the most widely utilized for both diagnostic and treatment planning.

7.4.1 INITIAL EXAMINATION

Because the ulcers were not healing, the ENT doctor suggested visiting an oncologist. Oncologists examined for symptoms of cancer or precancer in the mouth and throat. The doctor examined the inside of the patient's mouth and felt it with his gloved finger. The backside of the tongue had a hump that extended towards the neck. Other tests are performed to check for abnormal spots in the mouth or throat of the patient.

7.4.2 COMPLETE HEAD AND NECK EXAM

The doctor did a comprehensive head as well as neck check and ordered further exams and tests, because there were enough chances that the patient might have cancer. The doctor focused his attention on the head as well as the neck, looking for and testing any abnormalities. This exam involves a careful examination of the lymph nodes and nodules in the patient's neck for any swelling. Some sections of the oropharynx are difficult to notice since it is located deep within the neck. To examine these locations, the doctor employed mirrors or advanced fiber-optic scopes. By initially spraying the back of the neck and throat with numbing drugs to help make the exam easier, the doctor was able to look at these locations via the scopes to locate any tumors, check how enlarged they were, and see how long they had been spreading to neighboring places.

7.4.3 IMAGING TESTS

The patient was recommended to a radiologist for an imaging test. A computed tomography (CT or CAT) scan uses X-rays to make complete and detailed cross-sectional images of patients' bodies. It was recommended in order to see the width, breadth, and actual location of a tumor if it was invading into nearby tissues, that is, if it had already spread to lymph nodes in the neck or the respiratory

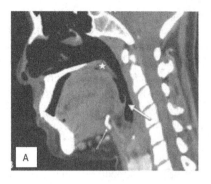 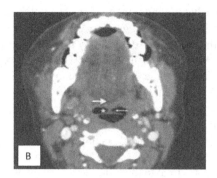

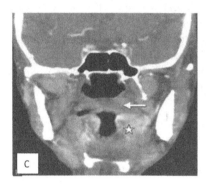 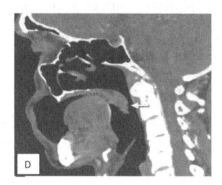

FIGURE 7.5   Normal patient's CT scan (A, B) of propharynx and their areas.[14]

FIGURE 7.5(B)   Oropharyngeal cancer patient (C, D) CT scan.[14]

TABLE 7.2

Complete Head and Neck Exam of Oropharyngeal Cancer Patient

Sequences	Serial axial section of the neck from the roof of the nasopharynx to lung apex with IV contrast medium. Sagital and coronal reconstruction are provided.
Abnormal clinical finding	Homogeneously enhancing mass lesion of 19 × 14 mm is seen in the right buccal mucosa.
	Retro-molar trigone, upper, and lower GBS appears uninvolved.
	No involvement of skin and subcutaneous tissue is seen.
	There is no evidence of significant cervical lymphadenopathy.
Normal clinical finding	Bilateral cricoarytenoid joint and parlaryngeal space are normal.
	Eustachian tube orifice and fossac of rossenmullar appear normal on both sides.
	The oropharynx and hypopharynx appear normal.
	Epiglottis, pre-epiglottic space, ary-epiglottic folds are normal.
	The hyoid bone, thyroid cartilage, and cricoids cartilages appear normal.
	The right and left lobes of the thyroid gland appear normal.
	Internal jugular vein and carotid arteries appear normal on both sides.
	Parotid and submandibular glands appear normal on both sides.
	The cervical spine appears normal.

---

system or other distant organs through metastasis. The images showed a tumor extending towards the neck. The CECT report revealed a homogeneously enhancing mass lesion of 19 × 14 mm in the right buccal mucosa and there was the instant need to perform a biopsy study (see Figure 7.5 and Table 7.2).

TABLE 7.3

Histopathological and Microscopic Examination of Isolated Tissues of Patient

HISTOPATHOLOGY REPORT—Request letter: Slide no SNDH-0545/2020
ADDITIONAL COMMUNICATION—Previous Biopsy—Well-differentiated squamous cell carcinoma
MICROSCOPIC EXAMINATION—Slide no SNDH 533–545/2020

Clinical findings	Complaining of ulcer in right buccal mucosa for three months.
Clinical diagnosis	**Carcinoma of right buccal mucosa**.
X-ray findings	CT neck 15–02–2020 Homogeneously enhancing mass lesion of size 19 × 14 mm on right buccal mucosa. **Features suggestive of neoplastic lesion**.
Right neck section diagnosis	Specimen of right hemandibulectomy of size 7.5 × 6.5 × 3 cm consists of half mandible two molar teeth with right buccal growth.
	Growth of size 2.9 × 2 × 1.8 cm. **Growth is solid grayish-white**.
Sections of resected margins away from tumor	Sections from anterior margin 14 mm away from the tumor (533).
	Sections from posterior margins 5 mm away from the tumor (534).
	Sections from superior margins 7 mm away from the tumor (535).
	Sections from inferior margins 2 mm away from the tumor (536).
	All appeared clear.
Specimens from ulcerated growth	Specimens from ulcerated growth (537–539) showed poorly differentiated cells.
Specimen of salivary gland	Neck dissection consists of salivary gland (540) of size 3 × 2.8 × 2 cm on cut gland appear normal.
Specimens of lymph nodes and free fatty tissues	All nodes submitted for processing (541–545).

7.4.4 BIOPSY STUDY

A tiny sample of tissue was extracted from any tumors or other abnormal areas to be examined more closely (biopsied) to discover if they contained malignancy. Biopsies are performed using specialized instruments that are inserted through scopes. Only a biopsy can determine whether or not oral cavity or oropharyngeal cancer is present, as well as the kind of malignancy. The diagnosis made from the biopsy study was a squamous cell carcinoma of right buccal mucosa grade I, and tumor infiltration up to 18 mm was noted. Also, the salivary gland had normal physiology and there wasn't any metastasis to the lymph nodes. The clinicoradiological correlation was suggested (see Table 7.3).

7.4.5 MAGNETIC RESONANCE IMAGING (MRI)

MRI and CT scans were recommended for obtaining a comprehensive picture of soft tissues in the body. Instead of X-rays, MRIs employ radio waves and powerful magnets. To produce clear photos, a contrast substance called gadolinium was injected into a vein before the scan. If there are several dental fillings that might affect the CT scan images, an MRI can be performed for oral cavity cancer. Also, check to determine if the cancer has spread to the bone marrow (Figure 7.6).

7.4.6 BLOOD TESTS BEFORE SURGERY

There is no blood test that can detect cancer in the mouth or oropharynx. Routine blood tests are still recommended to gain an indication of your general health, particularly before therapy. These tests can assist in the diagnosis of malnutrition and low blood cell counts. A complete blood count

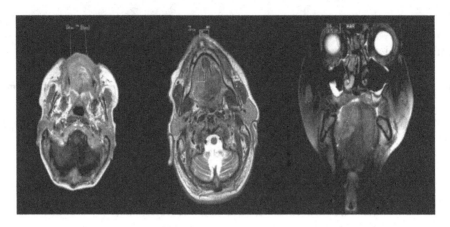

FIGURE 7.6   MRI scan of oropharyngeal cancer patient.[15]

TABLE 7.4

Hematology and Biochemical Tests of Oropharyngeal Cancer Patient

CBC Platelet, Differential Blood, and Biochemistry	Observed Value	Normal Range	Unit
White blood cell count	8.2	4.0–10.0	thou/ml
Red blood cell count	**3.12 Low**	4.5–5.5	million/mm3
Hemoglobin	**9.8 Low**	13.0–17.0	g/dl
Hematocrit	**30.6 Low**	40–50	%
Mean corpuscular volume	98.0	83–101	fL (femtoliters)
Mean corpuscular hemoglobin	31.5	27–32	pg (picograms)
Mean corpuscular hemoglobin concentration	32.1	31.5–34.5	g/Dl
Mean platelet volume	**6.7 Low**	6.8–10.9	fL
Width of red cell distribution	13.0	11.6–14.0	%
Neutrophils	71	40–80	%
Lymphocytes	20	20–40	%
Monocytes	6	2–10	%
Eosinophils	3	1–6	%
Basophils	0	0–2	%
Platelet count	**708 High**	150–410	thou/ul
Glucose random plasma	111.0	Non-diabetic < 200, diabetic > or = 200	mg/dl
Creatinine serum	**0.80 Low**	0.90–1.30	mg/dl
Alanine aminotransferase (ALT/SGPT)	15	<45	U/dl

(CBC) determines if the quantity of different types of blood cells in the blood is normal. It can reveal whether you are anemic, for example (have a low number of red blood cells). Blood chemistry testing can reveal how well your other vital organs, like the liver and kidneys, are functioning. The blood reports reported that there was a decrease in levels of RBC count, hemoglobin, hematocrit, mean platelet volume, and creatinine, whereas there was a drastic increase in platelet count (Table 7.4).

7.4.7 FUNCTION TESTS BEFORE SURGERY

After deciding on a surgical day and time, various important tests were conducted, including an electrocardiogram (ECG) to ensure that the heart was in good functioning order, liver function tests, kidney function tests, and hearing and speech exams. Before beginning any therapy for oral cavity and oropharyngeal cancer, the patient was advised to quit smoking. All of the function tests were found to be appropriate for surgical testing.

7.4.8 SURGERY

Before going in for surgery, the histopathological examination was done and reports were analyzed to check the suitability of the patient for the procedure. The patient had to undergo a surgical procedure to remove the whole affected portion. The patient had a procedure to remove the lesion and repair it using a split skin transplant. The reports stated that the tumor and the extra mass were successfully removed with the surgical procedure.

7.4.9 INTENSITY-MODULATED RADIATION THERAPY (IMRT)

IMRT is a sort of sophisticated radiation treatment that may be used to treat both malignant and noncancerous tumors. IMRT manipulates photon and proton beams of radiation to conform to the shape of a tumor using modern technologies. For accurate eradication of a tumor, IMRT employs many tiny photon or proton beams of various strengths. Each beam's radiation intensity is adjusted, and the beam form varies with every treatment. The purpose of IMRT is to confirm the radiation dosage to the target while avoiding or reducing radiation exposure to healthy tissue to prevent therapeutic adverse effects. The tumor was effectively eliminated and the spread was stopped, according to the radiation therapy treatment report (Table 7.5).

TABLE 7.5
Radiation Therapy Treatment Summary

CRN: 1920020228
Diagnosis: Cancer of right buccal mucosa; Post op(pT2pN0M0)

	Primary	Boost I
Intent of Rx	Adjuvant RT	Adjuvant RT
Rx technique	IMRT	IMRT
Site	PTV-1	PTV-1
Fields	7 fields	7 fields
Fields sizes	IMRT	IMRT
Treated with P/E	Photons	Photons
Energy	6MV	6MV
SSD/SAD	SAD	SAD
Prescribed depth/isodoce	95%	95%
Total RT dose delivered/no of fractions	50.4 Gy/28F	50.4 Gy/28F
Date	23/03/2020–30/04/2020	04/05/2020–14/05/2020

The head and neck region was immobilized with the thermoplastic mold with the patient in the supine position. RT planning CT scan was done GTV/CTV/PTV1, PTV2 and all QAR were delineated. Isocentre was extrapolated with simulation. The patient was planned and treated with the IMRT technique. Treatment was delivered in linear accelerator with photons after verification of set up fields

The total dose delivered to

1. Postoperative primary tumor bed—66.6Gy/37F.
2. Right neck nodal region (IB-V)—50.4Gy/28F.

The patient tolerated treatment well. Suggested to review back after four weeks.

7.4.10 POST-SURGERY TESTS

When surgery was undertaken, imaging using CECT and MRI was used to collect information on the procedure's outputs, the amount of resection, and reconstruction information. At a one-year follow-up, the outcomes of the treatment were also observed through CECT scanning. It was noticed that the patient remained free from disease.

7.5 DISCUSSION

Oropharyngeal cancer is becoming more common around the world, and this is partly due contemporary lifestyles and carcinogenic environmental factors such as smoking, nutrition, and pollution; these causes have led to increased cancer risk as well as longer life expectancy and gene heredity. Prevention, early detection, diagnosis, and time to time treatment of oropharyngeal cancer in a patient are very necessary. Traditional diagnostic techniques are time-consuming and do not determine a clear view of the disease and its spread. But nowadays the treatment starts with clinicoradiological studies, where physicians prefer recent advanced MRI, IMRT, CT, and X-ray imaging techniques along with histopathological and biopsy study because these techniques are easily affordable to patients and less time-consuming for diagnosis. Imaging techniques can show the clear location of a tumor present inside the body as well as its invasion in other tissues or metastasis, which will be helpful for early detection, evaluation of stage, depending upon the spread of the disease, decisions on quick surgery to remove a tumor, and management of the disease in early stages. It also provides information relating to the size of spread after surgical treatments.

7.6 CONCLUSION

From the above case study of the patient with oropharyngeal cancer, it can be concluded that imaging techniques are used in cancer in many ways. In clinical practice, imaging methods are increasingly being employed to conduct a non-invasive evaluation of tumor biology. Imaging studies produce conclusive details for early detection, confirmation, progression, and treatment of the disease. These techniques are proved to be crucially important in the overall management of cancer.

REFERENCES

1. Laprise C, Shahul HP, et al. Periodontal diseases and risk of oral cancer in Southern India: results from the HeNCe Life study. *Int. J. Canc.* 139:1512–1519;2016. https://doi.org/10.1002/ijc.30201.
2. Anjum F, Zohaib J. Oropharyngeal squamous carcinoma. *Definitions. StatPearls* (Updated ed.); 2021 https://doi.org/10.32388/G6TG1L.
3. CDC. Cancers Associated with Human Papillomavirus (HPV). *Centers for Disease Control and Prevention.* www.cdc.gov/cancer/hpv/basic_info/cancers.htm. Published March 29, 2016. Accessed March 7, 2017.
4. Gupta B, Bray F, Kumar N, et al. Associations between oral hygiene habits, diet, tobacco and alcohol and risk of oral cancer: a case—control study from India. *Cancer Epidemiol.* 51:7–14;2017. https://doi.org/10.1016/j.canep.2017.09.003.
5. Osborne RF, Brown JJ. Carcinoma of the oral pharynx: an analysis of subsite treatment heterogeneity. *Surg. Oncol. Clin. N. Am.* 13:71–80;2004.
6. Shah KV, Westra WH. Genital HPVs in the aerodigestive tract: etiologic association with a subset of oropharyngeal/tonsillar cancers and with recurrent respiratory papillomatosis. *Dis. Markers.* 23:235–245;2017.
7. Sharma S, et al. Oral cancer statistics in India on the basis of first report of 29 population-based cancer registries. *J. Oral. Maxillofac. Pathol.* 22:18–26;2018. https://doi.org/10.4103/jomfp.JOMFP_113_17.
8. Veluthattil A, et al. Effect of hypofractionated, palliative radiotherapy on quality of life in late-stage oral cavity cancer: a prospective clinical trial. *Indian J. Palliat. Care.* 25:383;2019. https://doi.org/10.4103/IJPC.IJPC_115_18.
9. Ajay P, Ashwinirani S, et al. Oral cancer prevalence in Western population of Maharashtra, India, for a period of 5 years. *J. Oral Res. Rev.* 10:11;2018. https://doi.org/10.4103/jorr.jorr_23_17.

10. Singh M, Prasad CP, et al. Cancer research in India: challenges & opportunities. *Indian J. Med. Res.* 362–365;2018. https://doi.org/10.4103/ijmr.IJMR_1711_18.

11. American College of Radiology and Radiological Society of North America. *Patient Safety: Radiation Dose in X-Ray and CT Exams Exit Disclaimer*; April 2012. Retrieved July 19, 2013. https://www.radiologyinfo.org/en/info/safety-xray.

12. Gupta S, et al. Relationship between type of smokeless tobacco & risk of cancer: a systematic review. *Indian J. Med. Res. Suppl.* 148:56–76;2018. https://doi.org/10.4103/ijmr.IJMR_2023_17.

13. Tibrewala S, Roplekar S, Varma R. Computed tomography evaluation of oral cavity and oropharyngeal cancers. *Int. J. Otorhinolaryngol. Clin.* 5(2):51–62;2013.

14. Pałasz P, et al. Contemporary diagnostic imaging of oral squamous cell carcinoma—a review of literature. *Pol. J. Radiol.* 82:193–202;2017.

15. Arya S, et al. Imaging in oral cancers. *Indian J. Radiol. Imaging.* 22(3):196–205;2010.

16. Huber MA, Tantiwongkosi B. Oral and oropharyngeal cancer. *Med. Clin. North Am.* 98(6):1299–1321;2014.

17. Kalavrezos N, Scully C. Mouth cancer for clinicians. Part 1: cancer. *Dent. Update.* 42(3):250–252: 255–256:259–260;2015.

18. Montero PH, Patel SG. Cancer of the oral cavity. *Surg. Oncol. Clin. N. Am.* 24(3):491–508;2015.

19. American Society for Gastrointestinal Endoscopy. *Understanding Percutaneous Endoscopic Gastrostomy (PEG).* Unders 27, 2018. https://www.asge.org/home/for-patients/patient-information/understanding.

20. Cigna E, Rizzo MI, Greco A, et al. Retromolar trigone reconstructive surgery: prospective comparative analysis between free flaps. *Ann. SurgOncol.* 22(1):272–278;2015. http://doi.org/10.1245/s10434-014-3963-4.

21. National Cancer Institute. *Oropharyngeal Cancer Treatment (Adult) (PDQ)—Health Professional Version.* May 8, 2020. www.cancer.gov/types/head-andneck/hp/adult/oropharyngeal-treatment-pdq. Accessed September 23, 2020.

22. National Cancer Institute. *Physician Data Query (PDQ). Lip and Oral Cavity Cancer Treatment (Adult)—Health Professional Version.* September 5, 2019. www.cancer.gov/types/head-and-neck/hp/adult/lip-mouth-treatment-pdq. Accessed September 21, 2020.

23. Gou L, Yang W, Qiao X, et al. Marginal or segmental mandibulectomy: treatment modality selection for oral cancer: a systematic review and meta-analysis. *Int. J. Oral. Maxillofac. Surg.* 47(1):1–10;2018.

24. Guyon A, Bosc R, Lange F, et al. Retrospective outcome analysis of 39 patients who underwent lip surgery for cutaneous carcinoma. *J. Maxillofac. Oral. Surg.* 15(4):478–483;2016.

25. Kerawala C, Roques T, Jeannon JP, Bisase B. Oral cavity and lip cancer: United Kingdom national multi-disciplinary guidelines. *J. Laryngol. Otol.* 130(S2):S83–S89;2016.

26. Arya S, et al. Imaging in oral cancers. *Indian J. Radiol. Imaging.* 22(3);2012.

27. Oral Cancer Screening in Mumbai. *India by Primary Health Care Workers.* Full Text View—ClinicalTrials. gov; n.d. https://clinicaltrials.gov/ct2/show/NC T00655421. Accessed April 13, 2020.

28. Warnakulasuriya S. Global epidemiology of oral and Oropharyngeal cancer. *Oral. Oncol.* 45(4–5):309–316;2009. http://doi.org/10.1016/j.oraloncology.2008.06.002.

29. Gillison ML, Koch WM, Capone RB, et al. Evidence for a causal association between human papillomavirus and a subset of head and neck cancers. *J. Natl. Cancer. Inst.* 92(9):709–720;2000.

30. Parvathaneni U, et al. Nivolumab for recurrent squamous-cell carcinoma of the head and neck. *N. Engl. J. Med.* 375(19):1856–1867;2016.

31. Advances in Diagnosis and Multi-disciplinary Management of Oro-pharyngeal Squamous Cell Carcinoma: State of the Art; 39:2055–2068;2019.

32. King AD, Tse GM, Yuen EH, et al. Comparison of CT and MR imaging for the detection of extranodal neoplastic spread in metastatic neck nodes. *Eur. J. Radiol.* 52(3):264–270;2004.

33. Yousem D, Chalian A. Oral cavity and pharynx. *Radiol. Clin. North Am.* 36(5):967–981;1998.

34. Trotla B, Pease C, Rasamny J, et al. Oral cavity and oropharyngeal squamous cell cancer. Key imaging findings for staging and treatment planning. *Radiographics.* 31:339–354;2011.

35. Wesolowski JR, Mukherji SK. Pathology of the pharynx. In: Som PM, Curtin HD, editors. *Head and Neck Imaging*, 5th ed. St Louis Mosby;2;1749–1810;2011.

36. Maravilla KR, Pastel MS. Technical aspects of CT scanning. *Comput. Tomogr.* 2(3):137–144;1978. http://doi.org/10.1016/0363-8235(78)90037-6.

37. Curran AJ, Toner M, Quinn A, Wilson G, Timon C. Mandibular invasion diagnosed by SPECT. *Clin. Otolaryngol.* 21:542–545;1996.

38. Weissman RA, Kimmelman CP. Bone scanning in the assessment of mandibular invasion by oral cavity carcinomas. *Laryngoscope.* 92:1–4;1982.

39. Pathak KA, Shah BC. Marginal mandibulectomy: 11 years of institutional experience. *J. Oral. Maxillofac. Surg.* 67:962–967;2009.

40. Rao LP, Das SR, Mathews A, Naik BR, Chacko E, Pandey M. Mandibular invasion in oral squamous cell carcinoma: investigation by clinical examination and orthopantomogram. *Int. J. Oral. Maxillofac. Surg.* 33:454–457;2004.

41. Sankaranarayan R, Masuyer E, Swaminathan R, Ferley J, Whelan S. Head and neck cancer: a global perspective on epidemiology and prognosis. *Anticancer Res.* 18:4779–4786;1998.

42. Close L, Larson D, Shah JP. *Essentials of Head and Neck Oncology*. Stuttgart, Germany: Thieme Medical Publishers;22–29;1998.

43. Som PM, Curtin HD. *Head and Neck Imaging*, 5th ed. Mosby: Elsevier;1623–1628;2011.

44. Grover VP, Tognarelli JM, Crossey MM, Cox IJ, Taylor-Robinson SD, McPhail MJ. Magnetic resonance imaging: principles and techniques: lessons for clinicians. *J. Clin. Exp. Hepatol.* 5(3):246–255;2015. http://doi.org/10.1016/j.jceh.2015.08.001.

45. Kuppersmith RB, et al. Intensity-modulated radiotherapy: first results with this new technology on neoplasms of the head and neck. *Ear. Nose Throat. J.* 78(4):238:241–246:248;1999.

46. Taylor A, Powell ME. Intensity-modulated radiotherapy—what is it? *Cancer Imaging.* 2004;4(2):68–73;2004. http://doi.org/10.1102/1470-7330.2004.0003

47. Teh BS, Woo SY, Butler EB. Intensity modulated radiation therapy (IMRT): a new promising technology in radiation oncology. *Oncologist.* 4(6):433–442;1999.

48. Siegel RL, Miller KD, Jemal A. Cancer statistics, 2017. *CA Cancer J. Clin.* 67(1):7–30;2017.

49. Bhatia A, Burtness B. Human papillomavirus-associated Oropharyngeal cancer: defining risk groups and clinical trials. *J. Clin. Oncol.* 33(29):3243–3250;2015.

50. Amin MB, Edge SB, Greene FL, eds., et al. *AJCC Cancer Staging Manual*. New York, NY: Springer, (8):220–226;2017.

51. Subramaniam RM, Truong M, Peller P, et al. Fluorodeoxyglucose-positron emission tomography imaging of head and neck squamous cell cancer. *AJNR.* 31:598–604;2010.

Part II

IOT and Smart Healthcare

8 Introduction to Smart Healthcare Using IoMT

Varsha Bendre and Deepti Khurge

CONTENTS

8.1 INTRODUCTION

A few years ago, diseases and abnormalities in the human body could be diagnosed only by undergoing a physical examination in a hospital. The majority of the patients had to be hospitalized for the duration of their therapy. This resulted in higher healthcare costs as well as complex and advanced healthcare facilities. Such facilities can be difficult to reach in rural and distant areas. The development in technology over more recent years has made it possible to diagnose and monitor

DOI: 10.1201/9781003272694-10

109

patients and their problems using tiny devices controlled over the internet. Recent technology has much more to offer to healthcare systems, making it patient-centric.

The Internet of Things (IoT), a new technology, has broad applications in a variety of fields, including healthcare. IoT is a network of physical devices that employs connectivity to allow data to be exchanged. IoT facilitates the connections of several medical devices, and these can measure medical and health data. It can use the smartphone's data connection to connect and transmit monitored information to a hospital or to a cloud platform. Using this technique, real-time monitoring of a health condition is available through the internet via a smart medical device connected to a smartphone app. Such healthcare applications using IoT systems can streamline diagnostic and monitoring processes. This helps to complete healthcare related tasks in a timely manner. The patient can remain connected to the healthcare execution. Such systems can be called the Internet of Medical Things (IoMT).

With the advent of technologies like artificial intelligence, big data analysis, IoT, mobile computing, etc., deployment of such communication services has become possible and has increased healthcare facility accessibility. It is true that technology cannot prevent the population from aging and cannot remove chronic diseases, but it is possible for advancements in technology to make healthcare more accessible to common people by providing cost-effective services and making medical services accessible to all. In the event of a medical emergency, remote health monitoring systems can use connected IoMT devices to save lives.

The IoMT ecosystem is expected to have a very complex architecture considering the security of data, responses of users, volume of data, and complexity of devices. In this system, multiple components interact with each other, and complex decision making is involved to aid in reaching accurate solutions for the end user. Many modules in the systems are dependent on each other, as real-time data acquisition is involved. Hence, device connectivity, data transfers, and analytics to control such as complex and non-delay margin communications become very crucial. IoMT systems can provide such a connected environment, including cyber physical systems and human intervention with computer-based systems, and facilitate data-driven decision processes. IoMT systems and the IoMT environment is capable of integrating grids, homes, and logistics when combined through sensors, actuators, and communication protocol networks. IoMT offers various real-time solutions through the integration of data analytics and sensors embedded on machines. Medical diagnostics and investigations account for a significant portion of hospital expenses. Such investigations, monitoring, and diagnostics can, to a few extents, be made available online. Physical records are maintained at hospitals for reference.

8.1.1 EMERGENCE OF IoMT

A few decades ago, when IoT were first introduced, most people never imagined how the internet and portable cellular devices might one day be utilized to offer healthcare. These technologies are impacting the healthcare sector now; however, there are still a lot of opportunities for advancement in the medical and health industry's adoption of new technologies [1]. In current hospital infrastructure, the information centers, medical issues, traditional nurse stations, and doctor stations are seen to be in need of more reliable methods, as per requirements of patients and the expanding medical needs of people. As a result, discovering new implementation strategies for medical infrastructure improvement, particularly smart medical information management systems that enable suitable and efficient medical staff administration, has become a major concern [2]. There are numerous ways that IoT equipment can be utilized to improve patient care in healthcare. Equipment like smart heart rate monitors, blood pressure measurement equipment, glucometers, asthma inhalers, thermometers, and pill bottles have reinvented as smart devices in the last several years, referred to as the emergence of the IoMT and resulted in self-reported increases in medical knowledge [4].

The rise of IoT technology has aided in information and communications technologies and intelligent building of medical and healthcare facilities. Medical administrators and academic staff have to upgrade themselves to use IoT technology in the medical field [7]. The vast majority of countries have begun to apply IoT technology to medical and health sectors in order to promote enhancement of the same by providing consumers with intelligent services that are always available.

With emergence of IoMT, sensors that can be embedded in or worn on the human body are now being used in healthcare applications to record physiological data from the patient's body. Parameters like temperature, pressure rate, electrocardiograph (ECG), electroencephalograph (EEG), etc., are measured. Other data related to patients, such as temperature, humidity, date, and time, are also captured and converted to big data to draw relevant and precise inferences about a patient's health. Because a large volume of data is acquired from several sources, data storage and accessibility are especially vital in the IoMT system. An ecosystem for such volumes of data has been developing with the emergence of IoMT. Sensing devices collect data and provide this to doctors, caretakers, counselors, and family members. The interchange and communication of such important data with healthcare practitioners via cloud facilitates faster diagnosis of patients and, as necessary, medical intervention. All the communication modules of IoMT must be working together, or providing successful deliverables to patients and medical users. The majority of IoMT systems include a user intervention in the form of a dashboard used by patients and medical providers, allowing them to control, visualize, and assess data. The IoMT system is a combination and integration of healthcare measuring, monitoring, control, security, and privacy.

Effectiveness of IoMT and infrastructure development promises a strong future in the healthcare sector. Nevertheless, for such infrastructure to flourish, the IoMT systems should take care of quality-of-service matrices, including privacy of information exchange, confidentiality, cost, and scalability. Such an ecosystem makes intelligent interconnections with sensors and signal converters, and communication modems can be added to existing medical equipment to turn them into IoMT devices. IoMT devices might interface with medical practitioners in remote places and appear in a range of formats, including smart wearable devices, home-use diagnostic supplies, instruments, point-of-care tools, and mobile healthcare applications. Such disruptive modes can be utilized for disease prevention, fitness promotion, and remote assistance in emergency cases, in addition to managing normal health status [3].

8.2 ARCHITECTURE OF IOMT

With fast advances in science, technology, and medicine, as well as the spread of smart medical devices, the healthcare ecosystem has changed substantially. Likewise, advances in communication technology have transformed many medical services into virtual systems and online applications that may be managed from a distance. The IoT and its integration into healthcare systems have had a huge influence on public life and the healthcare business. In order to deliver better, cheaper, and more accessible healthcare, researchers and enterprises are turning to IoMT applications. Patient, doctor, drug (pharmacist), and therapy are all part of the conventional medical ecology. A typical medical ecosystem is compared to a more sophisticated IoMT-based ecosystem, which incorporates cloud data, apps, wearable sensor devices, and security systems. The architecture is hence divided to work in layers of physical, information, and application using communication protocols.

The architecture for IoMT consists of three layers, as shown in Figure 8.1. There are three layers: a things layer called the physical layer, a fog layer referred as information, and a cloud layer referred to as the application layer. In IoMT architecture, healthcare professionals can connect directly with users through the routers and other interfaces available between the thing layer and the fog layer, making use of the local processing servers available at the fog layer.

The things layer (Figure 8.1a) comprises patient monitoring and measurement devices, sensors, and actuators. These devices act as a physical interface to the data. The data in a physical medium is to be maintained as medical records, pharmacy and medicine statistics, and nutrition schedules. All of these devices and data records are part of this layer. Devices in the IoMT ecosystem like controllers, firewalls, software interface, etc., are also part of physical layer. This layer is directly in contact

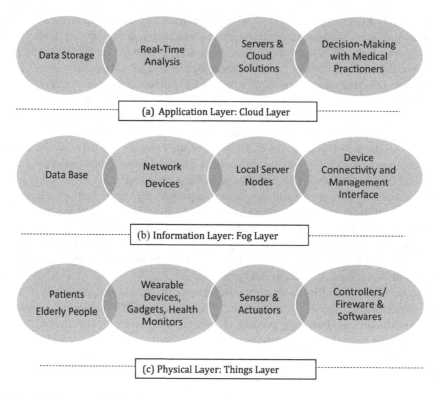

FIGURE 8.1   Architecture of IoMT.

with the users of the ecosystem. The data from devices such as wearables, patient monitoring data, and remote care data is measured and collected at this layer. The devices used in this layer should be secure and protected to ensure integrity and security of the data. So, by employing a firewall and other security systems, these also become part of the system. The local routers in the ecosystem collect the data from these devices by connecting them to the fog layer. The data is further processed at the fog layer and passed to the cloud layer to generate meaningful information. In order to reduce the delay, healthcare experts can get patient data through this router.

The fog layer (Figure 8.1b) operates between the cloud layer and the things layer. This layer comprises local servers and gateway devices for a sparsely distributed fog networking framework. Device connectivity and management interface are taken care of by this layer. The local processing of data is done by the previous layer to provide real-time responses to their users. The servers in this layer are also used to manage and administer the security and integrity of the system. The gateway devices at this layer do the work of redirecting the processed data from servers to the cloud layer for further processing.

The cloud layer (Figure 8.1c) consists of data storage and the computational resources required for data analysis and operate the decision-making systems based on it [6]. Servers and cloud solutions along with decision making with medical practitioners can be carried out in this layer. The cloud systems offer a vast memory and the bandwidth required to incorporate huge medical and healthcare data analysis and handle their day-to-day operations with ease. This layer consists of cloud resources where the data generated from the medical infrastructure will be stored and analytical work could be performed as required in the future.

When creating a new IoT-based medical healthcare system for real-time patient monitoring, it's essential to summarize all associated processes relevant to the targeted health application. The IoT system's success is determined by how well it meets the needs of healthcare providers. Because each condition necessitates a complicated set of healthcare actions, the diagnosis technique must adhere to medical norms and stages. As a result, a variety of cutting-edge technologies have been used to combine diverse healthcare applications with an IoT system.

8.3 RELATED WORKS

The IoMT has arisen by integrating IoT production with telemedicine along with telehealth systems. It is expected that the IoT industry will be worth $6.2 trillion by the year 2025. The medical sector is becoming so focused on IoT technology that healthcare will account for 30% of the IoT products' market share. The role of IoT in healthcare applications is manifold. In this section, a review of different healthcare applications of IoMT is presented [5]. The major concerns and consequences of implementing IoMT at various stages are also reviewed in this section.

The major applications possible due to IoMT are patient monitoring and recommendation systems. In these systems, the application of sensors for getting data related to various parameters like temperature, ECG, blood pressure, pulse, and heartbeat has revolutionized the accuracy of the data. Real-time monitoring of such health-related parameters has ultimately led to patients receiving improved service [11]. Patient health data is further utilized for nursing-recommended systems and hence effective nursing care plans. Such systems can assist as a support to current practice procedures by providing assistance in decision making for critical clinical investigations [12]. The application of rough sets, survival analysis approaches, and rule-based expert systems for developing the architecture of health recommendation system is proposed [13, 14]. This architecture utilizes the patients' self-reported data to recommend clinical examinations for patients as well as physicians. In [15], a new recommender systems approach in IoT-enabled mobile health (m-health) applications and specific case studies are presented.

In [11], the diagnosis and screening process of known COVID-19 patients from X-ray images and blood sample data using AI and ML solutions is proposed. Further, the application of deep convolution neural networks (CNN) intensifies the diagnosis process of the coronavirus disease significantly. Due to this, it became possible to develop tailored solutions for treatment and to control the spread of coronavirus infections in the initial period of the pandemic [16]. X-rays and CT scans are used for providing the solution in [16] for the screening of COVID-19 patients. This deep learning–based method has resulted in 100% accuracy in screening COVID-19 patients. The theoretical research to reconnoiter and explicate the possible applications of IoMT technology is done in [17]. The perspective roadmap to tackle the COVID-19 pandemic and various important applications of IoMT are also discussed.

Remote monitoring systems for brain and neurological diseases, cardiac diseases, and diabetic patients are discussed in [18,19]. The comparison of several ML algorithms like random forest, naive Bayes, and random tree and partial tree (PART) to reveal existence of brain tumors from magnetic resonance imaging (MRI) is presented in [20]. It is shown that PART beats all other considered ML algorithms in envisaging brain tumors. In [21], various AI/ML techniques are studied for monitoring of cardiovascular diseases. In [22], the application of neural network–based approaches for deep reinforcement learning is discussed for meeting a few performance parameters like latency, error rate, etc. A case study of remote monitoring of a diabetic patient using wearable sensors is presented in [23] using IoMT.

The major problem with the IoMT is the handling of large amounts of data while maintaining the security of the same. AI/ML-based solutions are generally preferred to maintain security and privacy of data in networks. In [24], an AI/ML-based method is explored to detect distributed denial-of-service (DDoS) and other privacy attacks. The use of blockchain technology in conquering security is discussed in [25–28]. In [29], the architecture of IoMT, emerging technologies in IoMT like blockchain, physically unclonable functions (PUF), AI, and software-defined networking (SDN), and their role in IoMT, are described in detail. Though it is possible to use blockchain technology for ensuring security in IoMT networks, resource overheads at end users are a major challenge. In [25], the secure architecture of detection and prevention of stress at end users using AI/ML-assisted blockchain technology is projected. In [26], a blockchain-based verification technique is proposed for medical devices.

In spite of many advantages to and applications of IoMT, maintaining the security of a patient's health-related data and keeping patients' identities confidential is still a challenge. Healthcare-related data in such systems must be secured at various stages like data collection, transmission, and storage. In a 2020 CyberMDX report, it was stated that nearly 50% of IoMT devices are susceptible to exploits and vulnerability attacks [30, 31]. The revealing of patients' identity and respective healthcare data can affect patients' lives and impose privacy concerns. An overview of the security requirements, state-of-the-art security techniques, and new types of attacks are discussed in [31], and the framework to meet all security requirements is also proposed in this paper. The secure management and practical needs of personal health records (PHR), electronic health records (EHR), and electronic medical records (EMR) using blockchain are explored in [27, 28]. Moreover, in [32], various cryptographic techniques are improved to encounter the safety necessities of medical data. In [33–35], privacy in the e-healthcare system is ensured using PUF-based devices. In [35], PUF-based sensor devices are used to ensure secure monitoring of COVID-19 patients. Secured contact tracing in densely populated areas using a PUF-based host tracking system is presented in [33]. Applications of PUF-based sensors for measurement of secure physical parameters is discussed in [25]. In [35], the development of new IoMT technologies using emerging AI, big data, and blockchain technologies in the context of COVID-19 are discussed.

SDN-based surgical training framework for various telehealth services like telemedicine and telemetry using IoMT is proposed in [37] and in [36]. Furthermore, in [38], an SDN-based e-healthcare management system is proposed with which different quality-of-service (QoS) requirements could be met using SDN based on different traffic requirements. The challenges faced by data-intensive ecosystems such as mobile healthcare environmental monitoring, security vulnerabilities, and solutions for big data systems are deliberated in [39]

The classification of the security techniques in IoMT and issues related to the authorization, availability, and intrusion detection systems (IDSs) are discussed in [31, 40]. In [41], the open issues in these networks, such as flexibility, single point of failure, and handling emergencies [9], are explicated. In [42], the design and security challenges for wearable devices in securing patient data in the cloud in IoMT systems are discussed. The application of AI/ML and the blockchain technology to secure IoMT systems and to enhance the systems' performance is discussed in [43, 44]. These methods can provide tolerance to some attacks like DoS attacks and a single point of failure.

8.4   IOMT APPLICATIONS

Applications of sensors, signal convertors, and different communication networking modules to sense and capture real-time data for remote patient monitoring and recommendation systems are now possible due to the emergence of IoMT. Various IoMT devices like smart wearable gadgets, home-care medical equipment, and e-mobile applications have made it possible to connect with healthcare professionals (HCP) even from distant places. IoMT is not only used for managing regular health statuses of the patient's remotely, but also useful in disease prediction and prevention, fitness preferment, and remote intervention in exigency. The various applications of IoMT are discussed in this section.

8.4.1   CHRONIC DISEASE MANAGEMENT

The most important application of IoMT devices is to supervise and manage chronic diseases like cardiac failure, hypertension, diabetes, etc. Blood pressure, blood sugar levels, and electrolyte concentrations inside the body are regularly monitored by such devices with the help of various integrated sensors. The real-time data sensed by these devices is regularly tracked, processed, and used for future treatment planning. This helps in suggesting appropriate medications, changes in doses, and prediction of progress of the diseases. Besides all these possibilities, the centralized data collection can be beneficial in reviewing epidemiological trends in specific diseases location-wise.

8.4.2 REMOTELY ENABLED ASSISTED LIVING

Centralized data storage at a physician's office can store compiled and patient-specific processed data. The quality of healthcare services provided will thus be enhanced as analyzing fresh data against old records can be automated by allowing service providers to route, monitor, and transfer tasks to IoMT machines. This can save the infrastructure cost of follow-up, equipment, and resources.

Moreover, remote monitoring helps in increasing the productivity of available resources and continuation in the treatment without a break due to any unavoidable situations. For cardiac monitoring, a kind of body guardian remote monitoring system is used. A major concern in such system is the security of the patient's data. The patient's identification information and monitoring data should be separately maintained to ensure security. For this, different encryption protocols can be used to store critical information.

8.4.3 WELLNESS AND PREVENTIVE CARE (LIFESTYLE ASSESSMENT)

Health supervision has become possible due to inventions like wearable devices, body-implanted chips, and embedded biomedical devices. Such devices can track and monitor a patient's activity continuously while making note of vital changes in the records. The advanced firmware, sensors, and convertors present in these IoMT-enabled devices give its users access to examine and relate vital events with their condition at personal levels. In case of emergencies, the remote networking facilities of the devices allow expert assistance to be provided even in remote locations.

8.4.4 REMOTE INTERVENTION

In emergencies, real-time data monitoring allows physicians to inject drugs and evaluate patient responses. This timely intervention offers advanced medical assistance and can also reduce hospitalization costs for patients.

8.4.5 WEARABLE DEVICES/GADGETS

Another promising application of IoMT is the use of wearable devices for real-time monitoring of various health-related parameters. These devices are designed by interfacing sensors with wearable equipment like wrist-watches, rings, necklace, shirts, caps, shoes, and so on [45, 46] and are noninvasive. The sensors attached to these accessories collect information about patient's health and surroundings. This information is uploaded to the cloud and used by HCP for the treatment of patients at a reduced cost. Such wearable devices can also be linked with various healthcare applications through mobile phones for easy access and monitoring. The network of connections of these wearable devices with a mobile application increases the computational capacity and utilization of such devices.

Various case studies explaining the application of these body-worn devices and their interconnectivity with mobile applications for real-time monitoring have been reported in literature [47–50]. Castillejo et al. have developed an internet-health mobile application for using a novel activity recognition method. In this application, wearable devices are integrated in a wireless sensor network [51]. Similarly, Jie Wan et al. invented a remote healthcare system using IoT and embedded systems. This system is capable of providing real-time data about patient's health like number of heartbeats, body temperature, and blood pressure. Bio-signals such as ECG and EMG signals are also analyzed with the help of IoT-enabled wearable systems [52].

8.4.6 PERSONAL RECOMMENDATION SYSTEMS

The health recommender system is indispensable for improving patients' healthiness conditions. Two such recommendation systems are proposed in [53] by Seda Erdeniz et al. for integration of novel applications, healthcare devices, and physical activity plans for patients. The two recommendation systems, Virtual Coach and Virtual Nurse, assist with real-time patient monitoring and aim to improve and maintain their health conditions. This improvement is provided by Virtual Coach, with planning of medication and diet suggestions for patients by Virtual Nurse.

An artificial intelligence–based automatic recommendation system for providing diet to the patients based on their disease is proposed in [54]. In this system, the data collected from an IoMT device is used for making a decision about the patient's diet. The decision is made in the proposed system by considering various physical parameters like gender, age, weight, and chemical parameters such as calories, protein, fat, sodium, fiber, and cholesterol. The proposed recommendation system model works in six different phases: data reading, preprocessing, optimal features visualization, training, testing, and evaluation. But, according to a survey of the most recent recommendation systems, there are critical challenges in terms of handling the preferences, present health status of the patient, and nutritional content in diet. Thus, still there is scope in the future for automating this system and adopting it with other e-health functionalities [55].

8.4.7 IMPLANTABLE TECHNOLOGIES

The most prominent application of IoMT is contactless portable devices and wearable gadgets. These body-worn implantable devices have various medical sensors and actuators integrated together. Such a network of various body-worn implantable devices is then interfaced with the cloud or server for monitoring of physiological conditions and neuromuscular stimulation. The data sensed by these body devices and current medical prescriptions are then used by HCPs to make changes in prescribed drugs and to actuate directives to a monitoring station as well as among networking devices present on both the surface of the body and embedded as implants. The advent of many such implantable technologies will transform the next generation of healthcare technologies.

In [56], a portable device for contactless monitoring of respiratory rate using capacitive sensor is proposed. This device can be implanted in a T-shirt or a vest and monitors chronic obstructive pulmonary disease (COPD) patients. This type of monitoring is essential for those patients who are advised to rest at home between respiratory rehabilitation exercises. The design and preliminary development of e-health platforms and applications based on the IoMT paradigm are also presented in the paper.

Hand rehabilitation is important after stroke or surgery. Conventional methods of rehabilitation necessitate a therapist, incurring high costs and stress for the patient. In [57], employing a multi-sensor approach, the Virtual Glove (VG), based on the simultaneous use of two orthogonal LEAP motion controllers, is described.

Temp Pal, a wearable IoMT device, has been developed by Taiwan's iWEECARE company to detect unnatural temperature variations and send alerts accordingly [58]. Temp Pal smart patches are connected to the patient's body and interfaced with Wi-Fi/BLE modules for real-time data collection related to the temperature of the patient. Thus, the IoMT system implemented using Temp Pal is used by hospitals and self-quarantined people for real-time monitoring. This will help in reducing the events of direct contact between patients and nursing people, thus restricting the spread of disease.

8.4.8 IoMT in Pharma

Some of the fastest growing IoMT applications across the pharmaceutical industries are drug discovery, development, management, remote patient access, and tracking of drug usage. One such potential smart IoMT device developed is "organ in a chip," which helps organizations to run real-life diagnostics scenarios [59]. Analyzing the information received through such devices with various recent technologies like big data, artificial intelligence, and cognitive systems makes viable an increase in the R&D productivity.

One more instance showing the importance of IoMT devices in pharma is "chip in a pill"—a special ingestible pill. On consumption of the pill, health status like drug effects on key organs is captured and forwarded to a wearable device on a body. This data is then sent as a report to the cloud to HCP for analysis and further diagnosis. IoMT is also proving extremely helpful for sales, marketing, manufacturing, and supply chain management in the pharma sector. IoMT-based radio frequency identification (RFID) tags achieve the task of drug availability and supply cost. Smart medication is possible by embedding sensors in individual tablets to monitor biomarkers in and on the body and antibiotic level in body fuel, and hence dosage monitoring. Naik et al. [60] also experimented and explained the use of CE-marked ingestible sensor to assess patients with persistent hypertension.

8.4.9 Tele-Dentistry

Due to the emergence of the COVID-19 pandemic across the word, tele-dentistry is gaining in attention to avoid physical visits to doctors and thereby reduce the exposure to the virus. In this, dentists are providing platforms for remote streaming of videos of patients in real time, collecting the photos and storing them in the form of EHR. Then the information gathered is used for the diagnosis and recommendation of medications. Such tele-diagnosis is facilitating remote consultations and taking care of an individual's oral health even in invasive situations.

8.4.10 Thermal Imaging Systems

Thermal imaging systems (TIS) are noninvasive and more quickly able to diagnose increases in temperature. TIS have inherent thermal infrared cameras with temperature references and are used to detect skin temperature precisely. The advantage of this system is that it is contactless, i.e., without any physical contact with the individual. If a significant change in body temperature is noticed, then an indication is sent to the HPC to test the patient for infection or disease. Mohammed et al. [61] designed an IoMT-based drone with an integrated thermal camera to capture thermal images for identifying temperature increase associated with coronavirus infection.

8.4.11 IoMT-Robotics

IoMT–robotics is the branch of IoMT systems that creates a smart and automated environment by integrating multiple sensors/devices and systems consisting of humans and cloud-based robots. These cloud-based robotics systems are capable of accessing and processing large amounts of data and converting it into suitable information. Based on the sensing and computing, various tasks can be performed automatically with the help of robots [10].

The main aim of growth of IoMT robotic technology is to accomplish human-like automation without actual human intervention. Primarily, various machine learning algorithms are employed for decision making based on sensed data, and thus train the robots accordingly. The application of IoMT-robotics is manifold, from service robots for elderly care to biomedical waste management in hospitals, drug and food supply for patients to floor disinfectants, etc. In order to deal with the current COVID-19 pandemic situation, aerial robotics systems can be used for surveillance in quarantine areas for supervision on whether people are maintaining social distancing and wearing masks. For contactless diagnosis of COVID-19, a wheeled tele-presence robot has been invented. This robot is capable of performing face-to-face patient assessment virtually and executing various investigative tests on swab samples collected from patients.

For collision avoidance, a special robot, "Lio," has been developed by Miseikis et al. [62] and can be used for safe navigation in a hospital by staff and patients. This robot uses various sensors and a combination of visual, audio, ultrasound, and laser for autonomous collision avoidance. Another such application, "Guido" [63], has been developed for visually impaired individuals for providing assistance in walking. This application uses a map-based navigation system that tracks nearby objects and creates a safe path without obstacles.

For providing assistance in lifestyle management and avoiding future complications, a Nao Robot" [64] has been designed by Ali et al. This robot analyzes patients' medical data, interacts with them, and accordingly guides them about their health status. This kind of robot is also helpful in prediction of various critical diseases like the risk of heart attack. Another such application, "ROBIN," is a rehabilitation robot developed by Loureiro et al. [65].

8.4.12 DIGITAL BIOMARKERS

These are self-powered IoMT diagnostic devices used for real-time monitoring, in and on the human/animal body, of sweat, urine, blood, etc. The information received is helpful for distinguishing between different kinds of infection before any physical symptoms appear. With the help of biomarkers, it becomes possible to closely monitor a patient's response to the treatment and help healthcare professionals to decide on their next line of treatment. Wessels et al. (2021) have developed a digital biomarker to predict lymph node metastasis [66]. This biomarker is implemented on the basis of primary tumor tissue analysis using convoluted neural networks

8.4.13 SMART OPERATING ROOMS

IoMT-enabled smart cyber operating theater (SCOT) with open resource interface for network (ORiN) technology to connect with medical devices was developed by Okamoto et al. [67]. Smart operation theaters with intelligent human robotic systems are developed that can replicate the hand movements of a surgeon. This system is implemented using haptic supported enhanced sensation ability and tissue recognition. The correctness of surgery is also improved due to reduction in human error and improved visualization provided by high-definition, three-dimensional (3D) video images. Tele-surgery is where surgeries are performed when the surgeon and patient are at different locations. This is done with the help of a robotic arm prepared and trained for specific surgeries.

8.4.14 SMART HOSPITALS

Setting up smart hospitals focused on creating conducive environments that can interconnect patients, healthcare workers, and IoMT-based machines that can improve patient care and safety, i.e., smart hospitals, is now also possible due to emergence of IoMT. The four main areas to focus on when establishing such hospitals are interfaces between patient and services; process administration; support services, organization, and logistics; and capability designing. Keeping in mind the current pandemic situation, the availability of such smart hospitals will be of great help to provide remote services and effective isolation. The telemedicine facility, remote monitoring, and use of robots will aid in improvement of healthcare quality provided to patients. Robot-enabled tasks like providing medicine, report delivery, transport, detecting abnormal activities, and collecting patient data will reduce close contact and prevent vast spread of infections.

Resource management can be done efficiently and at a reduced cost if AI-based machines are employed. Promising technologies such as 3D printing and virtual reality (VR) can also be employed to create precise operating instruments and virtual environments for rehabilitation and to strengthen patient state of mind. Additionally, better management and effective utilization of resources and health devices can be established through the use of RFIDs.

Many such applications of IoMT, like training courses and coaching representation to paramedical staff, assistance in rehabilitation and hospitalization, access to health information through EHR without loss of medical information, online protein analysis and accuracy of composition, etc., are possible. So, IoMT has the potential of changing the scenario of medical sectors and improving medical services.

8.5 BENEFITS OF IOMT

8.5.1 CUSTOMER SERVICES

With emergence of IoMT, patients can experience improved attention from healthcare assistants using wearable technology that includes fitness bands, vital health monitoring equipment like blood pressure and heart rate monitors, glucometers, and probably ECG monitoring machines. Such devices can be customized according to patient needs using technology to give personalized experiences and can be used to set patient reminders for blood pressure, sugar intake, calorie counting, exercise, etc. They are also helpful for senior citizens and pregnant women to maintain appointment logs, diet, and drug changes. IoMT can transform the lives of elderly patients by allowing for continuous monitoring of their health problems and even by relaxing family members who have to go out, leaving elderly people at home. The warning system provides messages to family members and worried health providers if a person's usual activities are interrupted.

Physicians can stringently monitor their patients' health by adopting wearable IoT-enabled remote monitoring technology. They can keep track of patients' parameters and know whether they are sticking to their treatment plans, or if they require emergency medical assistance. IoMT allows healthcare providers to be more observant and proactive in their conversations with patients. Data from IoMT devices can assist physicians in selecting the correct treatment method and to have quick discussions in case of emergency for their patients in order to accomplish the best health benefits.

8.5.2 INFRASTRUCTURAL DEVELOPMENT SERVICES

IoMT devices are effective in administration areas as well as patient monitoring systems in hospitals. For monitoring systems, hospitals can have medical equipment such as wheelchairs, heart monitors, nebulizers, oxygen pumps, etc., connected to central systems to track real-time data and usage using IoMT devices with sensors. Medical staff deployment at various sites may also be tracked in real time, and in case of emergency, services can be provided quickly. If all places in hospitals can be centrally connected with server using IoMT, then many things can be controlled at one point like arrival of any sort of emergency, any accidental mishappening in the hospital, spread of infectious diseases, and violation of rules for safety. IoT-enabled hygiene monitoring devices aid in the prevention of infection in patients. There are numerous opportunities for health insurers with IoT-connected intelligent devices.

IoMT devices also improve hospital management, for example pharmaceutical inventory control and environmental monitoring such as checking refrigerator temperatures and controlling humidity and temperature. Machine-to-machine communications, fast data exchange and analysis, automatic alerts, real-time data insights, and end-to-end connectivity allow medical organizations to significantly reduce costs and automate internal processes.

8.5.3 DISEASE MANAGEMENT

For disease management, whether chronic or normal, IoMT-enabled devices offer promising alternatives for managing disease conditions such as hypertension, cardiac problems, diabetes, and other illnesses requiring continuous monitoring. Vital parameters related to blood, weight, electrolyte concentrations inside the body, sleep pattern analysis, and other activities related to the brain can be monitored to understand and predict brain and other organ-related disorders as well as possible predictions of brain disease. The real-time vital data collected by these devices is processed at a higher level and used for future treatment modifications and dose changes, and to predict the disease's progress.

8.5.4 ASSISTED LIVING FOR ELDERS, PREVENTIVE CARE, REHABILITATION ASSISTANCE

Remote assisted living that helps with collecting data from network devices is registered at a central location at the doctor's clinic. Data analytics and processing and compiling patient-specific data enables healthcare automation. Continuous analysis of fresh data against past records allows for deciding the future course and providing predictions for elderly people and other patients in order to manage and prevent disease. This machine-assisted intelligence assists service providers in transferring scheduling, supervision, and field management activities to IoMT machines, reducing the cost of adopting follow-up personnel and maximizing infrastructure usage. Furthermore, remote monitoring has resulted in a reduction in client drop-out rates and enhancement in the utilization of healthcare resources.

Furthermore, encryption technologies are employed to transfer and store sensitive data, ensuring the solution's security. Lifestyle assessment and preventive care are next level achievements of IoMT-enabled devices that facilitate health supervision with monitoring systems. They include diet control, physical activity, and quality of life. Wearable gadgets, implanted chips, and embedded biomedical equipment are novel technologies that capture constant data on patient activities and associated essential changes. Smart gadgets with sensing technologies, convertors, and drivers allow users to assess and connect numerous vital events with local health problems. These instruments have remote networking capabilities in order to provide professional support in emergency circumstances at any distant location. In the event of an emergency, clinicians can use real-time data from sensors to prescribe medications and assess reactions. These prompt measures provide high-tech medical help while lowering hospitalization costs. Furthermore, centralized data gathering can aid in the research of epidemiological trends in certain diseases in a given community. Assistance in rehabilitation and hospitalization of patients can be easily managed using IoMT. Using textiles for including sensors for patient data collection is also a possibility. Textiles of very common use are perfect for building wearable health monitoring devices because of easy mode of usage and comfortable texture. Sensors can be attached to conductive textiles that capture data related to the human body. This system simplifies the development of wearable, intelligent medical garments, facilitating long-term measurement and monitoring of crucial physiological signals [8].

8.5.5 CHILD HEALTH INFORMATION

Child health information is a concept that is concerned with raising knowledge about a child's health. The fundamental goal is to inform and make children and parents aware of their all-round health, which includes nutritional standards, emotional and mental well-being, and behavioral patterns. The creation of a IoMT platform to monitor and manage a child's health will prove to develop concrete steps in achieving higher mental and physical health goals. Children with special abilities need constant monitoring, and IoMT platforms can be very beneficial. Parents can manage many crucial episodes of anxiety and management of kids. IoT-based systems for monitoring a child's mental and physical health in the event of an emergency are gaining attention and can help required actions to be done with the assistance of physicians and parents.

8.6 CHALLENGES IN IOMT

8.6.1 SAFETY AND PRIVACY

IoMT medical devices are susceptible to security threats like sensor attacks, false positive or negatives of data, sometimes denial of service from servers, nonlinearity of smart devices, and undesirable fatal results. Malicious devices give several fake identities to other network devices. If such an attack is launched on healthcare IoT devices, it can compromise the health system's entire functionality and significantly pose threats, as the compromised device may emerge in more than one place. In IoMT devices, keeping data private from attackers is a critical problem. Devices in the IoT-based health system focus on providing the end-user with smart services; however, they are often not conscious of privacy. This causes a huge disadvantage in installed sensors in or on patients' bodies as patient privacy may be leaked. Therefore, a threat to patient information is posed. Because of the possibility of data leakage, patient safety is now compromised [9]. High amounts of personal data are transmitted by the network of embedded controlled devices in IoMT applications, raising major privacy problems. Appropriate protection safeguards for end users are also to be implemented along with these devices. User and device authentication to a system should be built around the devices to guarantee that data is accurately measured and transferred and that content in the systems is only available to authorized healthcare providers or family personnel. The capacity to authenticate users of medical devices in the context of healthcare systems might be used to ensure the integrity of data. Patients' privacy becomes vulnerable when security is not considered during the deployment of new technologies in healthcare applications. This is not to suggest that data confidentiality protection has not always been present, but in an IoT-based healthcare system, possible vulnerabilities are very hard to detect and eliminate.

8.6.2 DESIGN CHALLENGES

Portability, storage capacity, and computation limitations are major challenges in designing IoMT devices. Healthcare IoT devices generally suffer from limited battery power and need charging at regular intervals; hence, portability becomes an issue. As data keeps on changing and involves a lot of powerful computational capabilities, the complexity of design increases, but area and speed can't be compromised. Small amounts of memory pose a serious challenge in executing security techniques such as encryption to protect the infrastructure. Hence, when designing any medical device or instrument, designers must consider whether their product should have security walls; no power-hungry solutions are tolerated. Choices for technology in terms of device fabrications and in terms of hardware to handle the complexity of algorithms running at the back end are of major concern.

Multiple devices exit and enter the network within an IoT-based healthcare system. This entry and exit feature makes the network topology complex, as it is difficult to know which device leaves and if a new device is joining the network. It is therefore challenging to design a scalable technique for this multi-protocol communication and complex network. Hence, dynamic communication protocols and topology for hardware integration are of great importance. Healthcare IoT devices may be stolen, and intruders or hackers can extract patient data and security features of the device, reprogram the stolen device, and redeploy them to the network. Hence, most secured operating systems are custom made.

8.6.3 AWARENESS OF PATIENTS

Though healthcare business is shifting from a hospital-centric to a patient-centric model, awareness of this model is yet to be common among citizens. Traditional methods of inspection, diagnosis, and interaction with health executives are still appreciated by citizens.

8.7 CONCLUSION

The chapter presents several important aspects of the IoMT system. The architecture of an IoMT system and its components have been discussed. This chapter provides information about current healthcare services where the IoMT-based technologies are being applied, along with their challenges and benefits. By employing the concepts of the IoT, IoMT technology can support and help healthcare professionals and family members to monitor and diagnose health issues, measure health parameters, and provide diagnostic facilities for remote locations. IoT intervention in the healthcare sector has transformed the healthcare industry from a hospital-centric system to one that is more patient-centric. The challenges and issues associated with the design, manufacturing, and use of the IoMT system are discussed in the chapter, which can provide a foundation for future advancement and research focus in the upcoming years.

REFERENCES

[1] T. G. Li, "Research on data communication between intelligent terminals of medical internet of things," in *Proceedings of the Industrial Control Network and System Research Room, CSA2015*, pp. 357–359, Wuhan, China, November 2015.

[2] F. Liu, Z. Chen, and J. Wang, "Intelligent medical IoT system based on WSN with computer vision platforms," *Concurrency and Computation Practice and Experience*, vol. 36, p. e5036, 2018.

[3] Z. Pang, L. Zheng, J. Tian, S. Kao-Walter, E. Dubrova, and Q. Chen, "Design of a terminal solution for integration of in-home health care devices and services towards the internet-of-things," *Enterprise Information Systems*, vol. 9, no. 1, pp. 86–116, 2015.

[4] H. Shull, J. Friedman, C. Tymchuk, R. M. Hoffman, T. Grogan, and J. Hamilton, "Evaluation of the UCLA department of medicine Malawi global health clinical elective: lessons from the first five years," *The American Journal of Tropical Medicine and Hygiene*, vol. 91, no. 5, pp. 876–880, 2014.

[5] Z. Ni, I. Craddock, and T. Diethe, "Bridging e-health and the internet of things: the SPHERE project," *IEEE Intelligent Systems*, vol. 30, no. 4, pp. 39–46, 2015.

[6] A. Håkansson and R. Hartung, "An infrastructure for individualised and intelligent decision-making and negotiation in cyber-physical systems," *Procedia Computer Science*, vol. 35, no. 1, pp. 822–831, 2014.

[7] A. Singh and B. Pandey, "A new intelligent medical decision support system based on enhanced hierarchical clustering and random decision forest for the classification of alcoholic liver damage, primary hepatoma, liver cirrhosis, and cholelithiasis," *Journal of Healthcare Engineering*, vol. 2018, pp. 1–9, 2018.

[8] M. Yapici and T. Alkhidir, "Intelligent medical garments with graphene-functionalized smart-cloth ECG sensors," *Sensors*, vol. 17, no. 4, p. 875, 2017.

[9] IoT-Based Applications in Healthcare Devices Bikash Pradhan, Saugat Bhattacharyya, Kunal Pal, *Department of Biotechnology and Medical Engineering, National Institute of Technology*, Rourkela 769008, India 2 School of Computing, Engineering & Intelligent System, Ulster University, Londonderry, UK.

[10] A. Williams, B. Sebastian, and P. Ben-Tzvi, "Review and analysis of search, extraction, evacuation, and medical field treatment robots," *Journal of Intelligent and Robotic Systems*, vol. 5, pp. 1–18, 2019.

[11] J. Sengupta, S. Ruj, and S. D. Bit, "A comprehensive survey on attacks, security issues and blockchain solutions for IoT and IIoT," *Journal of Network and Computer Applications*, vol. 149, pp. 1–20, 2020.

[12] L. Duan, W. N. Street, and E. Xu, "Healthcare information systems: data mining methods in the creation of a clinical recommender system," *Enterprise Information Systems*, vol. 5, no. 2, pp. 169–181, 2011.

[13] P. Pattaraintakorn, G. M. Zaverucha, and N. Cercone, "Web based health recommender system using rough sets, survival analysis and rule-based expert systems," in An, A., Stefanowski, J., Ramanna, S., Butz, C. J., Pedrycz, W., and Wang, G. (eds.), *RSFDGrC 2007. LNCS (LNAI)*, vol. 4482, pp. 491–499. Springer, Heidelberg, 2007.

[14] F. Narducci, P. Lops, and G. Semeraro, "Power to the patients: The HealthNetsocial network," *Information Systems*, vol. 71, pp. 111–122, November 2017.

[15] S. P. Erdeniz, I. Maglogiannis, A. Menychtas, A. Felfernig, and T. N. T. Tran, "Recommender systems for IoT enabled m-health applications," in Iliadis, L., Maglogiannis, I., and Plagianakos, V. (eds.), *Artificial Intelligence Applications and Innovations. AIAI 2018. IFIP Advances in Information and Communication Technology*, vol. 520. Springer, Cham, 2018.

[16] S. M. Tahsien, H. Karimipour, and P. Spachos, "Machine learning based solutions for security of Internet of Things (IoT): A survey," *Journal of Network and Computer Applications*, vol. 161, pp. 1–18, 2020.

[17] R. P. Singh, M. Javaid, A. Haleem, and R. Suman, "Internet of Things (IoT) applications to fight against COVID-19 pandemic," *Diabetes Metabolic Syndrome, Clinical Research & Reviews*, vol. 14, no. 4, pp. 521–524, July 2020.

[18] M. Kozlovszky, L. Kovacs, and K. Karoczkai, "Cardiovascular and diabetes focused remote patient monitoring," in Braidot, A., and Hadad, A. (eds.), *VI Latin American Congress on Biomedical Engineering CLAIB 2014*, Paraná, Argentina 29, 30 & 31 October 2014. IFMBE Proceedings, vol 49. Springer, Cham, 2015.

[19] S. Vishnu, S. R. J. Ramson, and R. Jegan, "Internet of Medical Things (IoMT)—An overview," in *2020 5th International Conference on Devices, Circuits and Systems (ICDCS)*, 2020, pp. 101–104. https://doi.org/10.1109/ICDCS48716.2020.243558

[20] S. R. Khan, M. Sikandar, A. Almogren, I. Ud Din, A. Guerrieri, and G. Fortino, "IoMT-based computational approach for detecting brain tumor," *Future Generation Computer Systems*, vol. 109, pp. 360–367, 2020.

[21] A. Kilic, "Artificial intelligence and machine learning in cardiovascular health care," *The Annals of Thoracic Surgery*, vol. 109, no. 5, pp. 1323–1329, 2020.

[22] H. Song, J. Bai, Y. Yi, J. Wu, and L. Liu, "Artificial intelligence enabled internet of things: Network architecture and spectrum access," *IEEE Computational Intelligence Magazine*, vol. 15, no. 1, pp. 44–51, 2020.

[23] O. AlShorman, B. AlShorman, M. Al-khassaweneh, and F. Alkahtani, "A review of internet of medical things (IoMT)—based remote health monitoring through wearable sensors: a case study for diabetic patients," *Indonesian Journal of Electrical Engineering and Computer Science*, vol. 20, no. 1, pp. 414–422, 2020.

[24] A. Abdelkefi, Y. Jiang, and S. Sharma, "SENATUS: an approach to joint traffic anomaly detection and root cause analysis," in *2018 2nd Cyber Security in Networking Conference (CSNet)*, pp. 1–8, Paris, France, 2018.

[25] L. Rachakonda, A. K. Bapatla, S. P. Mohanty, and E. Kougianos, "SaYoPillow: Blockchain-integrated privacy-assured IoMT framework for stress management considering sleeping habits," in *IEEE Transactions on Consumer Electronics*, vol. 67, no. 1, pp. 20–29, Feb. 2021. https://doi.org/10.1109/TCE.2020.3043683

[26] F. Fotopoulos, V. Malamas, T. K. Dasaklis, P. Kotzanikolaou, and C. Douligeris, "A blockchain-enabled architecture for IoMT device authentication," in *2020 IEEE Eurasia Conference on IoT, Communication and Engineering (ECICE)*, pp. 89–92, Yunlin, Taiwan, 2020.

[27] C. Esposito, A. De Santis, G. Tortora, H. Chang, and K.-K. R. Choo, "Blockchain: a panacea for healthcare cloudbased data security and privacy?" *IEEE Cloud Computing*, vol. 5, no. 1, pp. 31–37, 2018.

[28] F. Girardi, G. De Gennaro, L. Colizzi, and N. Convertini, "Improving the healthcare effectiveness: the possible role of EHR, IoMT and blockchain," *Electronics*, vol. 9, no. 6, p. 884, 2020.

[29] S. Razdan and S. Sharma, "Internet of Medical Things (IoMT): Overview, emerging technologies, and case studies," *IETE Technical Review*, pp. 1–14, 2021.

[30] CyberMDX, *2020 Vision: A Review of Major IT & Cyber Security Issues Affecting Healthcare* [Online]. Available: www.cybermdx.com/resources/2020-vision-review-major-healthcare-it-cybersec-issues [Accessed: 18-November-2020].

[31] A. Ghubaish, T. Salman, M. Zolanvari, D. Unal, A. Al-Ali and R. Jain, "Recent advances in the internet-of-medical-things (IoMT) systems security," in *IEEE Internet of Things Journal*, vol. 8, no. 11, pp. 8707–8718, June 1, 2021. https://doi.org/10.1109/JIOT.2020.3045653

[32] M. Noura, "Efficient and secure cryptographic solutions for medical data," Theses, Univ. Bourgogne Franche-Comté, July 2019.

[33] V. P. Yanambaka, A. Abdelgawad, and K. Yelamarthi, "PIM: A PUF based host tracking protocol for privacy aware contact tracing in crowded areas," *IEEE Consumer Electronics Magazine*, pp. 1–1, 2021.

[34] H. Ma, Y. Gao, O. Kavehei, and D. C. Ranasinghe, "A PUF sensor: Securing physical measurements," in *2017 IEEE International Conference on Pervasive Computing and Communications Workshops (PerCom Workshops)*, 2017, pp. 648–653. https://doi.org/10.1109/PERCOMW.2017.7917639

[35] M. Masud, G. Singh Gaba, S. Alqahtani, G. Muhammad, B. B. Gupta, P. Kumar, and A. Ghoneim, "A lightweight and robust secure key establishment protocol for internet of medical things in COVID-19 patients care," *IEEE Internet of Things Journal*, pp. 1–1, 2020.

[36] S. Liaqat, A. Akhunzada, F. S. Shaikh, A. Giannetsos, and M. A. Jan, "SDN orchestration to combat evolving cyber threats in internet of medical things (IoMT)," *Computer Communications*, vol. 160, pp. 697–705, 2020.

[37] J. Cecil, A. Gupta, M. Pirela-Cruz, and P. Ramanathan, "An IoMT based cyber training framework for orthopedic surgery using next generation internet technologies," *Informatics in Medicine Unlocked*, vol. 12, pp. 128–137, 2018.

[38] S. Badotra, D. Nagpal, S. Narayan Panda, S. Tanwar, and S. Bajaj, "IoT-enabled healthcare network with SDN," in *2020 8th International Conference on Reliability, Infocom Technologies and Optimization (Trends and Future Directions) (ICRITO)*, pp. 38–42, Noida, India, 2020.

[39] R. Atat, L. Liu, J. Wu, G. Li, C. Ye, and Y. Yang, "Big data meet cyber-physical systems: a panoramic survey," *IEEE Access*, vol. 6, pp. 73603–73636, 2018.

[40] J.-P. A. Yaacoub et al., "Securing internet of medical things systems: Limitations, issues and recommendations," *Future Generation Computer Systems*, vol. 105, pp. 581–606, 2020.

[41] A. Vyas and S. Pal, "Preventing security and privacy attacks in WBANs," in Gupta, B., Perez, G., Agrawal, D., and Gupta, D. (eds.), *Handbook of Computer Networks and Cyber Security*. Cham: Springer, 2020. https://doi.org/10.1007/978-3-030-22277-2_8

[42] D. Bhushan and R. Agrawal. "Security challenges for designing wearable and IoT solutions," in Balas, V., Solanki, V., Kumar, R., and Ahad, M. (eds.), *A Handbook of Internet of Things in Biomedical and Cyber Physical System*. Intelligent Systems Reference Library, vol 165. Cham: Springer, 2020. https://doi.org/10.1007/978-3-030-23983-1_5

[43] F. Pesapane, M. B. Suter, M. Codari, F. Patella, C. Volonté, and F. Sardanelli, "Chapter 52—Regulatory issues for artificial intelligence in radiology," in Faintuch, J., and Faintuch, S. (eds.), *Precision Medicine for Investigators, Practitioners and Providers*, pp. 533–543. Academic Press, 2020. ISBN 9780128191781. https://doi.org/10.1016/B978-0-12-819178-1.00052-6

[44] J. Sengupta, S. Ruj, and S. D. Bit, "A comprehensive survey on attacks, security issues and blockchain solutions for IoT and IIoT," *Journal of Network and Computer Applications*, vol. 149, pp. 1–20, 2020.

[45] Y. Zhang, J. Cui, K. Ma, H. Chen, and J. Zhang, "A wristband device for detecting human pulse and motion based on the internet of things," *Measurement*, vol. 163, 2020.

[46] K. Singh, "Role and impact of wearables in IoT healthcare," in *Proceedings of the Third International Conference on Computational Intelligence and Informatics*, pp. 735–742, Springer, Berlin, Germany, 2020.

[47] M. Mendonça, "An IoT-based healthcare ecosystem for home intelligent assistant services in smart homes," in *Proceedings of the EAI International Conference on IoT Technologies for HealthCare*, pp. 142–155, Braga, Portugal, December 2019.

[48] T. Mauldin, M. Canby, V. Metsis, A. Ngu, and C. Rivera, "SmartFall: a smartwatch-based fall detection system using deep learning," *Sensors*, vol. 18, no. 10, p. 3363, 2018.

[49] D. Kraft, K. Srinivasan, and G. Bieber, "Deep learning-based fall detection algorithms for embedded systems, smartwatches, and IoT devices using accelerometers," *Technologies*, vol. 8, no. 4, p. 72, 2020.

[50] N. S. Erdem, "Gait analysis using smartwatches," in *Proceedings of the 2019 IEEE 30th International Symposium on Personal, Indoor and Mobile Radio Communications (PIMRC Workshops)*, pp. 1–6, Istanbul, Turkey, September 2019.

[51] P. Castillejo, J.-F. Martinez, J. Rodriguez-Molina, and A. Cuerva, "Integration of wearable devices in a wireless sensor network for an E-health application," *IEEE Wireless Communications*, vol. 20, no. 4, pp. 38–49, 2013.

[52] A. Kelati, "Biosignal monitoring platform using Wearable IoT," in *Proceedings of the 22nd Conference of Open Innovations Association FRUCT*, pp. 9–13, Petrozavodsk, Russia, May 2018.

[53] A. Felfernig and T. Ngoc, "Recommender systems for IoT enabled m-Health Applications," *Artificial Intelligence: Applications and Innovations*, vol. 520, pp. 227–237, 2018

[54] C. Iwendi, S. Khan, J. H. Anajemba, A. K. Bashir, and F. Noor, "Realizing an efficient IoMT-assisted patient diet recommendation system through machine learning model," *IEEE Access*, vol. 8, pp. 28462–28474, 2020.

[55] C. Iwendi, M. Uddin, J. A. Ansere, P. Nkurunziza, J. H. Anajemba, and A. K. Bashir, "On detection of sybil attack in large-scale VANETs using spider-monkey technique," *IEEE Access*, vol. 6, pp. 47258–47267, 2018.

[56] D. Naranjo-Hernández, A. Talaminos-Barroso, J. Reina-Tosina, L. M. Roa, G. Barbarov-Rostan, P. Cejudo-Ramos, E. Márquez-Martín, and F. Ortega-Ruiz, "Smart vest for respiratory rate monitoring of COPD patients based on non-contact capacitive sensing," *Sensors (Basel)*, vol. 18, no. 7, p. 2144, 2018.

[57] G. Placidi, L. Cinque, A. Petracca, M. Polsinelli, and M. Spezialetti, "A virtual glove system for the hand rehabilitation based on two orthogonal LEAP motion controllers," in *Proceedings of the 6th International Conference on Pattern Recognition Applications and Methods*, ICPRAM 2017, Porto, Portugal, 24–26 February 2017, vol. 1, pp. 184–192.

[58] A. H. Mohd Aman, W. H. Hassan, S. Sameen, et al. "IoMT amid COVID-19 pandemic: application, architecture, technology, and security," *Journal of Network and Computer* Applications, vol. 174, p. 102886, 2021.

[59] Q. Wu, J. Liu, X. Wang, et al. "Organ-on-a-chip: recent breakthroughs and future prospects," *BioMedical Engineering OnLine*, vol. 19, no. 9, 2020.

[60] R. Naik, N. Macey, R. J. West, P. Godbehere, S. C. Thurston, et al. "First use of an ingestible sensor to manage uncontrolled blood pressure in primary practice: The UK hypertension registry," *Journal of Community Medicine & Health Education*, vol. 7, p. 506, 2017. doi:10.4172/2161-0711.1000506

[61] M. Nasajpour, S. Pouriyeh, R. M. Parizi, et al. "Internet of things for current COVID-19 and future pandemics: an exploratory study," *Journal of Healthcare Informatics Research*, vol. 4, pp. 325–364, 2020.

[62] J. Miseikis, P. Caroni, P. Duchamp, A. Gasser, R. Marko, N. Miseikiene, F. Zwilling, C. de Castelbajac, L. Eicher, M. Fruh, et al. "Lio-a personal robot assistant for human-robot interaction and care applications," *IEEE Robotics and Automation Letters*, vol. 5, pp. 5339–5346, 2020.

[63] G. J. Lacey and D. Rodriguez-Losada, "The evolution of Guido," *IEEE Robotics & Automation Magazine*, vol. 15, pp. 75–83, 2008.

[64] S. Ali, M. Samad, F. Mehmood, Y. Ayaz, W. M. Qazi, M. J. Khan, and U. Asgher, "Hand gesture-based control of NAO robot using myo armband," *Advances in Neuroergonomics and Cognitive Engineering*, vol. 953, pp. 449–457, 2020.

[65] R. C. Loureiro and T. A. Smith, "Design of the ROBIN system: whole-arm multi-model sensorimotor environment for the rehabilitation of brain injuries while sitting or standing," *Proceedings of the 2011 IEEE International Conference on Rehabilitation Robotics*, pp. 1–6, Zurich, Switzerland, IEEE, June 2011.

[66] F. Wessels, M. Schmitt, E. Krieghoff-Henning, T. Jutzi, T. S. Worst, F. Waldbillig, M. Neuberger, R. C. Maron, M. Steeg, T. Gaiser, A. Hekler, J. S. Utikal, C. von Kalle, S. Fröhling, M. S. Michel, P. Nuhn, T. J. Brinker, "Deep learning approach to predict lymph node metastasis directly from primary tumour histology in prostate cancer," *BJU International*, vol. 128, no. 3, pp. 352–360, 2021. http://doi.org/10.1111/bju.15386. Epub 2021 May 5. PMID: 33706408.

[67] R. Dwivedi, D. Mehrotra, and S. Chandra, "Potential of Internet of Medical Things (IoMT) applications in building a smart healthcare system: A systematic review [published online ahead of print, 2021 Dec 11]," *Journal of Oral Biology and Craniofacial Research*, vol. 12, no. 2, pp. 302–318, 2022. https://doi.org/10.1016/j.jobcr.2021.11.010.

9 A Webcam-Based Belt-System for Respiratory and Chest-Expansion Measurements

Niveditha, Rohan Gupta, Anup Bhat,
Kalyana Chakravarthy Bairapareddy,
Rahul Magazine, and Ramesh R. Galigekere

CONTENTS

9.1 INTRODUCTION

Respiration rate (RR) is a vital sign associated with the human health, and the shape of the respiratory waveform, i.e., the respiration pattern (RP), serves as an aid in clinical testing and monitoring. The assessment of RR and RP is crucial in physical examination [1,2,3]. Deviation in the rate or pattern can point to underlying physiological conditions/diseases, e.g., changes in RP can be helpful in the diagnosis of abnormal conditions such as apnea, Cheyne-Stokes breathing, Biot's respiration [3,4], etc., and may indicate disorders in the muscles connected with the respiration process. Further, RP is useful in various investigations, e.g., examining the effect of different types of breathing on heart rate variability [5,6]. Finally, monitoring RR and RP is very useful in clinical environments such as intensive and neonatal care units, as well as operation theaters (during surgical procedures and on sedated patients) [7]. Apart from RR and RP, chest expansion is useful in pulmonary assessment, e.g., in assessing chest-wall stiffness—towards studying several conditions such as chronic obstructive pulmonary disease, hyperinflation, dyspnea, etc. [8,9,10], apart from its utility during life-insurance examination [3,11]. Additionally, it is used for routine measurement in schools as well as for police and military recruitment.

This chapter describes a webcam-based belt-system—an inexpensive alternative to the respiratory belt transducer (RBT) such as the one in the AD Instruments' Power Lab system [12], or capacitive belt sensors in [13, 14]—to estimate RP, RR, and chest expansion. A literature survey outlined in the following helps build the context leading to the solution.

Minimal/non-contact methods for estimating RP and RR have assumed great significance over the decades [13–28, 32–35]. It becomes even more significant in the current circumstances

DOI: 10.1201/9781003272694-11

involving COVID-19. In 2009, a microwave sensor was used to transmit and receive continuous signals to estimate RR [15], followed by the use of a Doppler multi-radar system [16], and thermal, IR, and near-IR cameras [17–21]. However, such devices are expensive. The webcam was introduced for gating the data-acquisition sequence, for alleviating respiratory artifacts during CT imaging [22] (fixed environment), using three color fiducials on a Velcro belt over the abdominal region. The method presumes a range for RR and was limited to a supine position. In a similar application, RP was estimated by tracking the size of a light-dot projected from a source [23]. Bai et al. [24,25] used webcam(s) to image the bare chest for measuring RR and RP. A slightly different approach of indirect measurement of RR was introduced by Poh et al. [26] based on respiratory modulation of photoplethysmogram (PPG). Many publications have appeared since then [27], and the work is still continuing. However, it is often desirable to measure RR directly with robustness, and also to measure chest expansion. Shao et al. [28] used a webcam to estimate RR based on the movement of the shoulder-edge of a person sitting erect, using a manually selected ROI. However, shoulder is not a good location for measuring respiration waveform/RR—shoulder movement is associated with accessory muscles, which do not contribute much during regular breathing [29–31]. Makkapati et al. [32] presented a method based on optical flow of obtaining RR using a webcam, in neonates over a bare chest. Optical flow was used also in [33] to measure RR from a lateral perspective, although changing light conditions or movement were not addressed. Further, the camera was too close to the body (5–7 cm). The use of a Kinect camera was proposed to extract RR on a subject wearing form-fitting clothing by measuring depth-changes in the chest wall to reconstruct the 3D chest-wall image [34]. The method requires a pressure sensor (to force the subject to strictly adhere to a position) and a spirometer for calibration. Further, the measurement is susceptible to artifacts in the presence of bright light/surfaces in the vicinity of the camera. Recently, [35] proposed contactless monitoring of RP and RR at the neck-pit (selected by user-intervention), over a restricted frequency range ([0.05–2] Hz), on subjects seated still under stable lighting. However, the method reported some errors, perhaps due to non-stationarity of the signal.

Chest expansion is another measure used routinely in clinics, though there has not been much effort towards developing an automatic device, or a protocol, to estimate the same. An "inch-tape" at the nipple-level was being used for the purpose, though concerns were raised on its accuracy due to a lack of a protocol to measure the same [3]. Based on a detailed study of chest expansion by an inch-tape and calipers (for antero-posterior and transverse measurements) in 1972 [36], measurement at any plane—e.g., second or third intercostal space (ICS), or the xiphoid—by an inch-tape was recommended as being sufficient. Calipers were to be used only if the person was obese. However, tape measurement is error-prone due to the moving hands, mistakes due to poor light or weak eyes, and possible gliding of the tape on the surface [3]. Bockenhouer et al. [37] found it necessary to standardize the way in which the tape is held (without slipping), implying that measuring it individually without any help is prone to errors. Since recently, there have been efforts on measuring chest expansion using electronic devices. Ref. [38] reported the use of a belt with a DC motor, to measure the circumference. A laser-based system for measuring the depth differences was reported in [39,40]. However, the measurement, performed on a bare chest, was sensitive to even slight subject-motion, and the necessity for employing multiple laser sources (around the ribcage) was indicated. An ultrasound-based system proposed for estimating chest expansion [8] relied only on a single measurement. No waveform was acquired, and there were issues due to loose clothing. Arthittayapiwat et al. [41] used MEMS accelerometers to measure the lateral expansion of the chest over the sixth rib. In [42], the authors of [41] reported the use of six accelerometer sensors stuck on the bare chest at specified points, with the subject's arms elevated, to study 3D chest-wall movement.

The literature review outlined in the preceding reveals the scope for a simple, inexpensive, and minimal-contact device (along with a suitable protocol) for the measurement of chest expansion, and also to automatically estimate respiration waveform and rate, circumventing some of the issues/drawbacks associated with previously reported devices. This chapter reports the development of such a device/system.

The development of the system and the concomitant methods of measurement are described in the following section. The results of experiments, along with validation, are presented in section 9.3. Highlights, related issues/limitations of the current study, and applications are discussed in section 9.4. The chapter is concluded in section 9.5.

9.2 METHODS

The System: The system consists of a fiducial, which is a 3D-printed cube ("button") made of a light black plastic material (PLA) with a color sticker pasted on a side. It is fixed on a simple elastic tape to be worn around the chest at a clinically specified level. The sticker is made up of high-quality paper (matte finish) of a predetermined color, to allow easy and fast processing, i.e., image segmentation. Stickers with three colors, i.e., red (R), green (G), or blue (B), are reserved, so that the one providing maximum contrast (with that of the subject's clothing) can be used. Every measurement requires two fiducials—one on the belt for recording the signal, and the other on the side of the shoulder—to get the reference signal representing involuntary subject-motion. The signal acquisition system is a simple webcam, placed on the side of the subject, so that both the fiducials are visible. The system can also measure chest expansion with the help of a simple checkerboard calibration system.

Robustness: For color-representation and segmentation, the hue (H), saturation (S), and intensity (V) (HSV) color space [43] is used. Since H and S contain the color information independent of intensity and are less susceptible to variations in illumination, it is sufficient to use H and S for segmentation. To ensure robustness of segmentation, the variability of the color-parameters over a wide range of illumination (types of ambiences) was examined. Color-stickers were pasted on a flat surface in front of the camera, at about the same distance as that of the subject to be imaged. Each sticker was imaged for 10 s over a range of ambience. Different types of ambience were naturally available, as the experimental site was illuminated by a typical artificial light source, but also exposed to day (sun) light through a glass window (covered partially by a PVC vertical blinder allowing external light through the gaps) and a door with 50% glass at the top; another glass window faced the rest of the lab. Imaging was performed at different hours of the day from 9:00 AM to 7:00 PM, and repeated over six days. Since it was the monsoon season, a wide range of ambience/illumination was available: sunny, partially clouded, dark-clouded, rainy, sunny with very few clouds, and rainy with dark clouds.

The video-records, taken over different types of ambience, were processed to extract the values of H and S. To circumvent the discontinuity in the value of H for red, its range was shifted by $180°$ [44]. The clusters in the HSV space were found to be narrower over H (Figure 9.1 and Table 9.1), from which it is clear that the fiducial-segmentation is robust to changes in ambience. The range for fiducial-segmentation, pre-specified to lie within the range shown in Table 9.1, was found to be effective.

Location of the Belt: The subject is made to wear the belt and sit erect on a chair without a backrest, to facilitate imaging. For estimating the respiration waveform, the belt may be placed either over the thoracic region right above the xiphoid (or an inch or two below), as decided by the clinician. Initial experiments revealed that RR is not affected by the position of the belt. In the case of chest expansion, upper chest expansion is measured over the second, third, or fourth ICS. Expansion corresponding to the lower lobes of the lungs is measured at the xiphoid [35,36,44,45,46].

9.2.1 IMAGING AND IMAGE PROCESSING

Imaging: A simple webcam (Logitech C270; frame-rate: 30 fps) was used for recording the video. The subject is instructed to wear the belt and sit still on a chair, with the feet resting flat on the floor and the hands relaxing vertically down. The webcam, mounted on an adjustable camera-stand, is placed on a side—to ensure that the front of the chest with the fiducial on the belt is clearly exposed.

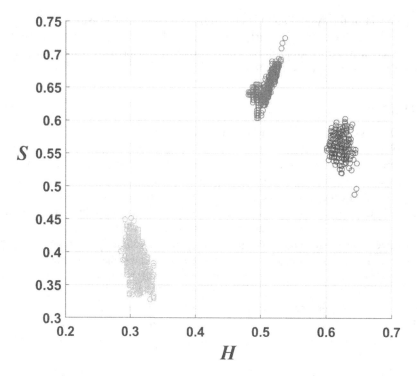

FIGURE 9.1   Scatter plot of hue (*H*, normalized to the interval [0,1]) and saturation (*S*), for red, green, and blue colors. Note that the hue values for red have been shifted by 180° and then normalized.

TABLE 9.1

Range of Hue (Normalized) and Saturation, for Red, Green, and Blue Buttons

	Red	*Green*	*Blue*
H	0.47–0.5511	0.23–0.3857	0.58–0.683
S	0.452–0.931	0.2525–0.645	0.347–0.76

Another fiducial is fixed on the side-arm of the subject (just below the shoulder), for recording the reference signal used to account for involuntary subject-motion. A video of the subject with the moving chest wall and the reference fiducials is captured for a minute.

Image Processing: The video-record is processed to segment and track the button over each frame, using the pre-specified range in the HSV space. Connected component labeling (CCL) [43] of each frame yields labeled blobs (binary regions/objects) with the respective areas. Noisy blobs are eliminated by retaining those with area within the range: [300,1200]. Morphological closing enhances the segmented fiducial-images. Finally, a constraint on the aspect ratio of the fiducial, to lie within the range [0.85, 1.15], yields the true (square) fiducial-image. The coordinates of the centroid of each of the fiducial are computed. The displacements of the coordinates, as a function of time, provide the raw time-series, to be processed to extract the respiration waveform and rate. With the addition of a calibration system, and the recorded waveforms according to a suitable protocol, one can estimate chest expansion.

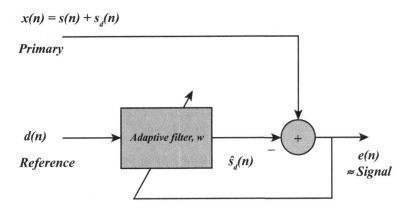

FIGURE 9.2 Adaptive filter to minimize the effect of subject-motion. The input $x(n)$ consists of the respiratory signal corrupted by subject-motion. The secondary input consists predominantly of subject-motion. The output yields the estimated respiratory waveform.

9.2.2 Signal Processing for Extracting the Respiration Waveform

The trajectory of the X-component of the centroid provides the raw waveform, which must be subjected to adaptive filtering to compensate for the involuntary subject-motion. The raw waveform after adaptive filtering provides RP. The location of the peak in the PSD estimated from the RP gives RR; the Welch method [47] is sufficient for the purpose. In (rare) cases wherein the subject changes the breathing rate during the recording, the time-varying frequency can be tracked by using the short-term Fourier transform (STFT).

Motion Compensation: Although the subjects are asked to sit still during the video-capture, one must compensate for the artifacts due to possible involuntary motion. Since the frequency-band pertaining to the motion-artifacts is unknown, conventional filters with fixed coefficients cannot be used. Instead, an adaptive filter [48] in which the filter-weights get adjusted automatically to the changes in the nature of the input(s) is required. One such filtering scheme is shown in Figure 9.2. Let $s(n)$ denote the signal, i.e., the trajectory of the chest-fiducial due to respiration alone. The measured signal $x(n)$ consists of $s(n)$ contaminated by $s_d(n)$ (assumed to be additive) due to subject-motion. The reference signal/disturbance $d(n)$, representing predominantly the motion of the body and not of the chest wall, is obtained by tracking the location of the fiducial on the upper arm of the subject. The adaptive filter works by estimating that part (denoted by $s_s(n)$) of the input $x(n)$ (primary) correlated with $d(n)$ and canceling it. The estimate of $s_d(n)$ is given by:

$$\hat{s}_d(n) = \sum_{i=0}^{N-1} w(i) d(n-i) = \mathbf{w}^T(n) \mathbf{d}(n), \tag{1}$$

where $w(n)$ is the vector of filter-weights at instant n. The rule for updating $w(n)$, obtained by the normalized least-mean-square (NLMS) criterion, i.e., by minimizing the normalized value of the mean of the squared values of the error-sequence $e(n) = x(n) - \hat{s}_d(n)$, is given in the following:

$$\mathbf{w}(n+1) = \mathbf{w}(n) + 2\mu(n) e(n) \mathbf{d}(n); \tag{2}$$

$$\mu(n) = \frac{\mu_s}{\left[\varepsilon + \mathbf{d}^T(n) \mathbf{d}(n) \right]} \tag{3}$$

In Equation (3), ε is a small constant, and μ_S is the "step-size" that determines the rate of convergence. The filter gradually learns the characteristics of the input, and its weights converge to the optimum values. If the input statistics change after convergence, the filter would respond by readjusting its weights to the new optimum values, and the process continues. Thus, changes due to subject-motion that are not very abrupt are tracked and subtracted from the primary input to yield the respiratory waveform.

Algorithm: The complete algorithm for processing the recorded video to extract the respiratory waveform, and the respiratory rate, is outlined in the following:

1. Perform color segmentation of the fiducial in the HSV space, followed by CCL—on each of the video-frames. Apply area constraints to eliminate noisy blobs.
2. Enhance the blobs (candidate fiducial-objects) by morphological closing and apply the aspect-ratio constraint to extract the fiducial-images (one on the belt, and the other on the shoulder).
3. Compute the centroid of each of the fiducials, in every frame, to extract the raw respiratory waveform—pertaining to fiducial on the belt; and the reference waveform—pertaining to the fiducial on the shoulder.
4. Perform adaptive filtering on the raw respiratory waveform using the reference waveform—to retrieve the respiratory waveform free of distortion due to subject-motion.
5. Compute the PSD of the respiratory waveform. The location of the peak in the PSD gives the value of RR. If the signal is non-stationary, use STFT to track the frequency as a function of time.

Note that characterizing and computing a single value of RR for the waveform assumes the waveform to be stationary—which was indeed the case in most of the measurements when recorded over a short interval of time (1 minute). On the other hand, adaptive approaches such as the STFT, or adaptive autoregressive model-based methods, can be used for tracking non-stationary signals over long intervals.

Comparison and Validation: The standard RBT connected to Power Lab (MLT 1132) [12] is used to compare the values of RR, and also the waveforms obtained by the webcam-based method. Note that the RBT measures changes in the circumference, and the webcam-based method estimates those in chest-wall displacements. While the waveforms from the two systems may not match exactly, the values of RR should. Further, if the two systems are not triggered simultaneously, there will be a short delay between the waveforms. This is not an issue for RR, and the RPs can be post-aligned for the sake of comparison.

9.2.3 MEASUREMENT OF CHEST EXPANSION

The webcam-based respiratory belt, along with a calibration-mechanism, allows estimation of chest expansion—when the subject is instructed to breathe according to a suitable protocol. For ensuring the visibility of the button at the xiphoid in the case of female subjects, a T-shaped extension may be used when required. In many subjects, at the xiphoid process or the third ICS, the fiducial was found to follow a curvilinear path. Hence, instead of mere depth-difference, the total distance traversed by the fiducial from the end of inhalation to the end of exhalation is recommended as the measure of chest expansion. To get the measure in physical units, calibration is required. In other words, one must get the pixel size in real units (e.g., mm). Calibration is performed by using an inexpensive and accurate technique of finding the intrinsic parameters of the camera and also the extrinsic parameters [49–51]. It involves a closed form solution obtained using singular value decomposition of a small $(2n \times 6)$ matrix, where n is the number of images of a "model plane," e.g., a simple checkerboard pattern, at different poses. The solution is made robust by subsequent refinement, by the maximum-likelihood method, requiring only 3–5 iterations to converge. The technique is applied on the frames pertaining to a 10 s "calibration video" of the model plane held next to the subject, at slightly different (random) poses. At 30 fps, this corresponds to about 300 frames, which is much more than sufficient for accurate calibration [51].

The procedure for measuring chest expansion is as follows:

1. The subject is instructed to sit erect on a chair with the hands down, so that the fiducial on the elastic belt is visible to the webcam on the side (~ 1 m from the camera). Another button is placed on the side of the arm (upper pat close to the shoulder) facing the camera.
2. The subject is asked to relax, while the instructor holds the checkerboard pattern and changes its pose continuously for 10 s while the calibration video is captured.
3. *Breathing protocol*: A study revealed that when the subjects were asked to perform three deep-breathing cycles consecutively, the second and third cycles yielded lesser displacement. To overcome this bias, the following procedure (protocol) is recommended at the prescribed belt-levels:
   (a) The subject is asked to breathe thrice normally, followed by one deep breath-cycle. Normal breathing provides rest to the subject—between the deep-breathing cycles.
   (b) The procedure is performed thrice.
4. The belt is removed. A tape measurement is performed very carefully, for three deep-breathing events.
5. Algorithm for processing the video:
   (a) The values of the intrinsic and extrinsic parameters of the camera are obtained using the frames of the 10-second calibration video. Note that the MATLAB toolbox for camera calibration pertaining to a single camera has all the requisite functions for the purpose.
   (b) The frames of the video recorded to estimate chest expansion are processed as outlined in the preceding subsection, up to the point of extracting the chest-waveform.
   (c) The displacement of the chest-fiducial, at the instances of deep inhalation and deep exhalation, respectively, corresponding to three deep-breathing cycles, are recorded. The values of displacements in terms of pixels are converted to real-world (physical) values, i.e., centimeters, using the camera-parameters obtained in step (a).
   (d) The maximum of the three displacements is considered to be the chest expansion capacity.

9.3 RESULTS

Ethical clearance for conducting the experiments was obtained from the Institutional Ethics Committee (IEC No. 864/2017), and the details were registered at the Clinical Trials Registry–India (CTRI/2018/06/014599). The experiment was explained to each of the subjects, and informed consent was obtained from each. Subsequently, the volunteer was made to sit on a chair and wear the RBT (for validation), and then the elastic belt with the fiducial, on top of it—so that the side of the cube with the color sticker would face the camera. The color of the fiducial was chosen for best color-contrast. The second fiducial was attached on the upper arm just below the shoulder-level, to extract the reference signal for motion compensation. In the case of some female subjects, when the chest-fiducial was not fully visible, it was positioned slightly below the xiphoid.

9.3.1 RESPIRATION WAVEFORM AND RATE

The volunteer was asked to breathe naturally for a minute, during which the video was captured. See Figure 9.3 for an illustration (with segmentation-results). Spurious points in the color-segmented image were removed by the area constraint. The result was enhanced by morphological closing by a square structuring element of side seven pixels. Finally, objects with the aspect ratio within

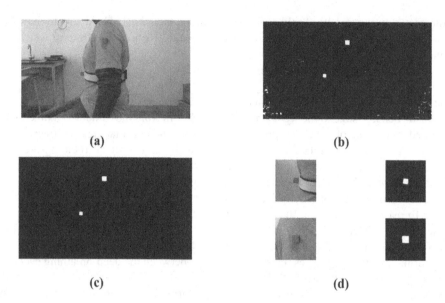

FIGURE 9.3 (a) Raw image from a frame, and (b) its color-segmented version. (c) The result of applying area constraint, morphological closing, and aspect-ratio constraint. (d) ROI of size 200 × 200—pertaining to the chest and the shoulder-buttons, and their segmented versions, respectively.

[0.85,1.15] correctly identified the fiducials. The centroids of the fiducial-regions were computed on the first frame. Since the motion of the chest-fiducial from frame to frame is not significant, one can restrict the computation over the subsequent frames to a smaller ROI, e.g., 200 × 200 around the centroid. Indeed, one as small as 51 × 51 was found to work. Respiratory waveforms, each given by the trajectory of the X-coordinate of the chest-fiducial-centroid as a function of time (from three arbitrary subjects), are shown in Figure 9.4. Note that the first few samples in the respiratory waveform acquired by the webcam-based system (WCS) (Figure 9.4(a)) appear slightly distorted, perhaps due to slight subject-motion in the initial stage—during which the adaptive filter-weights would have been adjusting. The subsequent samples of the WCS are seen to be very good. Further, since the two acquisitions are not triggered at the same time, there will be some delay between the two. Finally, note the phase difference of ~180° between the two waveforms—this is due to the placement of the camera by the side of the subject; it can be reversed by placing it on the other side of the subject; this can even be adjusted in the program. Thus, the delay-/phase-related differences are not an issue—particularly as far as computing the RR is concerned—and can be easily addressed (it was decided to display them as acquired). The PSDs associated with the webcam and the RBT signals, estimated by the Welch method [47] with three overlapping segments, are shown in Figure 9.5. Note the PSDs of the waveforms extracted by the webcam-based system to be fairly clean with a single peak, and close to those pertaining to the signal recorded by the RBT. Although other sophisticated methods—such as that based on autoregressive modeling—could have been used, the Welch method was found sufficient. An issue with model-based methods is that pertaining to the model-order, which needs to be estimated based on the data. Automatic estimation of the model-order is known to be a difficult task, in general. Such methods are generally preferred in the case of processing short-duration stationary signals with closely spaced peaks in the PSD that need to be resolved.

The values of RR estimated by the webcam-based system (in breaths per minute) of 21.7, 23.65, 18.72 were close to those obtained by the RBT: 21.3, 23.5, 18.6. The proximity of the values of RR demonstrates the efficacy of the webcam-based system.

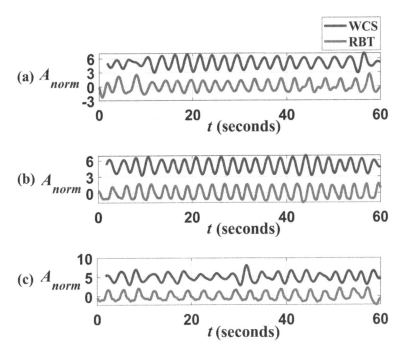

FIGURE 9.4 Respiratory waveforms recorded from three subjects, by the webcam-based system, and from the RBT. "A_{norm}" stands for amplitude normalized by the standard deviation. Note the phase difference of ~180° between the two waveforms (which is due to the placement of the camera by the side of the subject).

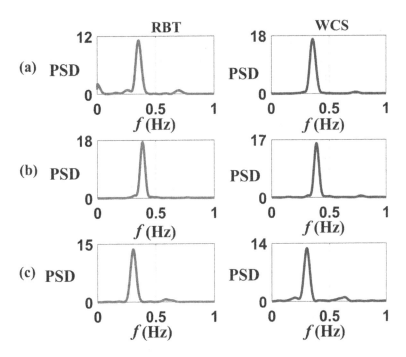

FIGURE 9.5 The PSDs of the three instances of the respiratory signals, measured from the webcam and the RBT signals (Figure 9.4). Note the corresponding PSDs to be close to each other.

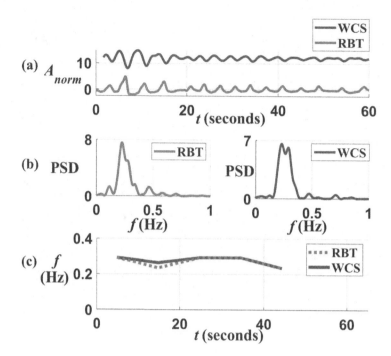

FIGURE 9.6   (a) Waveforms extracted from processing the webcam and RBT data, respectively. (b) PSDs of the two waveforms in (a). Note that the one pertaining to the webcam signal has two/split peaks. Observing (a) and (b) together indicate changing RR/frequency during data-acquisition. (c) Spectrogram computed from the RBT and webcam signals, showing the time-variation in RR.

Non-Stationary Case: Although the subjects were advised to relax and breath normally, the breathing pattern, in a few cases, changed during the recording. This is suspected to be due to their having been able to see the monitor, being biased, and changing the rate of breathing subconsciously. Fortunately, this provided an opportunity to study and address the issue. An example of such a non-stationary waveform, involving change in breathing frequency (RR) during acquisition, is shown in Figure 9.6(a). Such non-stationarity results in multiple peaks in the Welch-PSD, as demonstrated in Figure 9.6(b). The data was processed by the STFT with a 300-sample window to track the changes successfully. See Figure 9.6(c), in which the frequency-time plot pertaining to the webcam-based system, as well as that of the RBT, are given.

Quantitative Comparison: The values of RR were computed by the webcam and the RBT-based systems from 35 subjects (out of which four altered the breathing pattern and could not be characterized with a single value of RR). The mean absolute error (MAE) and the normalized root mean square error (NRMSE), associated with the estimates with respect to those of the RBT, were 0.29 and 0.021, respectively. These values show the accuracy of the estimates on the average. The proximity of the estimates is also indicated by the Bland–Altman plot [52]. The Bland–Altman plot (difference vs. mean), depicting the agreement of the estimates of RR obtained by the webcam-based system with those of the RBT, is shown in Figure 9.7 The preceding results demonstrate the efficacy of the webcam-based system.

Effect of Motion Compensation: The effect of motion compensation provided by the adaptive filter is demonstrated here by an illustrative example, in which the subject was asked to slowly move to and fro during video-capture, while breathing normally. The raw webcam-based signal (corrupted by subject-motion—induced deliberately by instructing the subject), the adaptive filtered signal, and the ground-truth (RBT signal)—pertaining to a sample subject—are shown in Figure 9.8.1. Note

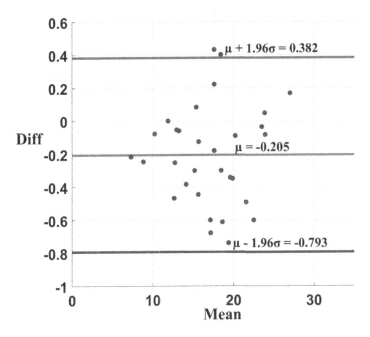

FIGURE 9.7 Bland–Altman plot (difference vs. mean) depicting the proximity of the estimates of RR obtained by the webcam-based system and the RBT.

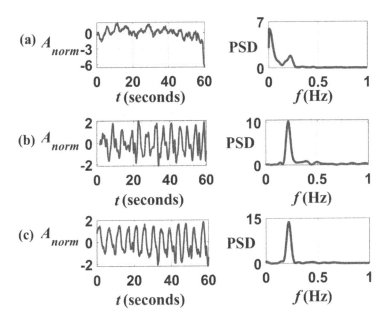

FIGURE 9.8.1 An example demonstrating the effect of motion (induced deliberately) and that of the adaptive filter in alleviating motion-artifacts. "A_{norm}" is the amplitude, normalized by the standard deviation. Left column: The webcam signal (a) before and (b) after adaptive filtering. (c) The RBT signal (ground-truth). The plots on the right column are the respective PSDs. The value of RR assessed from the motion-compensated waveform was 13.26 breaths per minute, while that pertaining to the RBT was 13.2 breaths per minute.

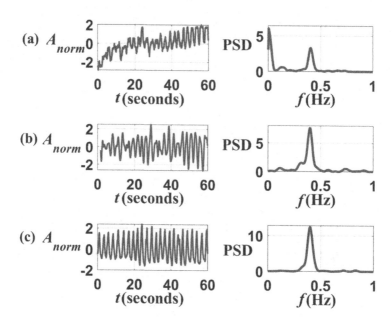

FIGURE 9.8.2 Another example demonstrating the effect of motion and that of the adaptive filter in alleviating the motion-artifacts. Left column: The webcam signal (a) before and (b) after adaptive filtering. (c) The
RBT signal (ground-truth). The plots on the right column are the respective PSDs. The value of RR assessed
from the motion-compensated waveform was 23.85 breaths per minute, while that pertaining to the RBT was
23.9 breaths per minute.

the raw waveform prior to adaptive filtering to be affected by subject-motion in terms of something
like "baseline wandering." Since the frequency-band pertaining to motion-artifacts is generally not
known, adaptive filtering is a better option than mere band-pass filtering. Indeed, one may observe
adaptive filtering to have corrected the motion-related artifact. The effect of the artifact may also be
observed on the PSD. Note that the PSDs of the adaptive filtered signal is close to that estimated by
the RBT signal (ground-truth). The values of RR estimated by the two were also very close to each
other (13.26 and 13.2 breaths per minute). The parameters of the filter were: order $M = 50$, step-size
$\mu_s = 0.1$, determined empirically. The filter was found to work even with minor changes around these
values. One more example is shown in Figure 9.8.2, in which the waveform, apart from the effect
similar to that of baseline wandering, also exhibits distortion. Adaptive filtering is seen to have
alleviated the effects of the artifacts, to yield the value of RR correctly (23.85 breaths per minute,
vs. 23.9 estimated from the RBT). In another trial, the estimate of RR from adaptive filtered signal
(20.25 breaths per minute) was close to that estimated by the RBT (20.16). However, the retrieved
waveform (e.g., Figure 9.8.2) still suffers from some distortions, which may be attributed to too
much motion, induced artificially by instructing the subject. Such motion was never encountered
naturally in normal subjects. Nevertheless, the study opens scope for further work, in the case of
involuntary motion that may be possible in patients with movement disorders (not related to mere
changing breathing rate, which can be tackled by adaptive frequency-trackers)—particularly when
breathing pattern is of importance.

9.3.2 Chest Expansion

The webcam-based system was used to estimate the chest expansion in 37 subjects, of whom eight
were assessed at the department of physiotherapy, Kasturba Medical College Hospital, Manipal.

FIGURE 9.9   First frame of the calibration video, showing the checkerboard pattern.

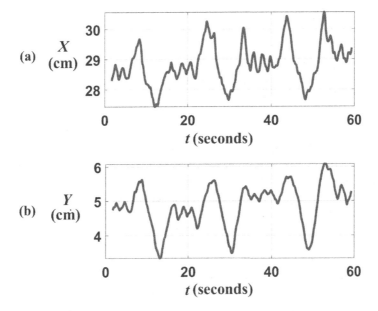

FIGURE 9.10   Waveforms (sequences) corresponding to: (a) the horizontal component/position X and (b) the vertical component/position Y, of the fiducial-centroid. The two sequences together define the points along the curvilinear path/trajectory of the fiducial. The sum of the distances between the successive points (corresponding to successive frames) along the trajectory gives the value of chest expansion.

Note that the latter measurements were performed in a completely different environment (the room was not so bright, and many people were around observing data collection during the recording). However, the range of H and V did not have to be changed, and the system was observed to perform well—indicating the robustness of the imaging system and of the image processing algorithms. For some female subjects, at the xiphoid, the T-shaped extension was required to make the fiducial visible. First, a 10 s calibration video with a checkerboard was recorded and processed. The first frame of the video with the checkerboard is shown in Figure 9.9.

After calibration, a 1.5–2.0 min. video of the subject, breathing as per the protocol (section 9.2), was recorded. The waveforms pertaining to the horizontal and vertical displacements of the centroid of the fiducial, extracted from a sample video, are shown in Figure 9.10. The sequences of X

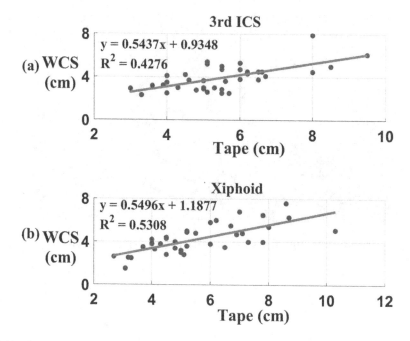

FIGURE 9.11 Scatter plot of chest expansion measurements taken by the webcam-based system (WCS) and a tape, at the (a) third ICS, and (b) xiphoid.

and Y locations of the fiducial-centroid, as a function of the frame-number, defines the trajectory of the button (assuming the motion to be approximately planar). The chest expansion is given by the total length of the path traversed by the fiducial-centroid—between the instances of extreme exhalation and extreme inhalation. It may be computed as the sum of the distances, between the successive X- and Y-coordinates of the fiducial-centroid. This measure, therefore, adds to the novelty of the proposed method. Note that it is different from mere (one-dimensional) depth-based measurements, performed by depth-cameras. In the specific example shown in Figure 9.10, note that the displacement in the Y-direction is higher than that in the X-direction, indicating that mere depth-measurement (horizontal displacement) is not sufficient to characterize chest expansion. For comparison, three tape-measurements each were also taken very carefully by a doctor (one of the authors of this chapter) as per the protocol, and the largest displacement was considered. The webcam-based measurements were found to be approximately linearly correlated with those of tape-measurements (circumference), at the third ICS as well as the xiphoid, as depicted in Figure 9.11. This is interesting because it brings out the potential of the new measure of chest expansion.

9.4 DISCUSSION

A novel webcam-based belt-system has been developed as an alternative to the expensive RBTs. The system (i) can be used to estimate both the respiratory waveform and the extent of chest expansion—directly at clinically recommended regions over the chest, (ii) has an adaptive filter-system to compensate for involuntary subject-motion, (iii) works in the presence of loose clothing, (iv) can be used on subjects in upright or supine positions, (v) is robust to fluctuations in illumination, (vi) can handle non-stationary waveforms, and (vii) involves a new measure of chest expansion, i.e., the length of the curvilinear trajectory of the fiducial during expansion—which accounts for the non-horizontal expansion. Note that the new measure of chest expansion is different from the mere (one-dimensional) depth-based measurements, performed by depth-cameras or equivalents. The proposed method overcomes some of the drawbacks associated with the use of tape/calipers. As indicated before, tape measurement is error-prone due to the moving hands, mistakes due to poor light or weak eyes, and possible gliding of the tape on the surface [3]. Calipers may be considered to be somewhat clumsy and limited in this age of technical advancements—indeed, it had been recommended only on obese subjects [36]. Measurement of chest expansion by the proposed device can be extended to identify uneven expansion by imaging with the fiducial(s) placed at the relevant side(s). While some of the image processing steps presented in this chapter were conceived independently, they turn out to be similar to those in a different context, i.e., respiratory-gating in CT imaging [22]. Such a similarity, however, should not be surprising because of the simplicity of the system proposed and the standard techniques in image processing. On the other hand, the proposed system can be used for estimating RP and RR under both supine and erect-positions of the subject, even under loose clothing, due to the use of an elastic belt. In addition, a calibration system and a breathing protocol have been developed towards measuring chest expansion. The system and the study presented, therefore, contribute significantly to the measurement and study of chest expansion for clinical applications. Chest expansion measurement is routinely taken in pulmonology and respiratory physiotherapy clinics. Accurate recording of chest expansion measurement is important for planning exercises to improve lung expansion, treat pathophysiological conditions leading to lung collapse, and plan comprehensive pulmonary rehabilitation program. The technique may help understanding the progression of respiratory diseases affecting the chest wall (such as kyphoscoliosis and scoliosis [53,54]), and also in identifying and documenting thoracic dominant dysfunctional breathing—particularly seen in people suffering from bronchial asthma and chronic obstructive pulmonary disease [55]. Since antero-posterior movements of the ribcage are limited in interstitial lung disease, the proposed device may help to document the limited movements in these patients [56]. The measurement of chest expansion and RR during procedures like flexible bronchoscopy (under sedation) can help the clinician in detecting respiratory depression and thus take measures to manage it. In such a situation, it can be potentially life-saving.

Very recently (over the past few months), a spurt of activity in the area of non-contact methods of assessing RR, by measurements over the upper body (UB) based on optical flow (OF), has been observed. Note that the use of OF was proposed in 2016, on UB of neonates [23], to estimate RR. Guo et al. [57] used OF and deep learning to estimate RR based on periodic motion over UB. However, they have not incorporated motion compensation. Romano et al. [58] also use an ROI of fixed dimensions over UB and employ OF to assess RR. However, their method of motion compensation based on a derivative is rather crude—being a high-pass filter, it exacerbates noise, and hence is not reliable; further, they remove motion-related segments. Hwang and Lee [59] perform motion-analysis over a manually selected ROI on UB and classify pixels having similar patterns by deep learning-based clustering to assess RR. However, the method cannot tackle subject-motion. Valenzuela et al. [60] reported the use of a (not so inexpensive) depth camera (at 15 fps) to estimate the RP/RR (in people over a restricted age range) over UB, based on an ROI determined at fixed distances from the face. However, they had to discard acquisitions with errors due to subject-movement/device-saturation. The measurement required stable lighting and was found susceptible to the presence of people in the background. None of the methods address the issue of loose clothing or chest expansion measurement. In contrast, the device described in this chapter is very simple, inexpensive, robust to fluctuations in ambience and to involuntary subject-motion, addresses the problem of loose clothing, and can perform chest expansion measurements at clinically specified levels. Therefore, the system and the concomitant methodology are useful in their own right.

9.4.1 LIMITATIONS AND FUTURE SCOPE

The proposed method involves the use of the NLMS algorithm, which is relatively slow in adaptation and may not be able to handle abrupt subject-motion. One can replace this algorithm by those that adapt faster, such as recursive least-squares (RLS) and its variants [48]. From a clinical perspective, this would be useful in the case of subjects with movement disorders. In this context, improving the performance of adaptive filters, and/or exploring alternatives to the same, towards suppressing the effects of such motion or of other similar defects/abnormalities would be helpful. Further, it may be useful to document chest expansion in patients who do not follow commands, e.g., as those with neurological conditions.

The method developed is an alternative to the more expensive RBT. However, such a "minimum-contact" device involves wearing a belt, though useful in its own right. Under the pandemic circumstances such as those prevalent now due to COVID-19, a completely contactless method would be desirable. It would therefore be useful to study and address the limitations of completely non-contact methods of estimating respiratory waveform and rate, particularly with respect to subject-motion.

The current method involves measurement of subjects sitting on a chair. It would obviously be useful to study its applicability—possibly in terms of the required modifications—under other postures and more complicated clinical situations, as in patients with breathlessness and those with spinal deformities, diaphragm paralysis, and other biomechanical changes in the thoraco-abdominal region.

In this chapter, the development of a system to estimate the respiratory waveform and RR has been reported. The working of the system has been tested on healthy subjects. Experiments with subjects under different physiological conditions, and patients with different types of diseases, and/ or under different circumstances, form the scope for future work. Accordingly, the development of suitable signal processing algorithms for the analysis and diagnosis of abnormalities/diseases—based on the respiratory and/or chest expansion waveforms/data—would be needed. The use of the wavelet transform, for example, would reveal the finer details pertaining to the respiration waveform/pattern. The support of machine and deep learning-based methods may also be explored in this context. Further, there is a vast scope for extensive investigations involving a processing of the respiratory waveform, in correlation with several other physiological waveforms such as the ECG/ PPG, breathing pattern extracted from (the region below the) nose, and naadi signals (signals arising at the Vaatha, Pittha, and Kapha spots on the wrist—used extensively in the Siddha system of medical practice in India), etc., towards understanding the physiological correlates.

9.5   CONCLUSION

This chapter described the design and validation of an inexpensive, multi-purpose, minimal-contact device—consisting of an elastic belt with a fiducial, which can be fitted around the chest of a subject to be imaged by a webcam—for recording respiratory pattern, respiration rate, and chest expansion. It is an inexpensive alternative to the standard RBT. In fact, the RBT cannot be directly used to measure chest expansion. For validating the respiration waveform/pattern and RR-estimates, the method has been compared with those obtained by the RBT with Power Lab. Chest-expansion measurements were found to be linearly correlated to those estimated carefully by an inch-tape. The proposed method allows the subjects to be clothed during the measurement. The performance of the method has been found to be good, as reflected by the results of the experiments. The utility of the device in a clinical setting has been discussed. Some of the limitations of the work performed, and the scope for future work, have also been discussed. Further, one can investigate the possibilities of approximating the chest-circumference, using more fiducials and an additional camera, and perform experiments with data corresponding to subjects under various health conditions. Finally, it would be relevant and interesting to look into the possibilities of modifying the current non-contact methods to impart the advantages of the system reported in this chapter.

ACKNOWLEDGMENT

The authors acknowledge the voluntary participation of many subjects in our study, and thank Dr. Amrutharaj H. Krishnan, Head of the Department of Media Technology, Manipal Institute of

Technology, Manipal, MAHE, Manipal, for providing us with good-quality color-printed stickers. The first author thanks James John for assistance on Bland–Altman analysis.

REFERENCES

[1] M. A. Cretikos, R. Bellomo, K. Hillman, J. Chen, S. Finfer, A. Flabouris, "Respiration Rate: The Neglected Vital Sign," *Medical Journal of Australia*, vol. 188, no. 11, pp. 657–659, 2008.

[2] D. R. Goldhill, A. F. McNarry, G. Mandersloot, A. McGinley, "A Physiologically-based Early Warning Score for Ward Patients: The Association Between Score and Outcome," *Journal of the Association of Anaesthesia of Great Britain and Ireland*, vol. 60, no. 6, pp. 547–553, 2005.

[3] R. Hogner, "Criticism on the Usual Method of Measurement of Chest-Expansion in Life-Insurance Examinations, and Ktethokyrtographical Studies of the Bilateral Expansion of the Chest," *Boston Medical and Surgical Journal*, vol. CXXXII, no. 19, pp. 453–458, 1895.

[4] G. Yuan, N. A. Drost, R. A. McIvor, "Respiration Rate and Breathing Pattern," *McMaster University Medical Journal*, vol. 10, no. 1, pp. 23–25, 2013.

[5] P. Raghuraj, A. G. Ramakrishnan, H. R. Nagendra, S. Telles, "Effect of Two Selected Yogic Breathing Techniques on Heart Rate Variability," *Indian Journal of Physiology and Pharmacology*, vol. 42, no. 4, pp. 467–472, November 1998.

[6] E. Helfenbein, R. Firoozabadi, S. Chien, E. Carlson, S. Babaeizadeh, "Development of Three Methods for Extracting Respiration from the Surface ECG: A Review," *Journal of Electrocardiology*, vol. 47, no. 6, pp. 819–825, 2014.

[7] P. Varady, T. Micsik, Z. Benyo, "A Novel Method for the Detection of Apnea and Hypopnea Events in Respiration Signals," *IEEE Transactions on Biomedical Engineering*, vol. 49, no. 9, pp. 936–942, September 2002.

[8] R. Dey, U. Thakur, L. Sunny, L. D. Almeida, K. Chakravarty, "Digital Chest Expansion Measurement & Its Biomedical Application," in *5th IEEE International Conference on E-Health and Bioengineering*, Romania, November 2015, pp. 1–4.

[9] C. Malaguti, R. R. Rondelli, L. M. Gouza, M. Domingues, S. D. Corso, "Reliability of Chest Wall Mobility and its Correlation with Pulmonary Function in Patients with Chronic Obstructive Pulmonary Disease," *Journal of Respiratory Care*, vol. 54, no. 12, pp. 1703–1711, December 2009.

[10] R. Carter, P. Riantawan, S. W. Banham, R. D. Sturrock, "An Investigation of Factors Limiting Aerobic Capacity in Patients with Ankylosing Spondylitis," *Respiratory Medicine*, vol. 93, no. 10, pp. 700–708, 1999.

[11] H. W. Goodall, J. L. Belknap, "A Critical Study of the Value of the Measurements of Chest Expansion and Lung Capacity," *Archives of Internal Medicine*, vol. 3, 1909.

[12] www.adinstruments.com/products/respiratory-belt-transducer

[13] S. D. Min, Y. Yun, H. Shin, "Simplified Structural Textile Respiration Sensor Based on Capacitive Pressure Sensing Method," *IEEE Sensors*, vol. 14, no. 9, pp. 3245–3251, September 2014.

[14] D. G. Kim, C. Wang, J. G. Ho, S. D. Min, Y. Kim, M. H. Choi, "Development and Feasibility Test of a Capacitive Belt Sensor for Noninvasive Respiration Monitoring in Different Postures," *Smart Health*, vol. 16, May 2020.

[15] D. Dei, G. Grazzini, G. Luzi, M. Pieraccini, C. Atzeni, et al., "Non-Contact Detection of Breathing Using a Microwave Sensor," *Molecular Diversity Preservation International Journal: Sensor*, vol. 9, no. 4, pp. 2574–2585, 2009.

[16] C. Gu, C. Li, "Assessment of Human Respiration Pattern via Non-Contact Sensing Using Doppler Multi-Radar System," *Molecular Diversity Preservation International Journal: Sensors*, vol. 15, no. 3, pp. 6383–6398, 2015.

[17] J. Fei, I. Pavlidis, "Analysis of Breathing Air Flow Patterns in Thermal Imaging," in *Proceedings of the 28th IEEE EMBS Annual International Conference*, New York City, September 2006, pp. 946–952.

[18] B. Xu, L. K. Mestha, G. Pennington, "Monitoring Respiration with a Thermal Imaging System," *U.S. Patent 20120289850*, May 9, 2011.

[19] M. Martinez, R. Stiefelhagen, "Breath rate monitoring during sleep using Near-IR Imagery and PCA," in *21st International on Pattern Recognition*, Tsukuba, Japan, January 2012, pp. 3472–3475.

[20] G. Sun, T. Negishi, T. Kirimoto, T. Matsui, S. Abe, "Noncontact Monitoring of Vital Signs with RGB and Infrared Camera and Its Application to Screening of Potential Infection," in *Non-Invasive Diagnostic Methods*, ed. M. Marzec, IntechOpen, December 2018.

[21] H. E. Elphick, A. H. Alkali, R. K. Kingshott, D. Burke, R. Saatchi, "Exploratory Study to Evaluate Respiratory Rate Using a Thermal Imaging Camera," *Respiration*, vol. 97, no. 3, pp. 205–212, 2019.

[22] S. Wiesner, Z. Yaniv, "Monitoring Patient Respiration Using a Single Optical Camera," in *29th Annual International Conference of IEEE EMBS*, Lyon, France, August 2007, pp. 2740–2743.

[23] V. Makkapati, S. S. Rambhatla, "Camera Based Estimation of Respiration Rate by Analyzing Shape and Size Variation of Structured Light," in *International Conference on Acoustics, Speech and Signal Processing*, IEEE, Shanghai, March 2016, pp. 2219–2223.

[24] Y. W. Bai, W. T. Li, C. H. Yeh, "Design and Implementation of an Embedded Monitor System for Body Breath Detection by using Image Processing Methods," in *International Conference of Consumer Electronics*, Las Vegas, January 2010, pp. 193–194.

[25] Y. W. Bai, W. T. Li, Y. W. Chan, "Design and Implementation of an Embedded Monitor System for Detection of a Patient's Breath by Double Webcams in the Dark," in *12th IEEE International Conference on e-health and Networking, Applications and Services*, Lyon, July 2010, pp. 93–98.

[26] M. Z. Poh, D. J. McDuff, R. W. Picard, "Advancements in Non-Contact, Multiparameter Physiological Measurements using a Webcam," *IEEE Transactions on Biomedical Engineering*, vol. 58, no. 1, pp. 7–11, 2011.

[27] P. H. Charlton, *et al.*, "Breathing Rate Estimation from the Electrocardiogram and Photoplethysmogram: A Review," *IEEE Reviews in Biomedical Engineering*, pp. 2–19, October 2017.

[28] D. Shao, Y. Yang, C. Liu, F. Tsow, H. Yu, N. Tau, "Non-Contact Monitoring Breathing-Pattern, Exhalation Flow Rate and Pulse Transit Time," *IEEE Transactions on Biomedical Engineering*, vol. 61, no. 11, pp. 2760–2767, November 2014.

[29] W. Sheel, "Respiratory Muscle Training in Healthy Individuals," *Sports Medicine*, vol. 32, no. 9, pp. 567–581, 2002.

[30] Physiopedia, *Muscles of Respiration*, December 2020, available: www.physio-pedia.com/Muscles_of_Respiration

[31] Kenhub, *Anatomy of Breathing*, October 2020, available: www.kenhub.com/en/library/anatomy/anatomy-of-breathing

[32] V. Makkapati, P. Raman, G. Pai, "Camera Based Respiration Rate of neonates by Modeling Movement of Chest and Abdomen Region," in *International Conference on Signal Processing and Communications (SPCOM)*, Bangalore, India, 2016, pp. 1–5.

[33] M. Mateu-Mateus, F. Guede-Fernandez, M. A. Garcia-Gonzalez, J. J. Ramos-Castro, M. Fernandez-Chimeno, "Camera-based Method for Respiratory Rhythm Extraction From a Lateral Perspective," *IEEE Access*, vol. 8, 2020, pp. 154924–154939.

[34] C. Sharp, V. Soleimani, S. Hannuna, M. Camplani, D. Damen, J. Viner, M. Mirmehdi, J. W. Dodd, "Toward Respiratory Assessment Using Depth Measurements from a Time-of-Flight Sensor," *Frontiers in Physiology*, vol. 8, no. 65, pp. 1–8, February 2017.

[35] C. Massaroni, D. S. Lopes, D. L. Presti, E. Schena, S. Silvestri, "Contactless Monitoring of Breathing Patterns and Respiratory Rate at the Pit of the Neck: A Single Camera Approach," *Journal of Sensors*, vol. 2018, pp. 1–13, 2018.

[36] J. M. H. Moll, V. Wright, "An objective clinical study of chest expansion," *Annals of Rheumatic Diseases*, vol. 31, no. 1, pp. 1–8, 1972.

[37] S. E. Bockenhauer, H. Chen, K. N. Julliard, J. Weedon, "Measuring Thoracic Excursion: Reliability of the Cloth Tape Measurement Technique," *JAOA*, vol. 107, no. 5, pp. 191–196, 2007.

[38] B. Padasdo, E. Shahhaidar, O. B. Lubecke, "Measuring Chest Circumference Change during Respiration with an Electromagnetic Biosensor," in *35th Annual International Conference of EMBS*, Osaka, Japan, July 2013, pp. 1936–1939.

[39] T. Konda, T. Uhlig, P. Pemberton, P. D. Sly, "Laser Monitoring of Chest Wall Displacement," *European Respiratory Journal*, vol. 10, no. 8, pp. 1865–1869, 1997.

[40] M. Norgia Milesi, P. P. Pompilio, C. Svelto, R. L. Dellaca, "Measurement of Local Chest Wall Displacement by a Custom Self-Mixing Laser Interferometer," *IEEE Transactions on Instrumentation and Measurement*, vol. 60, no. 8, pp. 2894–2901, August 2011.

[41] K. Arthittayapiwat, P. Pirompol, P. Samanpiboon, "Study on Chest Expansion in Lateral Plane Using Accelerometers," in *Proceedings of 139th The IIER International Conference*, Osaka, Japan, 8th–9th December 2017, pp. 4–8.

[42] K. Arthittayapiwat, P. Pirompol, P. Samanpiboon, "Chest Expansion Measurement in 3-Dimension by Using Accelerometers," *Engineering Journal*, vol. 23, no. 2, pp. 71–84, 2019.

[43]   R. C. Gonzalez, R. E. Woods, *Digital Image Processing*, 3rd ed., Pearson Education India, 2009.

[44]   Rohit Nayak, Pramod Kumar, Ramesh R. Galigekere, "Towards a Comprehensive Assessment of Wound-Composition Using Color-Image Processing," *Proc. 16th IEEE International Conference on Image Processing* (ICIP), Cairo, Egypt, November 7–9, pp. 4185–4188, 2009.

[45]   M. F. Olsen, H. Lindstrand, J. L. Broberg, E. Westerdahl, "Measuring Chest Expansion; A Study Comparing Two Different Instructions," *Advances in Physiotherapy*, vol. 13, no. 3, pp. 128–132, 2011.

[46]   R. S. Reddy, K. A. Alahmari, P. S. Silvian, I. A. Ahmad, V. N. Kakarparthi, K. Rengaramanujam, "Reliability of Chest Wall Mobility and Its Correlation with Lung Functions in Healthy Nonsmokers, Healthy Smokers, and Patients with COPD," *Canadian Respiratory Journal*, vol. 2019, no. 4, pp. 1–11, 2019.

[47]   A. E. Oppenheim, R. W. Schafer, *Digital Signal Processing*, Prentice Hall India Learning Pvt. Ltd., 2015.

[48]   A. H. Sayed, *Fundamentals of Adaptive Filtering*, Wiley India Pvt. Ltd., 2003.

[49]   Z. Zhang, "A Flexible New Technique for Camera Calibration," *IEEE Transactions of Pattern Analysis and Machine Intelligence*, vol. 22, no. 11, pp. 1330–1334, November 2000.

[50]   Mathworks, *What Is Camera Calibration?*, available: mathworks.com/help/vision/ug/camera-calibration.html

[51]   J. Bouguet, *Camera Calibration Toolbox for MATLAB*, available: www.vision,cltech.edu/

[52]   J. M. Bland, D. G. Altman, "Statistical Method for Assessing Agreement Between Two Methods of Clinical Measurements," *The Lancet*, vol. 327, no. 8476, pp. 307–310, February 1986.

[53]   J. C. Leong, W. W. Lu, K. D. Luk, E. M. Karlberg, "Kinematics of the Chest Cage and Spine During Breathing in Healthy Individuals and in Patients with Adolescent Idiopathic Scoliosis," *Spine*, vol. 24, no. 13, pp. 1310–1315, July 1999.

[54]   T. Kotani, *et al.*, "An Analysis of Chest Wall and Diaphragm Motions in Patients with Idiopathic Scoliosis Using Dynamic Breathing MRI," *Spine* vol. 29, no. 3, pp. 298–302, February 2004.

[55]   R. Boulding, R. Stacey, R. Niven, S. J. Fowler, "Dysfunctional Breathing: A Review of the Literature and Proposal for Classification," *European Respiration Review*, vol. 25, pp. 287–294, 2016.

[56]   N. J. Brenan, A. J. Morris, M. Green, "Thoracoabdominal Mechanics During Tidal Breathing in Normal Subjects and in Emphysema and Fibrosing Alveolitis," *Thorax*, vol. 38, no. 1, pp. 62–66, January 1983.

[57]   T. Guo, Q. Lin, J. Allebach, "Remote Estimation of Respiration Rate by Optical Flow Using Convolutional Neural Networks," *International Symposium Electronic Imaging*, pp. 267-1–267-10, January 2021.

[58]   C. Romano, E. Schena, S. Silvestri, C. Massaroni, "Non-Contact Respiratory Monitoring Using an RGB Camera for Real-World Applications," *Sensors*, vol. 21, no. 5126, pp. 1–16, 2021.

[59]   H. Hwang, E. Lee, "Non-Contact Respiration Measurement Method Based on RGB Camera using 1D Convolutional Neural Networks," *Sensors*, vol. 21, no. 3456, pp. 1–14, 2021.

[60]   A. Valenzuela, N. Sibuet, G. Hornero, O. Casas, "Non-Contact Video-Based Assessment of the Respiratory Function Using a RGB-D Camera," *Sensors*, vol. 21, no. 5605, pp. 1–17, 2021.

10 Novel Data Analysis Framework in Smart Healthcare

Swapnaja Hiray and Bhramaramba Ravi

CONTENTS

10.1 INTRODUCTION

Making use of the Internet of Things (IoT) in the healthcare industry takes it to next-generation smart digital environments and remote monitoring. Despite the potential advantages of a remote monitoring system using wearables, there are significant challenges ahead. Sensors in the IoT ecosystem create a vast volume of stream data. Analyzing the huge amounts of data generated by the sensor is the main challenge that needs to be addressed, as this can prevent obtaining accurate results. Generally, the data getting from the sensor is uncertain, so analyzing such uncertain data streams [1] in real time is quite difficult.

Due to the absence of suitable solutions in the recent state of the art, there is a need for a system that evaluates only important content from the continuous stream of data and sends only significant data over the cloud to reduce computational complexity. It is essential to have a system that can analyze and deliver a comprehensive analysis of data with greater accuracy for real-time decision-making on streaming data. Different techniques are available [1,2] for extracting valuable information from continuous data for post-event analysis that detect irregularities in real time. This identification has a significant impact on the event outcome. Unobservable actions can be detected via complex event processing (CEP), a developing area of research. It represents more relevant events from several sensors than the simple event, allowing for real-time insights. A single health sensor (e.g., temperature sensor) cannot diagnose a disease. Multiple sensor events passing a threshold provide information for higher-level decision-making. For instance, an arrhythmia can be recognized if the breathing and heart rate rise above a threshold limit in a specific period.

Because of sensor data resemblance and reliability, current complex event-processing (CEP) algorithms are inefficient. Such a system tries to send all primitive data to the cloud, which makes the system very complex, and it takes too long to upload the data. There are several methods found in the literature that provide predictive solutions in different domains; in [3], for instance, complex event-processing (CEP) detection is done using rule-based machine learning approaches. In addition, effort has already been taken to generate CEP using Esper, as Boubeta et al. [4] use the Xively IoT platform to combine Mule ESB and Esper engine technologies. However, due to the centralized framework, this does not allow for the dynamic communication protocol required for event-driven architecture, and it does not make use of the benefits of multi-cloud environments. Dong Wang et al. [5] use LAIPE (lightweight intelligent data analysis), a unique CEP engine, which analyzes events using a knowledge base with rules. With identical input events and used rules, LAIPE outperforms Esper. But measuring the LAIPE framework's performance is difficult because it is workload dependent. This study's major goal is to evaluate huge streams of data in real time to anticipate patient health and inform doctors. Creating complex events on a mobile device and forwarding such information to the cloud rather than streams of big data from several sensors might help to save the time required for data transfer and storage capacity. Esper will be used for data analysis in healthcare applications as part of the proposed CEP computing strategy. Such events aid in the prediction of patients' health and offer quick responses. Machine learning techniques (SVM and Viterbi) are used to improve the prediction of a patient's health. The data compression model plays a significant part in the business module/rule. Data compression is the process of modifying or encoding structured data to save space on a cloud server. Several algorithms are used to compress data. The given system compresses data utilizing the Lempel–Ziv–Markov chain technique (LZMA).

10.2 LITERATURE REVIEW

10.2.1 Event Generation and Pre-Processing

Bhargavi et al. introduced a framework (see Figure 10.1), which focuses on how primitive events are generated from the various sensor-generated values and how this is aggregated to generate a complex event. The term complex event represents a scenario of interest as well as a pattern. The event collection subsystem is in charge of gathering information from sensors to connect with the virtual environment. The following are some primitive events that are taken into consideration for the current study.

- Complex events are created when RFID readers and tags interact.
- A human movement in front of the sensor generates a PIR reading.
- The location of an event is determined using GPS data.
- Photographs were taken using a camera.
- Event generation (Level-0): Generating an event is considered the initial step towards complex event processing (CEP). This stage takes and prepares raw data from real-time sources like sensors.
- Event pre-processing (Level-1): Level-1 intrusion detection uses PIR, camera, RFID, and other sensors to detect intrusions. These sensors keep an eye on the changes in the real-time phenomenon and capture those changes. These phenomenon changes are observed along with specific information like an event occurrence time and its location details. Further communication is done with the central server for processing.

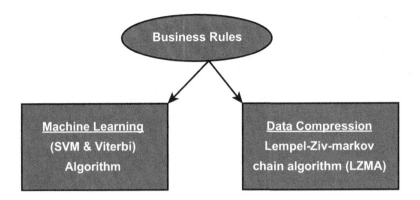

FIGURE 10.1 Categorization of algorithms used in first model (without CEP).

10.2.2 Afef Mdhaffar et al.

This research described a novel method for predicting cardiac failure. Here, the authors combine the complex event-processing (CEP) technique with statistical methodologies. To process the incoming health information, the CEP engine carries out threshold-based analysis. This arithmetical procedure calculates and updates the threshold based on historical evidence instead of manually setting up thresholds.

10.2.2 Yao et al.

Yao et al. introduced the complex event-based approach for processing RFID streams in the healthcare application. The authors also implement this model to visualize the critical situation and surgical events in the RFID-enabled hospitals. This framework was created and applied to monitor the patient's aberrant state in a real-time environment. CEP acts as the vital engine for data filtering and complex event detection, respectively.

10.2.3 Edge Computing IoT

Based on the Internet of Things, Dhillo et al. present complex event processing (CEP). Mobile devices as a bridge between sensors and the cloud server. The mobile device acts as an edge or a medium between sensors and the cloud server. The edge detects the complex events and sends them to the hospital servers for processing. Bluetooth or wireless connections enable wearable health sensors (WHS) to transfer sensor data to mobile devices, communicating with hospital servers via cellular or Wi-Fi networks. Complex event processing (CEP) on the mobile application gets the sensors' data, identifies complex events, and sends them to the hospital cloud server.

Advantages of CEP Technique

- The main advantage of CEP edge computing for IoT is to avoid out-of-order health sensor data delivery.
- Avoid hospital server queues.
- Costs of data transfer between edge devices and hospital cloud servers have been reduced. The key advantage of this technique is to generate an alert on a patient's side even if the mobile network to the hospital server is down.

The Constraints of the CEP

- The CEP is a mobile application that runs on a mobile device, and it is small enough to be used by persons. CEP utilizes mobile resources in conjunction with other mobile applications, which affects performance.
- The cell phone's storage space is limited, making it harder to save extra information. As a result, it must collaborate with remote IHS in order to analyze long-term data. The CEP is unsuitable for large-scale telemedicine surveillance due to its design limitations.
- The CEP only supports a few sensor types. The appropriate way to upkeep the new sensor is not fully described. Thus, uncertainty is observed in the scalability of the CEP.

The researchers provide numerous strategies for data streaming in diverse contexts. In the IoT domain, some applications like accident detection consider the security aspects and the required response time. There is an inconvenience to gathering the entire data from the sensors and deploying to the central cloud server to process.

PROACTIVE COMPLEX EVENT-PROCESSING PROCEDURE

Wang et al. proposed the proactive complex event-processing (Pro-CEP) procedure and methods used to process big traffic data sets. However, in the event of a system or network failure, Pro-CEP will cause a catastrophic crisis. So, the massive amounts information can be pre-processed and sent to the backend for processing. By following this process, the pre-processing burden is reduced, but the processing speed is also being improved.

10.2.4 K. HONG ET AL.

K. Hong et al. recommend mobile fog computing, which is considered as the high-level programming model used for distributed Geo-spatially, latency-sensitive, and large-scale future Internet applications. The occurrence of the low-latency processing at the edge and latency-tolerant large aggregation is performed on the powerful resource in the network core that is simply the cloud service. The mobile fog can handle the events and the functions that an application can call. This mobile fog is not considered as the generic model, although it is constructed for the particular application.

Advantage: Mobile Fog computing technique helps to minimize the latency as well as network traffic.

10.2.5 PATHAK AND VAIDEHI

Using CEP to monitor elderly patients has been discussed in depth by Pathak and Vaidehi. In order to collect data, the author uses a variety of biological sensors, the most important of which are heart rate, respiration rate, blood pressure, and an ECG. Real-time sensors such as accelerometers and GPS are used to identify contexts. The most important aspects are as follows:

- Stream the deployment to the Android phone.
- Compare with specified thresholds to spot irregularities and trigger alarms.

10.2.6 SENSOR PROCESSING ON MOBILE DEVICES

Considering the scenario of mobile applications in some special cases, mobile applications use sensor data instead of some restricted functionality like simple motions that can be used to control a video game or to see a digital spirit level. Advanced functions necessitate a complex event in terms of location and time. In recent years, CEP usage has been conducted to process mobile sensor information on the controlling backend server.

The mobile device that is the edge only serves the event source, and the processing of the entire event takes place on the remote cloud server. In [8], the author argues for pre-processing of the records from the sensor to achieve the key objective of context-event filtering. Thus, the client–server transmission is reduced; however, CEP is still in use on the server.

Advantages of Mobile CEP for Sensor Processing Low Latency for In-Memory Processing

- **Low Latency for In-Memory Processing:** The patient's various sensors continuously output vast amounts of sensor streams. The key purpose of the CEP is efficiently handled streaming of the inputted data directly in-memory.
- **Confidentiality of Sensor Info:** Confidential data stays on the phone (e.g., GPS coordinates).

10.2.7 WANG ET AL.

Wang et al. present an event-oriented framework for processing RFID data. Temporal restrictions for the event declaration include:

1. Define the "declarative rules" to support data transformation as well as run-time monitoring.
2. The framework for detecting the complex event of RFID. This complex event detection engine provides real-time support for RFID applications; the main objective is to track events and run-time monitoring. Hence, the focus was only on RFID streams.

10.2.8 HEAL

A framework called "HEAL" was established by Manashty et al. to recognize and forecast glitches in healthcare. HEAL uses the CEP engine to process real-time analysis rules and predict upcoming irregularities. This study is entirely based on relating the actual values with the threshold. The author declares that to set up the threshold values, historical data is used. Three layers are mentioned here, including:

- Service layer
- Control layer
- Data layer

10.3 DATA LAYER: METHODOLOGY AND EXPERIMENTAL SETUP

10.3.1 PROPOSED SYSTEM

10.3.1.1 Problem Statement

The suggestion of innovative architecture for data analytics in an IoT smart city environment and to check the computational performance improvement for healthcare smart city applications can, in short, be interpreted as "reduction in data transfer in smart healthcare application at the edge devices with improved computational performance."

Objectives

1. Develop smart healthcare management engine and calculate amount of data transferred and end-to-end data processing time.
2. Develop complex event engine at edge device.
3. Suggest new efficient framework for smart city healthcare applications.

The Proposed System and Experimental Setup
- **Input:** Sensor data, rules for alert generation.
- **Output:**
  - Generate alert to doctor as well as registered mobile.
  - Generate the simple event from the sensor data at the edge device.
  - Find the patterns for alert generation from complex events and push them on the cloud.

The various modules in the proposed system include:

1. Data Layer

A patient's sensors continuously relay data to an Arduino-like microcontroller. Different commercial wearable health sensors include temperature sensors, pulse oximeters, ECG sensors, and many more.

- **Hardware Interfaces**

  A patient's sensors continuously relay data to an Arduino-like microcontroller. Different commercial wearable health sensors can be used, like temperature sensors, pulse oximeters, ECG sensors, and many more.

2. Algorithms and Models Used
- **Machine Learning:** Using machine learning algorithms like SVM and Viterbi, we can better anticipate the patient's health in the next 24 hours and send alerts to the doctor and registered phone number.
  - **SVM:** Because SVMs can handle high-dimensional data with a small training set, they are becoming increasingly useful in medical applications. The ECG, HR, and SpO2 are the most complex health metrics considered by the SVM algorithm. SVM may also detect arrhythmia from ECG readings. SVM approaches are frequently advocated for healthcare anomaly identification and decision-making.
- **Data Compression:** The data compression model plays a significant part in the business module/rule. Data compression is the process of modifying or encoding structured data to save space on a cloud server. Data compression algorithms vary. Here we have used the Lempel–Ziv–Markov chain technique (LZMA) to compress the data.
- **AWS Server:** Here we collect data from the patient's sensor. The threshold values of each sensor are used to create complex events (CE). Only sophisticated event data is sent to the cloud, rather than large data streams from several sensors. It reduces data transport time and storage space. The complex events generated help to predict the patient's health within the next 24 hours and generate alerts to the doctor as well as the registered mobile.

In addition, electronic health records and some laboratory reports are pouring data into our cloud server. This will categorize the patient into the severity level for disease—type A, B, and C. After this very severe type, patients are provided with 24/7 monitoring facility, and then an alarm is generated with the critical condition. We have a CEP module for this module, where our research is focused on the edges of the network.

10.3.1.1.1   Edge Device Event Processing
Simple events (SE) are generated by considering the threshold values of each sensor. And only the significant events are sent to the complex event generation engine. Only complex events are pushed

to the cloud instead of essential data streams getting from various sensors. It helps to decrease the time for data transfer and storage capacity. The complex events generated helps to predict the patient's health within the next 24 hours and create alerts to doctors and registered mobile.

10.3.1.1.2   Complex Event Processing Systems CEP

It represents more relevant events from several sensors than the simple event, allowing for real-time insights. The given technology employs CEP to detect abnormalities in the patient's health. To generate real-time alerts, complex events (CE) are formed by combining sensor threshold values.

We all discussed standard methodologies used to achieve optimization while transferring data from sensors to cloud-based ML algorithms. But this architecture itself continuously pours "big data" in the network. And algorithmic level optimization cannot be sufficient to handle the data traffic. We worked with all architectural blocks and came up with a novel architectural solution to overcome this vast data transfer and associated problems by reducing and controlling the data traffic at the network's edges only.

We introduced the novel complex event generator block at the edges, and sensor events are converted to complex events with reduced data attributes and volume. Then these CEP events data are pushed on the cloud.

In this novel architecture, with this edge-situated, rule-based complex event-generation block, more relevant events from several sensors are generated than the simple event, allowing for real-time insights. The given technology employs CEP to detect abnormalities in the patient's health. To develop real-time alerts, CE are formed by combining sensor threshold values. We are using the hierarchical event model. We have three types of events as follows:

1. Raw sensor captured data streams (raw events).
2. Filtered atomic events, used some threshold value and windowing techniques, and removed unwanted values from raw events.
3. Complex events. Based on the domain knowledge and rule base, we generate the complex event.

Figure 10.2 gives the idea about the algorithm we have introduced at the edges of the smart applications. First, it will collect the input from the sensors. At the second level, it will generate the atomic events, and, lastly, depending upon use case domain knowledge, it will cause complex events.

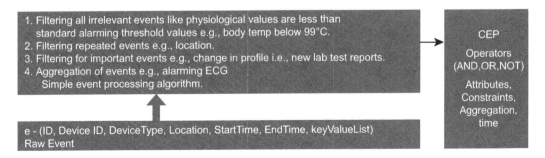

FIGURE 10.2   Suggested novel methodology for edge analytics.

An irregularity in a patient's health can be identified using complex event processing (CEP). CE are generated by considering the rule engines by setting it with the help of domain experts. We are using association rule methods for pattern matching. Values of each sensor and association with each other are stored as part of the rule and further used to generate alerts in real-time.

Esper is an available library in java that can be used for the CEP engine generation patch. Esper provides a high-performance, low latency, SQL-standard, real-time streaming processing engine for medium to high-volume data. Esper can describe complicated matching requirements such as temporal windows, joining several event streams, filtering, and sorting. It can also recognize patterns and sequences of unconnected occurrences.

10.4 RESULTS AND DISCUSSIONS

The proposed system (Figure 10.3.) is split into two key models:

1. Patient data transfer on the cloud
2. Complex event-generated data transferred on the cloud

Model 1: Patient Data Transfer on the Cloud

- **Input:** Sensor-generated data.
- **Output:** Generate alert to doctor as well as registered mobile.
- **Process:** Here, we will be collecting the patient's sensor data as a system input. The data files are stored on the cloud, respectively. Machine learning algorithms like SVM are used to classify the three categories of patients. These are 1) normal, 2) settled, and 3) critical and require 24/7 observations. Any classifier can be used, but for convenience, we have used the Naive Bayes algorithm. SVM algorithm is also used to predict the patient's health within the next 24 hours and generate alert to nearest hospital or send the notification to Dr. and registered mobile number of the caretaker.
- **Observation:** The time and space complexity for data transfer is calculated. It is observed that the time taken to store the file on the cloud is more as the file size is also large. As the file size is large, it may take sufficiently more space on the cloud to store.

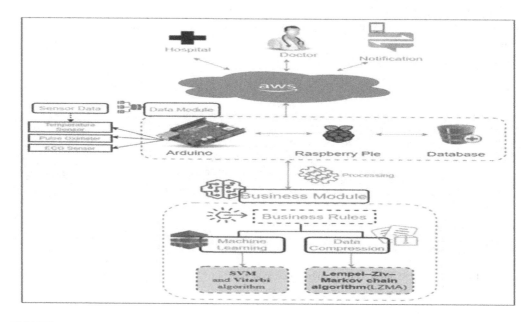

FIGURE 10.3 System architecture.

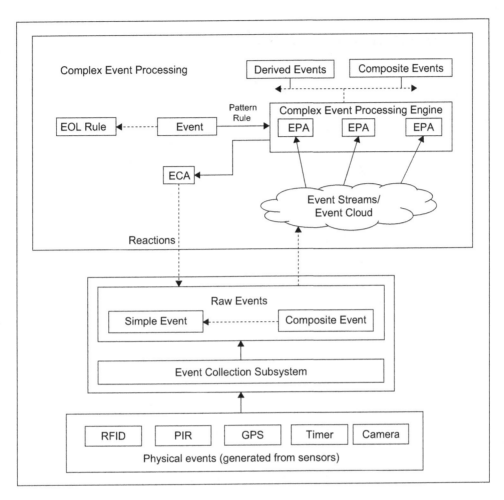

FIGURE 10.4   Complex event processing.

TABLE 10.1
Patient's Data Files Transfer in the Cloud

Sr. No	File Size (kb)	Internet Upload Speed (Kb/s)	Time Taken to Upload (Seconds)
1	1999	999	2.001001001
2	1577	753	2.094289509
3	3000	1152	2.604166667
4	4520	937	4.823906083
5	5950	1000	5.95
6	6520	1170	5.572649573

Table 10.1 and Figure 10.5 represent the patient's medical data file transfer on the cloud server. The file of the patient's data contains the sensor values and other detail. These sizes are bulky as they are in kilobytes (KBs). To store these files on the AWS cloud will take a lot of time and ample space. So, here, we found the research gap, and then we developed the innovative rule-based complex event-generated engine on edge devices.

The main problem observed here is that data processing is directly proportional to the data generated and transferred over the network. If we want to reduce this, we should think about reducing

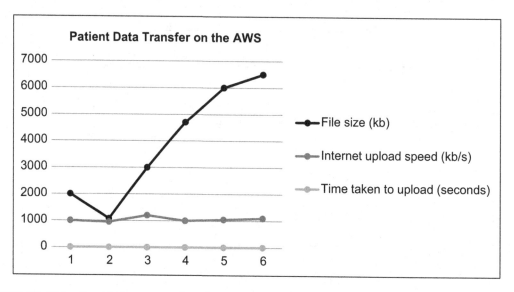

FIGURE 10.5 Graphical representation of the patient's data files transfer considering the threshold value mentioned; a complex event is generated if a value exceeds the normal range. Those generated events are only sent to the cloud.

the data resources only so that subsequent routing of data over the web will be avoided. We did the comparative analysis for data reduction with the help of various machine learning algorithms. We found that time and space complexity is the main problem with these resource-constrained edge devices and then came up with a complex event generation module.

Model 2: Complex Event-Generated Data Transferred on the Cloud

The proposed generates the complex event if three of the sensors exceed the threshold value among four sensors. Such complex events only will be sent to the cloud, which can reduce the data transfer time or memory space. The experimentation is carried out using ECG, SPO2, BPM, or temperature sensors.

In the case of the ECG sensor, the standard value for the RR interval ranges from 600–1500 ms. If the values from the sensor exceed this range, then it can cause problems. In this project, we consider the BPM values for patients above the age of 50. The average value of the BPM sensor for ordinary people is between 85 and 145 (PM).

Using the SPO2 sensor, blood oxygen levels can be measured. It helps to monitor diseases like congenital heart defects, heart failure, etc. The normal range for SPO2 is 90–100%. A value below 90 can cause severe problems to the user. Also, a temperature value above 97.7–99.5 (F) is dangerous.

10.5 CONCLUSION

This chapter presents a new computing methodology for analyzing the data using complex event processing (CEP) and machine learning in the IoT environment. The majority of the available CEP approaches take a long time as they do not consider parallel and redundant operations individually concerning basic events. The given system can be used for remote patient monitoring over a cloud environment. We conducted an empirical study on the memory data to investigate the applicability of a pattern-generating algorithm with business rules. The time required for data transfer is greatly reduced as only complex events are pushed over the cloud instead of the whole sensor data. The support vector machine (SVM) algorithm used provides the health prediction for that particular patient and alerts the doctor for further treatment. Esper is used for the generation of the CEP engine on the mobile. The system can analyze data and generate a real-time alert.

REFERENCES

1. Nijat Mehdiyev, Julian Krumeich, David Enke, Dirk Werth, Peter Loos. *Determination of Rule Patterns in Complex Event Processing Using Machine Learning Techniques.* Conference Organized by Missouri University of Science and Technology 2015-San Jose, CA.
2. https://smartcitiescouncil.com/system/tdf/main/public_resources/understanding-data-streams-in-iot-107491.pdf?file=1&type=node&id=3862&force=.
3. Nijat Mehdiyeva, Julian Krumeicha, David Enkeb, Dirk Wertha, Peter Loosa. *Determination of Rule Patterns in Complex Event Processing Using Machine Learning Techniques.* Complex Adaptive Systems, Publication Cihan H. Dagli, Editor in Chief Conference Organized by Missouri University of Science and Technology 2015-San Jose, CA.
4. Juan Boubeta-Puig, Guadalupe Ortiz, Inmaculada Medina-Bulo. *Approaching the Internet of Things through Integrating SOA and Complex Event Processing.* March 2014, www.researchgate.net/publication/261877904.
5. Dong Wang, Mingquan Zhou, Sajid Ali, Pengbo Zhou, Yusong Liu, and Xuesong Wang, Novel Complex Event Processing Engine for Intelligent Data Analysis in Integrated Information Systems. *International Journal of Distributed Sensor Networks*, 2016, Article ID 6741401: 14, http://dx.doi.org/10.1155/2016/6741401.
6. R. Bhargavi, V. Vaidehi. Semantic Intrusion Detection with Multi-Sensor Data Fusion Using Complex Event Processing. *Sadhana*, 2013, 38.
7. Yao W, Chao-Hsien Chu, Li Z. Leveraging Complex Event Processing for Smart Hospitals Using RFID. *Journal of Network and Computer*, 2011, 34(3): 799–810.
8. Wang Xue, Sheng Wang, Daowei Bi. Distributed Visual-Target-Surveillance System in Wireless Sensor Networks. *IEEE Transactions on Systems, Man, and Cybernetics*, 2009, 39(5): 1134–11463.
9. F. Wang, S. Liu, P. Liu, Y. Bai. *Bridging Physical and Virtual Worlds: Complex Event Processing for RFID Data Streams.* In 10th International Conference on Extending Database Technology (EDBT'2006), 2006.
10. R. Pathak, V. Vaidehi. *Complex Event Processing Based Remote Health Monitoring System.* In Proc. 3rd Int. Conf. Eco-Friendly Comput.Commun. Syst. (ICECCS), Dec. 2014, pp. 61–66.
11. A. Manashty, J. Light, U. Yadav. *Healthcare Event Aggregation Lab (HEAL), a Knowledge-Sharing Platform for Anomaly Detection and Prediction.* In Proc. 17th Int. Co+nf. E-Health Netw., Appl.Services (HealthCom), Boston, MA, USA, Oct. 2015, pp. 648–652.
12. Afef Mdhaffar, Ismael Bouassida Rodriguez, Khalil Charfi, Leila Abid, Bernd Freisleben. CEP4HFP: Complex Event Processing for Heart Failure Prediction. *EEE Transactions on Nanobioscience*, December 2017, 16: 8.
13. V. Vaidehi, R. Bhargavi, K. Ganapathy, C. S. Hemalatha. *Multi-Sensor Based in-Home Health Monitoring Using Complex Event Processing.* In Proc. Int. Conf. Recent Trends Inf. Technol., Apr. 2012, pp. 570–575.
14. S. Majumdar Dhillon, M. St-Hilaire, A. El-Haraki. *MCEP: A Mobile Device Based Complex Event Processing System for Remote Healthcare.* In Proc. IEEE Int. Conf. Internet Things (ICIOT), Jul./Aug. 2018, pp. 203–210.
15. Lina Lan, Ruisheng Shi, Bai Wang, Lei Zhang, Ning Jiang. A Universal Complex Event Processing Mechanism Based on Edge Computing for Internet of Things Real-Time Monitoring. *Digital Object Identifier, IEEE Access*, August 2019, 7, pp. 101865–101878. https://doi.org/10.1109/ACCESS.2019.2930313.
16. Jürgen Dunkel, Ralf Bruns, Sebastian Stipković. *Event-Based Smartphone sensor Processing for Ambient Assisted Living.* In 2013 IEEE: Eleventh International Symposium on Autonomous Decentralized Systems (ISADS).
17. D. Bade. Esper-Android: EventStreamProcessingonAndroid [Online], 2010. www.informatik.uni-hamburg.de/projects/esper-android/
18. D. Amade. Joining Oracle Complex Event Processing and J2MEto React to Location and Positioning Events [Online], 2009. Available Link:—www.oracle.com/technetwork/articles/amadei-cep-090595.html
19. J. Dunkel. *On Complex Event Processing for Sensor Networks.* In Proceedings of the International Symposium on Autonomous Decentralized Systems (ISADS), pp. 249–254, IEEE (2009).

20. I. Mohomed, A. Misra, M. Ebling, W. Jerome. *HARMONI: Context-aware Filtering of Sensor Data for Continuous Remote Health Monitoring*. In Proceedings of Pervasive Computing and Communications (PerCom), pp. 248, IEEE (2008), 978-0-7695-3113-7.

21. A. Ito, T. Ohta, Y. Kakuda, S. Inoue. *Safety Support System on School Routes Based on Grouping of Children in Mobile Adhoc Networks*. In Proceedings of the International Symposium on Autonomous Decentralized Systems (ISADS), pp. 533–538, IEEE (2011).

22. A. Mouttham, L. Peyton, B. Eze, A. El Saddik. Event-Driven Data Integration for Personal Health Monitoring. *Journal of Emerging Technologies in Web Intelligence*, November 2009, 1(2): 144–148.

23. S. Reddy, V. Samanta, J. Burke, D. Estrin, M. Hansen, M. Srivastava. *MobiSense—Mobile Network Services for Coordinated Participatory Sensing Autonomous Decentralized Systems (ISADS)*. In Proceedings of the International Symposium, 2009, pp. 1–6, IEEE.

24. Google Android Developer's Guide (2012, Oct) Content Provider [Online]. http://developer.android.com/guide/topics/providers/-content-providers.html

25. Google Android Developer's Guide. Using Databases [Online], October 2012. http://developer.android.com/guide/topics/data/data-storage.html#db

26. S.R. Jeffery, G. Alonso, M.J. Franklin, J. Widom, W. Hong. *A Pipelined Framework for Online Cleaning of Sensor Data Streams*. In Proceedings of the International Conference on Data Engineering (ICDE), pp. 140–142, IEEE (2006), 0-7695-2570-9.

27. D. C. Luckham. *The Power of Events: An Introduction to Complex Event Processing in Distributed Enterprise Systems*. Addison-Wesley, 2002.

Part III

Bio-Signal Processing

11 Evolution of Automatic Epilepsy Detection and Classification Techniques
A Survey

Neeta Hemant Chapatwala and Dr. Chirag N. Paunwala

CONTENTS

11.1 INTRODUCTION

Seizure and an epileptic seizure are different. An epileptic seizure is a momentary incidence of symptoms due to atypical extreme or synchronous neural activity in the brain, as per the definition given by the International League Against Epilepsy (ILAE) (Boonyakitanont et al. 2019; Blinowska and Zygierewicz 2011). It is a long-lasting ailment followed by recurrent, senseless seizures. It can cause a change in emotional state, consciousness levels, and physical activity. Less than 2% of the population suffers from seizures. The randomness of seizure occurrence is a primary reason for the debility linked with epilepsy. This ambiguity impacts the quality of life of patients, preventing them from daily activities like cooking, driving, sports activity, swimming, etc. With early and accurate detection, this uncertainty can be removed, which results in a significant quality of life improvement. Automatic feedback-based therapy like biofeedback, electrical stimulation, or drug infusion needs automatic seizure detection for treatment. Epilepsy is a disorder of the central nervous system, categorized by loss of awareness and convulsions. An electroencephalogram is the recording of brain activity due to electrical signals that used to analyze the epilepsy condition. Early detection of epilepsy plays a major role in improving risk factors of death and quality of life. Extracting various types of features from raw encephalography signals in the time domain, frequency domain, and joined time-frequency domain helps to detect and classify seizures.

Early detection of epilepsy is useful for hospitalized patients and those with recurrent epilepsy. Such patients can be treated in a better way to improve the quality of their life. Selecting and extracting the specific EEG features among time domain, frequency domain, and multi-domain

DOI: 10.1201/9781003272694-14

is a crucial part. Also, for the detection of seizures in advance, extraction of the pre-ictal state is challenging. Due to artifacts in EEG signals, classification of seizure and non-seizure becomes difficult. Another approach is to use raw EEG signals and directly train the model using deep learning methods. In this case, the issue is a requirement of handling a big database of raw EEG. There is potential for enhancement and optimization in seizure prediction and detection. Database selection, adequate pre-processing, channel selection, and machine learning considerations can be assessed to achieve more realistic performance.

Measurement of EEG can be done by placing electrodes at various locations and depths in the brain. Scalp EEG (sEEG) electrodes are mounted on the scalp; sEEG is known to be a non-invasive method, while in invasive method electrodes are placed directly on the cortex, known as an electrocorticogram (ECoG) or intracranial EEG (iEEG). Electric fields are measured with invasive methods, referred to as local field potentials (LFP). A normal subject's EEG, recorded with scalp electrodes, ranges between 10µV and 100µV during the awake state (Blinowska and Zygierewicz 2011). EEG signal amplitude increases in magnitude for epilepsy concerning normal cases. The size of electrode does not matter if placed on the scalp. In case of iEEG, the size of electrode matters as smaller electrodes give higher potentials.

11.1.1 Epilepsy Cycle

Epilepsy cycle refers to different stages, which include ictal, pre-ictal, interictal, and post-ictal stages. Ictal denotes a physiologic state such as a seizure, stroke, or headache (A. F. Hussein et al. 2018). The word ictal originates from the Latin word ictus, which means a stroke. In electroencephalography, the recording during a seizure is said to be "ictal." The basic epilepsy cycle is shown in Figure 11.1 (Bou et al. 2017).

- The state immediately before the actual seizure, stroke, or headache refers to pre-ictal.
- The state shortly after the event refers to post-ictal.
- The period between seizures or convulsions refers to interictal. People with epilepsy live more than 99% of their life in the interictal state. Neurologists frequently use the interictal period when diagnosing epilepsy.

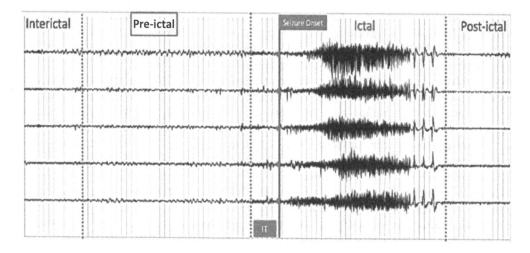

FIGURE 11.1   Four stages of typical epilepsy cycle.

Source: Bou et al. (2017)

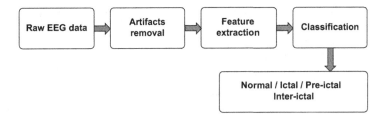

FIGURE 11.2   Block diagram of automatic epilepsy detection and classification.

11.1.2 TYPES OF EPILEPSY SEIZURES

An epilepsy seizure is defined clinically, per the International League Against Epilepsy (ILAE), if a minimum of two unprovoked seizures with a gap of more than a day occurs or one unprovoked seizure with a probability of more seizures (as a minimum 60%), happening over the following ten years diagnosis of an epilepsy syndrome.

Seizures can be broadly classified as partial and generalized seizures. Partial seizures start from an electric liberation of more than one localized area of the brain. They may or may not impair awareness. Generalized (non-focal) seizures involve electrical liberation in the entire brain. Signs could be the absence of awareness or loss of awareness.

A focal onset seizure may occur due to epilepsy or many other reasons like brain tumors or infections, heat stroke, or low blood sugar. Epilepsy is caused by excessive or abnormal electrical charge disruptions in the brain's various sections. Partial seizures initially affect one-half of the brain. Focal epilepsy can affect either the complete cerebral hemisphere or some parts of brain. Location of seizure onset can help medically to collect information as a pre-surgery preparation. To locate and identify epileptic seizures clinically, the encephalography signals in the brain need to learn in depth. These signals can provide meaningful data about the disease's location and pointers. The EEG waves are used to define rhythmic sinusoidal activities. For analyzing these signals, five frequency bands are normally used, i.e., delta (less than 4 Hz), theta (4 to 7 Hz), alpha (8 to 15 Hz), beta (12 to 28 Hz), and gamma (25 to 100 Hz; Li et al. 2020). A detailed block diagram for automatic epilepsy detection and classification is shown in Figure 11.2, which takes the raw EEG dataset from publicly available sources and then removes the noises, followed by feature selection and classification. Detail description of each block is discussed in the next section.

11.2 EEG DATASETS

Various raw EEG datasets are freely available. Normally used datasets are listed for ready references.

The epilepsy dataset by the University of Bonn (www.upf.edu/web/ntsa/downloads) contains five different sets of a database (A–E), in which non-epileptic data with eyes open and closed were labeled as "A" and "B" respectively. The epileptic interictal data and ictal data are labeled as "C, D," and "E" respectively. For each set of this dataset, 100 txt files, each of 4096 samples of one EEG time series in ASCII code, are given. Another widely used dataset of 23 subjects is the scalp EEG dataset from the Boston Children's Hospital-MIT (CHB-MIT) (https://physionet.org/content/chbmit), which includes 18 female and 5 male subjects of different age groups (2–22 years). The database from the University Hospital of Freiburg, Germany (http://epilepsy.uni-freiburg.de/freiburg-seizure-prediction-project/eeg-database), contains iEEG recordings of 21 patients with focal epilepsy. During monitoring of invasive pre-surgical epilepsy, recording was done. The EEG data of 128 channels were acquired using a Neurofile NT system. The Open Neuro and NEMAR databases (https://openneuro.org/datasets/ds003555/versions/1.0.0) include EEG recordings of 30 pediatric patients with epilepsy based on the 10–20 system and iEEG multicenter dataset of 35 subjects. A few databases are also available on Kaggle (www.kaggle.com/c/seizure-prediction/data), like iEEG data from Kaggle refractory drug-resistant focal epilepsy (three female subjects) and iEEG (pre-ictal and interictal) datasets of seven subjects by American Epilepsy Society Seizure Prediction Challenge Predict Seizures in Intracranial EEG recordings. The TUH EEG Epilepsy Corpus (www.isip.piconepress.com/projects/tuh_eeg/downloads/) includes 100 patients with epilepsy and 100 without epilepsy. The data was created in partnership with a variety of partners, including the National Institutes of Health (NIH).

11.3   ARTIFACTS REMOVAL

The raw EEG signal contains various noises to contaminate it, which leads to a serious delusion in EEG signal analysis and decision making. These contaminations are known as artifacts, which are signals that are not related to brain activity. Moreover, artifacts can result in considerable EEG measurement miscalculations, reducing the therapeutic use of EEG signals. It is very important to remove these artifacts employing signal processing to improve signal quality and to prepare signals for adequate feature extraction.

11.3.1   TYPE OF ARTIFACTS

Artifacts in EEG signals can be classified as interior artifacts and exterior artifacts (Motamedi-Fakhr et al. 2014), Interior artifacts include noise due to the subject's movement, such as:

- Ocular artifacts caused due to movements of an eye, either slow or fast.
- Muscle artifacts occupy a wide frequency range. These can appear in the form of spikes or continuous interference, for example electromyography (EMG) interference.
- Electrocardiogram (ECG) interference is an example of electric field changes induced by cardiac muscle depolarization, which inhibit EEG signals.
- Movements of human body parts, like the head, body, and chest.
- Sweat artifacts change electrolyte concentration at electrodes.

Exterior artifacts are due to outer environment noise like:

- Power line interference at 50 or 60 Hz depending on local standards.
- Digital artifacts such as loose wiring.
- Faulty electrode or poor placement.
- Noise due to ventilation, machine, etc.

The EEG dataset gives raw EEG signals that include supply line noise of 60 Hz (Motamedi-Fakhr et al. 2014). It also includes artifacts due to muscular movement, sweating, and movements of eyes, legs, hands, electrode misplacements, etc., which interfere with neuron information to misguide the findings (Jiang et al. 2019). Wavelet transform and its variants are commonly used to decompose the EEG signals into different rhythms. It also helps to remove some artifacts by using thresholding but fails to identify artifacts completely that overlap with the spectral properties. Breg and Scherg used principal component analysis (PCA) to remove ocular noises, while Casarotto et al. verified that PCA performs more efficiently than linear-regression methods. For muscular artifacts removal, empirical mode decomposition (EMD) is also used by many authors (Bajaj and Pachori 2013; Usman et al. 2021). The EMD technique decomposes the signal into intrinsic mode functions (IMFs). The advantage of this method is that a selection of the basis functions, like in wavelet decomposition, is eliminated. One drawback of EMD is due to noise sensitivity mode mixing complications (Xu et al. 2018). Independent component analysis (ICA) is the most popular technique, but it has the drawback of loss of relevant information, which is solved by canonical correlation analysis (CCA). Several researchers have proposed a hybrid approach by combining two different techniques, like enhanced EMD-ICA or multivariate EMD-CCA (Jiang et al. 2019).

11.4 FEATURE CLASSIFICATION

This section describes the features commonly used in the literature of EEG seizure detection, classification, or prediction. These features are categorized by: time, frequency, and time-frequency domains. A broad classification of features for epilepsy detection is shown in Figure 11.3.

Time-domain features (TDFs) are those calculated on raw EEG signals or pre-processed signals using time-dependent features, such as energy, variance, or EMD. Frequency-domain features (FDFs) are computed on raw EEG signals using discrete Fourier transform. Time-frequency domain features (TFDFs) contain both time and frequency characteristics, such as STFT, spectrogram, or DWT. Various features can be extracted from captured EEG. Features must be unique to the pertaining disease and should not overlap with any other diseases for perfect diagnosis.

11.4.1 TIME-DOMAIN FEATURES

From a timeseries, one can extract a lot of statistical information such as the Mean and the Standard Deviation (Harpale and Bairagi 2021). Other frequently used features are explained underneath: (Boonyakitanont et al. 2019; Harpale and Bairagi 2021).

$$\text{Mean } \mu = \frac{\sum x}{n} \tag{11.1}$$

where, x is the data and n the number of data samples.

$$\text{Coefficient of Variation} = \frac{\delta}{\mu} \tag{11.2}$$

where δ is the standard deviation given as

$$\delta = \sqrt{\frac{\sum (x - \propto)^2}{n-1}} \tag{11.3}$$

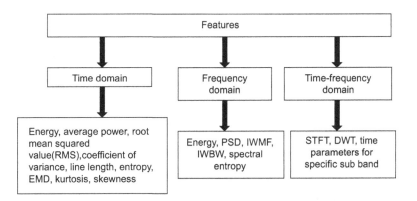

FIGURE 11.3 Feature classification for epilepsy detection.

RMS value is as per eq. 11.4, which is calculated as the square root of the average of the squared value of the signal.

$$RMS = \sqrt{\frac{1}{T}\int_0^T \left(x(t)\right)^2} \qquad (11.4)$$

Kurtosis is fourth-moment estimation of signal and given as

$$K = \frac{E\left(x-\mu\right)^4}{\delta^4} \qquad (11.5)$$

Approximate entropy (ApEn) is used to measure the signal's variety of variance. It examines the similarity of the samples using pattern length (m) and similarity coefficient to find changes in the underlying episodic behavior (r).

$$ApEn = \ln\left(\frac{C_m(r)}{C_{m+1}(r)}\right) \qquad (11.6)$$

Where, Cm(r) is the pattern mean of length m and Cm+1(r) is the pattern mean of length m +1. The data is considered to be skewed if the probability distribution of a real-valued random variable around its mean is asymmetrical. The equation for skewness (SK) is given as:

$$SK = E\left[\frac{\left(x-\frac{1}{4}\right)^3}{\bar{A}^3}\right] \qquad (11.7)$$

Where, E is the expectancy, μ is the mean and σ is the standard deviation.
Energy represents the EEG signal's intensity. Seizures are associated with high energy. If x(n) is an input signal, x(n)² is the signal's instantaneous energy. The average energy of the signal is given by eq. 11.8

$$Average\ Energy = \frac{1}{N}\sum_{n=1}^{N} x(n)^2 \qquad (11.8)$$

11.4.2 FREQUENCY DOMAIN FEATURES

EEG can be seen as a mixture of signals with different frequencies. EEG data can also be represented using a spectrogram. It is somehow a compromise between the time and frequency representation. EEG signal can be transformed into a frequency domain using discrete Fourier transform. To selectively represent the EEG samples signal, PSD estimation is used to compute the EEG signal. Using nonparametric methods, the PSD is calculated, and one of these methods is Welch's method (Boonyakitanont et al. 2020). Steps for this are described in the following:

- Partition of the data sequence.
- For each segment, compute a windowed DFT.
- For each segment, form the modified periodogram value.
- Average the periodogram values to obtain Welch's estimate of the PSD.

Power Spectral Density (PSD): The PSD calculates the average of the Fourier transform magnitude squared over a long time interval.

$$S_x = \lim_{T \to \infty} E\left\{\frac{1}{2T}\left|\int_{-T}^{T} x(t)e^{-j2\pi ft}dt\right|\right\} \tag{11.9}$$

Intensity Weighted Mean Frequency (IWMF): This feature gives the mean of the frequency distribution using the normalized PSD and is defined as

$$IWMF(X) = \sum_{k} X[k]f[k]. \tag{11.10}$$

Here, X[k] represents the normalized PSD at frequency f[k].

Intensity weighted bandwidth (IWBW): This is a measure of the PSD width in terms of the standard deviation and is defined as

$$IWBW(X) = \sqrt{\sum_{k} X[k](f[k] - IMWF(X))^2}. \tag{11.11}$$

The PSD is sharper during seizure events, according to seizure patterns in typical EEG data. As a result, during those activities, the IWBW is smaller.

Spectral Entropy (SEN): This is a normalized form of Shannon's entropy. It uses the power spectrum amplitude components of the time series for entropy evaluation:

$$SEN = \sum_{f} P_f \log\left(\frac{1}{P_f}\right). \tag{11.12}$$

11.4.3 TIME-FREQUENCY DOMAIN FEATURES

TFDFs (Boonyakitanont et al. 2019) are used to get the benefit of both time and frequency characteristics, such as STFT spectrogram or DWT. Because the EEG signal is nonstationary, time-frequency domain methods such as wavelet transform are the best way to extract features from raw data (WT). Any general function can be written as an infinite series of wavelets using a spectral estimating technique. The use of variable window size allows a more flexible representation of the signal in the time-frequency domain.

11.5 COMPARISON OF VARIOUS METHODS FOR SEIZURE DETECTION

After feature selection, the classifier plays an important role to detect a seizure. Many traditional methods like DWT, SVM, and EMD are used by researchers. SVM was used by Acharya at el., Cho et al., and Petrocian at el. For seizure detection. As shown in Table 11.1, Acharya at el. achieved 98.68% to 100% sensitivity, and Cho et al. got 83.17% accuracy for the CHB-MIT database in epilepsy detection. Kaur at el. used modified NN to achieve 0.02/hr false rate. Thomas Maiwald et al. (2004) used the dynamical similarity index method with a seizure prediction horizon of less than two minutes to predict the seizure with sensitivity between 21% and 42%.

This result was not sufficient for clinical use.

Interictal epileptiform discharges (IED) in EEG signal also play an important role for the epilepsy diagnosis (Indiradevi et al. 2008) as spikes are generated due to synchronous discharge of a group of neurons in the epileptic focus region. Due to the higher correlation between epileptic spike and scaling wavelet function of Daubechies 4 (DB4), this is selected as a base function. Sub-bands

TABLE 11.1

Comparison of Traditional Methods for Automatic Epilepsy Detection

References	Database	Feature	Classifier	Results	False Alarm Rate
Lasefr et al. (2017)	University of Bonn	Amplitude range —band power —crest range	ANN SVM KNN	Accuracy 96% 95% 98%	–
Kaur, Prakash, and Kalra (2018)	Montreal Neurological Hospital	Time and frequency domain	Modified NN	Sensitivity 100% Detection latency 9.35 s	0.02/hr
Petrosian et al. (2000)	Clinical data	DWT, morphology	SVM	Sensitivity 97% Detection latency 7.1 ± 1.9 s	6/hr
Acharya et al. (2018)	Freiburg CHB-MIT	Spectral power Kalman filter	SVM	Sensitivity: 100% Sensitivity: 98.68%	–
Cho et al. (2017)	CHB-MIT	Multivariate EMD	SVM	Accuracy: 83.17%	–

TABLE 11.2

Comparison of Traditional Methods for Early Detection of Epilepsy

Authors	Database	Features	Method	Results
Maiwald et al. (2004)	University Hospital of Freiburg, Germany 21 subjects Including ictal, pre-ictal, and interictal	SOP, SPH	Dynamical similarity index	Sensitivity for SPH < 2 min (21–42%)
Slimen et al. (2020)	CHB-MIT sEEG Database 23 subjects	No. of spikes in ictal, interictal, and pre-ictal in all channels	Threshold based on max spike in interictal	Prediction time, 1–23 minutes Prediction accuracy 92%
Usman et al. (2017)	CHB-MIT sEEG Database 22 subjects	Entropy, approximate entropy, spectral moments	EMD Classifier k-nearest neighbor classifier, naive Bayes, SVM	Avg prediction time 23.6 minutes Sensitivity 92.23%
Yang et al. (2018)	Feriburg iEEG Database 19 subjects	Permutation entropy	SVM	Average sensitivity 94% FPR 0.111 h−1. Avg. SPH =61.93 min

4 and 5 with a frequency range of 4–16 Hz were used to avoid other artifacts, like myogenic, within the range of 20 to 30 Hz over the anterior head region and 40 to 80 Hz over the temporal regions. Normal sleep activities like vertex sharp transients were excluded to avoid false detection from midline electrodes Fz, Cz, and Pz. The author used an adaptive threshold level to detect epileptic spikes and, after extracting spikes, the channel with maximum energy is used to locate the epileptic foci. The author claimed that the system was able to detect all types of IED spikes but failed to detect slow waves with amplitude much greater than a spike. The method correctly identified 627 of 687 IEDs and 1468 of 1644 non-epileptiform transients with 91.7% sensitivity, 89.3% specificity, and 90.5 % accuracy. Petrosian et al. (2000) worked on clinical data with DWT and SVM as a classifier with sensitivity 97% and detection latency 7.1 ± 1.9 s. Comparison of traditional methods is summarized in Table 11.1 and early detection methods are compared in Table 11.2.

Machine learning and deep learning approaches have attracted many researchers, as they can select features by training the model. Poomipat et al. (2019) proposed two approaches for seizure detection: convolution neural network (CNN) and artificial neural network (ANN). Based on CHB-MIT scalp EEG database, ANN detects abnormal samples better than CNN at a certain level, but CNN has more potential to classify normal samples. As per their experiments, CNN uses a raw database while ANN, with its dominant features, is better to detect the abnormality. ANN can perform with an overall accuracy of 98.62% and an F1-score of 77.04%, while CNN performs with 99.07% accuracy and an F1-score of 65.69%. Ihsan Ulah at el. (2018) proposed an automatic method for epilepsy identification that works with binary classification between epileptic and non-epileptic and ternary classification between normal, ictal, and interictal. The author developed a simple pyramidal one-dimensional deep convolutional neural network (P-1D-CNN) model that is memory efficient. To overcome the issue of a small dataset, two data augmentation schemes have been introduced for learning P-1D-CNN model. This system gives an accuracy of 99.1 ± 0.9% on the University of Bonn dataset. Fengshi Tian et al. (2021) proposed a new neuromorphic computing approach for epileptic seizure prediction as spiking CNN with reduced computation complexity by 98.58% compared to CNN. Comparison of CNN-based methods for epilepsy prediction is shown in Table 11.3 and other methods are also compared in Table 11.4.

TABLE 11.3
Comparison of CNN-Based Methods for Prediction

Authors	Database	Method	Results
Hussein et al. (2019)	iEEG data from Kaggle refractory drug-resistant focal epilepsy 3 Female: 22, 51, and 53 years	CNN	Average prediction sensitivity 87.85%
Tian et al. (2021)	CHB-MIT sEEG Database 22 subjects	Spiking CNN (Spiking NN+CNN)	Sensitivity 95.1% Specificity 99.2% Reduction in computation complexity by 98.58% compared to CNN
Usman et al. (2021)	CHB-MIT sEEG Database 22 subjects	EMD for noise removal Generative adversarial network (GAN) for class balance (Generative adversarial networks) 3-layer CNN	Sensitivity 93% Specificity 92.5% with average time of 32 min to predict the seizure's onset
Wang et al. (2021)	CHB-MIT sEEG Database 23 subjects	Multi-scale dilated 3D CNN	Sensitivity 85.8% Accuracy 80.5% Specificity 75.1%
Dissanayake et al. (2020)	CHB-MIT sEEG Database 23 subjects	Feature (MFCCs) 13 bank 1. CNN 2. Siamese architecture	CNN: Accuracy for pre-ictal–interictal state detection 88.81% Sensitivity 93.45% Specificity 81.64% ROC-AUC score 0.9273 Siamese architecture: Accuracy 91.54% Sensitivity 92.45% Specificity 89.94%. ROC-AUC score 0.9694
Zhang et al. (2019)	CHB-MIT sEEG Database 23 patients	Wavelet packet decomposition and common spatial pattern (CSP) for feature extraction and CNN	Sensitivity 92.2% FPR 0.12/h.

TABLE 11.4

Comparison of Epilepsy Prediction Methods

Author	Database	Features	Method	Results
Ali et al. (2019)	Kaggle (pre- and interictal) iEEG 7 subjects	PSD, Standard deviation	Bidirectional LSTM(ANN) Classifiers: Linear least squares Linear discriminant analysis Regularized SVM	Max AUC 0.84 for test set and split 1 Linear least squares AUC 0.78 Linear discriminant analysis AUC 0.69 Regularized SVM AUC 0.80
Yang et al. (2015)	The Children's Hospital of Philadelphia CEEG of 222 subjects under PICU without an epilepsy-related diagnosis prior to admission	Interictal epileptiform discharges Clinically evident seizures prior to CEEG Age and background	Multivariate logistic regression model	Sensitivity of 59% Specificity of 81%
Zacharaki et al. (2016)	Epilepsy Monitoring Unit, St. Luke's Hospital, Thessaloniki, Greece	Spike	Spike pattern recognition and supervised classification in low dimensional embedding space	F-score sensitivity (97%) False positive rate (0.1/min)
Das et al. (2020)	Own dataset 85-Male (67 seizure, 18 normal) 65-Female (36 seizure, 29 normal) Age-18–60 years	Current maxima lower threshold target point selection	Region identification with domain matching algorithm	True positive rate (TPR) 91.07% seizure 97.36% normal accuracy 92.66% F1-score 94.86%

11.6　CONCLUSION AND RESEARCH GAP

Automatic detection of seizures helps doctors to give proper treatment in a short time span. This chapter reviews numerous techniques starting from traditional methods and moving towards current state-of-the-art methods. Traditional methods give good performance in terms of accuracy with the only challenge selection of appropriate features. Also, features changes based on the patient's age, gender, medical history, mental state, etc., which makes it very difficult to develop a general algorithm. Removing artifacts is also important if raw EEG signals are used. Neural network–based classifiers give better accuracy and sensitivity as the system trains itself by learning the model and selecting features from raw EEG data automatically. For the deep machine learning approach, the major problem is a limited dataset of seizures and class imbalance issues due to a majority of data including non-seizure and interictal events. Data augmentation is used to increase the dataset and to remove the class imbalance problem. Also, a GAN is used by some researchers to generate synthetic data. In such cases, validation of synthetic data is necessary due to clinical use. Researchers can further work on a specific group of patients and also towards localization of seizures and for EEG data generations.

REFERENCES

Acharya, U. Rajendra, Yuki Hagiwara, and Hojjat Adeli. "Automated seizure prediction." *Epilepsy & Behavior* 88 (2018): 251–261.

Ali, Hazrat, Feroz Karim, Junaid Javed Qureshi, Adnan Omer Abuassba, and Mohammad Farhad Bulbul. "Seizure prediction using bidirectional LSTM." In *Cyberspace Data and Intelligence, and Cyber-Living, Syndrome, and Health*, pp. 349–356. Springer, Singapore, 2019.

Bajaj, Varun, and Ram Bilas Pachori. "Epileptic seizure detection based on the instantaneous area of analytic intrinsic mode functions of EEG signals." *Biomedical Engineering Letters* 3, no. 1 (2013): 17–21.

Blinowska, Katarzyna J., and Jarosław Żygierewicz. *Practical Biomedical Signal Analysis Using MATLAB®.* Boca Raton, FL: CRC Press, 2011.

Boonyakitanont, Poomipat, Apiwat Lek-Uthai, Krisnachai Chomtho, and Jitkomut Songsiri. "A review of feature extraction and performance evaluation in epileptic seizure detection using EEG." *Biomedical Signal Processing and Control* 57 (2020): 101702.

Boonyakitanont, Poomipat, Apiwat Lek-uthai, Krisnachai Chomtho, and Jitkomut Songsiri. "A Comparison of Deep Neural Networks for Seizure Detection in EEG Signals." *bioRxiv* (2019): 702654.

Assi, Elie Bou, Dang K. Nguyen, Sandy Rihana, and Mohamad Sawan. "Towards accurate prediction of epileptic seizures: A review." *Biomedical Signal Processing and Control* 34 (2017): 144–157.

Cho, Dongrae, Beomjun Min, Jongin Kim, and Boreom Lee. "EEG-based prediction of epileptic seizures using phase synchronization elicited from noise-assisted multivariate empirical mode decomposition." *IEEE Transactions on Neural Systems and Rehabilitation Engineering* 25, no. 8 (2016): 1309–1318.

Das, Khakon, Debashis Daschakladar, Partha Pratim Roy, Atri Chatterjee, and Shankar Prasad Saha. "Epileptic seizure prediction by the detection of seizure waveform from the pre-ictal phase of EEG signal." *Biomedical Signal Processing and Control* 57 (2020): 101720.

Dissanayake, Theekshana, Tharindu Fernando, Simon Denman, Sridha Sridharan, and Clinton Fookes. "Patient-independent Epileptic Seizure Prediction using Deep Learning Models." arXiv preprint arXiv:2011.09581 (2020). https://arxiv.org/abs/2011.09581

Harpale, Varsha, and Vinayak Bairagi. "An adaptive method for feature selection and extraction for classification of epileptic EEG signal in significant states." *Journal of King Saud University-Computer and Information Sciences* 33, no. 6 (2021): 668–676.

Hussein, Ahmed Faeq, N. Arunkumar, Chandima Gomes, Abbas K. Alzubaidi, Qais Ahmed Habash, Luz Santamaria-Granados, Juan Francisco Mendoza-Moreno, and Gustavo Ramirez-Gonzalez. "Focal and non-focal epilepsy localization: A review." *IEEE Access* 6 (2018): 49306–49324.

Hussein, Ramy, Mohamed Osama Ahmed, Rabab Ward, Z. Jane Wang, Levin Kuhlmann, and Yi Guo. "Human intracranial EEG quantitative analysis and automatic feature learning for epileptic seizure prediction." arXiv preprint arXiv:1904.03603 (2019). https://arxiv.org/abs/1904.03603

Indiradevi, K. P., Elizabeth Elias, P. S. Sathidevi, S. Dinesh Nayak, and K. Radhakrishnan. "A multi-level wavelet approach for automatic detection of epileptic spikes in the electroencephalogram." *Computers in Biology and Medicine* 38, no. 7 (2008): 805–816.

Jiang, Xiao, Gui-Bin Bian, and Zean Tian. "Removal of artifacts from EEG signals: A review." *Sensors* 19, no. 5 (2019): 987.

Kaur, Manpreet, Neelam Rup Prakash, and Parveen Kalra. "Early seizure detection techniques: A review." *Indian Journal of Science and Technology* 11 (2018): 1–8.

Lasefr, Zakareya, Sai Shiva VNR Ayyalasomayajula, and Khaled Elleithy. "An efficient automated technique for epilepsy seizure detection using EEG signals." In 2017 IEEE 8th Annual Ubiquitous Computing, Electronics and Mobile Communication Conference (UEMCON), pp. 76–82. IEEE, 2017.

Li, Gen, Chang Ha Lee, Jason J. Jung, Young Chul Youn, and David Camacho. "Deep learning for EEG data analytics: A survey." *Concurrency and Computation: Practice and Experience* 32, no. 18 (2020): e5199.

Maiwald, Thomas, Matthias Winterhalder, Richard Aschenbrenner-Scheibe, Henning U. Voss, Andreas Schulze-Bonhage, and Jens Timmer. "Comparison of three nonlinear seizure prediction methods by means of the seizure prediction characteristic." *Physica D: nonlinear phenomena* 194, no. 3–4 (2004): 357–368.

Motamedi-Fakhr, Shayan, Mohamed Moshrefi-Torbati, Martyn Hill, Catherine M. Hill, and Paul R. White. "Signal processing techniques applied to human sleep EEG signals—A review." *Biomedical Signal Processing and Control* 10 (2014): 21–33.

Petrosian, Arthur, Danil Prokhorov, Richard Homan, Richard Dasheiff, and Donald Wunsch II. "Recurrent neural network based prediction of epileptic seizures in intra-and extracranial EEG. " *Neurocomputing* 30, no. 1–4 (2000): 201–218.

Slimen, Itaf Ben, Larbi Boubchir, and Hassene Seddik. "Epileptic seizure prediction based on EEG spikes detection of ictal-preictal states." *Journal of Biomedical Research* 34, no. 3 (2020): 162.

Tian, Fengshi, Jie Yang, Shiqi Zhao, and Mohamad Sawan. "A New Neuromorphic Computing Approach for Epileptic Seizure Prediction." In 2021 IEEE International Symposium on Circuits and Systems (ISCAS), pp. 1–5. IEEE, 2021.

Usman, Syed Muhammad, Shehzad Khalid, and Zafar Bashir. "Epileptic seizure prediction using scalp electro-encephalogram signals." *Biocybernetics and Biomedical Engineering* 41, no. 1 (2021): 211–220.

Usman, Syed Muhammad, Muhammad Usman, and Simon Fong. "Epileptic seizures prediction using machine learning methods." *Computational and Mathematical Methods in Medicine* 2017 (2017).

Wang, Ziyu, Jie Yang, and Mohamad Sawan. "A novel multi-scale dilated 3D CNN for epileptic seizure prediction." In 2021 IEEE 3rd International Conference on Artificial Intelligence Circuits and Systems (AICAS), pp. 1–4. IEEE, 2021.

Xu, Xueyuan, Xun Chen, and Yu Zhang. "Removal of muscle artefacts from few-channel EEG recordings based on multivariate empirical mode decomposition and independent vector analysis." *Electronics Letters* 54, no. 14 (2018): 866–868.

Yang, Amy, Daniel H. Arndt, Robert A. Berg, Jessica L. Carpenter, Kevin E. Chapman, Dennis J. Dlugos, William B. Gallentine et al. "Development and validation of a seizure prediction model in critically ill children." *Seizure* 25 (2015): 104–111.

Yang, Yanli, Mengni Zhou, Yan Niu, Conggai Li, Rui Cao, Bin Wang, Pengfei Yan, Yao Ma, and Jie Xiang. "Epileptic seizure prediction based on permutation entropy." *Frontiers in Computational Neuroscience* 12 (2018): 55.

Zacharaki, Evangelia I., Iosif Mporas, Kyriakos Garganis, and Vasileios Megalooikonomou. "Spike pattern recognition by supervised classification in low dimensional embedding space." *Brain Informatics* 3, no. 2 (2016): 73–83.

Zhang, Yuan, Yao Guo, Po Yang, Wei Chen, and Benny Lo. "Epilepsy seizure prediction on EEG using common spatial pattern and convolutional neural network." *IEEE Journal of Biomedical and Health Informatics* 24, no. 2 (2019): 465–474.

12 Evaluation of Boosting Algorithms for P300 Detection in EEG Signals

Priyanka Jain, Subhash Tatale, Dr. Nivedita Bhirud, Rutuja Pote, Vinaya Kumar, Purvi Sampat, and N. K. Jain

CONTENTS

12.1 INTRODUCTION

Brain–computer interface (BCI) systems are a way to enable direct communication between humans and electronic devices by translating the patient's thoughts via signals into commands for the devices. The thoughts are interpreted through the various signals that they manifest. These signals are then recorded by placement of electrodes on the scalp of a person, while following the

DOI: 10.1201/9781003272694-15

international 10–20 system (Klem et al., 1999); the recording is termed electroencephalography (EEG). BCI systems have also been used to develop better, more natural prosthetics without the need to be invasive.

12.1.1 NEED

Neurological disorders are caused by malfunction or damage in the central nervous system (brain, nerves, and spinal cord). Amyotrophic lateral sclerosis (ALS), quadriplegia, epilepsy, and locked-in syndrome are some such disorders. In most of these diseases, the patient loses control over their body movements to different extents while retaining their cognition, but the negative impact on a patient's ability to move affects their ability to do day-to-day tasks. In these situations, brain–computer interface (BCI) technologies are quite useful because they allow patients to restore some independence. In 2017, (Hsieh et al. (2017) made a prototype where specially abled patients can operate household devices using auditory stimuli. In another study involving home automation, (Shivappa et al., 2018), Android smartphones were used to send commands to various devices. These systems help the patients to do their daily tasks. However, their movement is restricted. In a study by Rebsamen et al. (2008), a mind-controlled wheelchair is proposed. BCIs have also facilitated the inclusion of the specially abled in the digital space through applications like Neurophone (Campbell et al., 2010), SmileToPhone (Ammar & Taileb, 2017), and MindEdit (Elsawy et al., 2017), which enable users to use the basic features of a phone like calling, sending text messages, and setting alarms.

12.1.2 MOTIVATION

These applications are based on ERP systems i.e. signals related to external stimuli. These systems can be developed by depending on a specific component of an ERP signal like the P300. BCIs have also been used to make the lives of healthy people more convenient. They are used in recreational activities like gaming (Cattan et al., 2020). Real-time feedback to the brain, called neurofeedback, can be used to train the brain as reinforcement that facilitates learning. One such use case, called ACTA, has been tested for aiding the independent aging of senior citizens (Cisotto et al., 2021). Out of these applications of BCI, in this study, our focus is on P300 spellers. These are a type of BCI systems used for mind spelling. They are a means by which a person can use devices by just focusing on an item of choice. The increase in attention on seeing the item of choice causes an increase in the potential, also known as the P300 peak. The amplitude of the P300 in event-related potential is more distinct when the target stimuli occur much more rarely and is much more distinguishable than the non-target stimuli.

12.1.3 CHALLENGES

With all the advancements that have been made in BCI using EEG, some challenges still remain. In real-world scenarios, where BCI systems are used to improve a patient's mobility, the setup must be mobile as well. It has been discovered that the majority of accurate EEG recording setups are cumbersome and wired to some extent, obstructing movement and, as a result, obstructing ambulatory behavior. Because of the low signal-to-noise ratio in EEG, detecting the P300 component in a single stimulus is hard. As a result, the P300 speller requires multiple repeated stimuli to denoise by overlaying and averaging so that the spelling accuracy rate is decent.

This chapter consists of a relative study of various approaches that the authors have used for detecting this P300 peak, in EEG data. It proposes a feature extraction method and has provided a performance analysis. This chapter also proposes the comparison of various boosting algorithms like CatBoost, AdaBoost, LightGBM, and XGBoost.

The remaining space in this chapter is organized as follows; the second section gives background about related terminology in depth. The third section explains related work of existing approaches used for the P300 spellers. In the fourth section, the proposed approach is elaborated, and in section five, the obtained results are discussed. Sections six and seven offer the conclusion and avenues for future work.

12.2 BACKGROUND

Certain common terms and an awareness of the background are required to operate effectively with EEG signals. Therefore, the purpose of this section is to clarify thoroughly the terms associated with the P300. It begins with an introduction of event-related potentials, then moves on to P300, and lastly explores the paradigms employed.

12.2.1 EVENT-RELATED POTENTIAL (ERP)

Event-related potentials are small voltages, recorded from the scalp, that are evoked in response to external stimuli (auditory, visual, tactile, olfactory, or gustatory). In humans, ERPs are differentiated based on their latency and amplitude. There are various ERP techniques (Singla, 2018), the most common one being P300. Usually, it is elicited using the oddball paradigm. In this paradigm, low-probability target items are mixed with high-probability non-target (or "standard") items. It is a commonly used task for cognitive and attention measurement in ERP studies.

12.2.2 COMPONENTS OF ERP

The morphology of an ERP signal consists of various components that can be defined on the grounds of their polarity (positive or negative-going potential), timing, scalp distribution, and sensitivity to task computations. The components are C1, P100, N100, P200, N200, and P300. A summary of the components consisting of their respective name, range, and polarity is given in Table 12.1 and a graphical representation of these components can be seen in Figure 12.1.

As seen in Figure 12.1, the P300 is more distinct than other ERP components. Also, it performs quite well in character spelling applications. Hence, greater focus has been placed on P300 signal detection, which is a small but crucial part of the functioning of the P300 speller.

12.2.3 PARADIGM OF A P300 SPELLER

In the P300 speller paradigm, Donchin et al. (2000) have considered where 26 alphabets and 10 digits are shown on a screen in a 6 × 6 matrix. The flashing pattern on this paradigm could be row-column (RC), where an entire row is highlighted, or single character (SC), where only one character is highlighted (Figure 12.2) at a time. Each item in the matrix is highlighted a pre-decided number of times. The subject is then asked to count the number of times the target character is flashed. Whenever the target character is flashed, the subject is surprised or alerted and a high amplitude

TABLE 12.1

Components of ERP

Sr. No	Component	Range	Polarity
1	C1	65–90 ms	Negative or positive
2	P100	~100 ms	Positive
3	N100	80–120 ms	Negative
4	P200	150–250 ms	Positive
5	N200	200–350 ms	Negative
6	P300	250–500 ms	Positive

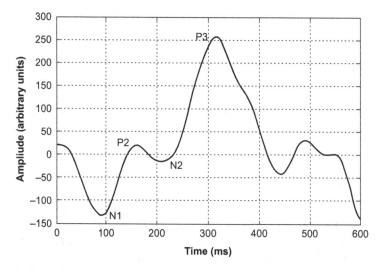

FIGURE 12.1   Components of an ERP with a distinct P300 peak.

Source: Hawking's Spelling Device and P300 | by Brainmab | Medium (n.d.)

a

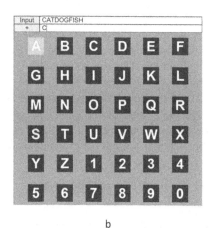

b

FIGURE 12.2   Flashing paradigms: (a) row–column paradigm with row highlighted; (b) single character paradigm.

Source: (a) Pan & Li (2011); (b) Schalk & Mellinger (2010)

positive potential (P300 peak) is seen in the subject's EEG roughly 300 ms later. This is termed as one trial of a P300 speller. A session, on the other hand, is a collection of words where each word is made up of multiple trials. The P300 amplitude is significantly high with a lower probability and a higher discriminability of targets.

12.3   RELATED WORK

The identification of the P300 peak in the EEG signal is basically a binary classification problem with "target" and "non-target" as the two classes. A review was undertaken based on the most regularly used classification algorithms and their derivatives. The most commonly used algorithms were found to be support vector machine (SVM), convolutional neural network (CNN), and linear discriminant analysis (LDA). The comparison of these approaches with respect to performance is explained in the next section.

12.3.1 LINEAR DISCRIMINANT ANALYSIS

LDA is a commonly used supervised classification method that is also used for dimensionality reduction. It allows us to divide two or more classes by projecting features from a higher dimensional space to a lower dimensional space. It was introduced to overcome the limitations of logistic regression, which is only useful for two-class classification.

Ahi et al. (2009) used various dimensionality reduction techniques like principal component analysis (PCA), channel selection, and spatial filtering and applied LDA to all of them for classification. The authors claim the accuracies are in the range of 75–100%. Chaurasiya et al. (2017) discussed the application of a P300 speller that uses an 8 × 8 matrix to display a different script i.e. Devanagari. It uses binary differential evolution (Binary DE) as the channel selection technique and LDA and stepwise SWLDA as classification models with an accuracy of 83% and 86% respectively. P300 spellers have also been developed for making smartphone user interface more intuitive (Guy et al., 2018; Kuo et al., 2018; Piña-Ramirez et al., 2018). Classification algorithms like LDA and SWLDA have been used along with feature extraction methods like PCA and stepwise regression for feature selection with accuracy ranging from 66.33% to 92.3%. LDAs have been implemented in applications that are used to assist specially abled people (Chaurasiya et al., 2016a; Cortez et al., 2021) with preprocessing methods like least absolute shrinkage and selection operator optimization and XDAWN having an accuracy of 94%. The studies using LDA have been tabulated in Table 12.2.

12.3.2 SUPPORT VECTOR MACHINE

The goal of SVM is to find a hyperplane in N-dimensional space (N—the number of characteristics) that categorizes the data points. The study (Chaurasiya et al., 2017) has made use of linear SVM and non-linear SVM (with Gaussian kernel) and has achieved accuracy of 84.72% and 89.7% respectively on BCI II dataset. The paper claims to have achieved an accuracy of 100% when it comes to target word prediction in five trials or less. It also claims that SVM is computationally cheap and light, making it suited for online applications, where the EEG signals are acquired and analyzed in real time. One such application is explored in Kuo et al. (2018); the study is carried out on three post-stroke patients, with one severe case. A prototype for smart home has been designed using a Gaussian SVM in (Cortez et al., 2021). An accuracy of 91.51% is obtained, although it uses just 16

TABLE 12.2
Studies Using LDA and Its Variants for P300 Detection

Sr. No.	Author Name	Preprocessing Method	Classification	Accuracy
1	Ahi et al. (2009)	PCA, channel selection, spatial filters	BLDA	75–100%
2	Elsawy & Eldawlatly (2015)	PCA	LDA	66.33%
3	Chaurasiya et al. (2017)	Filter 1–10 Hz, optimal channel selection using binary DE	LDA, SWLDA	83.6%, 85.9%
4	Guy et al. (2018)	Least absolute shrinkage and selection operator optimization	LDA	94%
5	Piña-Ramirez et al. (2018)	XDAWN	LDA	–
6	Martínez-Cagigal et al. (2018)	Stepwise regression (feature selection)	LDA	92.30%
7	Martínez-Cagigal et al. (n.d.)	–	SWLDA	90%

TABLE 12.3

Studies Using SVM and Its Variants for P300 Detection

Sr. No.	Author Name	Preprocessing Method	Classification	Accuracy
1	Chaurasiya et al. (2016b)	Preprocessed + normalization	SVM	linear—84.7% Gaussian—89.7%—fivefold cross validation—training 100% on testing in five trials
2	Chaurasiya et al. (2016a)	Optimized channel location—binary DE	WESVM	94.20%
3	Chaurasiya et al. (2017)	Optimized channel location—binary DE	SVM	SVM—86.8%
4	Turnip et al. (2017)	ICA; spatio-temporal features; minimum amplitude, maximum amplitude, mode amplitude, median amplitude, and mean amplitude	SVM	70.83%
5	Kundu & Ari (2018)	PCA	EWSVM	EWSVM 98% EWLDA 88% SVM and LDA 96%
6	Kuo et al. (2018)	Artificial bee colony optimization	SVM	86% before calibration and 90.25% after calibration
7	Cortez et al. (2021)	–	SVM, multi-layer perceptron (MLP)	SVM 91.51% MLP 91.79%

channels as opposed to the approach proposed in Chaurasiya et al. (2017), which uses 64 channels. This shows that SVM could be a good choice for mobile applications. In another study that involves character recognition, Chaurasiya et al. (2016a) have used PCA to reduce redundant features for feature extraction followed by an ensemble of weighted SVMs for classification. The dataset worked on is BCI Competition II and set II of BCI Competition III. Ensemble SVM (EWSVM) is employed to achieve a mean accuracy of 98%. Brain wave activity has also been used to assess whether a person is lying or telling the truth (Turnip et al., 2017), with an accuracy of 70.83 %. The study proposed the usage of independent component analysis (ICA) followed by SVM. The comparison of the different studies of SVMs for P300 detection is shown in Table 12.3.

12.3.3 CONVOLUTIONAL NEURAL NETWORK

The CNN is a supervised algorithm that has combined the feature extraction and classification tasks as one. The conventional, manually designed algorithms for classification and signal processing focus on the features known by the researcher. There are features that are important but are filtered out due to the researcher's limitations in identification and interpretation. CNNs, however, have shown the ability to identify EEG data and learn features on their own without much supervision. Another advantage is that it reduces the need for domain expertise to extract the features. In EEG, information can be found in spatial as well as temporal domains. Often, different algorithms are needed to extract these, whereas CNN has shown the ability to do both. Most studies that employ CNN have used a spatial filter followed by a temporal filter. However, Shan et al. (2018) claim that filtering in this order may result in losing important temporal features that may be present before spatial filtering. As a solution, it proposes using one convolution layer network (OCLNN) that filters both spatial and temporal features in the first layer itself. Kshirsagar and Londhe (2018) have used

TABLE 12.4

Studies Using CNN and Its Variants for P300 Detection

Sr. No.	Author Name	Preprocessing Method	Classification	Accuracy
1	Kshirsagar and Londhe (2018)	Preprocessed	DCNN	94.18%
2	Shan et al. (2018)	Raw	One convolution layer NN	92.41%
3	Li et al. (2020)	PCA	Parallel CNN—9 layers	D1 98%, D2 96%

TABLE 12.5

Studies Using CNN and Its Variants for P300 Detection

Sr. No.	Author Name	Preprocessing Method	Classification	Accuracy
1	Hoffmann et al. (2005)	Lowpass filtered between 0 and 9 Hz with a 7th order Butterworth filter and downsampled to 128 Hz	Gradient boosting in conjunction with ordinary least squares regression (OLS)	90–100%
2	Ludwig & Kong (2017)	Bandpass filtering, downsampling, winsorization, and normalization	RUSBoost, AdaBoost, and LogitBoost	62.30%, 62.25%, 61.08%
3	Sahu et al. (2020)	Feature extraction—wavelet transforms and power spectral density features	LogitBoost	71.05%

deep convolutional neural network (DCNN) for P300 detection, which can handle high dimensional and complex non-learning tasks that traditional algorithms fail to handle. This algorithm gave an accuracy of 94.18%. The results of these studies are tabulated in Table 12.4.

12.3.4 BOOSTING ALGORITHMS

Boosting is a supervised learning algorithm that reduces bias as well as variance by using the concept of re-weighting. In this concept, an ensemble of weak learners is trained iteratively and weights are re-assigned according to the results of the previous learner. This method converts these weak learners into better performing models. Since the development of AdaBoost in 1995, a lot of boosting algorithms have been developed but very few have been applied in the field of EEG. One such study, Hoffmann et al. (2005), has used a combination of gradient boosting and ordinary least squares regression for P300 detection. This method is known for its high classification accuracy and conceptual simplicity and has given accuracy in the range of 90–100%. In Ludwig and Kong (2017), various classifiers were experimented on; boosting algorithms in these experiments have been able to achieve an accuracy of 61.8% on average. Another recent study (Sahu et al., 2020) uses LogitBoost for classification, which yielded an accuracy of 71.05%. Table 12.5 summarizes the performances along with their methodology used.

12.4 PROPOSED WORK

In this study, we have focused on P300 detection, a major task in the P300 speller. This comes down to a case of binary classification—whether the signal portion (epoch) contains a P300 peak or not. In most applications of binary classification, it is observed that traditional machine learning (ML) methods and a few deep learning (DL) methods tend to overfit. Further, the DL methods are computationally expensive and take a lot of time and data to train the model. In most cases, ensemble

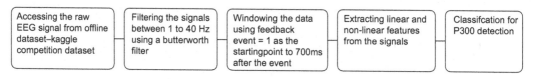

FIGURE 12.3 Proposed approach.

methods like boosting are used to minimize the overfitting while keeping the computational cost in check, thus leading to more generalized and accurate results. By using ensemble methods like boosting and overfitting, bias and the variance on data can be reduced considerably. Therefore, in this study, we have evaluated the performance of two recent boosting algorithms—CatBoost and LightGBM. Further, their performances are compared with those of popular algorithms—XGBoost and AdaBoost. Figure 12.3 describes the proposed approach that will be discussed in this section in detail.

12.4.1 Dataset

There are two modes in which BCI systems can be made to operate—online and offline. A robust BCI system should be able to execute in both modes. In offline analysis, the operation of the system is not real-time; it operates on already recorded EEG datasets.

On the other hand, online systems operate on real-time EEG data. In both modes, operations on data like preprocessing, feature extraction, and classification are performed.

The dataset used for this study is an open-source dataset from Kaggle's competition (BCI Challenge@NER 2015). The competition made available the dataset from Margaux et al. (2012). The dataset is collected from 26 healthy subjects (13 male, mean age = 28.8 ± 5.4 (SD), range 20–37), of which data from 16 subjects was used for training and the rest for testing. Fifty-six passive electrodes (passive Ag/AgCl EEG sensors) were used to record the subjects' brain activity. Signals were sampled at 600 Hz but were later downsampled to 200 Hz. The experimental setup used the international 10–20 system for the placement of electrodes. Apart from information regarding the potential in the 56 channels, information about timestamps, feedback events, and electrooculography (EOG) data (detecting eye movements) was also collected. The subjects had to undergo a total of five copy-spelling sessions. The first four sessions contained 12 five-letter words, whereas the fifth session consisted of 25-letter words. After the completion of each trial, the predicted item is shown in the middle of the screen as feedback. This feedback can be recorded and used for evaluating the performance of the online classifier.

12.4.2 Data Preparation

For the features to be extracted, the signals need to be denoised and filtered. This section talks about filtering and segmenting the signals into time-bound chunks so that further processing is easier.

12.4.2.1 Filtering the Signals

Raw EEG data encompasses a wide range of frequencies. These frequencies can be divided into bands of certain frequency ranges. Each band represents a different set of brain activities. Therefore, filtering enables the removal of unnecessary information in order to efficiently process the EEG signals. In this study, the signals have been filtered in the range of 1–40 Hz using a Butterworth filter.

12.4.2.2 Epoching the Data

The EEG recording consists of signals from target stimuli, non-target stimuli, and the time in between. For relevant data to be used for training, the window of interest (which is around 700 ms to 1000 ms post-stimuli) needs to be extracted. The proposed approach uses a 700 ms window of interest that is extracted post feedback.

12.4.3 FEATURE EXTRACTION

EEG signals are dynamic and chaotic in nature with all sorts of information embedded in them. Using these in their raw form can bring the curse of dimensionality and also the noise that the channels are vulnerable to. By feature extraction, we reduce the dimension, in turn reducing the computation time and increasing accuracy. These features are spread across domain-specific and signal-specific data. The domains are frequency and time, as well as signal properties like entropy. In this study, the performances are evaluated on the basis of two feature extraction methods. In the first method, XDAWN covariances projected in the tangent space are extracted. XDAWN is a spatial filter specially designed for P300, as proposed in Rivet et al. (2009).

The frequency domain is used to extract the ranges of frequencies present in a signal irrespective of when they occur. These ranges are usually found using fast Fourier transform (FFT). However, the features in time domain do not consider the presence of various frequencies. Both of these methods, if used individually, cause a loss of important information, because for P300, along with the frequency range and power, when the event occurs (around 300 ms after the stimuli) is also important. Considering this, the second feature extraction method uses a combination of:

1. **Statistical and Linear Features:** The mean, standard deviation, variance, and the peak-to-peak amplitude of each channel across every window was calculated.
2. **Non-Linear Features:** The features Higuchi's fractal dimension and Hurst exponent have been used to identify the signal's complexity and the range of the correlations in the given epoch. The signal's energy in each epoch is also estimated using the Shannon entropy. The time-frequency domain method that allowed us to get features in both the domains together was discrete wavelet transform (DWT).

After going through the feature extraction, the number of features is reduced from 7840 to 392 for every epoch. These features are then used for further identification of the P300 peak.

12.4.4 CLASSIFICATION ALGORITHMS

Out of the various classification algorithms available, boosting algorithms are comparatively lightweight and less complex in nature as opposed to the various neural architectures used. They have been employed in other classification problems but less so to the P300 classification problem. This study applies four boosting algorithms, namely AdaBoost, XGBoost, CatBoost, and LightGBM. These algorithms are further discussed in this section.

12.4.4.1 AdaBoost

AdaBoost, also known as adaptive boosting, is a supervised ML algorithm. It follows a decision tree model with a depth equal to one. AdaBoost reassigns weights with every iteration by putting more weight on misclassified instances and less on the correctly handled ones. This algorithm can solve classification as well as regression problems.

12.4.4.2 XGBoost

XGBoost focuses on model performance and computational speed. It consists of various weak learners arranged sequentially such that each learner corrects the error of the tree in the previous iteration. This algorithm has an option to penalize models through L1 (lasso regression) and L2 regularization (ridge regression). Regularization helps in preventing overfitting. XGBoost handles sparse data by incorporating a sparsity-aware split finding algorithm to handle different types of sparse patterns in the data.

12.4.4.3 CatBoost

CatBoost is a rather recent yet powerful machine learning algorithm that was introduced by Yandex. It can work on different types of datasets and provides very good accuracy. It is powerful since, unlike other ML models, it does not require intensive data training to yield good results. CatBoost name comes from two words "category" and "boosting". It works well with various categories of data like audio, text, image, etc. It can be used to convert categories into numbers (encoding) without any explicit preprocessing, needs less hyperparameter tuning, and has lower chances of overfitting, thus resulting in more generalized models.

12.4.4.4 LightGBM

LightGBM is a high-performance gradient boosting framework that is based on the decision tree algorithm. It is a popular ML algorithm for classification and ranking among others. Other boosting algorithms split the tree depth wise or level wise. LightGBM, however, splits the tree leaf-wise with the best fit. As we are growing on the same leaf in LightGBM, the leaf-wise algorithm reduces more loss than the level-wise algorithm. This is the reason why LightGBM yields better accuracy than previously existing boosting algorithms. Also, it is very fast, hence the word "light". Although leaf-wise splits lead to increases in complexity and may lead to overfitting, it can be overcome by specifying another parameter max-depth that specifies the depth to which splitting will occur.

12.5 RESULTS AND DISCUSSION

This section discusses the reasoning for the selection of the F1 score as a metric and then, further, the results obtained, using the proposed methodology.

12.5.1 Metric Used

Classification metrics are essential in evaluating the performance of a model. To do so, an understanding of these metrics would be imperative. The most common classification metrics are accuracy, precision, recall, and F1-score. These are discussed in the following:

1. Classification accuracy is the most common metric based on which a classification model is evaluated. It is the ratio of the total number of correct predictions made by the model to the total number of predictions made.
2. Precision gives the ratio between correctly predicted outcomes to the total number of positive predictions made by the model.
3. Recall, also called sensitivity, is the ratio of the correctly predicted outcomes with respect to the actual number of positive outcomes in the dataset.

F1-score can be mathematically defined to be the harmonic mean of precision and recall. This metric is preferably used whenever a balance between precision and recall needs to be attained.

Although in most cases, the accuracy metric is considered to be a crucial factor while comparing the efficiency of various classification models, this metric can also be pretty misleading whenever there's an imbalanced class distribution. Under such circumstances, the F1-score metric proves to be more dependable, as it is class dependent. Hence, the authors have used the F1-score of the target class as an evaluation metric.

12.5.2 Results

In this study, XDAWN covariances and a combined set of features (linear and non-linear) are used for feature extraction. Classification using XDAWN covariances have yielded F1 scores of 0.81, 0.77, and 0.84 for AdaBoost, XGBoost, and LightGBM respectively. These were evaluated with their default hyperparameters. In order to improve the metrics further, hyperparameters were tuned. There are various methods for hyperparameter tuning like randomized search, grid search, and genetic algorithms. Optuna is a framework that internally utilizes these methods to find the best possible hyperparameters. Using Optuna, F1 scores of 0.83, 0.75, 0.84, and 0.84 were obtained for AdaBoost, XGBoost, LightGBM, and CatBoost respectively. Table 12.6 represents these results on the BCI NER dataset with XDAWN covariances as the only features used. In Figure 12.4, a comparison of F1 scores obtained using boosting with XDAWN covariances as features is provided.

The same approach was applied to classification using the combined set of features, and the results can be seen in Table 12.7. The results obtained without hyperparameter tuning were 0.80,

TABLE 12.6
Results of Boosting with XDAWN Covariances as Feature Used

Sr. No	Model Applied	Hyperparameter Tuning	Accuracy	Precision	Recall	F1 Score
1	AdaBoost	None	0.72	0.78	0.84	0.81
2	AdaBoost	Optuna	0.72	0.72	0.99	0.83
3	XGBoost	None	0.69	0.81	0.72	0.77
4	XGBoost	Optuna	0.66	0.8	0.7	0.75
5	LightGBM	None	0.75	0.77	0.93	0.84
6	LightGBM	Optuna	0.76	0.77	0.93	0.84
7	CatBoost	Optuna	0.75	0.77	0.93	0.84

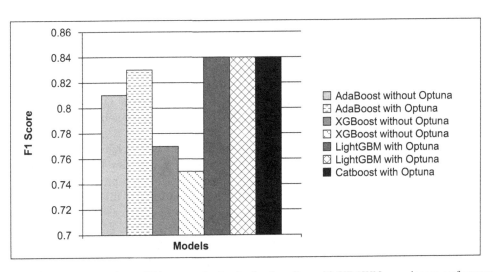

FIGURE 12.4   A comparison of F1 scores obtained using boosting with XDAWN covariances as features.

TABLE 12.7

Results of Boosting with a Combination of Linear and Non-Linear Features

Sr. No	Model	Hyper-parameter Tuning	Accuracy	Precision	Recall	F1 Score
1	XGBoost	None	0.62	0.74	0.72	0.73
2	AdaBoost	None	0.68	0.72	0.9	0.8
3	AdaBoost	Optuna	0.71	0.71	1	0.83
4	LightGBM	None	0.69	0.71	0.95	0.81
5	LightGBM	Optuna	0.71	0.72	0.97	0.83
6	CatBoost	Optuna	0.7	0.71	0.98	0.82

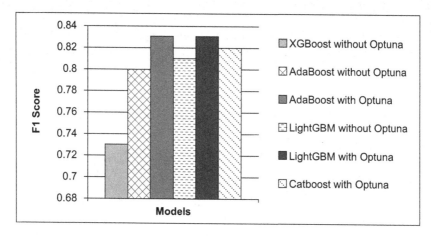

FIGURE 12.5 Comparison of F1 scores obtained using boosting with a combination of linear and non-linear features.

0.73, and 0.81 for AdaBoost, XGBoost, and LightGBM respectively and with hyperparameter tuning 0.83, 0.83, and 0.82 for AdaBoost, LightGBM, and CatBoost respectively. Thus, it can be observed that although both feature extraction approaches give a fairly comparable result, the best set of accuracy, precision, recall, and F1-score values are achieved by the combination of XDAWN for feature extraction followed by LightGBM with hyperparameter tuning using the Optuna framework. In Figure 12.5, a comparison of F1 scores obtained using boosting with a combination of linear and non-linear features is provided.

When compared to prior studies that have used complicated CNN architectures, our approach takes less time to train and is less expensive computationally, yet provides an AUC of 0.74. Whereas in EEGNET (Lawhern et al., 2018), a CNN-based model is proposed, it provides an AUC score of 0.738 when averaged over thirty-fold on the same dataset utilized in this study. In EEGNAS (Rapaport et al., 2019), neural architecture search is utilized in conjunction with genetic algorithms. Training the neural network takes roughly 34 hours, yet the AUC is only 67.3. Further, the AUC obtained by this study ranks in the top ten when compared with the results of the Kaggle competition leader board. The results obtained by the authors as compared to earlier methodologies are shown in Figure 12.6.

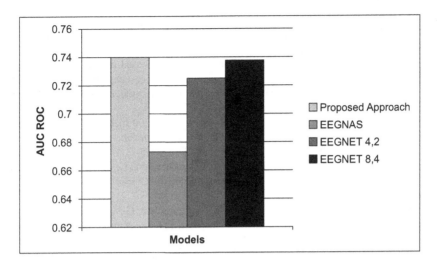

FIGURE 12.6   Results in comparison with previous studies.

12.6   CONCLUSION AND FUTURE SCOPE

P300 spellers have the potential to make quite an impact on a person's life. An important task in the making of P300 spellers is to detect the P300 peak. In this study, an investigation of the performances of four boosting algorithms—AdaBoost, XGBoost, LightGBM, and CatBoost—for the task of detection of the P300 peak is conducted. LightGBM and CatBoost are recent developments in boosting algorithms that have improved the performances of classifiers in other fields but have not yet been evaluated on EEG classification problems. In this study, these classifiers have been also compared on the basis of the features extracted. These feature extraction methods used XDAWN, a spatial filter specially designed for P300 and a combination of linear and non-linear features. It was observed that the best metric to identify this classification problem was the F1 score as it made sure that the tradeoff between precision and recall is maintained. Finally, using this approach, an F1 score of 0.84 is obtained using XDAWN covariances as the only feature and LightGBM for the classifier.

EEG signals contain a plethora of information, and various methods to extract more meaning to interpret brain activity can be further employed. Some of them involve channel selection. Some signals consist of unnecessary artifacts like muscle movements that reduce the efficiency of the model. Hence, instead of using data from all the channels, only those channels that have more P300 prominence can be selected. Other methods involve employing a different set of features and understanding the feature importance to improve the model's results.

REFERENCES

Ahi, S. T., Kambara, H., & Koike, Y. (2009). A comparison of dimensionality reduction techniques for the P300 response. *I-CREATe 2009 — International Convention on Rehabilitation Engineering and Assistive Technology*, https://doi.org/10.1145/1592700.1592732.

Ammar, H., & Taileb, M. (2017). SmileToPhone: A mobile phone system for quadriplegic users controlled by EEG signals. *International Journal of Advanced Computer Science and Applications*, 8(5). https://doi.org/10.14569/ijacsa.2017.080566

Campbell, A., Choudhury, T., Hu, S., Lu, H., Mukerjee, M. K., Rabbi, M., & Raizada, R. D. S. (2010). NeuroPhone: Brain-mobile phone interface using a wireless EEG headset. *Proceedings of the 2nd ACM SIGCOMM Workshop on Networking, Systems, and Applications on Mobile Handhelds, MobiHeld '10, Co-Located with SIGCOMM 2010*, 3–8. https://doi.org/10.1145/1851322.1851326

Cattan, G., Andreev, A., Mendoza, C., & Congedo, M. (2020). A comparison of mobile VR display running on an ordinary smartphone with standard PC display for P300-BCI stimulus presentation. *ArXiv*, 1502(c). https://doi.org/10.1109/tg.2019.2957963

Chaurasiya, R. K., Londhe, N. D., & Ghosh, S. (2016a). Binary DE-based channel selection and weighted ensemble of SVM classification for novel brain—computer interface using Devanagari script-based P300 speller paradigm. *International Journal of Human-Computer Interaction*, 32(11), 861–877. https://doi.org/10.1080/10447318.2016.1203047

Chaurasiya, R. K., Londhe, N. D., & Ghosh, S. (2016b). An efficient P300 speller system for Brain-Computer Interface. *Proceedings of 2015 International Conference on Signal Processing, Computing and Control*, ISPCC 2015, 57–62. https://doi.org/10.1109/ISPCC.2015.7374998

Chaurasiya, R., Londhe, N., & Ghosh, S. (2017). Comparison of Machine Learning Methods for Devanagari Script-based P300 Speller System. *International Journal of Control Theory and Applications*, 9, 477–485.

Cisotto, G., Trentini, A., Zoppis, I., Zanga, A., Manzoni, S., Pietrabissa, G., Usubini, A. G., & Castelnuovo, G. (2021). *ACTA: A Mobile-Health Solution for Integrated Nudge-Neurofeedback Training for Senior Citizens*. Retrieved from http://arxiv.org/abs/2102.08692.

Cortez, S. A., Flores, C., & Andreu-Perez, J. (2021). A smart home control prototype using a P300-based brain—computer interface for post-stroke patients. *Smart Innovation, Systems and Technologies*, 202, 131–139. https://doi.org/10.1007/978-3-030-57566-3_13

Donchin, E., Spencer, K. M., & Wijesinghe, R. (2000). The mental prosthesis: Assessing the speed of a P300-based brain-computer interface. *IEEE Transactions on Rehabilitation Engineering*, 8(2), 174–179. https://doi.org/10.1109/86.847808

Elsawy, A. S., Eldawlatly, S., Taher, M., & Aly, G. M. (2017). MindEdit: A P300-based text editor for mobile devices. *Computers in Biology and Medicine*, 80(August 2016), 97–106. https://doi.org/10.1016/j.compbiomed.2016.11.014

Guy, V., Soriani, M. H., Bruno, M., Papadopoulo, T., Desnuelle, C., & Clerc, M. (2018). Brain computer interface with the P300 speller: Usability for disabled people with amyotrophic lateral sclerosis. *Annals of Physical and Rehabilitation Medicine*, 61(1), 5–11. https://doi.org/10.1016/j.rehab.2017.09.004

Hawking's Spelling Device and P300 | by Brainmab | Medium. (n.d.). Retrieved June 24, 2021, from https://medium.com/@AliOztas/hawkings-spelling-device-and-p300-3d7693e693d2.

Hoffmann, U., Garcia, G., Vesin, J. M., Diserenst, K., & Ebrahimi, T. (2005). A boosting approach to P300 detection with application to brain-computer interfaces. *2nd International IEEE EMBS Conference on Neural Engineering*, 2005, 97–100. https://doi.org/10.1109/CNE.2005.1419562

Klem, G., Lüders, H., Jasper, H., & Elger, C. (1999). The ten-twenty electrode system of the International Federation. The International Federation of Clinical Neurophysiology. *Electroencephalography and Clinical Neurophysiology. Supplement*, 52, 3–6.

Kshirsagar, G. B., & Londhe, N. D. (2018). Deep convolutional neural network based character detection in Devanagari script input based P300 speller. *International Conference on Electrical, Electronics, Communication Computer Technologies and Optimization Techniques*, ICEECCOT 2017, 2018-January, 507–511. https://doi.org/10.1109/ICEECCOT.2017.8284557

Kundu, S., & Ari, S. (2018). P300 Detection with brain–computer interface application using PCA and ensemble of weighted SVMs. *IETE Journal of Research*, 64(3), 406–414. https://doi.org/10.1080/03772063.2017.1355271

Kuo, C. H., Chen, H. H., Chou, H. C., Chen, P. N., & Kuo, Y. C. (2018). Wireless stimulus-on-device design for novel P300 hybrid brain-computer interface applications. *Computational Intelligence and Neuroscience*, 2018. https://doi.org/10.1155/2018/2301804

Lawhern, V. J., Solon, A. J., Waytowich, N. R., Gordon, S. M., Hung, C. P., & Lance, B. J. (2018). EEGNet: A compact convolutional neural network for EEG-based brain-computer interfaces. *Journal of Neural Engineering*, 15(5). https://doi.org/10.1088/1741-2552/aace8c

Li, F., Li, X., Wang, F., Zhang, D., Xia, Y., & He, F. (2020). A novel P300 classification algorithm based on a principal component analysis-convolutional neural network. *Applied Sciences (Switzerland)*, 10(4), 1–15. https://doi.org/10.3390/app10041546

Ludwig, S. A., & Kong, J. (2017). Investigation of different classifiers and channel configurations of a mobile P300-based brain—computer interface. *Medical and Biological Engineering and Computing*, 55(12), 2143–2154. https://doi.org/10.1007/s11517-017-1658-2

Margaux, P., Emmanuel, M., Sébastien, D., Olivier, B., & Jérémie, M. (2012). Objective and subjective evaluation of online error correction during P300-based spelling. *Advances in Human-Computer Interaction*, 2012. https://doi.org/10.1155/2012/578295

Pan, J., & Li, Y. (2011). *A comparison of P300-speller stimuli presentation paradigms for Brain-computer interface.*

Piña-Ramirez, O., Valdes-Cristerna, R., & Yanez-Suarez, O. (2018). Scenario screen: A dynamic and context dependent P300 stimulator screen aimed at wheelchair navigation control. *Computational and Mathematical Methods in Medicine*, 2018. https://doi.org/10.1155/2018/7108906

Rapaport, E., Shriki, O., & Puzis, R. (2019). *EEGNAS: Neural architecture search for electroencephalography data analysis and decoding.*

Rebsamen, B., Burdet, E., Zeng, Q., Zhang, H., Ang, M., Teo, C. L., Guan, C., & Laugier, C. (2008). Hybrid P300 and mu-beta brain computer interface to operate a brain controlled wheelchair. *I-CREATe 2008 — International Convention on Rehabilitation Engineering and Assistive Technology 2008*, 51–55.

Rivet, B., Souloumiac, A., Attina, V., & Gibert, G. (2009). xDAWN Algorithm to Enhance Evoked Potentials: Application to Brain-Computer Interface. *IEEE Transactions on Biomedical Engineering*, 56(8), 2035–2043. https://doi.org/10.1109/TBME.2009.2012869

Sahu, M., Verma, S., Nagwani, N. K., & Shukla, S. (2020). EEG signal analysis and classification on P300 speller-based BCI performance in ALS patients. *International Journal of Medical Engineering and Informatics*, 12(4), 375–400. https://doi.org/10.1504/ijmei.2020.108240

Schalk, G., & Mellinger, J. (2010). A practical guide to brain-computer interfacing with BCI2000: General-purpose software for brain-computer interface research, data acquisition, stimulus presentation, and brain monitoring. In *A Practical Guide to Brain-Computer Interfacing with BCI2000: General-Purpose Software for Brain-Computer Interface Research, Data Acquisition, Stimulus Presentation, and Brain Monitoring*. Springer, London. https://doi.org/10.1007/978-1-84996-092-2

Shan, H., Liu, Y., & Stefanov, T. (2018). A simple convolutional neural network for accurate P300 detection and character spelling in brain computer interface. *IJCAI International Joint Conference on Artificial Intelligence*, 2018-July, 1604–1610. https://doi.org/10.24963/ijcai.2018/222

Shivappa, V. K. K., Luu, B., Solis, M., & George, K. (2018). Home automation system using brain computer interface paradigm based on auditory selection attention. *I2MTC 2018–2018 IEEE International Instrumentation and Measurement Technology Conference: Discovering New Horizons in Instrumentation and Measurement, Proceedings*, 1–6. https://doi.org/10.1109/I2MTC.2018.8409863

Singla, R. (2018). SSVEP-Based BCIs. *Evolving BCI therapy—Engaging brain state dynamics.* https://doi.org/10.5772/intechopen.75693

Turnip, A., Amri, M. F., Fakrurroja, H., Simbolon, A. I., Suhendra, M. A., & Kusumandari, D. E. (2017). Deception detection of EEG-P300 component classified by SVM method. *ACM International Conference Proceeding Series*, 299–303. https://doi.org/10.1145/3056662.3056709

13 Comprehensive Study of Brain–Computer Interface (BCI) with Emphasis on Strategies Used for Processing the Signals

Vrushali Ganesh Raut, Pranoti P. Mane, and Supriya O. Rajankar

CONTENTS

13.1 INTRODUCTION

Electrical signals corresponding to neural activities—which can be used for conveying a human's intent to a machine, leading to a strong interface between brain and computer—can be considered as disruptive developments in biomedical applications." Electroencephalography (EEG) collects signals from electrodes placed on a subject's scalp, acting as the efficient input for the brain–computer interface (BCI). These time-series signals, collected non-invasively by multiple electrodes from the region of interest, are weak in amplitude and experience interference from neighboring signal sources. Signal processing methodologies play a prominent role in processing the signal and making them capable for analyzing and detecting intent behind them.

BCI is a developing field, as it is evolving on almost all fronts, including input signals and the number of control signals derived from them, the method for acquiring the signals, signal processing

DOI: 10.1201/9781003272694-16

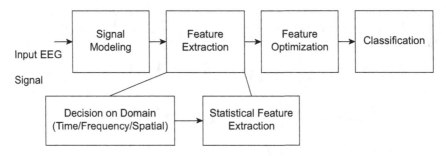

FIGURE 13.1 Signal processing requirement of brain–computer interface (BCI).

methodologies used, etc. Keeping the signal processing methodologies for non-invasive spontaneous BCI systems in consideration, this chapter carries out an exhaustive literature survey to throw light on different types of BCI systems, different available brain signals that can be used as inputs, various promising algorithms for artifact removal and modeling the signal and extracting the relevant features and classifying their underlying activity. This study follows the guidelines and framework given by Mason and Birch [1] regarding signal processing requirements (see Figure 13.1); this includes classification of BCI systems, comparative study of available inputs and resulting BCI performance, and thorough analysis of signal processing methodologies used in BCI. Concluding remarks on the research gaps found, given at every stage in this chapter, are helpful in judging the methodology used while giving thought to modifying the method.

13.2 CLASSIFICATIONS OF BCI SYSTEM

Systems developed for BCI are classified based on the type of input signal and the mechanism for generating those signals, which leads to dependent and independent BCI. The second classification gives synchronous BCI, working in the specific time slot, or asynchronous BCI, accepting and analyzing input signals over time. The third category is based on whether the method of collecting the signals is invasive/operative or non-invasive. These methods, along with their pros and cons, are described below.

13.2.1 Dependent and Independent BCI Systems

In dependent BCI systems, brain activity needs external stimuli (for evoking) and hence control of respective muscles in order to acquire those stimuli. The external stimulus required for SSVEP classifies a BCI system using SSVEP as a dependent BCI [2][3]. The subject has to gaze at a particular stimulus to generate the signal. Electrodes placed on the visual cortex of the brain capture this signal; signals collected from the occipital region of the brain gives maximum amplitude. Visually evoked potential is modulated on a frequency in the 5–20 Hz range [4]. A BCI system built using SSVEP provides comparatively higher ITR, while the training of the subject for generating the signal is minimal [5]. Gazing at the infrequent event gives a signal called P300, which can be collected from the parietal cortex of the brain approximately 300 ms after the event and used to make a dependent BCI system. In other words, P300 is generated 300 ms after the subject waiting for a particular stimulus positively got that stimulus [7]. Hybrid BCI incorporating both SSVEP and P300 signals are found to be promising solutions providing more control signals, speedy operation, and higher information transfer rates [8].

An independent BCI does not need any external stimulus to generate neural activity, and hence it is not dependent on any muscular organ to perceive it. The neural activities like motor imagery (MI) can be generated independently by just thinking about motor movement such as hand movement or leg movement etc. Systems using sensorimotor or MI signals are independent BCIs [9]. The hybrid method was tested for real-time control of wheelchair and was used to produce a binary command, "go/stop" [10].

13.2.2 SYNCHRONOUS AND ASYNCHRONOUS BCI SYSTEMS

Synchronous BCI system operates during a specific slot of time; the slot includes the onset, offset, and duration of the operation. More specifically, the system remains active during a specific period. It can also be referred to as cue-paced BCI [11]. Applications such as gaming can be developed using synchronous control. In such applications, the time slot or time period can be provided by a system in which the user can complete the control task, after which the system will initiate a new slot for the next control task [12].

In asynchronous BCI, the subject can any time perform the mental tasks, and the system will capture and react to it. Other states of the subject, such as rest and idle state, can also be detected by an asynchronous system [13]. The system has to remain active at all times to watch the signals coming from the user in order to respond. It increases the complexity of the system at the level of synchronization [14][15]. Hybrid BCIs using SSVEP and P300 in combination are also implemented in asynchronous mode [13].

13.2.3 INVASIVE AND NON-INVASIVE BCI

The implants directly placed on the part of the brain through invasive surgery extract the signals in invasive BCI. The limited region of the brain can be covered in this type as the surgical procedure is required to place the microelectrodes, and it cannot be moved to other parts of the brain [16]. The signals obtained by this system are strong, with minimal neighboring interferences, and is referred to as electrocorticography (ECoG). Major clinical risk and considerable technical difficulties are two major disadvantages of invasive BCI [17]

In non-invasive BCI, the signals are collected by mounting non-invasive electrodes on the scalp of the subject, referred to as electroencephalography (EEG) [18]. The obtained signals are noisy and weak, but the simple way of capturing the signals through placing the electrodes on any part of the brain makes this method popular for the research [19]. The signals collected in this manner carry interference from not only the neighboring EEG signals but also other electrophysiological signals like electrocardiogram (ECG) and electromyogram (EMG).

13.3 BRAIN SIGNALS FOR NON-INVASIVE BCI

Brain signals used in non-invasive BCI can be categorized as two types: evoked potential and spontaneous signals. Evoked potentials are further classified into SSVEP and P300, while SCP and SMR come under the category of spontaneous signals. The abovementioned signals are elaborated next.

P300 Evoked Potential: P300 is the potential variation captured from the occipital and parietal part of the brain, occurring approximately 300 ms after facing the surprising stimulus in the form of some event. It is a signal with a positive-going cycle, increasing the amplitude after paying attention to the particular event. The method for generating P300 generally uses a visual pathway with a rapidly and pseudo-randomly blinking LED character matrix. The potential will be evoked when the LED of the intended character glows. BCI is trained to detect the desired character, and accordingly, the control action will take place. The oddball paradigm is used to generate P300. The paradigm means producing the response to the column or row containing the planned character, and the response is different for the other combinations of row and columns [20][21]. Dochin et al. introduce the most commonly used paradigm for spelling application of event-related potential-based (ERP) BCI [22].

Reviewing the literature on P300 from a performance parameter point of view, it has been found that the system proposed by M. Chang et al. [23] gave five distinguishing control signals corresponding five different events with classification accuracy (CA) of 95%. In another approach by R. J. O. Naser Hamdi et al., six control signals were achieved with CA of 98.75% [24].

Steady-State Visual Evoked Potentials: Stimulus in the form of a visual event evoked the potential, which can be collected from the occipital cortex and is called steady-state visual evoked potential (SSVEP) [25]. The potential generated on the brain cortex has the same fundamental frequency as that of the stimulus [26][27]. These signals lie in the frequency band from 5 Hz to 60 Hz, a wideband frequency that can cover the number of control signals [28]. The muscular pathway controlling the vision to gaze at the target must be intact for generating SSVEP. Thus, it cannot be used for patients with advanced and severe neurological disorders. The lower training requirement for a BCI system using SSVEP increases its use and also provides a relatively higher information transfer rate (ITR) [29]. Summing up the advantages of BCI based on SSVEP: it offers high signal to noise ratio (S/N), high ITR [8], fewer artifacts related to eye movements and eye blink [9] and artifacts due to electromyography (EMG) signals [10], and, most importantly, is that less training is required [30][31][32][33].

To review the work on SSVEP: J. Pan et al. propose asynchronous BCI offering four control signals with 96% classification accuracy (CA) [4]. The optimized system suggested by H. Bakardjian et al. provides eight control signals and 98% CA with decent ITR of 50 bits/min [34]. P. Poryzala et al. offer the robust detection of signals with four control signals and 94% CA with ITR of 43 bits/min [35]. The system suggested by Y. Zhang et al. reaches a CA of 96% with four control signals and ITR of 50 bits/min [36]. The high speed BCI proposed by X. Chen et al. gave 40 control signals with ITR of 151 bits/min [37].

Slow Cortical Potential (SCP): SCPs are the signals collected from the brain cortex with a frequency shift occurring for 0.5–10 s. The negative trend in the SCP has an association with movements, whereas the positive trend in SCP is due to reduced cortical activation. SCP was used for necessary communication in people with late ametropic lateral sclerosis (ALS) [38]. Training is required for the users of the SCP-based BCI for modulating their SCP. Thus, it can be stated that a long training period and attention of professionals is a requirement of SCP-based BCI [39][40][41]. An SCP-based spelling device for paralyzed patients by N. Birbaumer et al. offers 75% CA and two control signals [42]. H. Bin Zhao et al. suggested a BCI with 89% CA and two control signals [5]. An SCP-based thought translation device by N. Birbaumer et al. offers 75% CA and two controls signals [43].

Sensorimotor Rhythms (SMR): Electrodes placed on the motor cortical and somatosensory regions can be used for extracting SMR with contralateral variations in the μ band ranging from 8 to 13 Hz and ipsilateral enhancement in the β band ranging from 18 to 26 Hz. Imagination or execution of motor movement decreases the amplitude of the signal in μ band, which is referred to as event-related desynchronization (ERD); in the β band, the signal indicates synchronization with the movement referred to as the event-related synchronization (ERS) band [44,45]. SMR is a beneficial control signal for persons with muscular disorders, as it helps in driving the systems performing motor activities [46]. Applications developed using SMR include prosthesis movement, driving a wheelchair, cursor control, and robot control [17]. Electrodes placed on the parietal and central part of the brain covering the motor cortex capture the distinction due to MI [47][48]. The SMR can be placed in the category of independent BCI as no external (e.g., visual) stimuli is required [49], resulting in effective communication for different MI [50][51]. Hence, the MI-based BCI suggests a promising alternative for the rehabilitation of the stroke patient [52].

Papers by Yousef Rezaei Tabar and Ugur Halici [53], proposes improved classification method for MI based BCI. Tao Wang et al. [54] uses a spatial approach for MI separation with CA of 80%. Miguel Almonacid et al. [55] offer improvement in CA for 2-class BCI. Boris Medina-Salgado et al. [56] propose 98% CA for 2-class BCI.

13.3.1 Input Signal Selection

The evoked potentials, particularly SSVEP and P300, due to its dependency on the external stimulus, can be used in the BCI where the subject is in a position to gaze at potential-evoking mechanism; this will lead to dependent BCI. BCI using SSVEP and P300 needs less training time and has a good information transfer rate (ITR). The remaining choices are SCP and MI; MI provides many variations in the signals corresponding to various movements, like hand movement, leg movement, etc., hence providing more control signals to the BCI. The subject has to be trained for generating MI variations.

13.4 SIGNAL PROCESSING STRATEGIES

EEG signals acquired from the scalp of the subject are very weak and have distortion and noise. After acquiring the input signals, the most critical part of BCI that follows is signal processing. Signal processing has to rebuild the source-specific signal, extract the features representing the task, and finally classify the task. Due to these requirements, major blocks of signal processing used are pre-processing of the signal or signal modeling, feature extraction, and task classification.

Signal spread in time, frequency, or spatial domain, its amplitude variations, frequency band covered by the signal—all these points play very important roles while selecting the signal processing strategy. The literature helps to peep into the methods used and justification provided to resolve for the techniques to be used. This chapter, in narrowing down on motor imagery signals, tries to explore the literature for different signal processing methods used for MI-based BCI. Signal processing as covered in this chapter is basically divided into signal modeling or signal pre-processing, which will rebuild the source-specific signal. Methodologies extracting the task-specific features are covered under feature extraction strategies, whereas linear and non-linear algorithms used for classification of the task from the extracted features are covered in classification methods.

13.4.1 Signal Modeling Methods

EEG signals are volume conducted as originated by the brain source; they have to cross the skull in between to reach to the capturing electrodes, leading to interference from neighboring signals as well as signals like ECG and EMG. Hence, signal modeling plays a significant role in EEG signals used for diagnostic purposes or for BCI. Various signal modeling methods from the literature are explored and their influence on system performance are tabulated in Table 13.1, and every method is analyzed further in what follows.

As mentioned in Table 13.1, Ran Xiao and Lei Ding propose temporal filtering using bandpass, notch filter, and spatial filtering by CAR. Signal modeling explores the time, frequency, and spatial domains for processing the signal. It claims the boosting of signal to noise ratio [46]. Kip A. Ludwig et al. use CAR and indicate the effect on boost in the performance is increased by 30% [57]. Adaptive CAR proposed by Liu Xinyu et al. works on the principle of adaptive noise cancellation by considering the common interfering noise and indicates excellent performance in low SNR compared to other artifact removal methods and the CAR method [58]. An experimental study by Herbert Ramoser et al. suggests the comparative analysis of small and large laplacian and CAR, concluding on the satisfactory performance using large laplacian [59].

Laplacian implementation using a 28-electrode array suggested by S. Syam et al. outperforms the CAR method, indicating the trend changing from average referencing to laplacian [60]. The paper by Jürgen Kayser and Craig Tenke emphasizes the use of SL as it effectively reduces interference of reference and adverse effect of volume conduction. It also clarifies the taboos surrounding the mathematical complexities of SL and the requirement of the electrode array for the SL [61]. The work presented by Claudio Carvalhaes et al. reviewed SL implementation by the finite difference method, highlighting its simplicity and computational cost and disadvantage of proneness to error

TABLE 13.1

Signal Modeling Methods Used in BCI Design and Its Effect on Performance

Signal Modeling Method	Concluding Remark
Temporal filtering and spatial filtering using common average referencing (CAR) [46]	Increases signal to noise ratio.
Common average referencing (CAR) [57]	CAR reduces noise by 30%, increasing the yield by 60%.
Adaptive common average referencing (ACAR) [58]	ACAR performs better compared to other artifact removal techniques and the standard CAR method.
Small laplacian, large laplacian, bipolar, and CAR [59]	Comparative study of referencing methods.
Laplacian and CAR [60]	The CA indicates the outperformance of laplacian filter over CAR.
Surface laplacian (SL) [61]	Interpolation of spherical spline is used to obtain the evaluations of radial current on the scalp.
SL [62]	Reviews the method of finite difference and splines interpolation and gives the mathematical modeling for it.
SL [63]	SL as a reference-free representation of the signal, without assumptions about functional brain anatomy and conductivity by tissue.
Spline estimate for SL [64]	Euclidian metric used for estimating the spline framework.
Editorial on SL [65]	Benefits of using SL for representing the source-specific EEG signal.
SL [66]	Accurate estimate of EEG signal for below-lying brain source.
ICA [67]	Helpful in separating original data and artifact.
Frequency band filtering, scaling the channels, selection of channel, spatial filtering, decomposition of frequency, and postprocessing [68]	Comparison of the methods, concluding on dataset-wise conscious selection of the methods.
CSP for pre-processing [69]	The discriminating spatial patterns are detected, sensitive to outliers.
Principal component analysis (PCA) used before ICA for signal analysis [70]	Decrease in the numbers of equivalent independent components (ICs) and thus not preferred before ICA.
ICA and SL [71]	Flexible spherical spline obtained in SL removes EMG, and ICA removes the EMG due to local muscles.

due to discretization. It elaborates spline implementation of SL as the regularization mechanism reducing the spatial noise, with comparatively increased mathematical and computational complexity [62]. Catching onto the trend of SL, the editorial by Jürgen Kayser and Craig Tenke gives its benefits of representing the underlying radial current source, which is the reference-free estimate of the neural source. The distinct topography of the SL estimate reduces the undesirable impact of volume conduction, and SL does not need any assumptions related to brain anatomy, tissue connectivity, and geometry of head [63]. A paper by Carvalhaes et al. proposes the spline framework for estimating the SL and demonstrated it [64]. J. Kayser et al. propose a contrast-enhancing effect of SL [66]. Surveying other trends of signal modeling/pre-processing, Izabela Reje proposes the use of ICA for pre-processing and measures its positive effect on system performance [67]. Paul S. Hammon and Virginia R. propose comparative analysis of pre-processing sets for different datasets and conclude with a careful selection of the steps for pre-processing [68]. Xinyi Yong et al. suggested robust CSP for pre-processing purposes of affecting positively on the performance [69]. Fiorenzo Artoni et al. suggested that PCA used for dimension reduction adversely affects the stability of following ICs used for decomposing the EEG data [70]. The SL of the EEG using a flexible spline for representing source-specific signals when combined with ICA claims to remove the EMG due to local muscles; this concept was proposed by S. Fitzgibbon et al. [71]. Analysis of the literature survey for signal modeling is discussed next.

13.4.2 ANALYSIS AND DISCUSSION ON THE RESEARCH GAP IN THE SIGNAL MODELING

The basic methods of signal modeling, such as filtering for noise removal and other methods like PCA and CSP, are used for EEG pre-processing but are not reported to enhance system performance. EEG being contaminated by its reference is found to be of concern along with artifacts from neighboring electrodes and other electrophysiological signals. Methods like average referencing and CAR are trying to normalize this interference, but are not able to completely remove it. SL emerges as the mathematical tool offering the reference-free EEG signal, and it also represents the source-specific signal removing interference due to the volume conduction. Spherical spline implementation of SL is further modifying the SL for accurate signal representation considering the spherical shape of the scalp. The research, though, highlights the advantages of SL, in that it does not show its effect on performance parameters and even does not elaborate on the number of electrodes required for SL transform; this research gap is addressed in this chapter.

13.4.3 FEATURE CONSTRUCTION AND EXTRACTION FOR MI

ERD and ERS are the variations reported in EEG signals due to MI, and they have spatial spread on the neighboring electrodes. ERD is event-related and short-lasting attenuations that are circumscribed and cover the μ band and lower β band. It starts with the activity planning stage and lasts until the onset of the movement. Enhancement in amplitude corresponding to motor movement is called the ERS. ERD can be collected from electrodes placed on the contralateral side, whereas ERS stems from the ipsilateral side of the brain [72].

ERD and ERS having spread in time, frequency, and spatial domain help to form the distinguishable features of MI. It poses a challenge for the feature extraction method to collect the motor movement-related variations. The feature extraction methods used in the literature are thus time-domain methods, frequency domain methods, spatial domain methods, or a combination thereof. The literature review presented in Table 13.2 examines the methods utilizing different domains based on performance reported.

TABLE 13.2
Literature Survey of Feature Extraction Methods and Its Effect on Performance

Method	Domain	Remark
Spectral representation using PSD techniques, atomic decompositions, energy distributions in t-f domain; CWT and DWT are the feature extraction approaches used [73].	Time-frequency	Band power features of MI are used for classification. PSD proves to be a superior robust approach.
Wavelet transform (WT) used to extract features.	Time-frequency	Change in non-stationary signal like EEG is detected using wavelet entropy (WE) and the relative value of WE (RWE) using localization characteristics of wavelet [74].
Appropriate time window and frequency band selected by using time-frequency (TF) [75].	Time-frequency	80% average and maximum 84.44% CA was achieved when tested on four subjects.

(Continued)

TABLE 13.2
(Continued)

Method	Domain	Remark
Relative wavelet energy calculated for detailed and approximate coefficients by applying DWT on EEG signals [76].	Time-frequency	98% CA is achieved. Classifiers used are SVM, K-nearest neighbor and multi-layer perceptron.
MI discriminations identified using CWT [77].	Time-frequency	Bayes linear discriminant analysis (LDA) used as classifier. 16.96% improvement in accuracy compared to FFT features.
MI features are represented by wavelet coefficients and autoregressive parameter [78].	Time-frequency	2-class MI classified using LDA with an error rate less than 10%.
Optimal WP decomposition for feature extraction [79].	Time-frequency	Fuzzy sets of features are created to represent the distinguishing features.
Brain rhythm represented by spectral band of interest using WT [56].	Time-frequency	98.44% CA obtained using K-NN and SVM.
3-class MI represented by wavelet coefficients [80].	Time-frequency	SVM and RBFN classify the features to give 99% accuracy.
Instantaneous power frequency band used as the features [81].	Time-frequency	CA of 90% during training and 77% for testing.
One-dimensional cursor control for the BCI using the spread of features in three domains [82].	Time-frequency-spatial	Obtained accuracy of 91.1% for two subjects under study.
Time-frequency synthesized spatial patterns [83].	Time-frequency-spatial	The instantaneous power of frequency bands represented by the envelope of oscillatory activity decides the features giving 80% accuracy.
Time-frequency based discriminative spatial filter [84].	Time-frequency-spatial	Non-homogenous spatial filter outdoes other competitive methods.
Spatial filter using array of electrodes for extracting discriminatory information representing the two populations [59].	Spatial	CA obtained for three subjects is 90.8%, 92.7%, and 99.7%.
Regularization and aggregation technique proposed for spatial pattern [44].	Spatial	Outperform the results obtained on the same dataset using other methods.
Methods used for constructing spatial filters are state-to-state and zero-training [85].	Spatial	Increases practicality of BCI.
Probabilistic CSP (P-CSP) is used for generic modeling of EEG [86].	Spatial	Demonstration of practical efficacy is done by successful applications to single-trial classifications of three MI EEG datasets.
Algorithm optimizing the CSP by considering subject-specific frequency band [87].	Spatial	Nave Bayesian Parzen window (NBPW) classifier gives 90.3% accuracy on spatial features.
The performance comparison of four methods for feature extraction [88].		Power Spectral Density based features gives higher CA compared to PLV based features. LDA with five-fold cross-validation used.
Analysis based on bi-spectrum to extract multiple high order spectra features of EEG [89].	C3, C4 electrodes	Two MI tasks distinguished with an accuracy of $90 \pm 4.71\%$.

The methods used for feature extraction are basically divided into the categories time-frequency, time-frequency-spatial, and spatial domain method, discussed next.

13.4.3.1   Time-Frequency Domain Method

Pawel Herman et al. proposed identification of MI patterns in frequency bands; power spectral density was found to be the efficient method [73]. WE and the relative wavelet entropy (RWE) computed from the wavelet bands are used for capturing the dynamics of the EEG signals by Osvaldo A. Rosso et al. [74]. Dipole analysis utilized for finding the difference between two movements, an idea proposed by Baharan Kamousi et al. [75]. Relative wavelet energy calculated from detailed and approximate coefficients, suggested by H. U. Amin et al., are used as features for classification of motor tasks [76]. The subject's own EEG signal is used as a mother wavelet for wavelet decomposition to give features [77] as proposed by W.-L. Yeh et al. B.-G. Xu et al. use the wavelet coefficients and autoregressive parameters as the features for classification [78]. The wavelet packet transform is also used for feature representation, and fuzzy discriminating features are represented with help of fuzzy sets [79]. Statistical representation of wavelet coefficients such as relative energy, variance, and standard deviation are used as the features for representing MI leading to good performance [56]. Wavelet coefficients are directly used as the features leading to good CA for 3-class BCI [80].

13.4.3.2   Time-Frequency Spatial (T-F-S) Domain Features

A paper by Nobuyuki Yamawaki et al., under this approach, downsamples the EEG signal and represents it in time domain for the frequency band of interest, and this representation is repeated for an array of the sensors, hence giving T-F-S representation [82]. A paper by Tao Wang et al. also tested the time variation of the signal in a selected frequency band for different combinations of spatial spread of the electrodes [83]. The proposed method by Tae-Eui Kam et al. derived the discriminative spatial pattern from the time and frequency information [84].

13.4.3.3   Spatial Domain

Ramoser et al. propose the spatial pattern filter, which optimizes the task specific variance of the signal when applied to it [59]. RCSP proposed by Haiping Lu et al. works efficiently for small training sets and outperforms the results obtained on same datasets [44]. The zero-training method for spatial filter design proposed in the work by Yijun Wang et al. claims to be a practical approach for BCI [85]. Efficient CSP was implemented by K. K. Ang et al., using a subject-specific filter band, and performance is given by yielding 0.569 and 0.600 as mean kappa value [87]. Probabilistic CSP (P-CSP) has been proposed by Wei Wu et al., as a generic spatio-temporal modeling structure for EEG that incorporates the algorithm of CSP and RCSP [86].

13.4.4   ANALYSIS AND DISCUSSION OF THE RESEARCH GAP IN THE FEATURE EXTRACTION

The feature extraction methods considered under time-frequency domain use the wavelet transform (WT) for representing the time-frequency variations of the EEG signal, but the search and analysis for matching wavelet function is not available. On the other hand, T-F-S techniques can be further improved by estimating parameters dependent on time for the spatially filtered EEG.

13.5   CLASSIFICATION TECHNIQUES

The study of classification techniques used for EEG-based BCI covers a wide range of linear and non-linear classifiers with supervised and unsupervised learning. The linear classifier proposed by Tao Wang et al. uses a weighting strategy for determination of the parameters and does not need a subject-specific setting [81]. Machine learning using SVM is the preferred algorithm for classification due to its adaptation with the dimensionality of feature space and ability to learn, as proposed by Y. P. A. Yong et al. [90] and S. Jirayucharoensak et al. [91]. The generalization of SVM with non-linear hyperplanes are the preferred classifiers in BCI [92] by Ercan Gokgoz et al. and [93] by Benjamin Blankertz et al. Classifiers like LDA, with small modifications, are commonly used in BCIs; results show the boosting in the performance, as suggested by W.-L. Yeh et al. [77], Chih-Yu Chen et al. [94], and P. Geethanjali et al. [95]. Preference given to non-linear classifiers is due to the significant amount of data with less knowledge. K-nearest neighbor classifier (K-NN) is a non-parametric classifier preferred for two-class BCI, as proposed by S. K. Bashar et al. [96]and M. Islam et al. [97]. Neural networks as the non-linear method for the classification method preferably used in BCI for its ability of pattern recognition is proposed by Rifai Chai et al. [98]. Genetic algorithm-based ANN are found to give good performance, as suggested by B. D. Seno [99].

13.5.1 ANALYSIS AND DISCUSSION OF THE RESEARCH GAP IN THE CLASSIFIER

Analyzing the methods preferentially used for classification in BCI, it can be concluded that non-parametric classifiers like SVM and K-NN are used as they fit into a large number of functional forms. Modifications or variations in kernel function used in the classifiers can boost system performance.

REFERENCES

[1] S. G. Mason and G. E. Birch, "A general framework for brain–computer interface design," *IEEE Trans. Neural Syst. Rehabil. Eng.*, vol. 11, no. 1, pp. 70–85, 2003, doi: 10.1109/TNSRE.2003.810426.
[2] E. Yin, Z. Zhou, J. Jiang, Y. Yu, D. Hu, and S. Member, "A dynamically optimized SSVEP brain–computer interface (BCI) speller," *IEEE Trans. Biomed. Eng.*, pp. 1–10, 2014, doi: 10.1109/TBME.2014.2320948.
[3] J. R. Wolpaw, N. Birbaumer, D. J. Mcfarland, G. Pfurtscheller, and T. M. Vaughan, "Brain–computer interfaces for communication and control," *Clin. Neurophysiol., Elsevier*, vol. 113, pp. 767–791, 2002.
[4] J. Pan, Y. Li, R. Zhang, Z. Gu, and F. Li, "Discrimination between control and idle states in asynchronous SSVEP-based brain switches: A," *IEEE Trans. Neural Syst. Rehabil. Eng.*, vol. 21, no. 3, pp. 435–443, 2013.
[5] H. Bin Zhao, H. Wang, C. S. Li, and Y. G. Li, "Brain–computer interface design based on slow cortical potentials using Matlab/Simulink," in 2009 IEEE International Conference on Mechatronics and Automation, ICMA 2009, 2009, pp. 1044–1048, doi: 10.1109/ICMA.2009.5246255.
[6] J. Long, Y. Li, H. Wang, T. Yu, J. Pan, and F. Li, "A hybrid brain computer interface to control the direction and speed of a simulated or real wheelchair," *IEEE Trans. Neural Syst. Rehabil. Eng.*, vol. 20, no. 5, pp. 720–729, 2012.
[7] Robbin A. Miranda, William D. Casebeer, Amy M. Hein, Jack W. Judy, Eric P. Krotkov, Tracy L. Laabs, Justin E. Manzo, Kent G. Pankratz, Gill A. Pratt, Justin C. Sanchez, Douglas J. Weber, Tracey L. Wheeler, Geoffrey S.F. Ling, DARPA-funded efforts in the development of novel brain–computer interface technologies, *Journal of Neuroscience Methods*, vol. 244, 2015, pp. 52–67, ISSN 0165-0270, https://doi.org/10.1016/j.jneumeth.2014.07.019.
[8] E. Yin, Z. Zhou, J. Jiang, F. Chen, and Y. Liu, "A speedy hybrid BCI spelling approach combining P300 and SSVEP," *IEEE Trans. Biomed. Eng.*, vol. 61, no. 2, pp. 473–483, 2014.
[9] A. Rodrigo and F. Cabrera, "Feature extraction and classification for brain–computer interfaces," PhD Thesis, (SMI) Department of Health Science and Technology Aalborg University, Denmark, 2009.
[10] Y. Li, J. Pan, F. Wang, and Z. Yu, "A hybrid BCI system combining P300 and SSVEP and its application to wheelchair control," *IEEE Trans. Biomed. Eng.*, vol. 60, no. 11, pp. 3156–3166, Nov. 2013, doi: 10.1109/TBME.2013.2270283.
[11] G. Pires and U. Nunes, "A brain computer interface methodology based on a visual P300 Paradigm," in IEEE/RSJ International Conference on Intelligent Robots and Systems, 2009.
[12] S. G. Mason and G. E. Birch, "A brain–controlled switch for asynchronous control applications," *IEEE Trans. Biomed. Eng.*, vol. 47, no. 10, pp. 1297–1307, 2000, doi: 10.1109/10.871402.
[13] Y. Li, J. Pan, F. Wang, and Z. Yu, "A hybrid BCI system combining P300 and SSVEP and its application to wheelchair control," *IEEE Trans. Biomed. Eng.*, vol. 60, no. 11, pp. 3156–3166, 2013.
[14] A. Bashashati, R. K. Ward, and G. E. Birch, "A new design of the asynchronous brain computer interface using the knowledge of the path of features," *2nd Int. IEEE EMBS Conf. Neural Eng.*, vol. 2005, no. Ic, pp. 101–104, 2005, doi: 10.1109/CNE.2005.1419563.

[15] M. Nakanishi, Y. Wang, Y. Te Wang, and T. P. Jung, "A comparison study of canonical correlation analysis based methods for detecting steady-state visual evoked potentials," *PLoS One*, vol. 10, no. 10, pp. 1–18, 2015, doi: 10.1371/journal.pone.0140703.

[16] D. Tan and A. Nijholt, "Brain–computer interfaces and human-computer interaction," in *Brain–Computer Interfaces Applying our Minds to Human-Computer Interaction*, 2010, pp. 3–19.

[17] J. R. Wolpaw and D. J. Mcfarland, "Control of a two-dimensional movement signal by a noninvasive brain—computer interface in humans," *PNAS*, vol. 101, no. 51, 2004.

[18] J. R. Millán, F. Renkens, J. Mouriño, S. Member, and W. Gerstner, "Noninvasive brain–actuated control of a mobile robot by human EEG," *IEEE Trans. Biomed. Eng.*, vol. 51, no. 6, pp. 1026–1033, 2004.

[19] E. W. Sellers, D. B. Ryan, and C. K. Hauser, "Noninvasive brain–computer interface enables communication after brainstem stroke," *Sci. Transl. Med.*, vol. 6, no. 257, 8 Oct. 2014.

[20] J. N. Mak et al., "Optimizing the P300-based brain–computer interface: current status, limitations and future directions.," *J. Neural Eng.*, vol. 8, no. 2, p. 025003, Apr. 2011, doi: 10.1088/1741-2560/8/2/025003.

[21] E. W. Sellers and E. Donchin, "A P300-based brain—computer interface: initial tests by ALS patients," *Clin. Neurophysiol., Elsevier*, vol. 117, pp. 538–548, 2006, doi: 10.1016/j.clinph.2005.06.027.

[22] P. B. C. Interface, E. Donchin, K. M. Spencer, and R. Wijesinghe, "The mental prosthesis: assessing the speed of a P300-based BCI," *IEEE Trans. Rehabil. Eng.*, vol. 8, no. 2, pp. 174–179, 2000.

[23] M. Chang et al., "Comparison of P300 responses in auditory, visual and audiovisual spatial speller BCI paradigms," in *the Fifth International Brain–Computer Interface Meeting 2013*, 2013, pp. 5–6, doi: 10.3217/978-3-85125-260-6-156.

[24] R. J. O. Naser Hamdi, "A comparison study on machine learning algorithms utilized in P300-based BCI," *J. Heal. Med. Informat.*, vol. 04, no. 03, 2013, doi: 10.4172/2157-7420.1000126.

[25] E. Yin, Z. Zhou, J. Jiang, Y. Yu, and D. Hu, "A dynamically optimized SSVEP brain–computer interface (BCI) speller.," *IEEE Trans. Biomed. Eng.*, vol. 9294, no. c, pp. 1–10, Apr. 2014, doi: 10.1109/TBME.2014.2320948.

[26] G. Pfurtscheller, G. R. Müller-Putz, R. Scherer and C. Neuper, "Rehabilitation with Brain-Computer Interface Systems," in *Computer*, vol. 41, no. 10, pp. 58–65, Oct. 2008, doi: 10.1109/MC.2008.432.

[27] Z. Wu, Y. Lai, Y. Xia, D. Wu, and D. Yao, "Stimulator selection in SSVEP-based BCI.," *Med. Eng. Phys.*, vol. 30, no. 8, pp. 1079–1088, Oct. 2008, doi: 10.1016/j.medengphy.2008.01.004.

[28] M. A. Lebedev and M. A. L. Nicolelis, "Brain–machine interfaces: From basic science to neuro-prostheses and neurorehabilitation," *Physiol. Rev.*, vol. 97, no. 2, pp. 767–837, 2017, doi: 10.1152/physrev.00027.2016.

[29] Y. U. Zhang, "Frequency recognition in SSVEP-based BCI using multiset canonical correlation analysis," *Int. J. Neural Syst.*, vol. 24, no. 4, 2014, doi: 10.1142/S0129065714500130.

[30] D. Lesenfants et al., "An independent SSVEP-based brain–computer interface in locked-in syndrome," *J. neural Eng. neural Eng.*, vol. 11, no. 3, p. 035002, Jun. 2014, doi: 10.1088/1741-2560/11/3/035002.

[31] M. Gray, A. H. Kemp, R. B. Silberstein, and P. J. Nathan, "Cortical neurophysiology of anticipatory anxiety: an investigation utilizing steady state probe topography (SSPT)," *NeuroImage, Acad. Press. Elsevier*, vol. 20, pp. 975–986, 2003, doi: 10.1016/S1053-8119(03)00401-4.

[32] Y. Zhang, G. Zhou, J. Jin, X. Wang, and A. Cichocki, "SSVEP recognition using common feature analysis in brain–computer interface," *J. Neurosci. Methods*, vol. 244, pp. 8–15, 2015, doi: 10.1016/j.jneumeth.2014.03.012.

[33] B. Z. Allison, D. J. McFarland, G. Schalk, S. D. Zheng, M. M. Jackson, and J. R. Wolpaw, "Towards an independent brain–computer interface using steady state visual evoked potentials," *Clin. Neurophysiol.*, vol. 119, no. 2, pp. 399–408, 2008, doi: 10.1016/j.clinph.2007.09.121.

[34] H. Bakardjian, T. Tanaka, and A. Cichocki, "Neuroscience letters optimization of SSVEP brain responses with application to eight-command brain—computer interface," *Neurosci. Lett. 469, Elsevier*, vol. 469, pp. 34–38, 2010, doi: 10.1016/j.neulet.2009.11.039.

[35] P. Poryzala and A. Materka, "Biomedical signal processing and control cluster analysis of CCA coefficients for robust detection of the asynchronous SSVEPs in brain—computer interfaces," *Biomed. Signal Process. Control. Elsevier 2014*, vol. 10, pp. 201–208, 2014, doi: 10.1016/j.bspc.2013.11.003.

[36] Y. Zhang, J. Jin, X. Qing, B. Wang, and X. Wang, "LASSO based stimulus frequency recognition model for SSVEP BCIs," *Biomed. Signal Process. Control*, vol. 7, no. 2, pp. 104–111, Mar. 2012, doi: 10.1016/j.bspc.2011.02.002.

[37] X. Chen, Y. Wang, S. Gao, and T. Jung, "Filter bank canonical correlation analysis for implementing a high-speed SSVEP-based brain—computer interface," *J. Neural Eng.*, vol. 12, no. 4, p. 46008, doi: 10.1088/1741-2560/12/4/046008.

[38] B. Fabio, "Brain computer interfaces for communication and control," *Front. Neurosci.*, vol. 4, pp. 767–791, 1900, doi: 10.3389/conf.fnins.2010.05.00007.

[39] J. S. Brumberg, A. Nieto-Castanon, P. R. Kennedy, and F. H. Guenther, "Brain–computer interfaces for speech communication.," *Speech Commun.*, vol. 52, no. 4, pp. 367–379, Apr. 2010, doi: 10.1016/j.specom.2010.01.001.

[40] A. Bablani, D. R. Edla, D. Tripathi, and R. Cheruku, "Survey on brain–computer interface," *ACM Comput. Surv.*, vol. 52, no. 1, pp. 1–32, 2019, doi: 10.1145/3297713.

[41] K. K. Ang and C. Guan, "Brain–computer interface in stroke rehabilitation," *J. Comput. Sci. Eng.*, vol. 7, no. 2, pp. 139–146, 2013.

[42] N. Birbaumer et al., "A spelling device for the paralysed," *Nature*, vol. 398, no. 6725, pp. 297–298, 1999, doi: 10.1038/18581.

[43] N. Birbaumer et al., "The thought translation device (TTD) for completely paralyzed patients," *IEEE Trans. Rehabil. Eng.*, vol. 8, no. 2, pp. 190–193, 2000, doi: 10.1109/86.847812.

[44] H. Lu, H. L. Eng, C. Guan, K. N. Plataniotis, and A. N. Venetsanopoulos, "Regularized common spatial pattern with aggregation for EEG Classification in small-sample setting," *IEEE Trans. Biomed. Eng.*, vol. 57, no. 12, pp. 2936–2946, 2010, doi: 10.1109/TBME.2010.2082540.

[45] G. Pfurtscheller and F. H. Lopes, "Event-related EEG/MEG synchronization and desynchronization: basic principles," *Clin. Neurophysiol.*, vol. 110, pp. 1842–1857, 1999, doi: 10.1016/S1388-2457(99)00141-8.

[46] R. Xiao and L. Ding, "Evaluation of EEG features in decoding individual finger movements from one hand.," *Comput. Math. Methods Med.*, p. 243257, Jan. 2013, doi: 10.1155/2013/243257.

[47] E. a. Carlo A. Porro, Maria Pia Francescato, "Primary motor and sensory cortex activation during motor performance and motor imagery: a functional magnetic resonance imaging study," *J. Neurosci.*, vol. 16, no. 23, pp. 7688–7698, 1996.

[48] E. Gerardin, A. Sirigu, and et al. Lehéricy, *Partially overlapping neural networks for real and imagined hand movements*, Oxford Univ. Press, pp. 1093–1104, 2000.

[49] C. U. Neuper and G. Pfurtscheller, "Event-related dynamics of cortical rhythms: frequency-specific features and functional correlates," *Int. J. Psychosiology*, 2001.

[50] J. Karat et al., *Human-Computer Interaction Series.* ISSN 1571-5035 ISBN 978-1-4471-2270-8 e-ISBN 978-1-4471-2271-5 DOI 10.1007/978-1-4471-2271-5

[51] I. Lazarou, S. Nikolopoulos, and P. C. Petrantonakis, "EEG-based brain—computer interfaces for communication and rehabilitation of people with motor impairment: a novel approach of the 21st century," *Front. Hum. Neurosci.*, vol. 12, no. January, pp. 1–18, 2018, doi: 10.3389/fnhum.2018.00014.

[52] K. K. Ang et al., "Facilitating effects of transcranial direct current stimulation on motor imagery brain–computer interface with robotic feedback for stroke rehabilitation," *Arch. Phys. Med. Rehabil.*, vol. 96, no. 3, pp. S79–S87, 2015, doi: 10.1016/j.apmr.2014.08.008.

[53] Y. R. Tabar and U. Halici, "A novel deep learning approach for classification of EEG motor imagery signals," *J. Neural Eng.*, p. 16003, doi: 10.1088/1741-2560/14/1/016003.

[54] T. Wang, J. Deng, and B. He, "Classifying EEG-based motor imagery tasks by means of time—frequency synthesized spatial patterns," *Clin. Neurophysiol., Elsevier*, vol. 115, pp. 2744–2753, 2004, doi: 10.1016/j.clinph.2004.06.022.

[55] M. Almonacid and J. Ibarrola, "Voting strategy to enhance multimodel EEG-based classifier systems for motor imagery BCI," *IEEE Sys.*, pp. 1–7, 2014.

[56] B. Medina-Salgado, L. Duque-Muñoz and H. Fandiño-Toro, "Characterization of EEG signals using wavelet transform for motor imagination tasks in BCI systems," Symposium of Signals, Images and Artificial Vision - 2013: STSIVA - 2013, 2013, pp. 1–4, doi: 10.1109/STSIVA.2013.6644931.

[57] K. A. Ludwig et al., "Using a common average reference to improve cortical neuron recordings from microelectrode arrays using a common average reference to improve cortical neuron recordings from microelectrode arrays," *J. Neurophysiol.*, vol. 101, pp. 1679–1689, 2009, doi: 10.1152/jn.90989.2008.

[58] L. Xinyu, W. Hong, L. Shan, C. Yan, and S. Li, "Adaptive common average reference for in vivo multichannel local field potentials," *Biomed. Eng. Lett.*, vol. 7, no. 1, pp. 7–15, 2017, doi: 10.1007/s13534-016-0004-1.

[59] H. Ramoser, J. M. Gerking, and G. Pfurtscheller, "Optimal spatial filtering of single trial EEG during imagined hand movement," *IEEE Trans. Rehabil. Eng.*, vol. 8, no. 4, pp. 441–446, 2000.

[60] S. H. F. Syam, H. Lakany, R. B. Ahmad, and B. A. Conway, "Comparing common average referencing to laplacian referencing in detecting imagination and intention of movement for brain computer interface," *MATEC Web Conf.*, vol. 140, 2017, doi: 10.1051/matecconf/201714001028.

[61] J. Kayser and C. E. Tenke, "Issues and considerations for using the scalp surface Laplacian in EEG/ERP research: A tutorial review," *Int. J. Psychophysiol.*, vol. 97, no. 3, pp. 189–209, 2015, doi: 10.1016/j.ijpsycho.2015.04.012.

[62] Claudio Carvalhaes, J. Acacio de Barros, The surface Laplacian technique in EEG: Theory and methods, *International Journal of Psychophysiology,* vol. 97, no. 3, 2015, pp. 174–188, ISSN 0167-8760, https://doi.org/10.1016/j.ijpsycho.2015.04.023.

[63] C. E. T. J. Kayser, "On the benefits of using surface Laplacian (Current Source Density) methodology in electrophysiology," *Int. J. Psychophysiol.*, no. jun., 2015, doi: 10.1016/j.ijpsycho.2015.06.001.

[64] C. G. Carvalhaes, R. De Janeiro, and P. Suppes, "A spline framework for estimating the EEG surface laplacian using the Euclidean metric," *Neural Comput. 23, Massachusetts Inst. Technol.*, vol. 3000, no. 2010, pp. 2974–3000, 2011.

[65] J. Kayser and C. E. Tenke, "Issues and considerations for using the scalp surface Laplacian in EEG/ERP research: a tutorial review," *Int. J. Psychophysiol.*, vol. 97, no. 3, pp. 189–209, 2015, doi: 10.1016/j.ijpsycho.2015.04.012.

[66] C. E. Tenke and J. Kayser, "Surface Laplacians (SL) and phase properties of EEG rhythms: Simulated generators in a volume-conduction model," *Int. J. Psychophysiol.*, vol. 97, no. 3, pp. 285–298, 2015, doi: 10.1016/j.ijpsycho.2015.05.008.

[67] Rejer, I., Górski, P. (2013). Independent Component Analysis for EEG Data Preprocessing - Algorithms Comparison. In: Saeed, K., Chaki, R., Cortesi, A., Wierzchoń, S. (eds) *Computer Information Systems and Industrial Management.* CISIM 2013. Lecture Notes in Computer Science, vol 8104. Springer, Berlin, Heidelberg. https://doi.org/10.1007/978-3-642-40925-7_11.

[68] P. S. Hammon and V. R. De Sa, "Preprocessing and meta-classification for brain–computer interfaces," *IEEE Trans. Biomed. Eng.*, vol. 54, no. 3, pp. 518–525, 2007.

[69] X. Yong, R. K. Ward, and G. E. Birch, "Robust common spatial patterns for EEG signal preprocessing," in 0th Annual International IEEE EMBS Conference Vancouver, British Columbia, Canada, 2008, pp. 2087–2090.

[70] F. Artoni, A. Delorme, and S. Makeig, "Applying dimension reduction to EEG data by principal component analysis reduces the quality of its subsequent independent component decomposition," *Neuroimage*, vol. 175, pp. 176–187, 2018, doi: 10.1016/j.neuroimage.2018.03.016.

[71] S. P. Fitzgibbon, D. Delosangeles, T. W. Lewis, D. M. W. Powers, and E. M. Whitham, "Surface Laplacian of scalp electrical signals and independent component analysis resolve EMG contamination of electroencephalogram," *Int. J. Psychophysiol.*, 2014, doi: 10.1016/j.ijpsycho.2014.10.006.

[72] M. P. G. Pfurtscheller, Ch. Neuper, D. Flotzinger, "EEG-based discrimination between imagination of right and left hand movement," *Electroencephalogr. Clin. Neurophysiol. ELSEVIER*, vol. 103, pp. 642–651, 1997.

[73] P. Herman, G. Prasad, T. M. McGinnity, and D. Coyle, "Comparative analysis of spectral approaches to feature extraction for EEG-based motor imagery classification," *IEEE Trans. Neural Syst. Rehabil. Eng.*, vol. 16, no. 4, pp. 317–326, 2008, doi: 10.1109/TNSRE.2008.926694.

[74] O. A. Rosso et al., "Wavelet entropy: a new tool for analysis of short duration brain electrical signals," *J. Neurosci. Methods, Elsevier*, vol. 105, pp. 65–75, 2001.

[75] B. Kamousi, Z. Liu, and B. He, "Classification of motor imagery tasks for brain–computer interface applications by means of two equivalent dipoles analysis," *IEEE Trans. Neural Syst. Rehab. Eng.*, vol. 13, no. 2, pp. 166–171, 2005.

[76] Amin, H.U., Malik, A.S., Ahmad, R.F. et al. Feature extraction and classification for EEG signals using wavelet transform and machine learning techniques. *Australas Phys Eng Sci Med* 38, 139–149 (2015). https://doi.org/10.1007/s13246-015-0333-x.

[77] W.-L. Yeh, Y.-C. Huang, J.-H. Chiou, J.-R. Duann, and J.-C. Chiou, "A self produced mother wavelet feature extraction method for motor imagery brain–computer interface.," in Conf. Proc. . . . Annu. Int. Conf. IEEE Eng. Med. Biol. Soc. IEEE Eng. Med. Biol. Soc. Annu. Conf., vol. 2013, pp. 4302–4305, Jan. 2013, doi: 10.1109/EMBC.2013.6610497.

[78] B. Xu and A. Song, "Pattern recognition of motor imagery EEG using wavelet transform," *J. Biomed. Sci. Eng.*, vol. 1, no. May, p. 64, 2008, doi: 10.4236/jbise.2008.11010.

[79] D. Li, W. Pedrycz, and N. J. Pizzi, "Fuzzy wavelet packet based feature extraction method and its application to biomedical signal classification," *IEEE Trans. Biomed. Eng.*, vol. 52, no. 6, pp. 1132–1139, 2005, doi: 10.1109/TBME.2005.848377.

[80] E. Mohamed, "Enhancing EEG signals in brain computer interface using wavelet transform," *Int. J. Inf. Electron. Eng.*, vol. 4, no. 3, pp. 234–238, 2014, doi: 10.7763/IJIEE.2014.V4.440.

[81] T. Wang and B. He, "An efficient rhythmic component expression and weighting synthesis strategy for classifying motor imagery EEG in a brain—computer interface," *J. Neural Eng.*, vol. 1, pp. 1–7, 2004, doi: 10.1088/1741-2560/1/1/001.

[82] N. Yamawaki, C. Wilke, Z. Liu, and B. He, "An enhanced time-frequency-spatial approach for motor imagery classification.," *IEEE Trans. Neural Syst. Rehabil. Eng.*, vol. 14, no. 2, pp. 250–254, Jun. 2006, doi: 10.1109/TNSRE.2006.875567.

[83] T. Wang, J. Deng, and B. He, "Classifying EEG-based motor imagery tasks by means of time—frequency synthesized spatial patterns," *Clin. Neurophysiol.*, vol. 115, pp. 2744–2753, 2004, doi: 10.1016/j.clinph.2004.06.022.

[84] T. Kam, H. Suk, and S. Lee, "Neurocomputing non-homogeneous spatial filter optimization for electroencephalogram (EEG)—based motor imagery classification," *Neurocomputing*, vol. 108, pp. 58–68, 2013, doi: 10.1016/j.neucom.2012.12.002.

[85] Y. Wang, Y. Wang, and T. Jung, "Translation of EEG spatial filters from resting to motor imagery using independent component analysis," *PLoS One*, vol. 7, no. 5, 2012, doi: 10.1371/journal.pone.0037665.

[86] W. Wu, Z. Chen, S. Member, and X. Gao, "Probabilistic common spatial patterns for multichannel EEG analysis," *IEEE Trans. Pattern Anal. Mach. Intell.*, vol. 37, no. March 2015, pp. 639–651, 2015, doi: 10.1109/TPAMI.2014.2330598.

[87] K. K. Ang, Z. Y. Chin, C. Wang, C. Guan, and H. Zhang, "Filter bank common spatial pattern algorithm on BCI competition IV Datasets 2a and 2b," *Front. Neurosci.*, vol. 6, no. March, pp. 1–9, 2012, doi: 10.3389/fnins.2012.00039.

[88] S. A. Park, H. J. Hwang, J. H. Lim, J. H. Choi, H. K. Jung, and C. H. Im, "Evaluation of feature extraction methods for EEG-based brain–computer interfaces in terms of robustness to slight changes in electrode locations," *Med. Biol. Eng. Comput.*, vol. 51, no. 5, 2013, doi: 10.1007/s11517-012-1026-1.

[89] B. Das, M. Talukdar, R. Sarma, and S. M. Hazarika, "Multiple feature extraction of electroencephalograph signal for motor imagery classification through bispectral analysis," *Procedia—Procedia Comput. Sci.*, vol. 84, pp. 192–197, 2016, doi: 10.1016/j.procs.2016.04.086.

[90] Y. Yong and N. Hurley, "Single-trial EEG classification for brain–computer interface using wavelet decomposition," in IEEE Signal Process. Conf. 2013, Antalya, Turkey, 2005 [Online]. http://signal.ee.bilkent.edu.tr/defevent/papers/cr1164.pdf.

[91] S. Jirayucharoensak, S. Pan-Ngum, and P. Israsena, "EEG-based emotion recognition using deep learning network with principal component based covariate shift adaptation," *Sci. World J.*, vol. 2014, 2014, doi: 10.1155/2014/627892.

[92] E. Gokgoz and A. Subasi, "Effect of multiscale PCA de-noising on EMG signal classification for diagnosis of neuromuscular disorders," *J. Med. Syst.*, vol. 38, no. 4, 2014, doi: 10.1007/s10916-014-0031-3.

[93] B. Blankertz, G. Curio, and K.-R. Müller, "Classifying single trial EEG: towards brain computer interfacing," *Adv. Neural Inf. Process. Syst. Conf.*, vol. 1, no. c, pp. 157–164, 2002, doi: 10.1.1.19.8038.

[94] C. Chen, C. Wu, C. Lin, and S. Chen, "A novel classification method for motor imagery based on brain–computer interface," in International Joint Conference on Neural Networks (IJCNN) Beijing, China, 2014, no. Mi, pp. 14–17.

[95] P. Geethanjali and Y. K. Mohan, "EEG data for Brain Computer Interface," in 9th International Conference on Fuzzy Systems and Knowledge Discovery (FSKD 2012), 2012, no. Fskd, pp. 1136–1139.

[96] S. K. Bashar, M. Imamul, and H. Bhuiyan, "Identification of motor imagery movements from EEG signals using automatically selected features in the dual tree complex wavelet transform domain," *Univers. J. Biomed. Eng.*, vol. 3, no. 4, pp. 30–37, 2015, doi: 10.13189/ujbe.2015.030402.

[97] M. Islam, M. R. Fraz, Z. Zahid, and M. Arif, "Optimizing common spatial pattern and feature extraction algorithm for brain computer interface," *2011 7th Int. Conf. Emerg. Technol.*, pp. 1–6, Sep. 2011, doi: 10.1109/ICET.2011.6048480.

[98] R. Chai, S. H. Ling, G. P. Hunter, and H. T. Nguyen, "Mental non-motor imagery tasks classifications of brain computer interface for wheelchair commands using genetic algorithm-based neural network," *Proc. Int. Jt. Conf. Neural Networks*, pp. 10–15, 2012, doi: 10.1109/IJCNN.2012.6252499.

[99] R. Chai et al., "Brain—computer interface classifier for wheelchair commands using neural network with fuzzy particle swarm optimization," *IEEE J. Biomed. Heal. INFORMATICS*, vol. 18, no. 5, pp. 1614–1624, 2014.

14 Fetal Electrocardiogram Extraction Using Adaptive Filters Approach

Manjiri A. Ranjanikar, Sagar V. Joshi, Jaishri M. Waghmare, Swati V. Shinde, and Rachana Y. Patil

CONTENTS

14.1 INTRODUCTION

Congenital heart abnormalities are one of the primary birth defects and the main reason for death from birth defects. The shape of cardiac electrical signals shows up in almost all cardiac abnormalities. The non-invasive analysis of fetal cardiac signals can be a useful tool for monitoring the unborn heart's health. This could be used to detect heart problems early on. The electrical potential created in connection with heart action is represented graphically by the ECG signal. It is one of the primary used physiological signals in medical backgrounds. A FECG signal can be used to determine the well-being and status of the fetus, much as it can be done in adults. Fetal electrocardiography, Doppler ultrasound, and fetal magnetocardiography are non-invasive fetal monitoring procedures. Doppler ultrasound is the most often utilized approach since it is inexpensive and easy to use. However, because this approach generates an averaged heart rate, it cannot provide beat-to-beat variability.

The advantage of a fetal ECG is that it can detect beat-to-beat variability. There are numerous procedural issues with non-invasive FECG extraction. Different forms of interference, such as maternal electrogram (MEMG), maternal electrocardiogram (MECG), baseline drift, and power line interference of 50 Hz contaminate the FECG signal. The extraction of FECG is stimulating because of the low amplitude of the signals, various forms of noise, and overlapping frequencies of the mother and FECG. The basic goals of electronic fetal monitoring are to abstract and examine the FECG signal. Digital signal processing methods were used extensively in the extraction of the neonatal ECG signal. The abdominal ECG signal (AECG) is thought to be a nonlinear mixture of the MECG, FECG signal, and numerous interference signals. The FECG is derived from two signals collected on the mother's skin in the thoracic and abdominal regions. The thoracic electrocardiogram (TECG) is thought to be nearly entirely maternal, but the abdominal electrocardiogram

DOI: 10.1201/9781003272694-17

(AECG) is thought to be compound since it includes both the mother's and the fetus's ECG signals. To extract the FECG, the MECG must be suppressed in the composite abdominal signal. When information about the thoracic signal is known, MECG cancellation is a particular example of the optimum filtering that can be achieved. Aside from the electrode positioning issue, noise from electrography activity degrades the signal owing to the fetus's low amplitude signal. The MECG, which is 5 to 10 times stronger than the FECG, is another interfering signal. The MECG impacts all electrodes on the chest (thoracic electrode) and those on the abdomen (abdominal electrode). Electrodes put on the thorax of pregnant women will barely capture any FECG because of the poor quality of the FECG. The FECG signal can be produced by eliminating the MECG element from the composite abdominal signal.

14.2   LITERATURE REVIEW

One of the most widely utilized physiological signals is the electrocardiogram (ECG). An ECG signal produced by measuring the potential difference of two locations on the skin may be used to observe heart activity, and this ECG can give significant cardiac information. For decades, monitoring and analyzing the ECG has been a helpful tool for diagnosing heart disease. Heart abnormality is one of the primary birth faults and a significant cause of birth-related fatalities. Every year, around one in every 125 infants is born with a congenital cardiac problem. The flaws may be minor, causing the infant to look healthy for many years after birth, or they may be serious enough to put the kid's life in jeopardy. Congenital heart defects develop during the first trimester of pregnancy when the heart is still forming, and they can affect any heart function. Cardiac abnormalities can be caused by hereditary diseases, genetic syndromes, and environmental causes such as drug usage or infection. They can also happen as a result of the umbilical cord being choked due to fetal positioning. The pediatric cardiologist can use frequent monitoring of the fetal heart, FECG, and early identification of any cardiac anomalies to prescribe appropriate medicines or evaluate the required measures to be taken before delivery or after birth. FECG monitoring is a method of getting vital information about the fetus's health throughout the early stages of pregnancy and before birth. The FECG can be used to determine the fetus's health and status. Methods based on Doppler ultrasound, wavelet transform, blind source separation, which uses independent component analysis (ICA) and principal component analysis (PCA), the mixture of adaptive neural networks, blind source separation method, support vector machines, wavelets, and adaptive neuro-fuzzy interference system have been proposed by various researchers [1–11] to extract FECG signal.

Sonali et al. [1] developed an enhanced technique for denoising the ECG using empirical mode decomposition (EMD) trailed by rotating average filter. EMD is a data-driven, adaptive approach that may be used to analyze any continuous signal. In this proposed work, to generate a noise-free ECG signal with a high signal to error ratio (SER), the decomposition of input ECG is performed into intrinsic mode functions (IMFs), and lower order IMFs are used to remove high-frequency noises.

Behar et al. [2] suggested an echo state neural (ESN) network-based filtering method for MECG cancellation, which was compared to recursive least square (RLS), least mean squares (LMS), template subtraction (TS), and adaptive filter techniques. The analysis was carried out on real signals captured from nine pregnant women with 37452 reference fetal beats totaling 4 hours and 22 minutes. The impacts of signal pre-processing were empirically examined, and the ESN-based method outperformed the others on the test data with an F1 measure of 90.2 percent.

For the removal of noise and extracting the decisive feature from continuous input ECG data, Lin et al. [3] suggested discrete wavelet transform (DWT). For the decomposition of recorded ECG signals, Symlets sym5 wavelet function is used. The soft-thresholding method is then used to detect features.

Ahmadieh et al. [4] suggested a non-invasive approach for differentiating the FECG from the MECG based on type-2 adaptive neuro-fuzzy inference systems. The proposed approach recognizes the mother's body's nonlinear dynamics. As a result, the MECG components are calculated based on the abdominal signal. The results reveal that the proposed type-2 neuro-fuzzy inference approach outperforms the polynomial networks methods and type-1 neuro-fuzzy inference, owing to its capacity to better capture the model's nonlinearities.

Fatemi et. al. [5] proposed an online subspace denoising approach tailored for MECG cancellation for the abstraction of signal subspace from multichannel data.

Jaros et al. [6] reviewed a wide range of literature on several nonadaptive signal processing approaches for FECG extraction and improvement. To obtain high accuracy with speedy operations, ICA, PCA, and wavelet transforms (WT) are recommended.

Li et. al. [7] proposed an improved fast ICA technique to extract FECG. The MECG was first centralized and whitened and then Newton's iterative algorithm was used to process randomly created original weight vector. To receive a clean fetal ECG signal, the MECG component in the individual channel was eliminated using the singular value decomposition (SVD) approach.

Mousavian et al. [8] proposed a twofold constrained block-term (DoCoBT) tensor decomposition approach for extracting FECG from maternal abdominal signals. The quasi-periodicity limitations of FECG and MECG signals limit this tensor decomposition method. Due to the use of additional information for source separation, tensor decompositions are more influential than matrix decompositions. It splits the subspaces of the mother, the fetus, and noise by tenderizing abdominal signals and employing periodicity restrictions of FECG and MECG. DoCoBT decomposition outperforms alternative tensor and matrix decomposition algorithms in noisy situations, according to quantitative and qualitative results.

Alshebly et al. [9] proposed a technique for extracting FECG by utilizing AECG to exclude all other signals. The developed algorithm works by weakening the MECG using wavelet analysis and filtering to locate the FECG and separating them based on their positions. The researchers employed two AECG signals recorded at distinct sites on the abdomen. MECG with a power of 5 to 10 times that of the FECG is included in the ECG data. The proposed method for FECG extraction is promising because it uses filtering and wavelet analysis. The approach used can be quickly altered based on signal strength levels, making it very adaptable to varying signals in various bio-signals applications.

Using ICA and adaptive filtering techniques, Mirza et al. [10] suggested a way for eliminating and filtering these artifacts. This method is a reliable way of non-invasively obtaining FECG signals from abdominal ECG. The SNR of the ICA approach is relatively high, and it is nonparametric.

Mohebbian et al. [11] proposed a method for developing a model that uses a fixed-point convolution kernel compensating adaptive filter, followed by an RLS algorithm to complete the deconvolution of the ECG signal. Deconvolution is used to denoise ECG signals with extremely low signal-to-noise ratios, as well as in blind source separating applications such as FECG separation from MECG.

Using the input mode adaptive filter (IMAF) and the output mode adaptive filter (OMAF), Taha et al. [12] developed two ways for FECG separation (OMAF). The LMS and RLS algorithms, as well as a single reference-generation block, are used in both techniques. The principal input of the IMAF filter is directly linked to the abdominal signal. The filter's primary input is connected to the OMAF's output stage of a blind source separation block. Windowing the raw FECG signal from the BSS output depending on the locations of the extracted MECG signal's QRS pulses creates the reference signal. In this study, the null space idempotent transformation matrix (NSITM) was used as the BSS algorithm. The FECG signal was successfully extracted using data from the Daisy and PhysioNet databases.

14.3 PROPOSED METHOD

The FECG signal can frequently offer crucial information for diagnosing an arrhythmia. Electrical measurements on the maternal abdomen can be used to acquire the FECG signal. The abdominal ECG signal, on the other hand, is made up of a mix of maternal, fetal, and interference

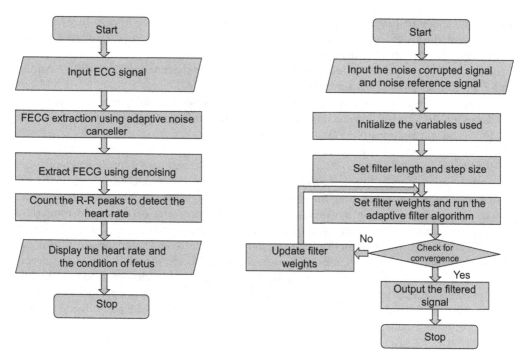

FIGURE 14.1   Flowchart of proposed approach and adaptive filters working.

signals. ECG signal processing can help get a fair approximation of the FECG signal since the amplitude of the MECG signal is generally significantly larger than the FECG signal and the interference signals. The proposed approach and flowchart of adaptive filters working are shown in Figure 14.1.

Fetal electrocardiography, Doppler ultrasonography, and fetal magnetocardiography are non-invasive fetal monitoring methods. Doppler ultrasonography is the most widely utilized technique since it is simple to use and inexpensive. However, because this technique generates an averaged heart rate, it cannot provide beat-to-beat variability. The advantage of a FECG is that it can detect beat-to-beat variability. There are several technical issues with non-invasive FECG extraction. Different forms of interference, such as maternal EMG, 50 Hz power line interference, and baseline drift, contaminate the FECG signal. The extraction of FECG is challenging because of the low amplitude of the signals, various forms of noise, and overlapping frequencies of the mother and FECG. Fetal heart rate fluctuations have been utilized as an indirect indication of fetal discomfort throughout pregnancy and childbirth. Longer durations of observation may give additional information regarding the fetus's condition. The challenge of detecting the fetal QRS complex from surface recordings is quite challenging, owing to the overlapping of the mother's ECG. The MECG and FECG have a skewed relationship. In addition, the MECG signal is significantly stronger than the FECG signal it contains. Depending on the gestation age, the noise in which FECG is enmeshed is likewise greater.

14.3.1   Least Mean Square (LMS Method)

The LMS algorithm is a type of adaptive filter that mimics the desired filter by determining the filter coefficients that provide the error signal with the least mean squares. It's a stochastic gradient

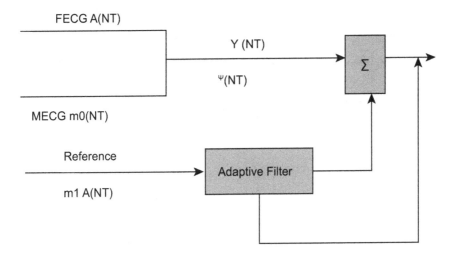

FIGURE 14.2 Extraction using LMS filter.

descent approach in which the filter is only adjusted in response to the current error. The LMS filter's main concept is to method the optimal filter weights (R-1P) by updating the filter weights in a way such that they converge to the optimum filter weight.

The procedure starts with tiny weights (zero in most situations), and the weights are changed at each step by calculating the gradient of the mean square error. That is, if the mean square error (MSE) gradient is positive, the error will continue to rise if the same weight is used for subsequent iterations, implying that the weights must be reduced. Similarly, if the gradient is negative, the weights must be increased. Equation (1) is the fundamental weight update equation.

$$W_{n+1} = W_{n-\mu\Delta\varepsilon[n]}, \tag{1}$$

where ε and μ denote mean square error and step size respectively. The negative sign indicates that the weights must be changed in the opposite direction of the gradient slope. That is, we approach the solution in a series of steps controlled by the step size μ, each time updating the gradient and the step size.

The measured MECG is used as the reference signal, and it is noticed that the heartbeat signal passes through the mother's body after passing through an LMS filter. The measured fetal electrocardiogram (MECG+FECG) signal is a mixed signal that includes the mother's heartbeat in the womb as well as the baby's heartbeat signal with noise. The baby's heartbeat with some noise comes after the measured fetal electrocardiogram (MECG+FECG) minus the filtered measured MECG using LMS filter, as shown in Figures 14.2 and 14.3.

The LMS method, which is reliant on the step size for convergence, is simple to develop and straightforward to use. By minimizing the error, LMS offers correct and fast solutions. So, using the deterministic gradient technique steepest descent algorithm, the filter adjusts the coefficient, then finds the error, finds the LMS of error, and minimizes the variance between error and input. It calculates the derivative of the error to determine the gradient and repeats the process until it reaches convergence, that is, until it obtains optimal MSE values and changes the optimal values. The weight, also called filter coefficients, is w, and the filter order is k. Here finite impulse response (FIR) filter is used, which is adaptive. The FIR filter is consistently steadier than the infinite impulse response (IIR) filter. From the chest to the stomach, the LMS filter imitates the mother's body. The order of the adaptive LMS filter is 8, and the w coefficient is initialized as shown in Figure 14.3.

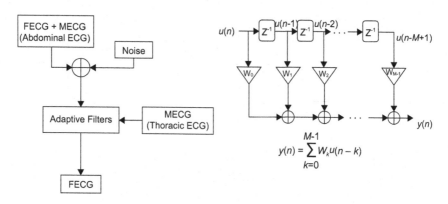

FIGURE 14.3   FECG extraction method and LMS algorithm.

The first of the two inputs of LMS is the abdominal ECG signal, which is a combination of MECG and FECG signals, i.e. $[m_0(NT)+A(NT)]$, and the second is a maternal signal, which is collected at the mother's chest or thoracic cavity (MECG) and includes broadband noise $[m_1(NT)]$. To generate the output, the adaptive filter A(NT) output is deducted from the input in Equation 2.

$$Y(NT) = A(NT) + m_0(NT) - \psi(NT). \tag{2}$$

To simplify each term, we square the result and make the (NT) implicit in Equation 3.

$$Y^2 = A^2 + (m_{0-\psi})^2 + 2A(m_{0-\psi}). \tag{3}$$

Applying expectations on both sides in equation 4,

$$E[Y^2] = [A^2] + \min E[(m_{0-\psi})^2]. \tag{4}$$

After minimization, the system generates the following output in Equation 5:

$$\min E[Y^2] = [A^2] + \min E[(m_{0-\psi})^2]. \tag{5}$$

A threshold value is then applied to the error and then the R-R peaks are detected to obtain the heart rate of the extracted FECG. Based on the results of heart rate, we can classify them as bradycardia and tachycardia. The MSE of $(m_{0-\psi})$ is reduced, and then the noise $(\psi \approx m_0)$ is synthesized adaptively, but changes to the filter do not affect $E[A^2]$. The ideal weight cannot be determined since the LMS algorithm fails to identify an accurate value.

14.3.2   QRS Peak Detection

The accurate identification of the QRS complex, which is a key help in detecting abnormalities in traditional ECG equipment, is a laborious and complicated operation in the ECG signal processing processes. The R peaks of the FECG signal must be ignored when calculating the fetal heart rate. The typical QRS wave is shown in Figure 14.4.

To count the R-R interval of the ECG signal, QRS detection is necessary. For QRS detection we may use bandpass filtering, the Pan Tompkins method. Based on the output of these methods, we are detecting the R-R peaks. Bandpass filtering, template matching, and Pan Tompkins techniques are among the known approaches for finding R-R peaks. All of these methods are based on differentiation. To find R peaks, we utilize a simple differentiation approach based on both derivatives

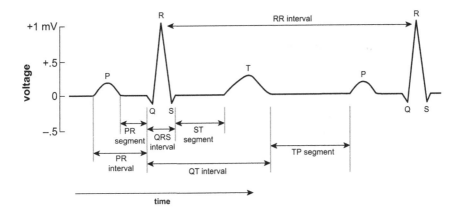

FIGURE 14.4 ECG signal source.

i.e. first and second-order. The ECG signal may be used to determine the absolute values of the first and second-order derivatives, as shown in Equations 6 and 7.

$$Y_0(N(T)) = |X(N(T)) - X(N(T) - 2T)|. \tag{6}$$
$$Y_1(N(T)) = |X(N(T)) - 2X(N(T) - 2(T)) + X(N(T) - 4(T))|. \tag{7}$$

These two data buffers, $Y_0(N(T))$ and $Y_1(N(T))$, are first scaled and then added to produce the following output in Equation 8.

$$Y_2(N(T)) = 1.3Y_0(N(T)) + 1.1Y_1(N(T)) \tag{8}$$

The scanning of buffering of the data $Y_2(N(T))$ is continued till a pre-defined threshold is not achieved in Equation 9.

$$Y_2(I(T)) \geq 1.0. \tag{9}$$

The comparison of the next 8 points with the threshold value gives the final output signal. This procedure recognizes the pulse and generates a pulse with a width relative to the complex.

14.4 RESULTS AND DISCUSSION

14.4.1 DATASET

A total of 447 records captured from five distinct sources are used for the analysis of the proposed system. Out of the five datasets, [16] and [18] are public and dataset [17] is artificial. The remaining two databases were given to PhysioNet for use in the system described in [15].

For the recording of the MECG signal, four non-invasive abdominal lead channels with a sampling frequency of 1 kHz and a recording time of 1 minute are used. Table 14.1 shows the details of FECG datasets.

14.4.2 RESULTS AND DISCUSSIONS

The experimental outcome of our suggested technique is tested on input sample data to extract the FECG signal. The use of adaptive noise cancellers in fetal ECG extraction is suggested and implemented. By modifying the tap-weight vector with the LMS algorithm, the FECG signals may be

TABLE 14.1

Details of FECG datasets [15]

Database Name	N Records
ADFECGDB [16]	25
Simulated FECGs [17]	20
NIFECGDB [18]	14
Non-Invasive FECG	340
Scalp FECG Database	48
Total	447

extracted from the abdominal electrocardiogram data. A software version of the LMS algorithm is provided to develop the adaptive noise canceller (ANC) system. The R-R interval's peaks are utilized to calculate fetal heart rate signals.

Thoracic and abdominal signals can be framed with overlapping signals to create training data. The suggested approach is carried out by synthesizing the thoracic and abdominal signals. As indicated in Figure 14.5.1, the three waveforms simulated are (a) noisy signal (thoracic signal), (b) raw signal (abdominal signal), and (c) LMS filtered output. The results of the proposed technique in this chapter show that the adaptive filter is a better technique for quality FECG signal from MECG signal. During experimentation, it has been observed that the average normal fetal heartbeats range between 110 to 160 beats per minute and are quicker than the maternal heart. It has been demonstrated that the proposed approach successfully eliminates MECG while extracting FECG. Although the FECG has a lesser amplitude than the MECG, the fetal heart beats faster than the maternal heart. The maternal component of the abdominal signal is in sync with the maternal component of the maternal signal. By subtracting the aligned maternal signal from the abdominal signal, FECG is obtained. In all situations, the extracted FECG may be provided a superior visual assessment. This means the suggested system outperforms the current system. The representative findings for several instances are depicted in Figures 14.5.1 to 14.5.4, which show abdominal, thoracic, and LMS filtered output for the sample four subjects from the dataset. From the experimentation, it has been observed that FECG extraction results are enhanced by eliminating the various disturbances. By overlapping each of the thoracic signals with abdominal signals, the training data is created. Figures 14.6.1, 14.7.1, and 14.8.1 depict the extraction of FECG from MECG for noisy inputs signals.

Table 14.2 gives the results of FECG extraction on input ECG form subject r01, r04, r07, and r08.

14.5   CONCLUSION AND FUTURE SCOPE

In this chapter, an effective FECG extraction technique based on adaptive noise cancellers is proposed and implemented. Based on the simulation results, one can conclude that using the LMS method to change the tap-weight vector, FECG signals may be recovered from abdominal electrocardiogram signals. To build the ANC system, a software implementation of the LMS algorithm is provided, and the suggested method is implemented using Simulink. The peaks of the R-R interval are used to derive fetal heart rate information. The goal of monitoring the fetus throughout pregnancy is to detect pathologic situations, such as asphyxia, early enough to allow the physician to intervene before irreparable alterations occur. The existing monitoring approaches, on the other hand, have major flaws. The noise-free FECG is required to overcome these limitations. Measurement of FECG is affected by many artifacts. The major artifact called MECG is cancelled from the FECG. In this chapter, we proposed a new approach for extracting FECG that uses adaptive filters and is more efficient than the previous technique. For precise FECG extraction to predict accurately

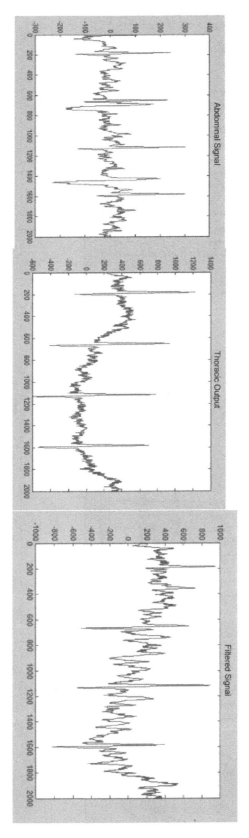

FIGURE 14.5.1 (a) Noisy signal (thoracic signal); (b) raw signal (abdominal signal); (c) LMS filtered output for input data: r01.

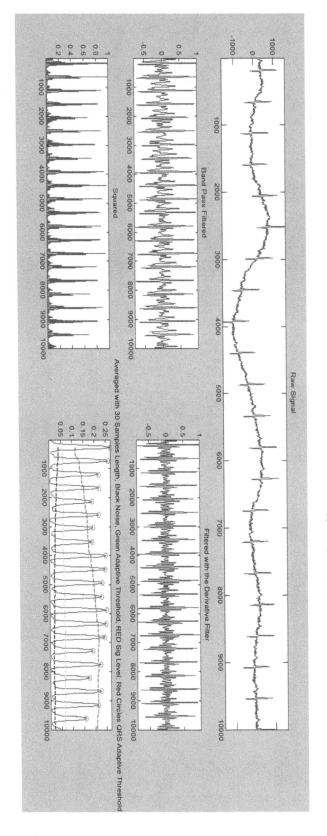

FIGURE 14.5.2   Derivative filtered signal for input data: r01.

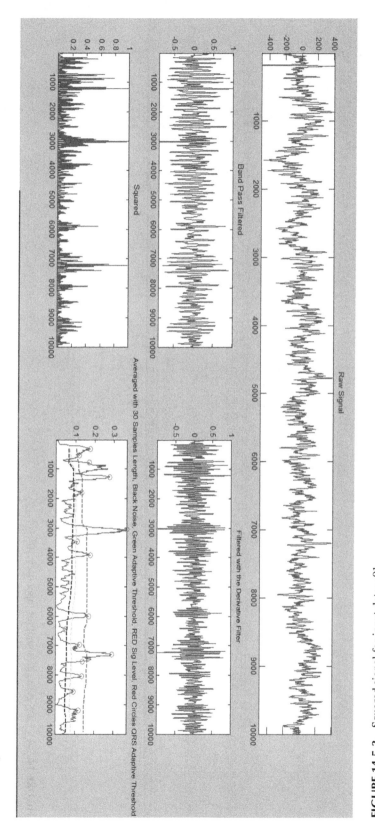

FIGURE 14.5.3   Squared signal for input data: r01.

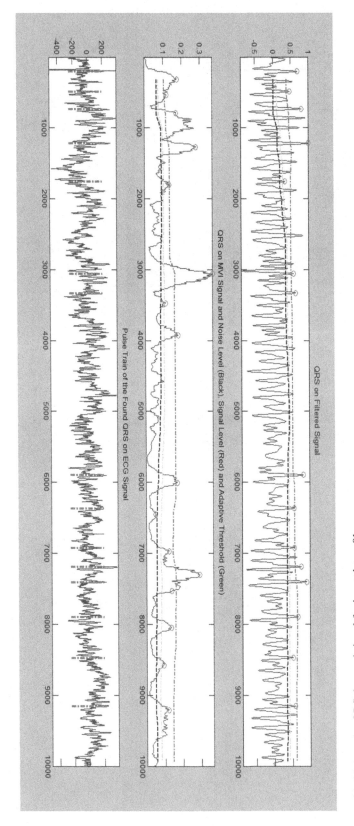

FIGURE 14.5.4　QRS detected signal for input data: r01.

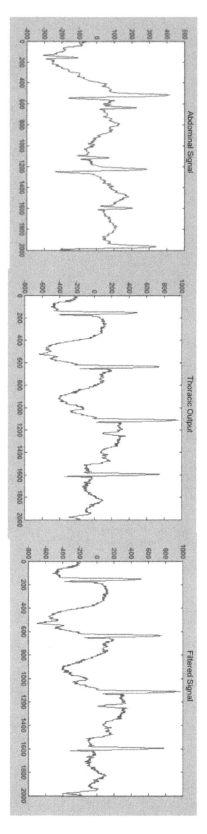

FIGURE 14.6.1 (a) Noisy signal (thoracic signal); (b) raw signal (abdominal signal); (c) LMS filtered output for input data: r04.

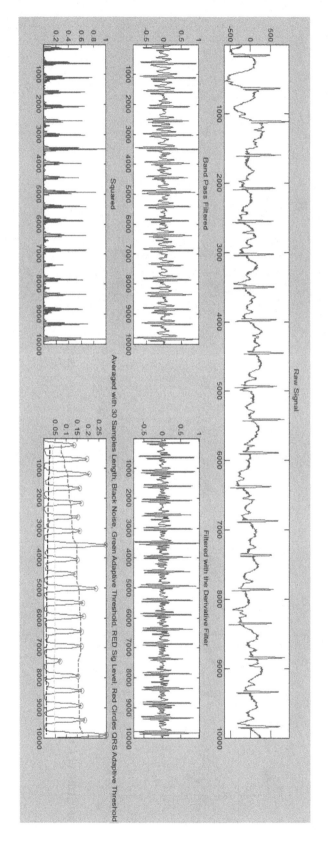

FIGURE 14.6.2 Derivative filtered signal for input data: r04.

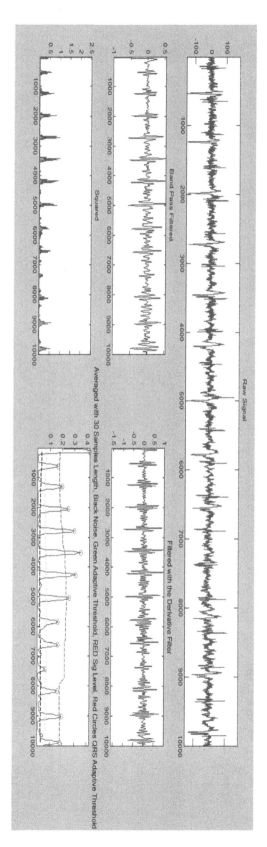

FIGURE 14.6.3 Squared signal for input data: r04.

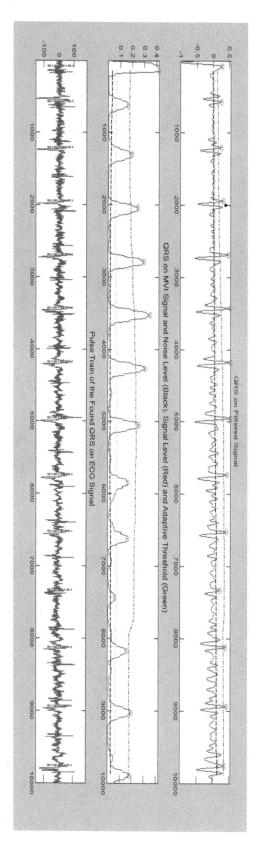

FIGURE 14.6.4   QRS detected signal for input data: r04.

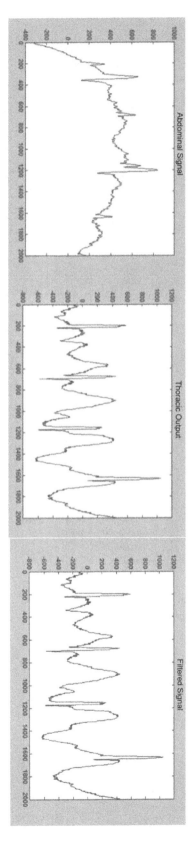

FIGURE 14.7.1   (a) Noisy signal (thoracic signal); (b) raw signal (abdominal signal); (c) LMS filtered output for input data: r07.

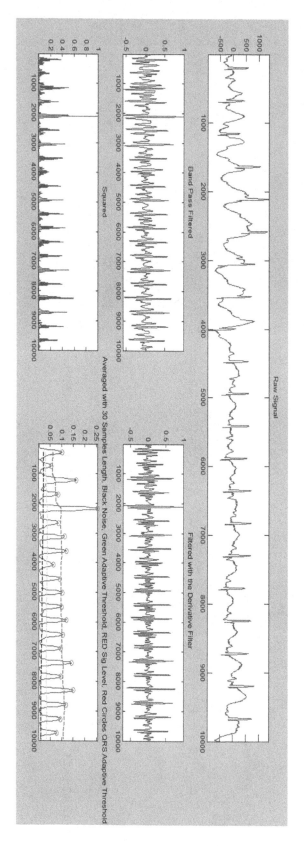

FIGURE 14.7.2   Derivative filtered signal for input data: r07.

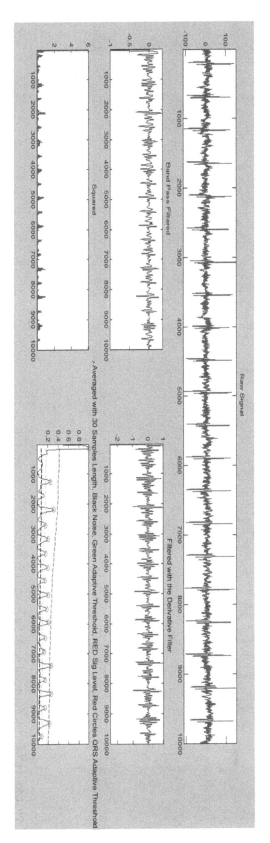

FIGURE 14.7.3   Squared signal for input data: r07.

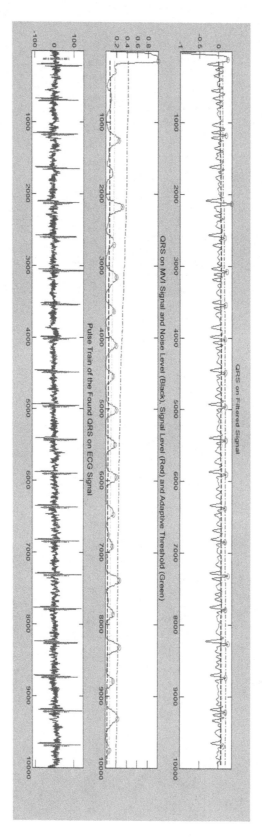

FIGURE 14.7.4   QRS detected signal for input data: r07.

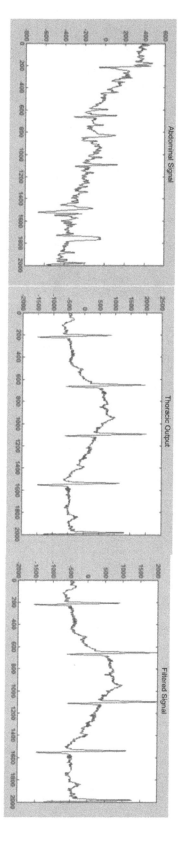

FIGURE 14.8.1 (a) Noisy signal (thoracic signal); (b) raw signal (abdominal signal); (c) LMS filtered output for input data: r08.

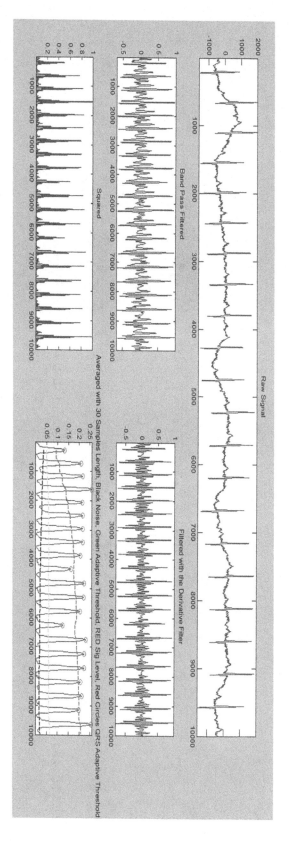

FIGURE 14.8.2   Derivative filtered signal for input data: r08.

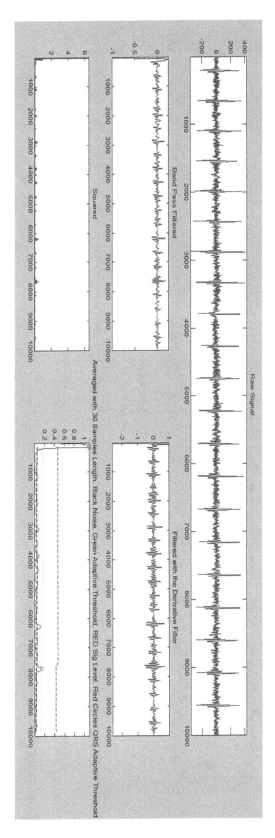

FIGURE 14.8.3 Squared signal for input data: r08.

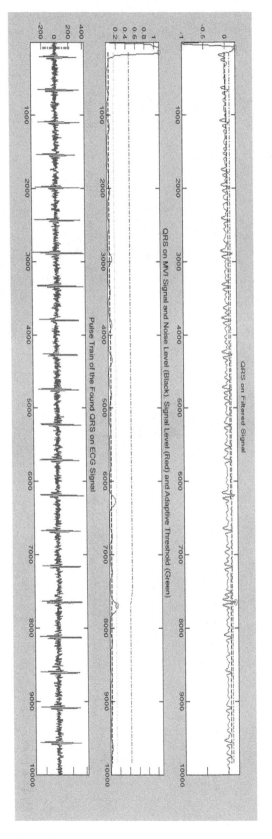

FIGURE 14.8.4   QRS detected signal for input data: r08.

TABLE 14.2
Results of FECG Extraction on Sample ECG Data

Sr. No.	Input ECG from Subject	Maternal Heart Beat (BPM)	Fetal Heart Beat (BPM)	Condition
1.	r01	93.8443	128.3285	Normal
2.	r04	80.5868	123.9285	Normal
3.	r07	112.8645	126.7293	Normal
4.	r08	7.9271	128.2462	Normal

a fetus's alive or dead condition, twin pregnancies, and fetal success, more patients and longer recordings are needed with more leads.

Furthermore, a labeled collection of data is required that contains marking the ST segments and QT intervals under a variety of normal and pathological circumstances. The challenge of fetal motion tracking utilizing non-invasive ECG recordings has piqued researchers' interest in recent studies. The herein proposed approaches can be coupled with these developments in future research to produce an integrated extraction of FECG and motion tracking system.

REFERENCES

[1]. S. Sonali, O. Singh, R.K. Sunkaria, *ECG signal denoising based on empirical Mode decomposition and moving average filter*, 2013 IEEE International Conference on Signal Processing, Computing and Control, ISPCC 2013 (2013).

[2]. Behar, Joachim, et al. "A comparison of single-channel fetal ECG extraction methods." *Annals of biomedical engineering* 42.6 (2014): 1340–1353.

[3]. H.-Y. Lin, S.-Y. Liang, Y.-L. Ho, Y.-H. Lin, H.-P. Ma, Discrete-wavelet-transform-based noise removal and feature extraction for ECG signals, *IRBM* 35 (December (6)) (2014) 351–361.

[4]. Hajar Ahmadieh, Babak Mohammadzadeh Asl. "Fetal ECG extraction via type-2 adaptive neuro-fuzzy inference systems." *Computer Methods and Programs in Biomedicine* 142 (2017): 101–108.

[5]. Marzieh Fatemi, Reza Sameni. "An online subspace denoising algorithm for maternal ECG removal from fetal ECG signals." *Iranian Journal of Science and Technology, Transactions of Electrical Engineering* 41.1 (2017): 65–79.

[6]. Rene Jaros, Radek Martinek, Radana Kahankova. "Non-adaptive methods for fetal ECG signal processing: A review and appraisal." *Sensors* 18.11 (2018): 3648.

[7]. Li Yuan, et al. "An improved FastICA method for fetal ECG extraction." *Computational and Mathematical Methods in Medicine* 2018 (2018): 1–7.

[8]. Iman Mousavian, Mohammad Bagher Shamsollahi, Emad Fatemizadeh. "Noninvasive fetal ECG extraction using doubly constrained block-term decomposition." *Mathematical Biosciences and Engineering: MBE* 17.1 (2019): 144–159.

[9]. Y. S. Alshebly, M. Nafea. "Isolation of fetal ECG signals from abdominal ECG using wavelet analysis." *IRBM* 41.5 (2020): 252–260.

[10]. Sarfaraj Mirza, Kalyani Bhole, Prateek Singh. *Fetal ECG extraction and qrs detection using independent component analysis*, 2020 16th IEEE International Colloquium on Signal Processing & Its Applications (CSPA). IEEE, 2020.

[11]. Mohammad Reza Mohebbian, et al. "Single channel high noise level ECG deconvolution using optimized blind adaptive filtering and fixed-point convolution kernel compensation." *Biomedical Signal Processing and Control* 57 (2020): 101673.

[12]. Luay Yassin Taha, Esam Abdel-Raheem. "Fetal ECG extraction using input-mode and output-mode adaptive filters with blind source separation." *Canadian Journal of Electrical and Computer Engineering* 43.4 (2020): 295–304.

[13]. Rachana R. Vaidya, N. Chaitra. *Comparison of adaptive filters in the extraction of fetal ECG*, 2020 International Conference on Smart Electronics and Communication (ICOSEC), pp. 1066–1070. IEEE, 2020.

[14]. H. Biglari, R. Sameni, "Fetal motion estimation from noninvasive cardiac signal recordings." *Physiological Measurement* 37.11 (November 2016): 2003–2023.

[15]. Gari D. Clifford et al. "Non-invasive fetal ECG analysis." *Physiological Measurement* 35.8 (2014): 1521–1536. doi:10.1088/0967-3334/35/8/1521

[16]. Adam Matonia, Janusz Jezewski, Tomasz Kupka, Krzysztof Horoba, Janusz Wrobel, Adam Gacek. "The influence of coincidence of fetal and maternal QRS complexes on fetal heart rate reliability." *Medical and Biological Engineering and Computing* 44.5 (2006): 393–403.

[17]. Joachim Behar, Fernando Andreotti, Sebastian Zaunseder, Qiao Li, Julien Oster, Gari D. Clifford. "An ECG simulator for generating maternal-fetal activity mixtures on abdominal ECG recordings." *Physiological Measurement* 35.8 (2014): 1537.

[18]. Ary L. Goldberger, Luis AN Amaral, Leon Glass, Jeffrey M. Hausdorff, Plamen Ch Ivanov, Roger G. Mark, Joseph E. Mietus, George B. Moody, Chung-Kang Peng, H. Eugene Stanley. "PhysioBank, PhysioToolkit, and PhysioNet: Components of a new research resource for complex physiologic signals." *circulation* 101.23 (2000): e215–e220.

15 Detection of Heart Functioning Abnormalities (Arrhythmia) Using ECG Signals
A Systematic Review

Ketan Sanjay Desale, Swati V. Shinde,
Vaishnavi Patil, and Parth Shrivastava

CONTENTS

15.1 INTRODUCTION

An electrocardiogram or an ECG estimates the electrical activity of the heart. Arrhythmia is an agent kind of disease that alludes to any unpredictable change from ordinary heart rhythms. While single arrhythmia heartbeat probably won't essentially affect life, nonstop arrhythmia thumps may bring about lethal conditions. Hence, by utilizing better treatment techniques, it is critical to intermittently screen heart rhythms to forestall cardiovascular diseases (CVDs). It has been for the most part utilized for identifying heart illnesses because of its straightforwardness and ready-to-distinguish heartbeat defects with high exactness. By dissecting the electrical sign of every heartbeat, which contains various impulses and waveforms, we can separate the development of various cardiovascular tissues found in the heart. Following these waveforms will make it easy to detect heart abnormalities.

In all the papers on the subject, authors have used the MIT-BIH dataset and CYBHi dataset (off the person category). The sampling rate was held at 360 Hz for 180 hours. The organization of this chapter is similar, in that this section is the introduction; Section 15.2 covers ECG signal pre-preparing, heartbeat division strategies, feature extraction strategies, and algorithms used for labeling. Section 15.3 includes the comparison of all the different techniques with the optimal solution, and section 15.4 involves the overview of the model.

15.2 LITERATURE REVIEW

The most recent decade of the 19th century witnessed the growth of a replacement period in which doctors used innovation with traditional history taking and physical examination to detect cardiac

DOI: 10.1201/9781003272694-18

sickness. The first electrocardiograph utilized a string galvanometer to record the likely respect between the limits coming about because of the heart's electrical initiation.

Electrocardiography today is a significant piece of the underlying assessment for patients with cardiovascular grievances. In particular, it assumes an urgent part as a non-intrusive, practical apparatus to measure arrhythmias and an ischemic heart condition. As an essential line demonstrative device, medical services suppliers at various degrees of instructing and ability regularly think that it's basic to have the ability to decipher electrocardiograms; nonetheless, a high pace of distortion has been noted among non-particular doctors, particularly among learners.

15.2.1 PREPROCESSING

When an ECG signal is recorded, it consists of various types of noises that need to be discarded before carrying out any further process of detection or extraction. The standard wander influences the recognition of arrhythmia and makes it difficult for an expert to analyze the ECG signal. The basic idea behind preprocessing is to remove noises such as baseline wandering, motion artifacts, and other false interpretations recorded in the ECG signal. The objective here is to improve the ratio of sound-noise. Various preprocessing techniques have been carried out earlier to improve the SNR ratio.

[1] uses ECG signal preprocessing and a support vector machine–based arrhythmia beat order to organize data into typical and unusual subjects. The handling of the electro cardiac signal is carried out using an LMS (least mean square) adaptive filtering technique to accomplish a fast and low blunder plan with less intricacy. A discrete wavelet change is set on the handled ECG signal to include extraction and an SVM (support vector machine) and other popular classifiers are used to classify beats. Results based on the SVM classifier have more accuracy compared to other classifiers based on machine learning. The denoising of the ECG signal is needed to abolish the baseline wander and different commotions in the electro cardiac signal. Many siftings and clamor evacuation methods have been used for commotion expulsion. An (LMS) adaptive filtering commotion evacuation strategy is applied in this work. The LMS calculation is the most mainstream procedure for versatile filtering on account of its computational straightforwardness. In every loop of the standard LMS calculation, the FIR channel coefficient is altered depending on the accompanying condition:

$$m(n + 1) = m(n) + \mu y(n)e(n), \qquad [1]$$

where n is defined as the time step $m(n)$ is the old weight and $m(n + 1)$ is the refreshed weight. u is the progression size that is utilized to control the strength. The versatile sifting yield $z(n)$ is then determined depending on the refreshed loads and contribution as $z(n) = w(n)y(n)$.

One strategy is for the arrangement of different kinds of arrhythmia utilizing morphological and dynamic highlights dependent on the time-space and recurrence area [2]. A discrete wavelet transform (DWT) is set forward on every heartbeat to get the powerful highlights of the ECG signal. Nonlinear elements of RR stretch are determined utilizing teaser energy administrator, which improves the arrhythmia characterization. More than 12 coefficients are chosen as morphological highlights. These highlights are used in a neural organization to arrange arrhythmia. The outcomes are tried on the MIT-BIH arrhythmia database utilizing 22151 beats.

The procedure is divided into four sections: ECG signal pre-preparing, heartbeat division strategies, feature extraction strategies, and algorithm used for labeling. Baseline wander mostly affects ECG signals. Various methods are imposed to eliminate these sorts of noise from the ECG signal. For removing the baseline wander, a bandpass filter was used in which the projected rate of the signal is generally deducted from the rudimentary electro cardiac signal to acquire an accurate ECG waveform utilizing $X[n] = xl[n] - u$ where $x[n]$ is defined as the denoised signal, $xl[n]$ addresses the rudimentary ECG sign, and μ is the math methods for the rudimentary EEG signal. The preprocessing stage is followed by heartbeat segmentation in which the QRS complex and the T and the P wave are detected. This involves the acknowledgment of the boundaries and peaks of these focuses. A solitary heartbeat comprised of about two hundred examples together with the R-wave and tests round the peak.

In [3], the authors have imposed a 12-layer deep CNN to categorize the five sub-classes of the heartbeats. The MIT-BIH database is utilized for the classification of the heartbeat, which contains 48 ECG recordings of 30 min, and a threshold denoising method is also used here. The preprocessing of the ECG signal is done using the wavelet transform method, which discards signals from various frequency bands. The convolutional modal has features to extract features from inside the signal; only simple filtering is applied in this work. Each pulse is marked with a disease label in the MIT-BIH database. In [3], five classes of heartbeats are used for classification. It uses the Pan-Tompkins algorithm, which is used to detect the R-waves, and the complete dataset is sectioned into 360 samples in this chapter; 16 recordings out of 48 recordings are used that contains all five classes of heartbeats that are needed to classify. The heartbeats of around 32,000 people are taken and divided into ten groups. The training procedure is divided into nine groups, with one remaining group used for testing and validation. The test data is shifted ten times during this operation, and performance is computed each time. Given the gradient descent, it uses a backward propagation algorithm of the convolutional neural network. The output vector is represented by the hyperparameters generated by the loss function. There are two phases to it: forward and backward propagation. The training data into the neural network is used as input. The middle and output layers are generated as the output in the form of vectors. The output vectors are compared to expected output vectors in backward propagation, and the loss is determined using the loss function. The weights are changed once the loss is re-input to the first layers using the gradient descent algorithm. After many iterations, the training comes to a conclusion when it reaches the set mistake.

The classification results of the convolutional neural network were found to have an overall classification accuracy count of 97.41%. The anticipated CNN algorithm has more accuracy than the BP neural network or the random forest network. It has a feature of weight sharing that improves its optimization process. It also shows good results in deriving local features that are required to categorize various forms of heartbeats. The number of convolutional layers and the filter size are also larger than the compared CNN networks.

A brief study on deep learning systems that was recently prepared on the picture dataset aims to recognize arrhythmia by diagnosing a patient's ECG signals [4]. A transferred deep convolutional neural organization is utilized to separate the highlights and a basic back engendering to process end grouping. The fundamental focal point of this work was to carry out a straightforward, solid, and effectively relevant deep learning algorithm to categorize three different cardiac conditions. The authors divided the work into five categories, namely, data acquisition, signal preprocessing, QRS detection, feature extraction, and ECG classification. For this study, the MIT-BIH arrhythmia database was used, consisting of over 4000 ECG recordings, although the ECG signal obtained from the recording is not the exact one because it contains noise that needs to be discarded from the ECG signal. Here at the first step, a method of mean removal is applied in which the aggregate of the ECG signal is subtracted from every point. The dc component is deleted, and the baseline is reset to zero. The high-frequency noise generated by the contraction of muscles is removed using a 10-point moving average filter that permits low frequencies but discards high frequencies. The low-frequency noise that causes baseline wandering is removed using high pass filters, which attenuates low-frequency noises. Preprocessing is followed by detection of QRS wavelet. It is a crucial element of the electro cardiac signal. The Pan-Tompkins algorithm was applied to detect the QRS wavelet. In the algorithm, a series of methods are carried out from derivation, squaring, integration, and adaptive thresholding for detection of R-peaks of the ECG signal.

ECG data acquired from the MIT-BIH database is refined; QRS complexes are detected and features of R-T interval are extracted. Finally, the resultant ECG signal is classified using a deep neural network of multiple layers for pattern recognition. When all the testing is carried out, it is found that the imposed deep learning extraction resulted in almost 100% recognition rates and

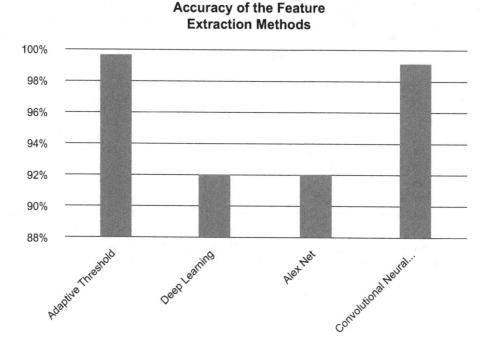

Accuracy of the Feature Extraction Methods

FIGURE 15.1   Accuracy comparison of feature extraction methods.

almost 96% accuracy during the training phase. During the testing phase, the recognition rate was found to be 98.5% with an average accuracy of 92.4%. As a result, the identification methods based on transferred learning extraction showed better results on the non-deep learning-based approach. Figure 15.1 gives the comparative analysis of various feature extraction methods.

15.2.2   HEARTBEAT SEGMENTATION

Heartbeat segmentation is a process where the QRS complex is detected from ECG successfully for future diagnosis. There are two parameters to evaluate the accuracy of heartbeat segmentation:

- Sensitivity (SN) = PT/(PT + NF)
- Positive Predictivity (PP)= PT/(PT + PF),

where PT indicates the count of correctly segmented heartbeats. PF—count of segmentations that do not correspond to the heartbeats. NF—count of segmentation that wasn't achieved by the most selected approach. Thus, we have studied different methods proposed on heartbeat segmentation in different papers and evaluated them on the above-mentioned parameters.

An analysis on arrhythmia by performing ECG classification applying CNN is done in [5]. The authors have used SVM for the feature analysis. First, the waves are preprocessed in two steps:

Step 1: Higher order statistics
Step 2: Hermit classification of R-waveform of the predefined electrocardiogram waves.

Then the segmentation process is done by applying the Pan-Tompkins algorithm. This technique is based on the recurring nature of the R-peaks strategy in electrocardiogram records. If the R-wave is not discovered once it is 166% of the recent average range, the maximum point in that range is chosen as the R-peak between the two threshold levels. The algorithm picks a single lead from the database, and all segments are normalized using the Z-score method.

$$Z = [x(i) - y]/SD, \qquad (2)$$

Where $x(i)$—heartbeat pin, (y)—mean heartbeat, and SD—standard deviation of wavelet. Thus, the dataset is further divided into 360 sections and is centered around the R-complex.

In [6], a faster-CNN established system is proposed that has been specially trained to handle electrocardiogram input. To classify inter-pulsation input, they have made use of inverted residual blocks. The key difference between this and the other models is that it has a 1D ECG sequence and outputs segmented heartbeat along with their labels. This model takes into account the relation between two waves. To perform the process of heartbeat segmentation and the classification simultaneously, these steps are followed:

- A filter networks
- Down sampling of block
- A region pooling block
- A backbone network
- A region proposal network (RPN)
- A region classification network (RCN)

An attainable and run-time method was used as a verification methodology for segmentation of the heartbeat by outsourcing the R-complex detection process, as proposed in [7]. It is established on CNNs, which may be encapsulated in the required hardware. Other methods generally tend to detect the false alarms in the classification stage, but in this process, the false alarms are detected in the segmentation stage itself. Rather than relying on input quality or disruption, the sense the ECG repeat format, i.e., identifying a heartbeat just by its frame. The third-party Pan-Thompkins algorithm is used herein to detect the R-peaks.

A modification of the algorithm was used here, i.e., decreasing the predefined threshold levels by half to increase the SN value. Two additional parameters were added to the study. These were the distance between two consecutive R-waves, which should be a minimum of two hundred meters from corporal view, and the model approach, which should tap the parameters to every patient continuously. Tompkins enforced a sliding window, which results in a satisfactory and sturdy approach to shed the disturbances. Therefore, it restrains the false-positive outcomes. Before CNN is trained, a human expert segments and labels a piece of data, and the output is a binary classification issue with the output of a heartbeat or no heartbeat.

In [4], a successful deep learning-based electrocardiogram classification system is used to do automated ECG arrhythmia diagnostics by categorizing patient ECGs into adjusting two distinctive cardiovascular conditions, namely, ordinary and paced. Pre-trained Alex Net is moved and utilized as a component extractor for the required task. The haul-out highlights are taken care of in a basic backpropagation NN to classify the info of ECG R-R. The algorithm recognizes QRS complexes based on digital inclination, quantitative measure, and breadth assessments. A digital filter lowers false detections in ECG signals produced by numerous types of interference. Because of this filtering, low thresholds can be used, boosting detection sensitivity. The system adjusts thresholds and settings regularly to respond to ECG changes like wave-frame or beats per minute. In [8], the authors recommended an innovative method for segmentation of electrocardiogram signals that does not necessitate removal of any interference from the signals. The proposed method states that the wave should initiate from R-wavelet and end when it approaches the consecutive R-wavelet in a ten-second window gap; this is in contrast to the traditional method, which starts from P-wavelet and ends at T-wavelet. Thus, an R-R complex is considered a unit, and the data consists of information regarding all three intervals. This method doesn't require resizing of the

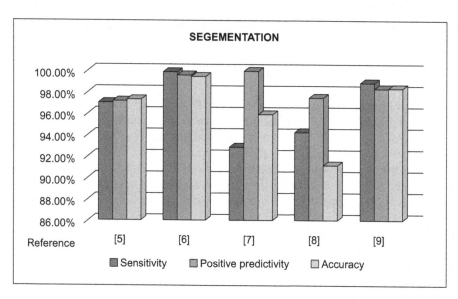

FIGURE 15.2   Comparison of segmentation methods based on sensitivity, positive predictivity, and accuracy.

blocks as they are already of the same size when they are procured from the ECG. This abnormal segment procedure on the information records is utilized to enhance the highlights settled in each portioned heartbeat, consequently causing an increase in precision. The comparative analysis of segmentation methods based on sensitivity, positive predictivity, and accuracy metrics is shown in Figure 15.2.

15.2.3   Feature Extraction

The paper [9] focuses upon examination for ECG errors using Hilbert change as well as the versatile edge strategy to recognize the genuine R-peaks from all the obtained signals. Extraction is applied to mostly three unique sorts of pulses, which are the typical pulses, untimely ventricular constriction, and atrial untimely compression. The requirement for adaptive threshold was necessary as it can be seen that a high threshold can lead to absent answers, whereas a lower threshold will lead to imprecise recognitions. Any threshold that is fixed will pose a difficulty to the detection of the T and P waves. To counter all these flaws, an adaptive threshold method is used to implement multiple thresholds simultaneously on different parts of the wave, declining the prospect of missing the QRS complexes.

The filtering technique used in [9] allows us to remove baseline wander along with higher frequencies. It also abates the T and P waves to make the most of the QRS complex. Next, the first derivative is used so that we can specify the lower and the upper slope of the ECG to gather the new points. The adaptive threshold is applied afterward, for QRS discovery from the produced wave. The method is achieved through the use of a pair of edge limiting values named as the upper threshold (uth) and lower threshold (lth).

Initially, the upper edge is characterized by the condition uth = 0.5 × auth, where α is the most extreme worth achieved y(k) over the point where k = 1. This should be done until n − 1. The bottom limit is characterized by the condition: lth = 0.1 × a. The edge esteems are refreshed in emphasis time, where the quantity of distinguished tops over the lth limit is gotten, and the quantity of recognized tops above uth is determined. In this way, Nlth is the quantity of QRS edifices distinguished by lth, and Nuth is the quantity of QRS buildings recognized by uth. The edges are refreshed after each integration while the quantity of recognized limits is changed.

Using the above methodology, automatic detection and extraction of data at a significant precision were able to be accomplished. The method proposed scored 96.28% and P = 99.71 for more than 44,715 heartbeats. Therefore, the paper [9] has obtained a unique technique for discovering the QRS complex using the electrocardiogram signals. This method for QRS abnormality discovery presents an adaptive threshold method to expand the precision of QRS complexes uncovered in accounts with low amplitude peak, negative polarities, and low SNR.

The primary purpose of [4] was aimed to prepare an advanced computer-aided analytic system that assists experienced cardiologists. This is done by providing cost-effective, brilliant, and efficient arrhythmia diagnostics that will save time. Traditional ECG signal processing methods, as well as excellent deep learning approaches, are used to detect ECG arrhythmia to achieve this goal for detecting heart arrhythmia. At the present state, the structure that has been proposed in this paper can distinguish and categorize heart arrhythmias effectively. In this paper [4], some major phases are used for the functionality of solving the ECG design recognition and classification of the problem. Some of the steps include QRS detection, preprocessing of the signal, ECG feature extraction, and the signal arrangement. We will be focusing on the feature extraction process to better understand it.

Using transferable deep learning to extract ECG features, it can be seen that the structures can readily distinguish between each class that falls between the R-T interval. This allows the determination of each member of a class that is capable of displaying the same form at the same time. In this case, more than 200 points were obtained following each R-peak, which were retrieved and fed into the deep learning algorithm. All the remaining portions of the ECG signal, which may hamper the identification, were removed. Alex Net is a deep learning structure grounded on a CNN that is capable of using more than one million RGB images of good resolution and being trained on the ImageNet dataset. The system can categorize and split the images into 1000 dissimilar groups with excellent performance. There are eight layers to the construction of the Alex Net CNN: three fully connected layers and five other layers. These layers are learned using ImageNet's generic imageries. As stated in the previous study, deeper layers of a deep learning (DL) framework completed on a big dataset can generally be transferred to and utilized on another organization assignment. These productivities of the Alex Net's deeper layers will be mined as structures for the assumed ECG inputs for the intended ECG arrangement system. Another paper we studied [11] offers a new and complete review study on DL approaches given to the ECG signal for arrangement purposes. The main objective of the learning is to educate a variety of DL topics in arrhythmia classification. This examination considers different kinds of the DL strategies like CNN and deep belief network (DBN). CNN is predominantly seen as the most effective procedure for highlight extraction, seen in 52% of the examinations. CNN is perhaps the most mainstream profound learning model that is generally prepared by slope-based streamlining. All in all, a CNN comprises various consecutive layers associated in a forward way.

Counting all the levels is the most important layer of this procedure. Extracting features is the responsibility of the first several levels. Other layers, such as the fully connected layers, are responsible for classification. The organization of many CNN architectures that have varied efficiency but have been demonstrated for several issues is represented by a universal CNN design. The element that was chosen by DL speeds up the cycle. The outcomes were not extraordinary for disclosure of unusual heartbeat. The framework was approved and tried with information from the MIT-BIH database. The proposed plan of this method was to consider the way there was no necessity aimed at information to decline through feature extraction.

We have considered the appropriateness of some significant DL algorithms used to predict ECG arrhythmia order. Plainly, from the outcome, CNN is the most encouraging technique for feature extraction (with 52% commitment). Also, we can sum up that we considered arrhythmia dependent on the most announced execution concerning the characterization techniques for all the contemplated arrhythmia.

In most of the papers that were applied in this survey [11], in any event, one sort of DL strategy for feature extraction was applied. As per the outcomes from the trials, DL calculations are demonstrated to be strong and effective. By using LSTM, a remarkable result on recognizing VEB and SVEB could be achieved. The DNNs can give the ideal outcomes; a few cases show a violation because of the immutable vulnerability in the extracted signals to noise. The results show gathering arrhythmia data from ECG signals using several DL techniques provided great results. The goal was to find and track the most effective DL algorithms for distinguishing between different types of arrhythmias.

The paper [10] was intended for the diagnosis of cardiac arrhythmia based on the wave features that continuous PR intervals greater than 0.2 s are indicative of first-degree blockage (I-AVB). The PAC and PVC identify the aberrant place. It's either a symptom of the STD or the STE is more than 0.1 mV if the ST segment is irregular. Significant activity is required to reliably distinguish these compound CA that are linked to ECG features. The difficulty is worsened by the huge expansion of the noise, which increases the effort. Emerging computer algorithms that can produce accurate outputs and programmed diagnoses to assist clinicians will help to alleviate the problem. The best-authenticated outcomes were nominated for further evaluation [10] to harvest several skilled models that are generated. The models with similar construction were also the result of this process. With correct validation of the methods, a satisfactory result was attained with a more optimal performance than that which could be achieved by individual models. In terms of predicting CA types, each of these new studies received a score of 0.82–0.84 on average. When compared to general practitioners and cardiologists, simulated intelligence-based ECG analysis has been shown to significantly improve conclusion accuracy. These AI algorithms can eliminate clinical overburden and decisions on the doctors. It's important to remember that until a significant percentage of the "underlying data" CA analysis needed to determine AI models is performed by expert cardiologists, the model's precision will suffer.

15.2.4 Algorithm and Classification

In [12], the electrocardiogram (ECG) is a test that detects and records the intensity and timing of the electrical activity in your heart. P, QRS, and T waves are examples of ECG waveforms. The most essential wave is the QRS complex. The spike-wave is a two-phase or three-phase wave with a period of 1 mV and an amplitude of 1 mV (80 to 100 milliseconds). The highest point of the QRC section of the ECG is represented by R when the regular rhythmic activity of the gut (the amplitude, duration, and shape of the amplitude) is disrupted. For many heart diseases, the EKG, particularly its QRS complex, remains the most straightforward approach.

Hermite basic features extend another representation of the ECG waveform, i.e., has outgrown Hermite basic features. It uses the similarity between the functional form of the ECG signal and the QRS complex number. The characteristics that determine the best shape of ECG are given by the expansion coefficients of the basic function of Hermite. Let us use the QRS complex number of the ECG curve. Including it in the Hermite series will display listing. A generic classification system that employs a large number of classifiers where the expansion coefficient is, the width parameter is, and the Hermite basic function, and is the Hermite polynomial of numerical experiments employing recursive relations to obtain Hermite polynomial findings. We use a system that combines the two classifiers discussed in this section (both support SVM classifiers). Since SVM is input, the feature vector used is different. In the first method, the feature HOS forms/defines the input vector (called HOS), while in the second method, the feature vector is formed by Hermite coefficients. In the database, there are 52 patients with ECG beats. The amount of knowledge associated with each type of time varies due to a shortage of data matching to particular types of time. Limiting some of the beats, we tried to provide the best minimum balance for the beats in the category under examination so as to provide the best minimum balance for the beats in the category under consideration. The total knowledge utilized to learn the neural network amounts to 6,690 when picking data. In addition, 6,095 data points are kept for testing purposes. In these circumstances, the SVM neural network has one output and equal inputs (17). To understand the problem of identifying multiple categories, we apply the one-to-many strategy to many network structures that adapt to popularity between the two categories at the same time. We use the radial Gaussian kernel. The parameter C was used in the experiment.

These values were chosen after multiple experiments on training and test data, urging that the required generalization potential should be selected so that the number of support vectors is as small as possible to provide the best network performance on the observed test data. As a result of this learning process, there are SVM networks, and the number of potential units (supporting vectors) is changed from one network to another. The total number of support vectors for all networks is bounded by 1200. The dataset has fixed network parameters and recovery mode, so it is not used in training.

In [13], SVM is a new paradigm learning system. Due to its generalizability, it is used to solve supervised classification problems. Here, given the radial basis function (RBF) using a nonlinear binary tree, SVM has read for multiple class classification problems. When using the SVM model, determining the kernel function and its limit values is essential. It should be that the simplified limit incorporates the sigma coefficient used in the kernel function.

All the examples at a node are assigned two sub-hubs obtained by the similarity of the most recently selected class. This process is rehashed on each hub until each node contains only one instance of the class. The main advantages of the SVM-BDT tree architecture include the computational efficiency and high-order precision of SVM. The RBF function is widely used in SVM classification. The width of the function Cris and Ix-Zl two are expressed as the squared Euclidean distance between two feature vectors. It tends to assume that using SVM, which relies on the wavelet energy histogram method to construct a rendering frame, can achieve a high permutation rate, reaching 99.75% for 0.9 sigma priority. The 16-layer deep convolutional network is designed in [14] to identify ECG signals based on cardiovascular arrhythmias. This deep network model can automatically classify segments (input) through the structure without any manual feature extraction. The deep neural network structure is made up of traditional CNN layers, but the one-dimensional CNN design is transcendent. In the "one-dimensional convolutional layer", the specular map described as ECG points undergoes convolution processing under different loads and uses 128 wt vectors to perform a one-dimensional convolution on the ECG information signal in the main layer of the model.

The deep network proposed has a smoothing layer in the fourteenth layer, so the element mapping obtained from the thirteenth layer can be converted into a required size to contribute to the resulting layer of the network. This layer changes the multidimensional input that the vector contains to one-dimensional output information. The bright spots obtained from the leveling layer will be processed into a thicker layer of 512 units of associated neural tissue. In the last layer of the network, there is a SoftMax layer, which is the unit of the number of output categories. Using the SoftMax layer, the category expectations of the input information can be determined. The developed 16-layer model provides the highest grouping results for large-scale ECG signals. The main disadvantage of this analysis is that it decomposes a small number of ECG signal slices (1000 out of 45 patients). You are also unable to classify ECG signal segments containing more than one category. The 1D-CNN model has an accuracy of 91.33% for 17 cardiovascular arrhythmias (classes), and the combined time is 0.015 s. It is used to check the ECG test every 10 s.

Optimal path forest (OPF), seen in [15], is a pattern classifier framework designed by Papa et al. (2009, 2012), based on best graphics partitioning where every sample is a node of the entire graph, and the arc between them is weighted by the distance of its corresponding feature vector. The concept is to use the competitive process between prototypes to divide the graph in an optimal path tree (OPT), rooted in each prototype. We have samples belonging to the same OPT that are more closely related to the root (prototype) than any other sample in the forest with its best path. The prototype assigns a cost to each node (that is, its path of least weight or the maximum arc weight along the path); the prototype that provides the best path cost will conquer that node and use the same tag for the prototype. In essence, the OPF classifier creates a distinct optimal partition, so that can classify any sample based on the partition. This obtained partition is the best path forest (OPF) calculated

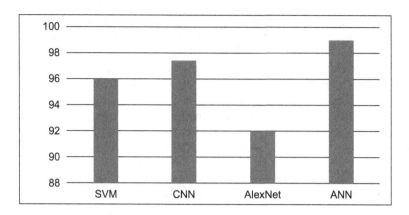

FIGURE 15.3   Classifier performance (accuracy) comparison.

in Rn by the image forest transformation algorithm. Figure 15.3 shows the comparison of accuracy of various classifiers.

15.3   RESULTS AND DISCUSSION

After reviewing several papers and numerous methodologies for detecting arrhythmia using ECG signals and abating the risk of death from CVD, we concluded that in the heartbeat segmentation process, the use of the Pan-Tompkins algorithm will be most optimum. It lies on R-wave detection with an accuracy of 97.41%. The adaptive threshold method was the best method to use. It provides better accuracy than any other proposed method (99.7%) and holds better noise immunity. DL methods have a better approach and may provide better results but are highly prone to noise and so can be unreliable in many cases.

15.4   CONCLUSION

After surveying numerous research papers on arrhythmia and its detection, we have proposed this methodology for the classification of arrhythmia using ECG signals. We would use adaptive digital filtering, difference operation method, adaptive threshold, and SVM to achieve the decided and accurate results. We believe that with our research, we can use ECG signals to detect arrhythmias in patients accurately and reduce the number of mortalities by a significant amount, and thus save lives.

REFERENCES

[1] C. Venkatesan, P. Karthigaikumar, A. Paul, S. Satheeskumaran, and R. Kumar, "ECG Signal Pre-processing and SVM Classifier-Based Abnormality Detection in Remote Healthcare Applications", *IEEE Access*, vol. 6, pp. 9767–9773, 2018, https://doi.org/10.1109/ACCESS.2018.2794346.
[2] Syed Muhammad Anwar, Maheen Gul, Muhammad Majid, and Majdi Al-nowami, "Arrhythmia Classification of ECG Signals Using Hybrid Features", *Computational and Mathematical Methods in Medicine*, vol. 2018, Article ID 1380348, pp. 8, 2018, https://doi.org/10.1155/2018/1380348.
[3] Mengze Wu, Yondi Lu, Wenli yang, and Shen Yuong Wong, "A Study on Arrhythmia via ECG Signal Classification Using the Convolutional Neural Network", *Frontiers in Computational Neuroscience*, vol. 14, 2021, https://doi.org/10.3389/fncom.2020.564015.
[4] Ali Isin and Selen Ozdalili, "Cardiac Arrhythmia Detection Using Deep Learning", *Procedia Computer Science*, vol. 120, 2017, https://doi.org/10.1016/j. procs.2017.11.238.3.

[5] Wu Mengze, Lu Yongdi, Yang Wenli, and Wong Shen Yuong, "A Study on Arrhythmia via ECG Signal Classification Using the Convolutional Neural Network", *Frontiers in Computational Neuroscience*, vol. 14, 2021.

[6] X. Qiu, S. Liang, and Y. Zhang. Simultaneous ECG Heartbeat Segmentation and Classification with Feature Fusion and Long-Term Context Dependencies. In: Lauw H., Wong R.W., Ntoulas A., Lim E.P., Ng S.K., Pan S. (eds) *Advances in Knowledge Discovery and Data Mining. PAKDD 2020*. Lecture Notes in Computer Science, vol 12085. Springer, Cham, 2020, https://doi.org/10.1007/978-3-030-47436-2_28.

[7] P. Silva, E. Luz, G. Silva et al. Towards Better Heartbeat Segmentation with Deep Learning Classification. *Scientific Reports* 10, pp. 20701, 2020, https://doi.org/1 0.1038/s41598-020-77745-0.

[8] Taissir Fekih Romdhane, Haikel Alhichri, Ridha Ouni, and Mohamed Atri, "Electrocardiogram Heartbeat Classification Based on a Deep Convolutional Neural Network and Focal Loss", *Computers in Biology and Medicine*, vol. 123, 2020.

[9] R. Rodríguez, A. Mexicano, J. Bila, S. Cervantes, and R. Ponce, "Feature Extraction of Electrocardiogram Signals by Applying Adaptive Threshold and Principal Component Analysis", *Journal of Applied Research and Technology*, vol. 13, 2015.

[10] Tsai-Min Chen, Chih-Han Huang, Edward S.C. Shih, Yu-Feng Hu, and Ming-Jing Hwang, "Detection and Classification of Cardiac Arrhythmias by a Challenge-Best Deep Learning Neural Network", *iScience*, vol. 23, 2020.

[11] Zahra Ebrahimi, Mohammad Loni, Masoud Daneshtalab, and Arash Gharehbaghi, "A Review on Deep Learning Methods for ECG Arrhythmia Classification", *Expert Systems with Applications: X*, vol. 7, 2020.

[12] A. S. Barhatte, R. Ghongade, and A. S. Thakare, "QRS Complex Detection and Arrhythmia Classification Using SVM", *2015 Communication, Control and Intelligent Systems (CCIS)*, pp. 239–243, 2015, https://doi.org/10.1109/CCIntelS.2015.7437915.

[13] S. Osowski, L. T. Hoai, and T. Markiewicz, "Support Vector Machine-Based Expert System for Reliable Heartbeat Recognition", *IEEE Transactions on Biomedical Engineering*, vol. 51, no. 4, pp. 582–589, April 2004, https://doi.org/10.1109/TBME.2004.824138.

[14] Eduardo José da S. Luz, Thiago M. Nunes, Victor Hugo C. de Albuquerque, João P. Papa, and David Menotti, "ECG Arrhythmia Classification Based on Optimum Path Forest", *Expert Systems with Applications*, vol. 40, 2013.

[15] Özal Yıldırım, Paweł Pławiak, Ru-San Tan, and U. Rajendra Acharya, "Arrhythmia Detection Using Deep Convolutional Neural Network with Long Duration ECG Signals", *Computers in Biology and Medicine*, vol. 102, 2018, https://doi.org/10.1016/j.compbiomed.2018.09.009.

16 Heart Rate Variability Analysis in Healthy Male Subjects with Comprehensive Age Groups

Anjali C. Birajdar and Vijaya R. Thool

CONTENTS

16.1 INTRODUCTION

The heart and the brain are the most important organs of the cardiovascular and nervous systems, respectively, of human physiology. The functioning of the cardiovascular system and the nervous system are assessed individually by electrocardiogram (ECG) and electroencephalogram (EEG), respectively. However, heart rate variability (HRV) analysis provides a single and simple technique to understand the functioning of both cardiovascular and nervous systems, specifically, the heart and autonomic nervous system (ANS), and also the interrelation between them. It manifests the subtle variations available in each successive beat intervals, which are under the control of the ANS. HRV is the beat-to-beat changes occurring in the successive heart beat from a continuous ECG signal [1].

HRV analysis gained enough appreciation as a simple and non-intraoperative tool to investigate cardiac abnormalities and autonomic functioning. Wide-ranging studies on heart rate variability have been undertaken, ranging from physiological modeling and interpretation, diagnostic tools in different pathologic states, and detection of stress levels to observation under various physiological and pharmacological interventions. In contemporary times, practically all electrocardiogram recording equipment has modules for computing time and spectral parameters of HRV; moreover, such systems are used in modern hospitals to observe and verify a patient's condition specifically in intensive and coronary care sections.

In pursuit of robust techniques for heart rate variability analysis and measurements, researchers have come up with various signal processing techniques and algorithms for its measurement in time and spectral domain methods. The increasing applications of time and spectral methods in clinical settings have demonstrated the diagnostic and prognostic inter-relevance of several features that are analyzed by HRV dynamics [2]. Rompelman et al. [3] utilized the computational efficiency of the personal computer for frequency domain analysis of HRV, to provide more accurate results. A simple and efficient algorithm used for derivation of equispaced RR sequence from the electrocardiogram was proposed by Berger et al. [4]. Luczak and Lurig presented and established the superiority of the spectral analysis method of HRV measurement [5]. Impacts of undesired artifacts on HRV measurement have been also evaluated by other works [6,7]. Merri et al. [8]

DOI: 10.1201/9781003272694-19

proposed a sampling frequency of 250 Hz or more for ECG recording to avoid errors in inter-beat interval calculations.

Huikuri et al. described the spectral domain method to analyze HRV to evaluate the temporal variations before immediate serials of ventricular tachycardia by spectral indices measures for verification of quantity difference analysis [9]. A. J. Camm et al. provided standard HRV analysis guidelines in TD and FD features with its clinical interpretation for clinical use [1]. The idea of sympathovagal balance has been seriously criticized, as changes in LF/HF or in normalized LF and HF powers have been interpreted as if sympathetic and parasympathetic activities always change reciprocally. However, while the sympathetic and vagal nervous system act in parallel in some situations, such as cold immersion of the face, the interpretation may not be physiologically justified in all situations [10]. Tiran et al. analyzed HRV by spectral domain to distinguish normal subjects and sarcoidosis patients by observing features like powers in LF, HF, and its ratio [11]. Pichon et al. described the effect of spectral analysis by HRV on healthy subjects at rest and during an orthostatic stress and found that both methods have same trend [12]. Belova et al. [13] proposed and developed a better approach using wavelet transform to access instantaneous variations in the HRV. Kuss et al. performed the HRV analysis by TD and FD on simulated data to quantify the statistical errors of both methods and show that TD has fewer statistical errors [14]. Montano et al. explored HRV analysis by experimenting on posture such as rest and 90-degree tilt in young subjects [15]. Bravi et al. analyzed the biomedical time series signal by time domain measures to provide significant information to clinical use [16]. Faust et al. reviewed and presented the features calculated from linear methods along with other methods to explore changes by HRV in normal subjects and diabetic patients [17]. Silva et al. calculated the TD and FD indices to examine the effect of physical training in normal individuals by HRV analysis with different age groups [18]. Voss et al. computed the TD and FD features of HRV analysis to observe in healthy persons the effect of age and gender [19]. Heart rate variability indices evaluated with a non-parametric approach are assumed to be a reference due to their dependency on actual data stream with certain data length and segment length.

Nonlinear methods were discussed earlier for the time series; later, around 1995, these methods were used for biomedical signals for analysis and interpretation. HRV analysis by nonlinear methods through considering its respiratory dynamics was proposed and developed to provide the simple analysis of chaotic non-stationary biomedical signal by Hoyer et al. [20]. M. Brennan et al. [21] proposed and implemented the Poincare plot nonlinear method, which is very simple in nature for heart rate variability analysis. Beckers et al. described HRV analysis with the help of nonlinear indices to investigate the effect of age and gender along with variation of day and night [22]. Ding et al. [23] proposed a technique of nonlinear dynamic pattern fluctuation to study the nonlinear and non-stationary signals of HRV by analyzing normal, healthy subjects in two different age groups. Voss et al. described an extensive review of HRV analysis using more nonlinear methods by different researchers and also the application of these nonlinear methods in particular areas, such as healthy subjects with aging effect and sex [24]. Vigo et al. [25] proposed the nonlinear method along with the FD method of HRV analysis within an independent frequency component during sleep–wake cycle in healthy volunteers. Singh et al. explored the effect of the presence of ectopic beat and ectopic beat editing in analyzing data by HRV nonlinear methods using ApEn and SampEn on healthy individuals and acute MI patients [26]. Voss et al. computed the nonlinear indices of HRV analysis to provide the information of age and gender in a healthy population [27]. Jelinek et al. presented an analysis of HRV by Poincare plot method on sedentary male individuals with high- and low-intensity exercises to find out the effect of temporal dynamics of circadian rhythm [28].

A sample representation of ECG signal and its HRV signal are portrayed in Figure 16.1. In this case, at the top is the ECG signal with time along the x-axis, active potential along the y-axis, and its R peaks at t1, t2, etc. However, at the bottom, a generated HRV signal of the same ECG signal with time along the x-axis and RR interval along the y-axis has been manifested.

For the analysis of time series HRV data, various methodological aspects have been proposed, including simple basic statistical, time domain (TD) methods [29, 30], fast Fourier transform (FFT)

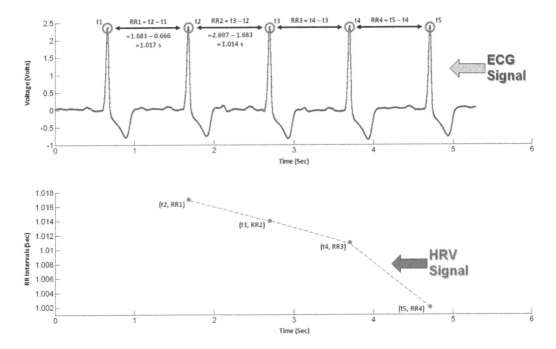

FIGURE 16.1 Representations of ECG signal and HRV signal.

based spectral or frequency domain (FD) methods [30, 31], and different nonlinear techniques [31–33]. More influencing parameters on HRV such as age, gender, life style, eating habits, etc., in healthy volunteers have been confirmed by many researchers [34–39]. Short-term frequency domain analysis of HRV using FFT technique has shown that heart rate variability is influenced more by age effects compared to gender, which is shown by a decrease in total power by spectral analysis [40–42]. The present study aims to compute aging effects in healthy males with wide age group from boys to the elderly with the help of significant features from TD and FD by FFT of linear methods and SD1, SD2 of Poincare plot, ApEn, and SampEn.

The chapter is organized as follows: In section 16.2, materials and methods are presented with the help of HRV analysis methods that include ECG and HRV data as well. In section 16.3, the results and discussion are illustrated with detailed tables and figures. The conclusion is presented in section 16.4, and the reference list follows.

16.2 MATERIALS AND METHODS

16.2.1 HRV DATA

ECG signal using Lead-II was recorded by a 16-channel BIOPAC™ MP160 system and its supporting AcqKnowledge software. The system set-up for recording is shown in Figure 16.2. The data was acquired with an amplifier module ECG 100C using one of 16 available channels in normal male subjects in supine rest condition. Disposable electrodes were used for acquisition. Expert observers examined the data to confirm acceptable signal quality prior to its processing for analysis, but no efforts were made to exclude data simply on the basis of low values. The channel has been well calibrated prior to the recording. The sampling frequency used at the time data acquisition was 500 Hz [43].

ECG signals of 223 healthy male subjects were selected after considering the precise exclusion/inclusion criteria from additional recorded signals by considering an age group of 10–75 years at

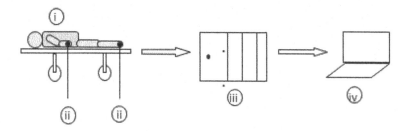

FIGURE 16.2   ECG data acquisition system set-up: (i) subject in supine rest condition; (ii) ECG leads; (iii) recording system amplifier modules; (iv) laptop.

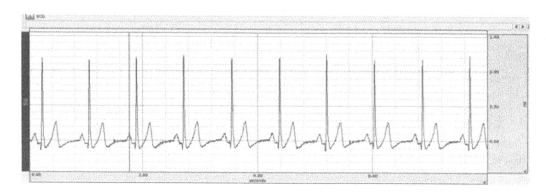

FIGURE 16.3   Sample image of recorded ECG of normal subject with time (sec) along x-axis and potential (mV) along y-axis.

M. B. E. Society's College of Engineering Ambajogai, Maharashtra, India. These data have been categorized into five subsets as 10–15 years old (A), 18–30 years old (B), 31–45 years old (C), 46–60 years old (D), and 61–75 years old (E). The number of subjects in each subset is 62, 52, 47, 34, and 28 in the categories of A, B, C, D, and E respectively. In this present work, the healthy male subjects considered for this study did not have any kind of habits. The entire ECG data recording was carried out in a noise-free, controlled environment in the supine rest condition. A noted consent form has been received from every volunteer before recording the data that says that they have been made aware of the purpose of recording and that it will not cause any kind of harm to the subjects' body. Placement of the electrode, applying the jelly at the location of electrode, and proper lead selection have been carefully verified in each subject before beginning the recording. Subjects were acquainted with the situation through relaxing for few minutes in a supine condition. While recording the data, care was taken such that the recording data follows as per ideal expectation by monitoring continuously towards recording data and electrode positions. These recorded ECG data were then converted into heart rate variability data in tachogram format. In all cases, AcqKnowledge software of BIOPAC™ system was used to generate RR tachogram. Figure 16.3 and Figure 16.4 depict the typical representation of recorded ECG data and HRV RR interval signal respectively. Figure 16.5 is the simple workflow representation of the complete notion.

16.2.2   HRV ANALYSIS: LINEAR AND NONLINEAR TECHNIQUES

The insightful meaning of the status of the subject can be obtained from an HRV analysis derived by different linear and nonlinear methods. In time domain methods, the heart rate variability indices are evaluated from normal-to-normal (NN) interval series. The time domain methods are simple

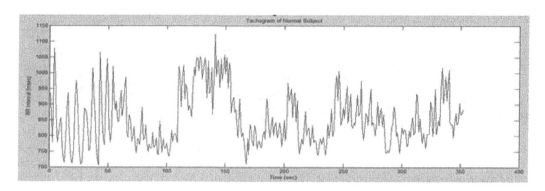

FIGURE 16.4 Sample image of tachogram of normal subject with time (sec) along x-axis and RR interval (msec) along y-axis.

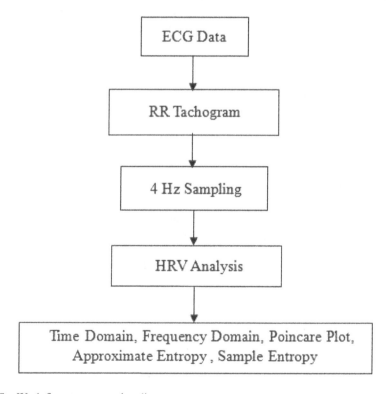

FIGURE 16.5 Work flow representation diagram.

methods represented in statistical format, but yet are much better to observe the overall changes in the signal [44]. The TD indices considered significant are briefed as follows. Mean heart rate (HR_{mean}), as the name suggests, is the mean value of the heart rate (HR) of an entire ECG signal. HR is the reciprocal of the RR interval measured in beats per minutes. Variance is a change occurring in RR interval with respect to its mean and is expressed in ms^2. Standard deviation of normal-to-normal intervals (SDNN) is simple and an important basic feature that computes the standard deviation (SD) of a NN interval. SDNN is a standard deviation of the NN intervals, which is the square root of their variance and is expressed in milliseconds. SDSD is the standard deviation of successive difference between adjacent normal-to-normal RR intervals and is expressed in milliseconds.

RMSSD is the root mean square of successive difference and is expressed in milliseconds. CV% is the coefficient of variance expressed in percentage of normal-to-normal RR interval series. pNN50 is the percentage of the number of adjacent normal-to-normal RR intervals having more than 50 ms. In spectral, analysis of HRV is performed by the FFT technique. The frequency domain methods are not as simple as time domain methods, as more emphasis is on sympathetic and vagal activity. Power spectral density (PSD) has been used to compute the power in spectral analysis. The complete frequency range has been subdivided into three frequency components, namely, power in very low frequency (P-VLF): 0.0033 Hz to 0.04 Hz; power in low frequency (P-LF): 0.04 Hz to 0.15 Hz; and power in high frequency (P-HF): 0.15 Hz to 0.4 Hz. The entire frequency range is total power (P-Total). In the present work, powers in very low frequency, low frequency, high frequency, and entire range of frequency, and also LF/HF, have been calculated. Here, to calculate the HRV indices using the FFT technique, a 4 Hz resampling of RR interval data, 512 samples, 50% overlapping area, Hann window, and Welch periodogram are preferred to estimate the power spectral density.

Nonlinear methods of HRV analysis have the ability to extract the inherent feature of a biomedical signal like non-stationarity and nonlinear dynamics. Nonlinear methods, with features like Poincare plot (SD1, SD2), approximate entropy (ApEn), and sample entropy (SampEn), have been carried out for HRV analysis. Poincare plot portrays a RR interval variation with respect to current and its successive RR intervals along the x-axis and y-axis respectively [21, 44–46]. Approximate entropy is a measure of the complexity or irregularity of a signal, where the more regular or predictable the RR interval series, the lower the value of *ApEn* and vice versa [46,47]. The conditional probability's negative natural logarithm is nothing but a sample entropy. It is yet another algorithm that computes the complexity or irregularity in the signal, similar to that of approximate entropy, but it avoids similarities in the matching.

16.3   RESULTS AND DISCUSSION

Comparative result analysis of all five age groups with respect to time domain, FFT-based spectral domain, and nonlinear methods like Poincare plot (PP), ApEn, and SampEn have been compiled and discussed. All the features considered here are significant based on P-values of student T-test and values expressed in terms of mean ± standard deviation. Table 16.1 provides comparison of time domain indices like HR_{mean}, variance, SDNN, SDSD, RMSSD, CV%, and pNN50. All the TD features declined with increasing age, mostly with linear change and a few with precipitous nature. However, HR_{mean} declined gradually in the initial four age groups, but increased in the elderly age group because of higher age. Interestingly, though HR_{mean} has increased in the elderly age group, HRV wasn't enhanced but rather diminished linearly, which is evident from the feature variance. Features such as SDNN, SDSD, and CV% have linear change, suggesting that the sympathetic and parasympathetic activity of ANS is a balancing act, and that features like RMSSD and pNN50, although they may appear linear, are in fact less steep comparatively since these exhibit parasympathetic dominance. In general, all time domain features follow a similar trend when compared with earlier research, though the data recording is from the South Asia region. Figures 16.6, 16.7, 16.8, and 16.9 highlight the insight of comparative analysis of all age groups in terms of indices, specifically SDSD, RMSSD, CV%, and pNN50, respectively. It is evident from these comparison figures that values are decreasing with increasing age groups.

Table 16.2 sums up the comparison of all FD features by FFT such as powers in very low, low, high, and entire range of frequencies and also LF/HF. The feature P-VLF shows gradual decline from lower age group to higher age groups, which is mainly because of the vascular mechanisms system caused by negative emotions, worries, etc. Features P-LF, P-HF, and P-Total show a steep decline in the age group from A to B and then follow a linear decline in the age group C to D and then in the last age group, a U type change occurs. Feature P-LF inter-relates sympathetic and parasympathetic tone, whereas feature P-HF inter-relates parasympathetic tone and feature P-Total reflects a combination of all three. The parameter LF/HF follows the similar pattern of P-LF and

TABLE 16.1
Comparative Analysis of Time Domain Features in Normal Male Subjects with Different Age Groups

Features Age Group	A	B	C	D	E
HR$_{Mean}$ (bpm)	82.26 ± 6.24	76.17 ± 9.34	74.94 ± 9.03	70.18 ± 9.59	79.0 ± 4.82
Variance (ms²)	3783.70 ± 900.3	2834.58 ± 555.8	2335.97 ± 457.1	2044.48 ± 414.3	1903.01 ± 509.9
SDNN (ms)	59.7 ± 5.05	55.48 ± 4.44	47.16 ± 4.94	41.92 ± 5.38	37.76 ± 3.89
SDSD (ms)	56.67 ± 5.27	46.52 ± 4.24	39.65 ± 3.2	35.14 ± 3.27	22.58 ± 2.82
RMSSD (ms)	56.90 ± 8.01	45.68 ± 3.32	37.9 ± 3.54	36.45 ± 3.86	21.59 ± 2.35
CV%	9.61 ± 1.19	8.0 ± 0.3	7.06 ± 0.34	6.35 ± 0.4	5.29 ± 0.44
pNN50 (%)	39.1 ± 3.34	30.23 ± 3.61	21.10 ± 2.21	12.68 ± 2.34	5.95 ± 0.58

Values expressed in mean ± standard deviation

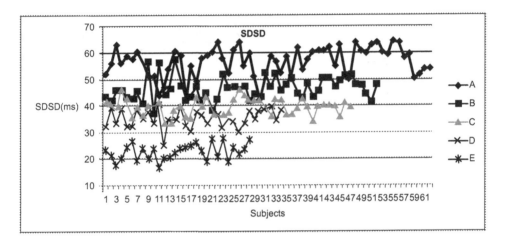

FIGURE 16.6 Comparison of SDSD with different age groups.

P-HF but in a reverse way i.e. escalates from age group A to D and then shows a down surge in the last age group, E, since LF/HF corresponds to sympathovagal balance. Figures 16.10, 16.11, 16.12, 16.13, and 16.14 correspond to age groups A, B, C, D, and E respectively and show the typical representation of the power distribution in the VLF, LF, HF, and entire frequency range with the help of PSD computed using FFT. Figures 16.15–16.18 illustrate juxtapose of features, P-VLF, P-LF, P-HF and P-Total respectively of all age groups A–E. A notable discrimination can be observed in these figures that signifies the different range of values in all age groups.

Table 16.3 outlines the compiled result of features from nonlinear HRV methods like SD1, SD2 obtained from Poincare plot, ApEn, and SampEn by considering all age groups. Nonlinear techniques of HRV analysis have an ability to extract the inherent characteristics of biomedical signal like non-stationarity and nonlinear dynamics. All the nonlinear indices exhibit decremental feature values with increasing age groups, which corresponds the physiological and psychological aging of human organs. Both ApEn and SampEn, which describe the periodicity of the data for normal subjects, basically have a smaller overall range to express themselves but have slightly diminished values with increasing age groups. The parameter SampEn in age group A has a mean value of 1.6993

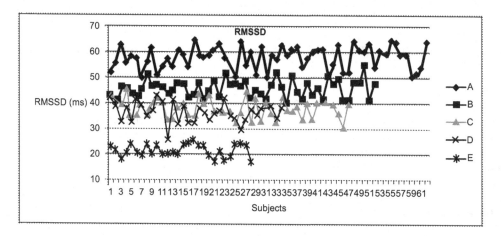

FIGURE 16.7   Comparison of RMSSD with different age groups.

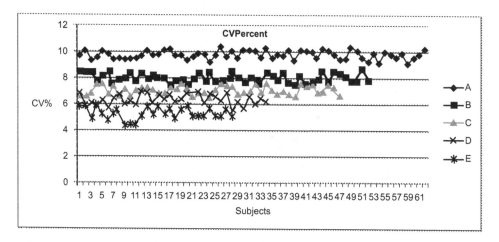

FIGURE 16.8   Comparison of CV% with different age groups.

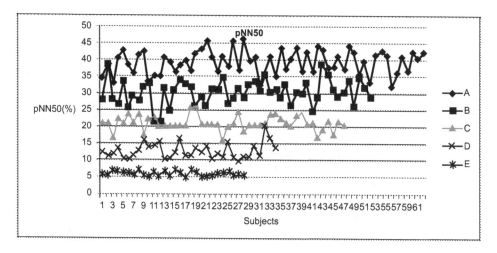

FIGURE 16.9   Comparison of pNN50 with different age groups.

TABLE 16.2

Comparative Analysis of Frequency Domain (FFT) Features in Normal Male Subjects with Different Age Groups

Features Age Group	A	B	C	D	E
P-VLF (ms²)	479.51 ± 23.5	444.11 ± 29.19	335.70 ± 20.49	287.61±29.59	268.37 ± 26.37
P-LF (ms²)	413.23 ± 7.83	352.18 ± 41.34	249.31 ± 10.88	167.59±12.91	188.52 ± 12.17
P-HF (ms²)	374.56 ± 37.37	214.15 ± 23.07	189.53 ± 18.07	127.35±5.08	144.62 ± 7.75
P-Total (ms²)	1267.58 ± 50.66	1010.37 ± 25.99	775.52 ± 14.26	582.71±18.64	601.31 ± 23.23
LF/HF	1.55 ± 0.15	2.29 ± 0.32	2.54 ± 0.51	2.74±0.11	2.24 ± 0.1574

Values expressed in mean ± standard deviation

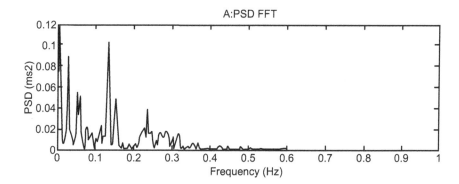

FIGURE 16.10   Typical representation of PSD spectral analysis by FFT of age group A.

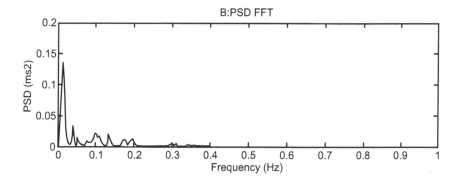

FIGURE 16.11   Typical representation of PSD spectral analysis by FFT of age group B.

and is declining as age increases i.e. 1.6090 for age group B, 1.5835 for age group C, 1.542 for age group D, and 1.3189 for age group E, which suggests the more random or non-periodic nature of HRV data in lower age groups than higher age groups. Figures 16.19, 16.20, and 16.21 portray the typical Poincare plot of age groups A and B; C; D and E respectively. SD1 and SD2 indicate the short- and long-term variability respectively. For most normal healthy subjects, considerations of

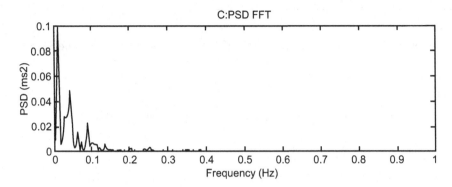

FIGURE 16.12 Typical representation of PSD spectral analysis by FFT of age group C.

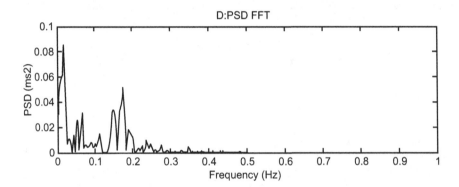

FIGURE 16.13 Typical representation of PSD spectral analysis by FFT of age group D.

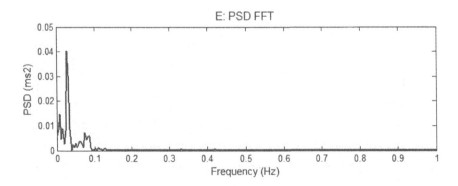

FIGURE 16.14 Typical representation of PSD spectral analysis by FFT of age group E.

Poincare plot representation are a non-uniform spread of the data in the elliptical form with SD2 comparatively much higher than SD1 in quadrant diagonal format; the position of elliptical spread data should be at the center of the quadrant and higher individual values of both SD1 and SD2 indices. Similar trends can be observed in these figures with the lower age group much healthier with its shape, size, and position.

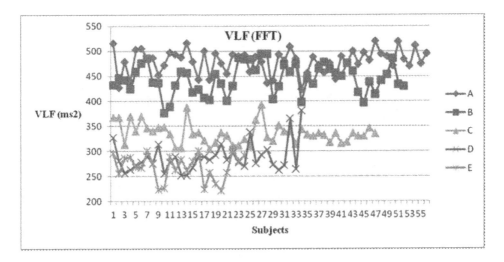

FIGURE 16.15 Comparison of P-VLF (FFT) in different age groups.

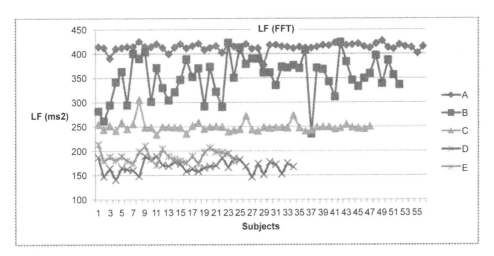

FIGURE 16.16 Comparison of P-LF (FFT) in different age groups.

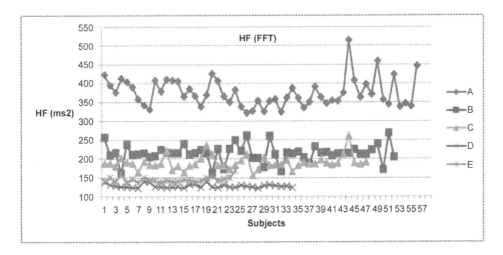

FIGURE 16.17 Comparison of P-HF (FFT) in different age groups.

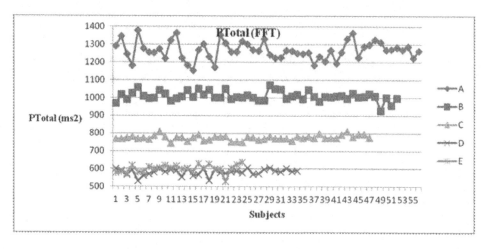

FIGURE 16.18 Comparison of P-Total (FFT) in different age groups.

TABLE 16.3

Comparative Analysis of Nonlinear Features in Normal Male Subjects with Different Age Groups

Features Age Group	A	B	C	D	E
SD1 (ms)	40.87 ± 2.92	30.94 ± 8.49	20.34 ± 5.19	19.56 ± 3.966	18.44 ± 3.49
SD2 (ms)	70.59 ± 13.3	66.63 ± 13.20	58.24 ± 10.46	52.29 ± 9.84	52.30 ± 4.66
ApEn	1.145 ± 0.0763	1.1327 ± 0.0637	1.0941 ± 0.0641	1.0605 ± 0.1030	1.0115 ± 0.1678
SampEn	1.6993 ± 0.2499	1.6090 ± 0.1750	1.5835 ± 0.2359	1.542 ± 0.3328	1.3189 ± 0.1271

Values expressed in mean ± standard deviation

16.4 CONCLUSION

Analysis of heart rate variability by the parameters computed from linear methods like basic time domain, FFT-based spectral domain, and nonlinear techniques from healthy male individuals with five different age groups has been attempted to diagnose the variations available in each age group. This present study regarding HRV parameter variations with aging of normal male gender individuals might be helpful to establish suitable HRV parameter ranges in these five psychosomatically different phases of total life-span, which are affected by different psycho-physiological conditions of the body. The trend of variations in heart rate variability indices is measure based, but most of the heart rate variability indices decline with age. However, their normalized contribution towards autonomic control activity clearly shows the heart rate variability indices change with the aging process. Nonlinear methods of HRV analysis provide supportive significant information along with linear methods, which are simple, basic methods and yet effective measures to observe the discriminative idea of different age groups in normal healthy subjects. Hence, the proposed methodology offers a better tool to discriminate between normal healthy subjects with different age groups and to optimize the values of typical HRV parameter ranges in different phases of the life-span from pediatric subjects to elderly men.

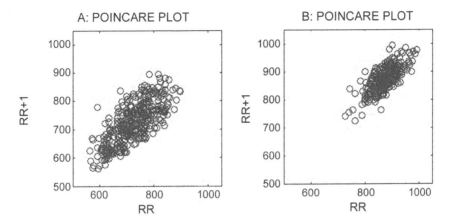

FIGURE 16.19   Poincare plot of age groups A and B.

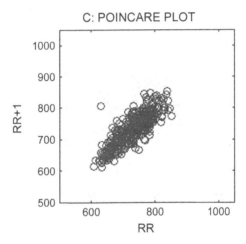

FIGURE 16.20   Poincare plot of age group C.

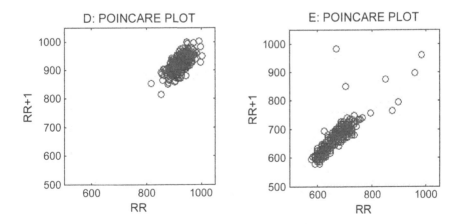

FIGURE 16.21   Poincare plot of age groups D and E.

REFERENCES

[1] A. J. Camm, M. Malik, J. T. Bigger, G. Breithardt, S. Cerutti, R. J. Cohen, P. Coumel, E. L. Fallen, H. L. Kennedy, R. E. Kleiger, F. Lombardi, A. Malliani, A. J. Moss, J. N. Rottman, G. Schmidt, P. J. Schwartz, D. H. Singer. 1996. Heart rate variability: standards of measurement, physiological interpretation and clinical use. *Circulation. Task Force of the European Society of Cardiology and the North American Society of Pacing and Electro-Physiology* 93: 1043–1065.

[2] M. Di Rienzo, G. Parati, Editorial. 2001. Heart rate variability and blood pressure analysis. *IEEE Engineering in Medicine and Biology* 20: 12.

[3] O. Rompelman, J. B. I. M. Snijders, C. J. Spronsen. 1982. The measurement of heart rate variability spectra with the help of a personal computer. *IEEE Transactions on Biomedical Engineering* 29: 503–510.

[4] R. D. Berger, S. Akselrod, D. Gordon, R. J. Cohen. 1986. An efficient algorithm for spectral analysis of heart rate variability. *IEEE Transactions on Biomedical Engineering* 33: 900–904.

[5] H. Luczak, W. Laurig. 1973. An analysis of heart rate variability. *Ergonomics* 16: 85–97.

[6] G. G. Berntson, J. R. Stowell. 1998. ECG artifacts and heart period variability: don't miss a beat. *Psychophysiology* 35: 127–132.

[7] M. Malik, R. Xia, O. Odemuyiwa, A. Staunton, J. Poloniecki, A. J. Camm. 1993. Influence of the recognition artefact in automatic analysis of long-term electrocardiograms on time-domain measurement of heart rate variability. *Medical and Biological Engineering and Computing* 31: 539–544.

[8] M. Merri, D. C. Farden, J. G. Mottley, E. L. Titlebaum. 1990. Sampling frequency of the electrocardiogram for spectral analysis of heart rate variability. *IEEE Transactions on Biomedical Engineering* 37: 99–106.

[9] H. V. Huikuri, J. O. Valkama, K. E. Airaksinen, T. Seppänen, K. M. Kessler, J. T. Takkunen, R. J. Myerburg. 1993. Frequency domain measures of heart rate variability before the onset of nonsustained and sustained ventricular tachycardia in patients with coronary artery disease. *Circulation* 87: 1220–1228.

[10] D. L. Eckberg. 1997. Sympatovagal balance: A critical appraisal. *Circulation* 96: 3224–3232.

[11] Tiran Boaz, Israel Heller, Aharon Isakov, Ofer Barnea, Joel Greif, Marcel Topilsky. 2004. Heart rate variability in sarcoidosis: a frequency domain analysis. *European Journal of Internal Medicine* 15: 518–522.

[12] P. Aurelien, R. Manuel, A. J. Sophie, B. Claire de, D. Andre. 2006. Spectral analysis of heart rate variability: interchangeability between autoregressive analysis and fast Fourier transform. *Journal of Electrocardiology* 39: 31–37.

[13] Nina Y. Belova, Stoyan V. Mihaylov, Boriana G. Piryova. 2007. Wavelet transform: A better approach for the evaluation of instantaneous changes in heart rate variability. *Autonomic Neuroscience* 131: 107–122.

[14] Kuss, Oliver, Barbara Schumann, Alexander Kluttig, Karin Halina Greiser, Johannes Haerting. 2008. Time domain parameters can be estimated with less statistical error than frequency domain parameters in the analysis of heart rate variability. *Journal of Electrocardiology* 41: 287–291.

[15] Montano Nicola, Alberto Porta, Chiara Cogliati, Giorgio Costantino, Eleonora Tobaldini, Karina Rabello Casali, Ferdinando Iellamo. 2009. Heart rate variability explored in the frequency domain: a tool to investigate the link between heart and behaviour. *Neuroscience & Biobehavioral Reviews* 33: 71–80.

[16] Bravi Andrea, André Longtin, A. J. Seely. 2011. Review and classification of variability analysis techniques with clinical applications. *Biomed Eng Online* 10: 90.

[17] Faust Oliver, V. Ramanan Prasad, G. Swapna, Subhagata Chattopadhyay, Teik-Cheng Lim. 2012. Comprehensive analysis of normal and diabetic heart rate signals: a review. *Journal of Mechanics in Medicine and Biology* 12 no. 05: 1–13.

[18] Silva Carla Cristiane, Ligia Maxwell Pereira, Jefferson Rosa Cardosa, Jonathan Patrick Moore, Fábio Yuzo Nakamura. 2014. The effect of physical training on heart rate variability in healthy children: a systematic review with meta-analysis. *Pediatric Exercise Science* 26: 147–158.

[19] A. Voss, R. Schroeder, A. Heitmann, A. Peters, S. Perz. 2015. Short-term heart rate variability—influence of gender and age in healthy subjects. *PLoS ONE* 10: e0118308.

[20] D. Hoyer, K. Schmidt, R. Bauer, U. Zwiener, M. Kohler, B. Luthke, M. Eiselt. 1997. Nonlinear analysis of heart rate and respiratory dynamics. *Engineering in Medicine and Biology Magazine, IEEE* 16: 31–39.

[21] Palaniswami Brennan M., Kamen P. 2001. Do existing measures of Poincare plot geometry reflect nonlinear features of heart rate variability? *IEEE Transaction on Biomedical Engineering* 48: 1342–1347.

[22] Frank Beckers, Bart Verheyden, and André E. Aubert. 2006. Aging and nonlinear heart rate control in a healthy population. *American Journal of Physiology-Heart and Circulatory Physiology* 290: H2560–H2570.

[23] Hang Ding, Stuart Crozier, Stephen Wilson. 2007. A new heart rate variability analysis method by means of quantifying the variation of nonlinear dynamic patterns. *IEEE Transaction on Biomedical Engineering* 54: 1590–1597.

[24] Andreas Voss, Steffen Schulz, Rico Schroeder, Mathias Baumert, and Pere Caminal. 2009. Methods derived from nonlinear dynamics for analysing heart rate variability. *Philosophical Transactions of the Royal Society, Mathematical, Physical and Engineering Sciences* 367: 277–296.

[25] Daniel E. Vigo, Javier Dominguez, Salvador M. Guinjoan, Mariano Scaramal, Eduardo Ruffa, Juan Solernó, Leonardo Nicola Siri, Daniel P. Cardinali. 2010. Nonlinear analysis of heart rate variability within independent frequency components during the sleep—wake cycle. *Elsevier, Autonomic Neuroscience: Basic and Clinical* 154: 84–88.

[26] Butta Singh, Dilbag Singh, A. K. Jaryal, K. K. Deepak. 2012. Ectopic beats in approximate entropy and sample entropy-based HRV assessment. *International Journal of Systems Science* 43: 884–893.

[27] A. Voss, R. Schroeder, C. Fischer, A. Heitmann, A. Peters, S. Perz. 2013. Influence of age and gender on complexity measures for short term heart rate variability analysis in healthy subjects. *Engineering in Medicine and Biology Society, 35th Annual International Conference of the IEEE*: 574–5577.

[28] F. Herbert Jelinek, C. Karmakar, A. M. Kiviniemi, A. J. Hautala, M. P. Tulppo, T. H. Mäkikallio, H. V. Huikuri, A. H. Khandoker, M. Palaniswami. 2015. Temporal dynamics of the circadian heart rate following low and high volume exercise training in sedentary male subjects. *European Journal of Applied Physiology*: 1–12.

[29] U. R. Acharya, K. P. Joseph, N. Kannatha, C. M. Lim, J. S. Suri, 2006. Heart rate variability: a review. *Medical & Biological Engineering & Computing* 44: 1031–1051.

[30] M. Teich, S. K. Lowen, C. H. Vibe-Rheymer. 2001. Heart rate variability: measures and models in nonlinear biomedical signal processing. dynamic analysis and modelling. *IEEE Press, New York* 2: 159–213.

[31] V. C. Kunz, E. N. Borges, R. C. Coelho, L. A. Gubolino, L. E. B. Martins, E. Silva. 2012. Linear and nonlinear analysis of heart rate variability in healthy subjects and after acute myocardial infarction in patients. *Brazilian Journal of Medical and Biological Research* 45: 450–458.

[32] P. Melillo, M. Bracale, L. Pecchia. 2011. Nonlinear heart rate variability features for real-life stress detection. case study: students under stress due to university examination. *BioMedical Engineering OnLine* 10: 96.

[33] M. P. Tarvainen, P. O. Ranta-Aho, P. A. Karjalainen. 2002. An advanced detrending method with application to HRV analysis. *IEEE Transactions on Biomedical Engineering* 49: 172–175.

[34] R. K. Sunkaria, V. Kumar, S. C. Saxena. 2013. Aging effects on dynamics: a comparative study with FFT and AR models. *International Journal of Signal and Imaging Systems Engineering* 6: 240–249.

[35] U. R. Acharya, N. Kannathal, O. W. Sing, L. Y. Ping, T. Chua. 2004. Heart rate analysis in normal subjects of various age groups. *BioMedical Engineering OnLine* 3: 24.

[36] M. G. Poddar, V. Kumar, Y. P. Sharma. 2013. Linear-nonlinear heart rate variability analysis and SVM based classification of normal and hypertensive subjects. *Journal of Electrocardiology* 46: e25.

[37] M. G. Poddar, V. Kumar, Y. P. Sharma. 2014. Heart rate variability based classification of normal and hypertension cases by linear-nonlinear method. *Defence Science Journal* 64: 542–548.

[38] M. G. Poddar, V. Kumar, Y. P. Sharma. 2015. *Heart rate variability: analysis and classification of healthy subjects for different age groups.* In Proceedings of IEEE International Conference on Computing for Sustainable Global Development, New Delhi India.

[39] M. G. Poddar, V. Kumar, Y. P. Sharma. 2015. Automated diagnosis of coronary artery diseased patients by heart rate variability analysis using linear and non-linear methods. *Journal of Medical Engineering & Technology* 39: 331–341.

[40] R. M. Carney, J. A. Blumenthal, P. K. Stein, L. Watkins, D. Catellier, L. F. Berkman, S. M. Czajkowski, C. O'Connor, P. H. Stone, K. E. Freedland. 2001. Depression, heart rate variability, and acute myocardial infarction. *Circulation* 104: 2024–2028.

[41] A. Alyahya, A. Fuller, N. Okwose, S. Charman, G. G. Macgowan, D. Jakovljevic. 2021. The effect of age and gender on heart rate variability in healthy individuals. *European Journal of Preventive Cardiology* 28: i237.

[42] J. Choi, W. Cha, M. G. Park. 2020. Declining trends of heart rate variability according to aging in healthy Asian adults. *Frontiers in Aging Neuroscience* 12: 610626.

[43] Biopac information. *Downloaded on 1.10.2021.* Available at www.biopac.com/product/mp150-data-acquisition-systems/

[44] Kampouraki Argyro, George Manis, Christophoros Nikou. 2009. Heartbeat time series classification with support vector machines. *IEEE Transaction on Information Technology in Biomedicine* 13: 512–518.

[45] Singh Dilbag, Kumar Vinod. 2005. Effect of RR segment duration on short-term HRV assessment using Poincare plot. In *Proceedings of IEEE International Conference on Intelligent Sensing and Information Processing*: 430–434.

[46] M. G. Poddar, V. Kumar, Y. P. Sharma. 2013. Linear—nonlinear heart rate variability analysis and SVM based classification of normal and hypertensive subjects. In *Proceedings of the 40th International Congress on Electrocardiology Glasgow, Scotland*: 89–95.

[47] M. G. Poddar, Anjali C. Birajdar, Jitendra Virmani, et al. 2019 Automated classification of hypertension and coronary artery disease patients by PNN, KNN, and SVM classifiers using HRV analysis. In *Machine Learning in Bio-Signal Analysis and Diagnostic Imaging Elsevier*: 99–125.

Part IV

Electronic Health Records

17 Electronic Health Records
Need, Challenges, and Future Scope

Priya M. Shelke and J. V. Bagade

CONTENTS

17.1 INTRODUCTION TO EHR

In the shift to "digital health," the usage of electronic health records (EHRs) is crucial. Information technology (IT) has become an important element of many businesses' efforts to enhance job quality. Healthcare can improve care quality by utilizing advanced technologies. For many businesses, investing in IT has become a means of enhancing communication, quality, task performance, profit, and safety. As a result, digitization in the form of EHR is used in healthcare. EHRs are primarily used to handle patient health data. The EHR is viewed as a good, and its adoption is on the rise across the world. The EHR allows each region to share data. EHR is viewed as a road map that helps hospitals function more efficiently [1].

An electronic health record is a patient's medical history in electronic form and includes key administrative clinical data, lab tests and results, imaging, diagnosis, demographics, treatment reports, issues, medicines, important symptoms, medical history, and vaccinations, among other things. In the e-Health transition, EHRs or EMRs appear to be highly important. They ensure the security and privacy of patient data while also improving the efficiency and outcomes of health systems at a lower cost [2].

These records aren't just large; they're also complicated, come in a variety of forms, and can be structured or unstructured. The production and access aspects of a health record may be categorized into two. During the creation stage, healthcare professionals collect data directly from patients or via the use of sensors. The acquired data is then saved in a database in a specified manner. And they are checked against a variety of processes and criteria to verify that they meet the requirements. The access stage is in charge of determining who has access to the data kept, as well as maintaining the security and confidentiality of medical information [3].

17.2 FEATURES OF HEALTH RECORDS

The life cycle of the health record determines the features of the health record, as shown in Figure 17.1. The 7Vs may be used to define the features of health records, with each V indicating a distinct feature [4]. The 7Vs will be explained further on.

- **Volume**

The amount of health records created is measured in bytes and is referred to as volume. We can't foresee or set a capacity limit since, due to modern technology, more and more records are created and stored every day. Big data processing in real time is no longer a wonder [5].

- **Velocity**

Velocity refers to the rate at which health records are produced, processed, and assessed. Organizations processing large-scale data just put it in databases and analyze it in bits due to the difficulties of analyzing huge amounts of unstructured data. Using machine learning techniques, it is now feasible to extract meaningful information from structured and unstructured data at a quicker rate. However, examination of health records is still a time-consuming procedure for time-sensitive data that must be acquired in real time utilizing sensors or similar devices [5].

- **Variety**

Variety refers to data's structural heterogeneity, or the reality that health records are created and maintained in a variety of formats, including structured, semi-structured, and unstructured.

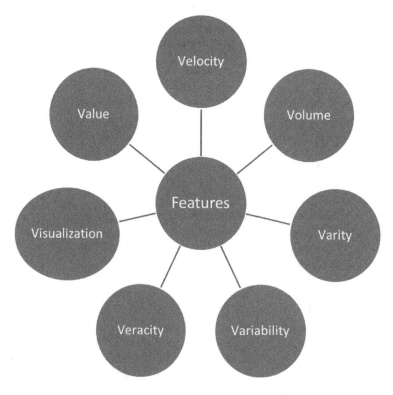

FIGURE 17.1   Features of health records.

Laboratory findings, vital signs, and an international classification of diseases (ICD) number are all included in structured health records. Pictures and graphics, visit notes, and free text, discharge summaries, and major complaints are examples of unstructured data. Prescriptions and medicines are semi-structured materials [6].

- **Variability**

Variability refers to the various capabilities that health records may have, even though they appear to be the same. Attempting to examine health records in pieces may result in incorrect findings. The integration of multiple types of information, on the other hand, allows for a deeper comprehension of the issue. Treatment action plans may generally be determined based on the doctor's report and lab test results, but if the patient's family history is known, an alternative treatment strategy may be explored. As a result, accounting for variation in health data is critical [7].

- **Veracity**

The correctness of health records is known as veracity. This includes not only data quality but also data understanding and inconsistencies, as health records are frequently inadequate and contain incorrect data [7,8].

- **Visualization**

The use of technologies that create graphs, pictures, diagrammatic representation, or animation for collecting information from health records, exhibiting readily comprehensible information, and helping in interacting with the data, therefore aiding knowledge discovery, is known as health records visualization. A strong health records visualization enables fast analysis of health information and visual story-telling, catching an audience's attention and enabling simple knowledge extraction at a faster pace with less mental labor [9]. The adoption of an effective and engaging visualization type is required for a strong health records visualization approach.

- **Value**

Actionable information, knowledge, and any other valuable information gained from health data are examples of value. It is the main purpose for keeping health records. Health records are extremely important because they represent a reservoir of data that, if retrieved, may frequently provide considerable societal advantages. Aside from its primary application in patient personal care, the information gathered might be useful for future service planning, resource allocation, standard development, preventative campaigns, health facility audits, and clinical research, among other things [8].

17.3   NEED OF EHR

Figure 17.2 demonstrates the evolution of electronic health records in the last century. Medical documents written on paper may be illegible, which can lead to medical errors. To enhance the trustworthiness of paper medical records, pre-printed forms, standardization of abbreviations, and handwriting standards were recommended. Medication administration is an example of a probable medical error. Medication is a treatment that can swiftly change a person's condition from stable to unstable. It is quite possible to not correctly document the administration of medication, the time provided, or mistakes such as administering the "wrong drug, dose, form, or not screening for allergies" using paper documentation, which might have a detrimental impact on the patient. Because records are now electronic and require specific measures to minimize errors, it has been stated that these errors have been decreased by 55–83%.

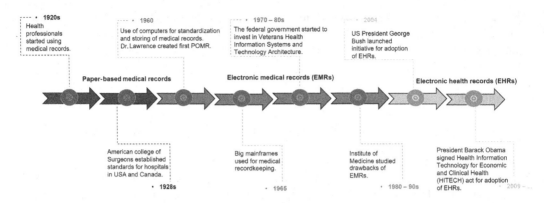

FIGURE 17.2 Evolution of EHRs.

Standardization of forms, language, and data input may be aided by electronic recordkeeping.

The digitization of forms makes data gathering for epidemiological and clinical research easier. Overall, individuals who used EMRs with automated notes and records, order input, and clinical decision assistance had fewer problems, lower death rates, and reduced expenditures.

EMRs can be updated on a regular basis. It would be easier to coordinate healthcare delivery at nonaffiliated healthcare institutions if the capacity to exchange records between different EMR systems could be developed by addressing the issue of interoperability. In addition, we may anonymize data in electronic form and utilize it for data analysis and presentation in areas such as health promotion, strategic planning, and primary care infectious disease monitoring. However, removing data from its context is challenging [10].

EHRs give access only to authorized persons and utilize encryption to secure sensitive medical information, unlike paper medical records, which can be left out or misplaced, making them vulnerable to browsing by unauthorized users. Audit trails are also available in EHRs, enabling knowledge of who accessed a patient's EHR, when they did so, and whether or not that access was allowed. Furthermore, remote EHR backup assures that you may access patient information even if you lose access to physical records due to natural disasters or other occurrences.

17.3.1 NEED OF EHR FROM THE PERSPECTIVE OF THE PATIENT

EHR improves patient care by enhancing all elements of healthcare, including safety, efficacy, patient-centeredness, communication, education, timeliness, efficiency, and equity.

It also improves health by encouraging healthier habits in the whole community, such as greater physical activity, improved diet, avoidance of behavioral hazards, and higher use of preventative care. Patients' healthcare costs can be reduced because they do not have to undergo clinical tests on a regular basis. It will also save the patient's time and physical strain. Patient data will be stored in an enhanced format and with all privacy measures [11].

17.3.2 NEED OF EHR FROM THE PERSPECTIVE OF HOSPITAL PROFESSIONALS

- **To Provide Better Care**

By allowing rapid access to patient records, EHRs aid in the provision of better treatment for their patients. They also contribute to therapeutic efficacy while enhancing the practice's operational efficiency. Most EHRs give clinicians health analytics that aid in the recognition of trends, the prediction of diagnoses, and the recommendation of viable treatment choices. Rather that depending on trial-and-error approaches, these analytics lead to more effective overall patient results the first time. Historical medical information such as lab and imaging results, medicines, diagnoses, and so on may be seen by gaining access to patient portals. The portal may be used by both clinicians and patients to follow an individual's treatment progress. This also simplifies preventative care [12].

- **To Provide Accurate, Real-Time Data across Various Providers**

EHR removes the danger of sensitive data theft, misplacement, damage, or manipulation. Mistakes and errors caused by handwriting and legibility difficulties can also be avoided with digital documents. Physicians may update patient information in real time, providing other healthcare providers with an accurate and up-to-date patient record. This electronic record can link every doctor or expert involved in a patient's healthcare. Continuity is extremely beneficial, particularly when a patient changes providers or visits a new physician, because it provides clinicians with a full backdrop of the patient's medical history rather than having them to start from beginning [12].

- **Interoperability**

EHR systems communicate with other systems, allowing medical practitioners to enhance continuity of care. When patients need to see specialists, manage chronic diseases like diabetes, or plan to transfer to a home healthcare setting for recovery or hospice, an EHR system with interoperability is essential [12].

- **Increased Efficiency and Revenue**

EHR systems expedite appointments and office visits, allowing health practitioners to meet more patients on a daily basis, ultimately increasing revenue. EHRs have built-in templates to assist clinicians in documenting frequent patient concerns or complaints. These templates are frequently adapted to certain specializations or are modifiable to meet the specific needs of a physician. Billing and payment features are provided by EHR to help manage money and assure payment. Claims can be automatically cleansed of flaws and errors that would otherwise result in rejections. This feature improves the acceptance rate of insurance claims the first time they are submitted, allowing for faster payouts with no lost or delayed claims. EHR also enables clinicians to document every element of a patient's visit, making it simple to give proof for specific claims. The government offers financial incentives for practices that adopt and employ EHR systems. The expense of establishing an EHR is quite high; however, government incentives allow healthcare firms to do so [12].

17.3.3 NEED OF EHR FROM THE PERSPECTIVE OF PHARMACISTS

Although pharmacists have always kept patient medication records, tracking patient care activities has not been a component of community pharmacy practice. Community pharmacists are increasingly offering innovative services to help patients with chronic illnesses and meet local public health requirements. There is now an urgent need for pharmacists to record information of the treatment they give in order to assist the consultation process, create a medicolegal record, justify service provision, and track outcomes [13].

17.3.4 NEED OF EHR FROM THE PERSPECTIVE OF CLINICAL RESEARCHERS

Clinical research encompasses a wide range of research issues and techniques. The pharmaceutical business places a strong emphasis on controlled clinical trials, which are critical. There is a need to enhance trial efficiency and decrease costs while responding to regulatory bodies' rising requests for more and higher quality evidence of efficacy and outcomes. Clinical research is confronted with difficulties such as rising trial recruiting hurdles, onerous and intrusive data collecting, and questionable generalizability of outcomes. For observational research, randomized trials for post-marketing registry, or comparative efficacy studies, EHRs are used as the primary source of data. EHRs may also be used to generate hypotheses, test feasibility, enhance performance, and ensure adherence to guidelines, among other things. Moving forward with this approach to randomized clinical trials, electronic health records could be used for appointment scheduling, healthcare evaluations, and practical trials (e.g., PROBE architecture), and to try new intervention strategies, populate registers, standardize data gathering and follow-up, and more [14].

Randomized controlled trials (RCTs) employing EHRs may be immediately incorporated into normal treatment, allowing for large-scale, pragmatic studies with near-perfect generalizability. Decision-support systems can be assessed as changes or additions to the EHR infrastructure. EHR infrastructure is increasingly being used for patient recruitment or outcome evaluation to assist studies evaluating traditional treatments.

Randomized controlled trials inside EHRs may overcome the constraints of traditional RCTs by enhancing generalizability, lowering costs and time, broadening research domains, and democratizing research objectives [15].

17.3.5 Need of EHR from the Perspective of Insurance Companies

EHR systems are a large collection of codified data that seems more trustworthy since clinicians enter the information manually. Insurers can discover crucial data on allergies, medicines, surgical procedures, test findings, and social determinants of health in this section. It undoubtedly aids in reducing application processing time. Cashless or reimbursement claims can be automatically cleared of errors and mistakes that would otherwise lead to rejection. This feature increases the likelihood that insurance claims will be accepted the first time they are filed, allowing for speedier payouts with no lost or delayed claims. EHRs can shorten application times while enhancing client satisfaction [16].

17.4 WORLDWIDE STATUS OF ELECTRONIC HEALTH RECORDS SYSTEM

The following sections provide an overview of the state of electronic health records systems in developed and developing nations. It is clear that EHR is still in its infancy and has a long way to go before it is fully implemented, even in wealthy nations.

- **Australia**

Since July 2016, Australia's Australian Digital Health Agency has been charged with overseeing the country's digital health strategy. With over 6 million registered patients and 13.4 million providers, the e-Health platform works on unique IDs. Since February 2019, all Australians have been able to access a My Health Record, which keeps track of prescriptions, imaging, and lab results, etc. [17].

- **Brazil**

In the late 1990s, Brazil implemented the Brazilian Ministry of Health's National Health Card system. They introduced the e-SUS software, which works in tandem with other programs. In 2017, computers were used by 90% of public-sector healthcare practitioners. In 2018, more than 45% of primary care practices used an EHR system provided by the government or on their own [17].

- **China**

In China, the use of an EHR system is commonplace. It works with health insurance companies to make the claim settlement process easier. Interoperability and compatibility of EHR systems between hospitals and organizations, on the other hand, are important concerns. If patients wish to see doctors in other hospitals, they must frequently bring a printed health record with them. Even if two hospitals are controlled by the same municipal health department or connected with the same university, they may utilize separate EHR systems [17].

- **Denmark**

In Denmark, the National Agency for Health IT funds the implementation of an EHR system in every suitable institution. Every resident has an electronic medical card with a unique electronic personal identity number on which medical data is encrypted and may be utilized in all public registers, including health databases, as well as shared with necessary healthcare providers.

Denmark's official health information website, Sundhed.dk, is quite helpful. It provides fundamental health information and treatment options for patients, as well as medical handbooks, research papers, and treatment suggestions for health professionals, and it allows access to individual's medical data and history for the general public [17].

- **England**

Since April 2015, all GPs (general practitioners) in England have been mandated to provide patients the option of booking appointments and ordering medicines online. In general practices, all patient records are digitized. Diagnosis, treatment, lab tests, vaccines, and medicine are all part of a patient's record [17].

- **India**

In 2013, India's Ministry of Health and Family Welfare established a committee to ensure that EHRs are effectively adopted and implemented across the country. India, however, lags far behind than other developing and developed nations in terms of EHR system deployment [17].

- **United States**

The Office of the National Coordinator for Health Information Technology, which was established in 2004, is in charge of electronic health records. More than 90% of acute-care hospitals and clinicians used an EHR system in 2017. Monitoring patient data, listing medications, keeping clinician notes and lab tests, imaging findings, and tracking prescription orders are all elements of an EHR. The usage of EHRs in general is encouraged by the 21st Century Cures Act, which was approved in 2016. It requires all healthcare providers to generate electronic health records for all of their patients and to make them available upon request [17].

17.5 CHALLENGES FOR EHR SYSTEM

Thanks to electronic health records, medical data can be promptly exchanged among stakeholders, and patient data can be retrieved and updated as a patient receives treatment. While cutting costs, IT in the health sector can increase healthcare outcomes efficiency and patient safety. Electronic health records may provide advantages like cost savings by digitizing data systems and a centralized location medical information [18], since, long term, health statistics primarily relied on paper data. However, with the increased use of health information technology over the previous three decades, there have been significant developments. The use of information and communication technology (ICT) in support of health and health-related sectors is known as e-Health. Telehealth, telemedicine, mobile health (mHealth), electronic medical or health records (eMR/eHR), big data, wearables, and even artificial intelligence are all part of it. The importance of e-Health in achieving broad health goals like universal health coverage (UHC) and the Sustainable Development Goals has been recognized (SDGs).

However, digitizing medical records is insufficient because it might generate issues with privacy, speed, technical scalability, and usability. One of the issues that health information systems throughout the world face is figuring out how to share patient records with a variety of stakeholders for a variety of purposes while maintaining personal privacy and integrity. Some of the problems are covered in depth in this section.

- **Insufficient ICT Infrastructure**

Computers, internet connectivity, printers, and energy are all lacking in developing countries' ICT infrastructure for e-Health. Furthermore, computers and the internet are only accessible to a small percentage of the population. Even in certain countries, internet connectivity remains out of reach for most people. Furthermore, the power supply is insufficient to enable e-Health operations and is unavailable. On the other hand is the long amount of time it takes to buy hardware and develop customized software. The program is ready for use and the hardware has become obsolete [19].

- **Economic Problem**

E-Health systems are exorbitant to purchase, implement, and utilize. According to the World Health Organization (WHO), one of the major barriers to e-Health adoption in developing countries is a lack of finance [20]. For the most part, governments must rely on wealthy countries, the World Bank, and foreign investors to carry out huge projects. Funding is a key barrier to the implementation of e-Health systems in poor nations, according to researchers [21].

- **Reluctant to Change**

Older administrative workers in medical sectors are accustomed to the manual method, and no one wants to introduce fresh ideas into an outdated system. The lack of motivation, often characterized as resistance to change or fear of new technologies, is a well-documented problem [22]. Administrative personnel, policymakers, physicians, and nurses are all opposed to the usage of e-Health for a variety of reasons. One of the main reasons is that they are afraid that computerization of various healthcare operations will render certain individuals redundant, and they are also reluctant to any variation in their acquainted working environment [23]. Researchers discovered that hospitals used few e-Health options and that numerous clinicians were apprehensive of implementing e-Health systems. In addition, employees reported a lack of motivation and encouragement when it came to introducing and adopting new ICTs.

- **Stakeholder Acceptance**

Government service providers are well versed in e-Health applications. However, service beneficiaries are unfamiliar with this application. As a result, their awareness of e-Health isn't ideal. Users' hesitance to utilize this system to document patient info will have a negative impact on their desire to accept and practice e-Health. The general community from developing countries are ignorant of this service. Only a small percentage of the population uses e-Health services. Furthermore, the majority of people lack sufficient expertise about how to use computers, the internet, or electronic service delivery. The majority of the population living in rural regions depend on traditional rather than low technology ICT methods to get health data [19].

- **Insufficiency of Regulation and Policy**

Healthcare is a delicate field in which people's lives are on the line. If a system is to be employed, specific processes and guidelines must be created and followed to guarantee that healthcare services are provided in a safe manner; otherwise, serious consequences may result. National regulatory/legal regimes have not yet been updated to meet the expanding demands of electronic e-Health. Nonetheless, an email doesn't have legal standing and also can't be regarded as an appropriate form of reporting in government agencies. There are weak anti-cybercrime laws or electronic authentication laws in place [23].

- **Standardization of Systems**

Because they were created by diverse software vendors, universities, enterprises, and research centers, the bulk of e-Health systems in developing countries are isolated [24]. Interoperability among heterogeneous systems and compatibility among different platforms and software applications are critical for a fully functional "fit for purpose" e-Health to enable the electronic transfer of health data among dissimilar systems and empower the conveyance of safe and effective patient care. The government did not create a central database that citizens could access over the internet. Even in government facilities, no information about any citizen is available to use in an emergency healthcare issue. As a result, physicians in government hospitals have a hard time identifying patients and their healthcare needs.

- **Lack of Training and Awareness**

The majority of doctors and nurses are unaware of e-Health and its potential benefits. There is a need for education on how to use these systems. Doctors, nurses, and patients need training to get familiar with the system and overcome their anxieties. Training programs in public and private hospitals must be requirement-based and scheduled throughout the execution stage of an e-Health project [24].

E-Health solutions must be simple to use and navigate. To satisfy the individual needs of patients, systems must be modified. Furthermore, there is a necessity of enhancing the system awareness in public as well as private hospitals. All stakeholders in the e-Health initiative must be involved for the project to be successful. It will not be a successful project unless the users are involved. As a result, the government should take initiatives to encourage citizens to practice e-Health services in their everyday lives. Governments, private organizations, and non-governmental organizations can host a variety of seminars, symposiums, short film screenings, and radio and television advertisements [19].

- **Legal and Security Challenges**

Security risks arising from information and technology developments have been discussed in the present literature [25, 26], for example, maintaining health records on remote servers managed by third-party cloud service providers. All IT systems utilized in storing, retrieving, processing, exchanging, and sending health data, as well as supporting healthcare delivery and system administration, are referred to as health information technology. Privacy, security, and confidentiality are all challenges that must be addressed in an EHR system [27]. Despite the fact that privacy and security are closely related but fundamentally different, security is defined as the level at which access to personal information is restricted and allowed only to authorized users [28, 29]. Privacy is the right that somebody has to govern for themselves when, how, and to what extent personal information is shared by others. When sensitive health data is transferred or shared without authorization, it might result in a data breach. In many circumstances, privacy can be violated by unavoidable systemic credentials that come out of the e-Health infrastructure, as well as by server technologies and third parties that monitor the behavior of staff and patients [29]. However, in other situations, pharmaceutical companies, the government, researchers, employers, and laboratories may have legitimate reasons to retrieve patient health records in order to obtain data, and the healthcare practitioner may inadvertently or willfully abuse the health records access [30]. Physicians are usually concerned that an unauthorized individual could gain access to patient information kept in EHR systems and misuse it, resulting in legal issues as a result of a break in the privacy of the patients' records [31]. According to Wikina [32], doctors are more concerned about safety and privacy issues than patients are. The majority of clinicians who utilize e-Health records believe that paper records are considerably safer and more confidential than e-Health records. This demonstrates how seriously the problem of EMR privacy and security is taken. Patients may elect to withhold information to stop unsuitable usage if they are not assured of privacy [33, 34].

The use of shared e-Health records exposes up an entire new world of opportunities for flexible and effective collaboration between healthcare professionals across institutions, all for the assistance of patients. However, there are unresolved security and legal issues. The overall goal of the section is to bring out legal and security issues that should be examined before implementing EHR systems.

- **Dissemination of Accountability**

Whenever health services are provided in a conventional way, the determination of roles, responsibilities, and liabilities of the participating personnel can be accomplished at any moment by establishing physical boundaries. The general regulation is that the GP is responsible for care while the patient is in his or her home municipality and receives services from local health personnel. When a patient is admitted to a hospital for further diagnosis and treatment, the hospital holds responsibility for the patient until the treatment is completed. Once a patient is medicated concurrently by doctors from various levels or institutions, each stage is accountable for their portion of the treatment and must mention it in health record systems. The physical borders between healthcare practitioners from different institutions are blurred when they communicate through a web-based health record system or other telemedicine options. At first glance, it may not be clear who is responsible for what.

Because the role is going along with a number of job responsibilities and duties outlined in health regulation, the participating personnel must discuss and explain who is accountable for the patient's treatment from the start. This is critical for the protection of patients' rights. Patients must know who to contact if they need to speak with someone involved in their medical treatment [35].

- **Accessibility to Documentation**

The absence of connectivity among internal EHR systems as well as the limitation on multiple documentation present unique issues. Due to the legal prohibition on multiple recording, patient data on the treatment registered in the shared EHR system will be obtainable only by the person who is engrossed in the treatment and thus has obvious access to the shared EHR. These treatment data will not be made available to the remaining healthcare staff in the collaborating facilities. Health staff treating the identical patients in emergency circumstances and for additional conditions may find information contained in the web-based record interesting and significant, but it is unavailable. There is clearly a need for shared EHR, as legislators have stated. However, in order to make widespread use of such systems practicable, access control integration difficulties must be overcome, as detailed later. Thus, integrated shared health record systems might be significantly more widely used than they are now [35].

- **Data Breach**

Authorized providers are said to use their smartphones, which contain potentially sensitive information, to send and receive personal emails, browse the web, and watch videos. According to reports,

80% of healthcare workers use their smartphones for work-related tasks [36, 37]. As a result, the system creates an environment in which an entire ecosystem of apps may dwell in the device, potentially exposing the device to a variety of accidental yet harmful dangers [38]. The number of people affected by the loss of electronic material was higher than the number of people harmed by illegal access or human error. Internal employees occasionally share passwords and send emails to the wrong addressee, exposing the personal information of some patients. They don't always follow the rules and end up with the inappropriate rights or authorizations unintentionally. Unauthorized access also includes patient credit card hacking and system hacking, as well as unauthorized staff accessing protected health information [39]. Individuals' trust in the EHR system is being eroded as a result of these data breaches. Data security technology can help to mitigate these vulnerabilities, but it can't completely eliminate them. Nonetheless, EHR security protection is a critical component of any successful EHR adoption since it is a condition of their societal acceptability and trustworthiness [40, 41].

Data breach notification is critical for e-Health systems because customer trust is built on transparency, which requires that all parties be kept up to date on how data is managed. The term "data breach" refers to incidents such as computer hacking, storage device theft, unintended personal information release, and inappropriate storage equipment decommissioning. Employees' misuse of personal information, on the other hand, can be regarded as a sort of data breach. Data breaches are important with regard to information privacy law because data subjects, who have some control over their data, plainly ought to be informed about breaches of their personal information, particularly those that occur in specialized settings like healthcare.

- **Medical Identity Theft**

The growth of healthcare technology has given criminals additional opportunity to steal identities. Medical identity theft can now affect a broader segment of the population thanks to electronic health records. Medical identity theft is when a patient's personal information is used to receive medical services or goods illegally. The information can also be sold to larger organized crime groups all throughout the world [42].

If a criminal alters a medical record, the victim may suffer injury if they are given incorrect treatment based on the erroneous information contained in the file. As more healthcare organizations adopt an electronic medical record format, more patient data is stored in computer systems. The ability to download thousands of documents from a computer terminal thousands of kilometers away makes medical record theft incredibly appealing [43, 44]. Because medical facilities get new patients on a daily basis, there are always new identities to steal, making systems more appealing for recurrent attacks. Because of the potentially dangerous modifications involved, getting a medical record corrected after medical identity theft can be a difficult task [45, 46].

- **Unavailability of Access Control Integration Among Systems**

Because they work in multiple health institutions, users of shared EHR systems are enrolled as users in user directories owned and maintained by different organizations. Furthermore, they must be members of the shared EHR system's user directory in order to access the system's health records. These numerous user access choices are not yet connected in any way, although EHR system suppliers and national health authorities in countries perceive the usefulness of doing so. Establishing a standardized and safe method for federating verification authorizations across all EHR systems in a specific area or country, for example, could be one way to gradually overcome the issues associated with the absence of access control integration between different EHR systems. The Norwegian Directorate of e-Health (NDE) has begun work on a project to develop a national secure authentication service for the healthcare sector. One example is a provisioning service (SPS) with a "trust anchor." It provides a security token service that allows users' authentication data to be transmitted across systems. When practicing an SPS, a security token comprising a unique user ID and credible info about the security level used for user verification in the inner system is provided to the external system via the "central trust anchor" to administer for access. Such a system must incorporate technical solutions and organizational agreements to attain the essential level of confidence among the entities accountable for the systems. The technological portion of the national authentication service in the Norwegian project stated has accomplished a pilot phase. Furthermore, each firm that wishes to use the solution must build the essential capabilities into their own infrastructure [35].

17.6   FUTURE ELECTRONIC HEALTH RECORD SYSTEM

It's long past time for an upgrade to the electronic health record. Rather than simply enhancing the GUI and compatibility, it must rectify the basic issues brought to light by the covid epidemic. The reform must also enhance providers' capacity to implement the novel value-based care healthcare model of business. This model pays clinicians for results rather than number of services and focuses on proactive health management rather than reactive illness care.

A redesign of the EHR is essential. EHRs are quite effective at the "record" aspect, but they must grow to handle the "health" component by assisting doctors in planning for what they want to happen. If we build EHRs with that objective in mind, they might become instruments for developing such goals and keeping them on track [47].

Future EHR systems should incorporate the following features:

- It should be plan-centric, which means that a collection of care plans covering a broad array of scenarios should be provided. Differences in the plans would be dictated by variations in the patient's circumstances and preferences.
- A master plan would integrate suitable methods for treatment, eliminating conflicts and redundancies automatically.
- The master plan and the patient's specific to-do list would be accessible to all team members, including the patient's primary care doctor, experts, registered nurses, chemists, and the patient. Members of the team might delegate duties to one another.
- The plan would have to move in tandem with the patient. Providers would have access to interoperable systems, allowing them to adopt a patient's plan regardless of where it came from.
- When patient states and care requirements change, the system must alert team members of upcoming and overdue actions, propose plan modifications, and route messages regarding new test findings or patient activities to the appropriate team member.
- It should be able to analyze both individual patients and entire groups.
- It should be converted from a transactional to an intelligence-based system.
- The present EMR standards are quite permissive. To attain true ease of use, future EHR systems should place a greater emphasis on standardization. Standardization promotes interoperability, encourages all suppliers and stakeholders to participate and adopt, keeps implementation costs as low as possible, and takes into account best practices, experiences, policies, and frameworks [48].
- Practitioners will be eager to see more usage of AI and IoT in EHR systems. IoT devices are becoming more popular, particularly in the healthcare industry. Artificial intelligence is also being used in a number of clinics to assist physicians in making diagnoses and identifying patient health trends. Many firms are investigating the use of AI to bring speech recognition to EHR software [50].
- By providing safer procedures for medical data sharing in the healthcare industry, as well as preserving it through a decentralized peer-to-peer network, blockchain might revolutionize the way patients' electronic health records are exchanged and maintained. By solving concerns such as interoperability of healthcare databases, recording medical reports,

controlling access to patient medical information, and sharing EHR among multiple institutions, blockchain technology would significantly change the present EHR system in near future. Although the usage of blockchain is still in its early stages, numerous EHRs have already included it to assure security, scalability, and secrecy [49].

- Patients have become more conscious of their healthcare indicators as wearable gadgets have grown in popularity. Data integration between wearable devices and EHR systems allows for improved patient care [50].

17.7 FURTHER DISCUSSION

Because of their improved convenience and productivity, electronic health records have become a crucial aspect of hospitals' patient data management. Increased awareness of the usage and necessity of EHR systems, as well as technological improvements in the field of healthcare IT, has led in a growth in demand for EHR systems all over the world. Furthermore, increased government support and spending for the development of healthcare IT solutions is encouraging the global use of electronic health records [51].

The worldwide electronic health records market was estimated at USD 26.8 billion in 2020, with a compound annual growth rate (CAGR) of 3.7% predicted from 2021 to 2028. The primary driver of this market is government measures to increase the use of healthcare IT.

In contrast to previous projections that the EHR market will grow to about USD 29.15 billion by 2020, the market shrank by 2.7% from 2019 to 2020. In 2020, the EHR market was influenced by the pandemic effect, EHR software, and service installation issues.

Client-server or web-based EHR systems are both available. In 2020, the web-based EHR segment dominated the market, accounting for more than 54% of worldwide sales. Web-based EHRs are becoming increasingly popular since they can be implemented without the need for in-house servers and can be customized and improved as needed.

In 2020, North America had the greatest revenue share in the worldwide EHR market, accounting for approximately 45%. Even during the predicted years, the region will remain dominant. During the projected period, however, Asia Pacific is expected to be the fastest-growing regional market [52].

REFERENCES

1. Mohammed, A., A. Mehrez, and L. Aladel. "Investigating the impact of electronic health record on healthcare professionals." *International Journal of Data and Network Science* 5, no. 1 (2021): 63–74.
2. Keshta, Ismail, and Ammar Odeh. "Security and privacy of electronic health records: Concerns and challenges." *Egyptian Informatics Journal* 22, no. 2 (2021): 177–183.
3. Latha, N. Anju, B. Rama Murthy, and U. Sunitha. "Electronic health record." *International Journal of Engineering* 1, no. 10 (2012): 25–27.
4. Umejiaku, Afamefuna, and Tommy Dang. "Visualising Developing Nations Health Records: Opportunities, Challenges and Research Agenda." In The 12th International Conference on Advances in Information Technology, pp. 1–9, Association for Computing Machinery, New York, United States. 2021. https://doi.org/10.1145/3468784.3471607
5. Gandomi, Amir, and Murtaza Haider. "Beyond the hype: Big data concepts, methods, and analytics." *International Journal of Information Management* 35, no. 2 (2015): 137–144.
6. Forestiero, Agostino, and Giuseppe Papuzzo. "Natural language processing approach for distributed health data management." In 2020 28th Euromicro International Conference on Parallel, Distributed and Network-Based Processing (PDP), pp. 360–363. IEEE, 2020. https://doi.org/10.1109/PDP50117.2020.00061.
7. Sivarajah, Uthayasankar, Muhammad Mustafa Kamal, Zahir Irani, and Vishanth Weerakkody. "Critical analysis of Big Data challenges and analytical methods." *Journal of Business Research* 70 (2017): 263–286.

8. Shah, Shahid Munir, and Rizwan Ahmed Khan. "Secondary use of electronic health record: Opportunities and challenges." *IEEE Access* 8 (2020): 136947–136965.

9. Nazir, Shah, Muhammad Nawaz Khan, Sajid Anwar, Awais Adnan, Shahla Asadi, Sara Shahzad, and Shaukat Ali. "Big data visualization in cardiology—A Systematic review and future directions." *IEEE Access* 7 (2019): 115945–115958.

10. Agrawal, Abha. "Medication errors: prevention using information technology systems." *British Journal of Clinical Pharmacology* 67, no. 6 (2009): 681–686.

11. The Office of the National Coordinator for Health Information Technology (ONC)(16 May 2019). www.healthit.gov/faq/what-are-advantages-electronic-health-records

12. Dugar, Divya. *Key benefits of electronic health records (EHR).* www.selecthub.com/medical-software/benefits-of-ehr-systems/

13. Nelson, Scott D., John Poikonen, Thomas Reese, David El Halta, and Charlene Weir. "The pharmacist and the EHR." *Journal of the American Medical Informatics Association* 24, no. 1 (2017): 193–197.

14. Cowie, Martin R., Juuso I. Blomster, Lesley H. Curtis, Sylvie Duclaux, Ian Ford, Fleur Fritz, Samantha Goldman et al. "Electronic health records to facilitate clinical research." *Clinical Research in Cardiology* 106, no. 1 (2017): 1–9.

15. Mc Cord, Kimberly A., and Lars G. Hemkens. "Using electronic health records for clinical trials: Where do we stand and where can we go?" *CMAJ* 191, no. 5 (2019): E128–E133.

16. Shestel, Alex (29 Jan 2019). https://belitsoft.com/custom-application-development-services/healthcare-software-development/how-can-EHRs-change-life-insurance-industry

17. The commonwealth fund. *Health System Features* (5 June 2020). www.commonwealthfund.org/international-health-policy-center/system-features/what-status-electronic-health-records

18. Curry, Adrienne, and Gail Knowles. "Strategic information management in health care-myth or reality?" *Health Services Management Research* 18, no. 1 (2005): 53–62.

19. Hoque, Md Rakibul, Md Fahami Ahsan Mazmum, and Yukun Bao. "e-Health in Bangladesh: Current status, challenges, and future direction." *The International Technology Management Review* 4, no. 2 (2014): 87–96.

20. World Health Organization. *Program and project: Publication: Global observatory for eHealth* (2010). Retrieve August 17, 2013, from World Health Organization. http://whqlibdoc.who.int/publications/2011/9789241564168_eng.pdf

21. Fryatt, Robert, Anne Mills, and Anders Nordstrom. "Financing of health systems to achieve the health Millennium Development Goals in low-income countries." *The Lancet* 375, no. 9712 (2010): 419–426.

22. Khalifehsoltani, Sayed Nasir, and Mohammad Reza Gerami. "E-health challenges, opportunities and experiences of developing countries." In 2010 International Conference on e-Education, e-Business, e-Management and e-Learning, pp. 264–268. IEEE, 2010.

23. Uddin, Giash. "E-Governance of Bangladesh: Present scenario, expectation, ultimate target and recommendation." *International Journal of Scientific and Engineering Research* 3, no. 11 (2012): 1–20.

24. Gao, Xiangzhu, Jun Xu, Golam Sorwar, and Peter Croll. "Implementation of E-health record systems and E-medical record systems in China." *The International Technology Management Review* 3, no. 2 (2013): 127–139.

25. Achampong, Emmanuel Kusi. "Electronic health record (EHR) and cloud security: The current issues." *International Journal of Cloud Computing and Services Science (IJ-CLOSER)* 2, no. 6 (2013). doi: 10.11591/closer.v2i6.5343

26. Dorgham, Osama, Banan Al-Rahamneh, Ammar Almomani, and Khalaf F. Khatatneh. "Enhancing the security of exchanging and storing DICOM medical images on the cloud." *International Journal of Cloud Applications and Computing (IJCAC)* 8, no. 1 (2018): 154–172.

27. Alanazi, Hamdan O., A. A. Zaidan, B. B. Zaidan, ML Mat Kiah, and S. H. Al-Bakri. "Meeting the security requirements of electronic medical records in the ERA of high-speed computing." *Journal of Medical Systems* 39, no. 1 (2015): 1–13.

28. Gupta, Brij B., ed. *Computer and cyber security: principles, algorithm, applications, and perspectives.* Boca Raton, FL: CRC Press, 2018.

29. Sittig, Dean F., and Hardeep Singh. "A new socio-technical model for studying health information technology in complex adaptive healthcare systems." In *Cognitive informatics for biomedicine*, pp. 59–80. Springer, Cham, 2015.

30. Cifuentes, Maribel, Melinda Davis, Doug Fernald, Rose Gunn, Perry Dickinson, and Deborah J. Cohen. "Electronic health record challenges, workarounds, and solutions observed in practices integrating behavioral health and primary care." *The Journal of the American Board of Family Medicine* 28, no. Supplement 1 (2015): S63–S72.

31. Miotto, Riccardo, Li Li, Brian A. Kidd, and Joel T. Dudley. "Deep patient: An unsupervised representation to predict the future of patients from the electronic health records." *Scientific Reports* 6, no. 1 (2016): 1–10.

32. Wikina, Suanu Bliss. "What caused the breach? An examination of use of information technology and health data breaches." *Perspectives in Health Information Management* 11, no. Fall (2014).

33. Hussain, Muzammil, Ahmed Al-Haiqi, Aws Alaa Zaidan, Bilal Bahaa Zaidan, M. Kiah, Salman Iqbal, Shaukat Iqbal, and Mohamed Abdulnabi. "A security framework for mHealth apps on Android platform." *Computers & Security* 75 (2018): 191–217.

34. Keshta, Ismail, and Ammar Odeh. "Security and privacy of electronic health records: Concerns and challenges." *Egyptian Informatics Journal* 22, no. 2 (2021): 177–183.

35. Christiansen, Ellen K., Eva Skipenes, Marie F. Hausken, Svein Skeie, Truls Østbye, and Marjolein M. Iversen. "Shared electronic health record systems: key legal and security challenges." *Journal of Diabetes Science and Technology* 11, no. 6 (2017): 1234–1239.

36. Piliouras, Teresa, Pui Lam Yu, Housheng Huang, Xin Liu, Vijay Kumar Ajjampur Siddaramaiah, and Nadia Sultana. "Selection of electronic health records software: Challenges, considerations, and recommendations." In 2011 IEEE Long Island Systems, Applications and Technology Conference, pp. 1–5. IEEE, 2011.

37. Delbanco, Tom, Jan Walker, Sigall K. Bell, Jonathan D. Darer, Joann G. Elmore, Nadine Farag, Henry J. Feldman et al. "Inviting patients to read their doctors' notes: a quasi-experimental study and a look ahead." *Annals of Internal Medicine* 157, no. 7 (2012): 461–470.

38. Markle Foundation. "Markle survey: the public and doctors agree on importance of specific privacy protections for health I.T.," *Markle Survey on Health in a Networked Life* (2011). https://markle.org/app/uploads/2022/03/7_PrivacyPolicies.pdf

39. Rezaeibagha, Fatemeh. "Privacy and Data Security of Electronic Patient Records (EPR) Sharing: Case studies: Iran and Sweden." (2013). (Dissertation). http://urn.kb.se/resolve?urn=urn:nbn:se:ltu:diva-56989

40. MEDHOST Solutions Corp (2013) "It's time to meet physicians' concerns about ehrs." https://emrindustry.com/wp-content/uploads/2014/05/Physicians-Concerns-About-EHRs-whitepaper-web.pdf

41. Mathai, N., M. F. Shiratudin, and F. Sohel. "Electronic health record management: expectations, issues, and challenges." *Journal of Health & Medical Informatics* 8, no. 3 (2017): 1–5.

42. Portela, Filipe, Marta Vilas-Boas, Manuel F. Santos, António Abelha, Jose Machado, Alexandra Cabral, and Irene Aragão. "Electronic health records in the emergency room." In 2010 IEEE/ACIS 9th International Conference on Computer and Information Science, pp. 195–200. IEEE, 2010.

43. Grana, Manuel, and Konrad Jackwoski. "Electronic health record: A review." In 2015 IEEE international conference on bioinformatics and biomedicine (BIBM), pp. 1375–1382. IEEE, 2015.

44. Pereira, Rui, Júlio Duarte, Maria Salazar, Manuel Santos, António Abelha, and José Machado. "Usability of an electronic health record." In 2012 IEEE International Conference on Industrial Engineering and Engineering Management, pp. 1568–1572. IEEE, 2012.

45. Steininger, Katharina, Barbara Stiglbauer, Bernd Baumgartner, and Bernhard Engleder. "Factors explaining physicians' acceptance of electronic health records." In 2014 47th Hawaii international conference on system sciences, pp. 2768–2777. IEEE, 2014.

46. Ben-Assuli, Ofir. "Electronic health records, adoption, quality of care, legal and privacy issues and their implementation in emergency departments." *Health Policy* 119, no. 3 (2015): 287–297.

47. Glaser, John. *Harvard business review. Analytics and data science. It's time for a new kind of electronic health record* (Jun2 12,2020). https://hbr.org/2020/06/its-time-for-a-new-kind-of-electronic-health-record

48. Bajpai, Nirupam, and Manisha Wadhwa. "India's national digital health mission." (2020). https://csd.columbia.edu/sites/default/files/content/docs/ICT%20India/Papers/ICT_India_Working_Paper_36.pdf

49. Mayer, André Henrique, Cristiano André da Costa, and Rodrigo da Rosa Righi. "Electronic health records in a blockchain: a systematic review." *Health Informatics Journal* 26, no. 2 (2020): 1273–1288.

50. Dugar, Divya. Future of Electronic Medical Records: Experts Predict EMR Trends in 2021 (2021). www.selecthub.com/medical-software/emr/electronic-medical-records-future-emr-trends/

51. ReportLinker. Global Electronic Health Records (EHR) market is forecast to grow from an estimated $ 30 billion in 2020 to $ 40 billion by 2025 (May 27, 2020). www.prnewswire.com/news-releases/global-electronic-health-records-ehr-market-is-forecast-to-grow-from-an-estimated-30-billion-in-2020-to-40-billion-by-2025-301066044.html

52. Market Analysis Report. Electronic Health Records Market Size, Share & Trends Analysis Report By Type (Post-acute, Acute), By End-use (Ambulatory Care, Hospitals), By Product (Web-, Client-server-based), By Business Models, And Segment Forecasts, 2021–2028 (April 2021). www.grandviewresearch.com/industry-analysis/electronic-health-records-ehr-market

18 Role of EHR in Cancer Detection
Need, Challenges, and Future Scope of EHR

Pratiksha R. Deshmukh and Rashmi Phalnikar

CONTENTS

18.1 INTRODUCTION

In the medical domain, electronic health records (EHRs) contain knowledgeable information that is required for the prognosis and treatment of the patient [1]. Natural language processing (NLP) performs an important part in extracting prognostic information from an EHR because most EHRs are represented in natural language [2]. EHRs related to cancer contain prognostic information regarding cancer stage, which includes location and size of lesion, count of lymph nodes, spread of cancer in different body parts, and cancer grade. Most of the EHRs are in an unstructured form and require processing on text to get prognostic information from them. This is a complicated job because there are variations in the interpretation of EHRs, use of medical concepts and their description, context of clinical terms, the format of the EHR, and the writing style of EHRs of different institutions.

An EHR describes pathological and clinical test results, history, a summary of diseases, etc. [3]. Based on information included in EHRs, clinicians treat patients. Most clinicians have to manually classify the severity of disease from EHRs, which takes time, and this is a difficult task to manage [4]. Hence, there is a need to automatically extract information from EHRs to classify the severity of diseases. As EHRs contain patients' confidential information, it's difficult to access these EHRs for research without consent. Researchers have to get approval from the ethics committee to study EHRs for research [5]. As these EHRs are not easily accessible, this is a major challenge for research in the medical domain.

DOI: 10.1201/9781003272694-22

Some EHRs include codes given by ICD (international classification of disease) with different versions like ICD-9, ICD-10, etc. [6]. Some EHRs use medical coding methods, like the systematized nomenclature of medicine clinical terms (SNOMED CT) [7], whereas some EHRs use the unified medical language system (UMLS) [8]. All of these coding systems need to update for easy integration into automatic extraction systems.

The organization of this chapter is as follows. Section 18.2 represents details of EHR structure. Section 8.3 provides different ways to extract information from EHRs. Section 18.4 discusses the needs and challenges of EHRs, and, finally, the chapter concludes in section 18.5 with future directions.

18.2   STRUCTURE OF EHR

EHRs like histopathology and mammography records contain prognostic factor details. But most of these EHRs are in an unstructured form, represented in natural language, and require processing on text to extract prognostic information from them, and this is a complicated job. Figures 18.1 and 18.2 show examples of histopathology and mammography record respectively.

These records consist of different sections, such as the nature of the specimen, clinical details, gross examination, microscopic examination, and impression part [9]. These records are given as an input to the system, and text processing is performed on these records. Prognostic factors such as T, N, M, and G are extracted from these records to predict the cancer stage. The following section shows how prognostic information can be extracted from EHRs for disease prognosis.

18.3   INFORMATION EXTRACTION FROM EHR

EHRs related to cancer contain prognostic information of cancer. While extracting data from these EHRs, the details of each feature have to be considered to identify the exact stage of the cancer. The prognostic information used to determine cancer stage includes location and size of lesion, count of lymph nodes (LN), spread of cancer in different body parts, and cancer grade [10, 11]. For example, Figure 18.3 shows the classification of prognostic factors while extracting from EHRs for prognosis.

Representation of these prognostic factors' information varies from hospital to hospital. There is a different synonym for each medical term, abbreviations, and variations in spellings. Every pathologist has their way of representing context, etc. Considering all these challenges, the system should extract accurate prognostic factors T, N, M, etc., and G.

In the case that the initial stage tumor can't be checked, then the T value will be Tx; if there is no evidence of initial stage tumor, then T value will be T0, and as tumor size starts increasing, T value will increase from T1 to T4. N value will be Nx when the LN can't be checked; if there is no evidence of affected lymph node, then N value will be N0, and as lymph node metastasis starts increasing, N value will increase from N1 to N3. Similarly, when metastasis information can't be checked, the value of M will be Mx, if proof of distant metastasis is not found, then the value of M will be M0, and if distant metastasis is found, then it will be M1. Grade value is divided as grade-1, grade-2, and grade-3 cancer. When cancer cells are well differentiated, the grade will be G-1; when cancer cells are moderately differentiated, then the grade will be G-2; and when cancer cells are poorly differentiated, the grade will be G-3 [12, 13, 14].

This information is given in EHRs, and it is a complicated task to extract it from unstructured EHRs. Some researchers have used machine learning (ML) techniques, and some researchers have used NLP to extract prognostic details for prognosis. Using machine learning for prognostic factors' extraction requires many EHRs, which is difficult in the medical domain. The use of NLP for extraction includes a number of tasks like pattern matching and rule-based method, dictionary creation, named entity recognition, context identification, information extraction, etc. This section represents how researchers have used machine learning and NLP for detail extraction from unstructured EHRs.

Nature of Specimen
1. Left breast lumpectomy
2. Revised posterior margin
3. Axillary dissection.

Clinical Details
K/C/O ca breast
FNAC s/o IDC, NST Grade 2
Gross Examination
1] Received oriented specimen of left breast lumpectomy measuring 5.5x4.5x2.5 cm. Skin eclipse measures 5x2 cm. Cut section a well defined, whitish, gritty tumour identified measuring 2.6x2.4x2.2cm .
Margin are as follows
Superior – 1.5 cm away.
Inferior – 0.5 cm away.
Lateral – 1.5 cm away.
Media – 1 cm away.
Anterior – 1.5 cm away.
Posterior – 0.5 cm away.

2] Specimen labelled as revised posterior margin : Received two fragments of fibrofatty tissue. Larger measures 5x2.5x0.5 cm, smaller is 2.5x2x0.2 cm. Inked surface identified. Cut surface is unremarkable.
3] Specimen labelled as axillary sampling: Received multiple fragments of fibro fatty tissue measuring 11x9x5 cm. Dissected 24 lymph nodes. Largest node measures 1.5x1x1 cm Cut surface is whitish.
Blocks:
1. Tumour with inferior margin
2. Tumour with posterior margin
3. Tumour with medial margin
4. Tumour with inferior margin
5. Tumour with superior margin
8. Tumour with posterior margin
6. Lateral margin
7. Tumour with skin
8. Tumour with adjacent breast
9-10. Revised posterior margin
11-16. Axillary lymph nodes
Microscopic Examination
- Paraffin sections confirm the findings of frozen section.
- Sections study reveal infiltrating ductal carcinoma, NST, Grade 2.
- Nottingham's score 3+2+1 = 6.
- Intervening stroma is desmoplastic with mild chronic inflammation .
- Lymphovascular invasion seen. No perineural invasion.
- Posterior margin is positive for tumour. All other margins are free of tumour.
- Overlying skin is unremarkable.
- Revised posterior margin is free of tumour.
- Dissected 24 axillary nodes out of which 4 shows tumour metastasis.

FIGURE 18.1   Sample histopathology report showing prognostic information.

18.3.1   Using Machine Learning

ML is used for prediction and prognosis of diseases. Machine learning is also used in cancer prediction when given clinical data is in a structured form.

Earlier studies have used ML for prognostic factors extraction from EHRs [15, 16, 17, 18]. McCowan et al. [19] detected the lung cancer stage from pathological EHRs with good accuracy at

MAMMOGRAPHY WITH ULTRASOUND CORRELATION BOTH BREASTS

Left breast upper & outer quadrant shows hypoechoic mass measuring 18 X 15 mm (Axillary tail region mass).

Central portion of left breast shows intraductal filling defect.

Fibroglandular tissue appears normal.

No cystic changes seen.

Retroareolar area appear normal.

IMPRESSION: -

LEFT BREAST UPPER & OUTER QUADRANT MASS (AXILLARY TAIL REGION MASS).

CENTRAL PORTION LEFT BREAST INTRADUCTAL FILLING DEFECT.

FIGURE 18.2   Sample mammography report showing prognostic information.

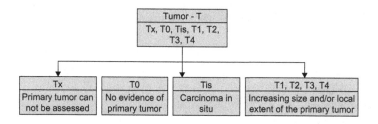

FIGURE 18.3A   Classification of tumor (T).

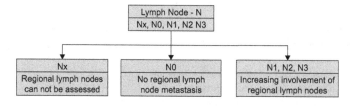

FIGURE 18.3B   Classification of lymph node (N).

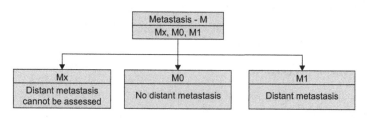

FIGURE 18.3C   Classification of metastasis (M).

FIGURE 18.3   Classification of prognostic factors during extraction from EHRs.

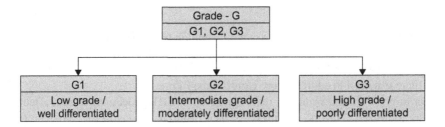

FIGURE 18.3D Classification of grade (G).

FIGURE 18.3 (Continued)

74% for T and 87% for N attributes. Lopez et al. [20] developed a computerized decision support system using naïve bayes to predict risk in breast cancer and obtained good outcome.

Rajguru et al. [21] used the logistic regression technique to extract tumor-node-metastasis (TNM) factors from a structured database. McCowan et al. [22] presented classification for TNM factors extraction using a support vector machine. Afzal et al. [23] introduced a system with a CART algorithm to extract details from EHRs of cancer.

18.3.2 USING NATURAL LANGUAGE PROCESSING

If EHRs are represented in the natural language, then NLP is used in disease prognosis. Extracting prognostic information from such unstructured EHRs is a complex task because there are variations in the interpretation of EHRs, use of medical concepts and their description, context of clinical terms, the format of EHRs, and the writing style of EHRs of different institutions.

Spasic et al. [24] used a semantic rule-based method and pattern matching to extract medication information. Liu et al. [4] discussed the role of NLP and electronic health records for clinical research. Buckley et al. [25] proposed a novel approach using NLP and checked the feasibility of medical information extraction from EHRs using their method.

In NLP methodology, EHRs are given as input to a system. Record preprocessing where tokenization, stemming, the normalization process is performed. Feature extraction plays a major role while extracting information from EHRs. For example, Figure 18.3 shows details of feature information required during cancer prognosis information extraction from EHRs. Techniques like UMLS, ICD, SNOMED CT, etc., are used for feature selection, but they have some constraints that affect the outcome's accuracy. Hence, the following section discusses the needs and challenges while extracting information from EHRs.

18.4 NEEDS AND CHALLENGES OF EHR

18.4.1 DATASET

Accessing the dataset is the main challenge in this research because of the privacy and confidentiality of patients' information. EHRs cannot be freely available for research without consent. Researchers have to obtain approval from the ethics committee to study EHRs for research. As these EHRs are not freely available, it causes the main bottleneck for research in the medical field.

18.4.2 UMLS

A UMLS can be used to implement a generalized system for disease prognosis. However, many EHRs include grammatical errors, spelling mistakes, different synonyms for medical terms, typing errors, different abbreviations, etc. Most of the abbreviations or synonyms are related to a particular disease, and it is difficult to find them in standardized dictionaries like UMLS.

18.4.3 SNOMED

SNOMED CT provides a framework to extract information from EHRs and can be used to improve the generalization of classifiers for all cancer subtypes. But this framework has limitations, for instance, concept model attribute and expression-based subsumption querying should be available [8]. Hence, there is a need to address these issues in the future.

To further improve the performance, there is a need for EHR processing to deal effectively with issues such as grammatical errors, spellings mistakes, different synonyms for medical terms, typing errors, different abbreviations, etc. There is a need to use the ML approach because text mining in the biomedical domain has shown promising results. ML approaches need a vast amount of training data, but EHRs cannot be freely available for this research because of confidentiality and the security of patient information [26]. Hence, using SNOMED CT with ML approach is another challenge in this research. Furthermore, a complete disease ontology is required to facilitate semantic modeling of unstructured data contained in EHRs.

18.4.4 STANDARDIZATION

Some prognostic factors have numerical value and dimension measures. There is a need for standardization of measure and value because several elements can be represented in different measurements and standards. For example, tumor dimensions are represented in various forms of centimeters and millimeters. Sometimes values are numeric, and sometimes these are described in words; hence, value standardization is also needed.

18.4.5 DICTIONARY

To extract prognostic information from EHRs, some researchers have proposed dictionary concepts for that particular disease [27]. There are a number of ways to represent clinical terms; hence, a generalized dictionary should be created for a specific disease that will include all medical terms related to that particular disease and consider variation in clinical terminology description, diversity in spellings of medical terms, and different synonyms for medical terms.

18.4.6 PATTERN MATCHING

Pattern matching is used while extracting prognostic information from EHRs. Some previous studies [28] used a regex pattern for extraction, but concrete filtering is complex using this pattern. For example, extracting tumor size considering only dimension is not sufficient because it can also be the size of any other element. Hence, pattern matching [29] with range analysis and setting priorities to confirmation words is the better solution to extract prognostic information from EHRs.

18.4.7 CONTEXT IDENTIFICATION

The rule-based method is used while extracting prognostic information from EHRs. In the rule-based approach, different weightage should be given to positive and negative findings, and priorities should be set according to their weightage [30]. For these findings, context identification [31] should be made, assigning weight to medical terms according to their importance.

18.5 CONCLUSION AND FUTURE SCOPE

This chapter briefly discussed the current status, structure, needs, and challenges of electronic health records. It also explained how NLP and ML can be used for the prognostic factor's extraction from EHRs for disease prognosis. This chapter discusses constraints while using these techniques for information extraction from EHRs.

For a strong framework in the future, machine learning techniques and information extraction systems should be incorporated. For more practical applicability of the medical research, a number of EHRs should be freely available. EHRs of different institutions belonging to different regional areas should be collected to implement the generalized method of extracting prognostic factors from EHRs. This generalized method will be unique to all institutions. In addition to this, a dictionary-based approach related to specific diseases should also be explored for generalization.

REFERENCES

[1] F. H. Saad, B. de la Iglesia, G. D. Bell, "Comparison of Documents Classification Techniques to Classify Medical Reports", pp. 285–291, Springer 2006.

[2] Wen-wai Y., Meliha Y., "Natural language processing in oncology a review", *Journal of the American Medical Informatics Association*, 2 (6): 797–804, https://doi.org/10.1001/jamaoncol.2016.0213, 2016.

[3] Meystre S. M., Savova G. K., Kipper-Schuler K. C., Hurdle J. F., "Extracting information from textual documents in the electronic health record: a review of recent research", *IMIA Yearbook of Medical Informatics*, 35(128):44, 2008.

[4] Liu F., Weng C., Yu H., Natural language processing, electronic health records, and clinical research, in: *Clinical Research Informatics*, Springer, London, 2012, pp. 293–310.

[5] Irena S., Jacqueline L., John A. K., Goran N., "Text mining of cancer-related information: Review of current status and future directions", *International Journal of Medical Informatics*, 83: 605–623, https://doi.org/10.1016/j.ijmedinf.2014.06.009, 2014.

[6] Indian Council of Medical Research, www.icmr.nic.in/. Accessed by 02–09–2020.

[7] Johanna J., Gladis D, Joy J. M., "SNOMED CT Annotation for improved pathological decisions in breast cancer domain ", *International Journal of Recent Technology and Engineering* (IJRTE), ISSN 8 (3): 2277–3878, https://doi.org/10.35940/ijrte.C6519.098319, September 2019.

[8] U.S. National Library of Medicine. Unified medical language system (UMLS), www.nlm.nih.gov/research/umls/2008.

[9] Coden A., Savova G., Sominsky I., Tanenblatt M., Masanz J., Schuler K., et al. "Automatically extracting cancer disease characteristics from pathology reports into a disease knowledge representation model", *Journal of Biomedical Informatics* 2009; 42(5): 937–949.

[10] Deshmukh P. R., Phalnikar R., "TNM cancer stage detection from unstructured pathology reports of breast cancer patients", Proceeding of International Conference on Computational Science and Applications, Algorithms for Intelligent Systems, CH 40: 411–418, https://doi.org/10.1007/978-981-15-0790-8_40, Springer 2020.

[11] Jiang D., Liao J., Duan H., Wu Q., Owen G., Shu C., Chen L., He Y., Wu Z., He D., Zhang W., and Wang Z., "A machine learning-based prognostic predictor for stage III colon cancer", *Scientific Reports*, 10: 10333, https://doi.org/10.1038/s41598-020-67178-0, 2020.

[12] Edge S. B., Byrd D. R., Compton C. C., Fritz A. G., Greene F. L., Trotti A., *AJCC Cancer Staging Manual Seventh Edition*, Springer, ISBN 978-0-387-88440-0.

[13] Gabriel N. H., James L. C., Carl J. D., Stephen B. E., Elizabeth A. M., Hope S. R., Lawrence J. S., Donald L. W., David J. W., and Armando G., *AJCC Cancer Staging Manual Eighth Edition*, 1–50, https://doi.org/10.1007/978-3-319-40618-3_48, 2018.

[14] Wong R. X., Wong F. Y., Lim J., Lian W. X., Yap Y. S., "Validation of the AJCC 8th prognostic system for breast cancer in an Asian healthcare setting", *The Breast, Elsevier*, 40: 38–44, https://doi.org/10.1016/j.breast.2018.04.013, 2018.

[15] Dursun D., Glenn W., Amit K., "Predicting breast cancer survivability: a comparison of three data mining methods", *Artificial Intelligence in Medicine*, Elsevier, 34: 113–127, https://doi.org/10.1016/j.artmed.2004.07.002, 2005.

[16] Joseph A. C., David S. W., "Applications of machine learning in cancer prediction and prognosis", *Cancer Informatics*, 2: 59–77, PMID: 19458758, PMCID: PMC2675494, 2006.

[17] Mogana D. G., Nur A. T., Yip C. H., Pietro L., and Sarinder K. D., "Predicting factors for survival of breast cancer patients using machine learning Techniques", *BMC Medical Informatics and Decision Making*, 19: 48, https://doi.org/10.1186/s12911-019-0801-4, 2019.

[18] Ravi K., Ramachandra G. A., Nagamani K., "An efficient prediction of breast cancer data using data mining techniques", *International Journal of Innovations in Engineering and Technology (IJIET)*, 2(4): 139–144, SSN: 2319–1058, 2013.

[19] Iain A. M., Darren C. M., Anthony N. N., Rayleen V. B., Belinda E. C., Edwina E., Mary-Jane F., "Collection of cancer stage data by classifying free-text medical reports", *Journal of the American Medical Informatics Association*, 14(6): 736–745, https://doi.org/10.1197/jamia.M2130, 2007.

[20] Lopez J., Palacios-Alonso D., Tortajada S., Moreno A., Casitas E., García-Gómez J., Otal R. G., Perez-Gonzalez A., Martinez A., Calderon C. P., et al., "Computerized decision support system and naïve bayes models for predicting the risk of relapse in breast cancer", *International Journal of Radiation Oncology - Biology - Physics*, 90(1): S593–S594, 2014.

[21] Rajaguru H., Vasanthi N. S., Balasubramani M., "Performance analysis of artificial neural networks and statistical methods in classification of oral and breast cancer stages", *International Journal of Soft Computing and Engineering (IJSCE)*, 2(3) ISSN: 2231–2307, July 2012.

[22] Iain M., Darren M., Mary-Jane F., "Classification of cancer stage from free-text histology reports", *International Conference of the IEEE Engineering in Medicine and Biology Society*, 1–4, https://doi.org/10.1109/IEMBS.2006.259563, 2006.

[23] Muhammad A., Maqbool H., Wajahat Ali K., Taqdir Ali, Sungyoung Lee, Eui-Nam Huh, Hafiz Farooq A., Arif J., Hassan I., Muhammad I., Manzar Abbas H., "Comprehensible knowledge model creation for cancer treatment decision making", *Computers in Biology and Medicine, Science Direct*, Elsevier, 82: 119–129, https://doi.org/10.1016/j. compbiomed.2017.01.010, 2017.

[24] Spasic I., Sarafraz F., Keane J. A., Nenadic G., "Medication information extraction with linguistic pattern matching and semantic rules", *Journal of the American Medical Informatics Association*, 17: 532–535, 2010.

[25] Buckley J. M., Coopey S. B., Sharko J., "The feasibility of using natural language processing to extract clinical information from breast pathology reports", *Journal of Pathology Informatics*, 3: 23, https://doi.org/10.4103/2153-3539.97788, 2012.

[26] David M., Graham P., Andrew M., Lawrence C., "Cross-hospital portability of information extraction of cancer staging information", *Artificial Intelligence in Medicine*, Elsevier, 62: 11–21, 2014.

[27] Deshmukh P. R., Phalnikar R., "Anatomic stage extraction from medical reports of breast cancer patients using natural language processing", *Health and Technology*, 10: 1555–1570, https://doi.org/10.1007/s12553-020-00479-6, 2020.

[28] Giulio N., Colin F., Richard M., David C., "Pattern-based information extraction from pathology reports for cancer registration", *Cancer Causes Control*, 21: 1887–1894, https://doi.org/10.1007/s10552-010-9616-4, 2010.

[29] Amjad H., Rola A., Dima S., "Four sliding windows pattern matching algorithms", *Journal of Software Engineering and Applications*, 8(3): 154–165, https://doi.org/10.4236/jsea.2015.83016, 2015.

[30] Chapman W. W., Bridewell W., Hanbury P., Cooper G. F., Buchanan B. G., "A simple algorithm for identifying negated findings and diseases in discharge summaries", *Journal of Biomedical Informatics*, 34(5): 301–310, https://doi.org/10.1006/jbin.2001.1029, 2001.

[31] Deshmukh P. R., Phalnikar R., "Identifying contextual information in medical document classification using term weighting", *8th International Advanced Computing Conference*, DOI-978-1-5386-6678-4/18, IEEE, 2018.

Part V

Recent Devlopement in Biomedical Applications

19 Implantable Pacemaker Low Power Telemetry Unit

Santosh D. Chede

CONTENTS

19.1 INTRODUCTION

Blood pumping is caused by heart muscle movement. The body's natural pacemaker (sinoatrial node) generates electrical impulses responsible for blood pumping. Heart muscle movement is synchronized by electric muscles i.e. whole heart pulse. The electrical pulse proceeds to the atrioventricular (AV) node after the atria contracts. After a certain delay, the impulse reaches the atrioventricular node, which allows time for contraction of the atria. These pulses travel towards bundle of His, the right and left bundle branches, the Purkinje fibers just below the AV node, and ultimately leads to ventricle contraction. This conduction system is responsible for electrogram as well as electrocardiogram [3].

An artificial pacemaker is implanted within the heart in case of a damaged intrinsic conduction system. Heartbeat rate is initially monitored by the implanted pacemaker, which provides required impulses to heart muscles when beat rate is low or zero. To stimulate a diseased heart artificially to operate at a normal rate, cardiac pacing plays a very crucial role. It is mostly preferred to have an implantable pacemaker that is smaller in size and less in weight, and has ultra-low power consumption. This helps with respect to increasing battery life, to extending the surgery period and the patient's comfort [4, 6, 12, 19]. A pacemaker consists of a magnetically operated reed switch. A reed switch consists of two hermetically sealed iron and nickel ferromagnetic blades in a glass capsule. The blades overlap internally in the glass capsule with an appropriate gap between them. A suitable magnetic field is responsible for making a switching contact between two blades [19]. Tachycardia and bradycardia are the major problems considering heart beats. With tachycardia (AOO), the heart beats faster, and with bradycardia (VOO), the heart beats slower. In order to treat a patient in such condition, the reed switch is used to alter the mode of the implantable pacemaker, thereby using the magnet externally. Reed switch activation will temporarily affect the mode of pacing, pacing output energy, and paced rate for the duration of magnet placement only. Similarly, this reed switch can be used to check battery status. As mentioned, in a TEROS SSI R 603 pacemaker, in magnet mode at EOL (end of life) of battery rate set is 96 beats per minute (bpm) and at BOL (Beginning of life) of battery rate set is 84 bpm [16]. In case of EOL, a pacemaker will experience pacing output

DOI: 10.1201/9781003272694-24

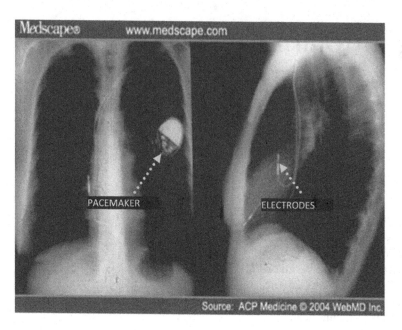

FIGURE 19.1 Implantable pacemaker and electrodes.

instability and in severe instances will cease to provide a paced output. When the external magnet is placed, the reed switch will be switched on and the mode of operation will be altered to asynchronous (VOO) mode and hence battery status will be identified [6]. When this switch is closed, the pacemaker operates at test rate, which decides battery status. On removal of the magnet, the pacemaker will alter to normal pacemaker mode after 30 seconds. Inappropriate activation of the magnetic reed switch could occur when the magnet is placed in close proximity to the implanted device [7]. Figure 19.1 shows an implantable pacemaker and electrodes.

19.2 MODES OF OPERATION

North American Society of Pacing and electrophysiology (NASPE) and British pacing and Electrophysiology (BPEG), as shown in Table 19.1, specifies nomenclature significance of various Modes VVI, VVT, VOO, AAI, AAT, and AOO for pacemaker classification [5]. Features like pacemaker sense the ventricle and pace the ventricles in inhibited mode as specified by VVI. Asynchronous mode is where the ventricle is paced with no chamber sensed and no response to sensing i.e. irrespective of the heart signal, the pacemaker generates pacing pulses at a set rate, which is specified by VOO.

19.3 WPAN STANDARDS

IEEE standards define network protocol and compatible interconnection for data communication devices using low data rate, low power, and low complexity, and short-range radio frequency (RF) transmission in a wireless personal area network (WPAN) [11]. For short distance data communication, WPAN, a network that involves little or no infrastructure, is used. Benchmarks for a system wireless communication design with low cost, ultra-low power consumption, ultra-low complexity, and low data rates—250 kbps (maximum) to 20 kbps (minimum)—are provided by these standards. For wireless connectivity in applications with limited power and relaxed throughput requirements, an efficient, low cost, low rate (LR) WPAN is used. LR WPAN is

TABLE 19.1
NASPE/BPEG CODE

Position	Category	Code
I	Chamber(s) paced	O = None
		A = Atrium
		V = Ventricle
		D = Dual (A + V)
II	Chamber(s) sensed	O = None
		A = Atrium
		V = Ventricle
		D = Dual (A+V)
III	Response to sensing	O = None
		T = Triggered
		I = Inhibited
		D = Dual (A + V)
IV	Rate responsive	O = None
		R = Rate modulation
V	Multirate pacing	O = None
		A = Atrium
		V = Ventricle
		D = Dual (A + V)

significantly used due to low cost, ease of installation, reliable data transfer, short range operation, reasonable battery life, and 'simplified flexible' protocol. Characteristics of low rate IEEE 802.15.4 WPAN are:

- Over the air data rates of 250 kbps, 40 kbps, and 20 kbps and star to peer-to-peer operation.
- Allocated 16-bit short or 64-bit extended addresses.
- Allocation of guaranteed time slots (GTSs).
- Carrier sense multiple access with collision avoidance (CSMA-CA) channel access.
- Fully acknowledged protocol for transfer reliability.
- Low power consumption.
- Energy detection (ED).
- Link quality indication (LQI).
- 16 channels in the 2450 MHz band, 10 channels in the 915 MHz band, and 1 channel in 868 MHz band.
- Compatible for systems with long battery life, selectable latency for controllers, sensors, remote monitoring, and portable electronics. It can be configured for maximum battery life equal to the 'shelf life' of most batteries.
- Transmission range of 30–100+ meters.

19.4 LOW POWER TELEMETRY STRATEGY

Main emphasis is given to the low power design approach for wireless battery status investigation of the implantable pacemaker, and transmission power is estimated with respect to transmission period. Considering magnet mode as mentioned in section 19.1, a record of bpm investigates battery status i.e. EOL, ERI etc. A magnet of suitable strength is placed in close proximity to the implanted device, thereby switching the reed switch. The RF wireless method with SimpliciTi protocol [20] is realized for battery voltage investigation instead of reed switch. An inbuilt 10-bit ADC is used to sense and convert battery voltage into a digital signal. IOT is an effective communication medium today. However, IOT has several security and other limitations, such as hacking in crucial biomedical applications like pacemakers [2]. IOT is mostly preferable and flexible with respect to connectivity and criticality and will allow ad hoc, mobile network structures. It also comprises less stringent timing and reliability requirements but is not desirable for medical applications [1]. Hence, other wireless methodology is being experimented with.

There are basically two types of heart signal i.e. ECG and EGM. ECG, as shown in Figure 19.3, is sensed by surface electrodes, and intracardiac electrodes are used to sense EGM. EGM contains valuable diagnostic information for cardiologists. Figures 19.3 and 19.5 show epicardium and endocardium nodes respectively. EGM signals sensed at these nodes are shown in Figures 19.4 and 19.6 [20]. For

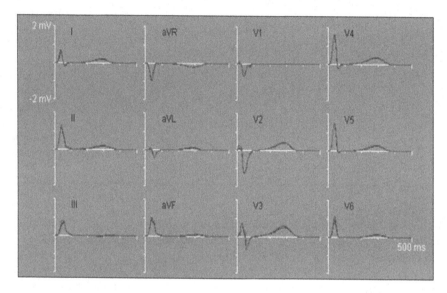

FIGURE 19.2 Twelve lead ECG.

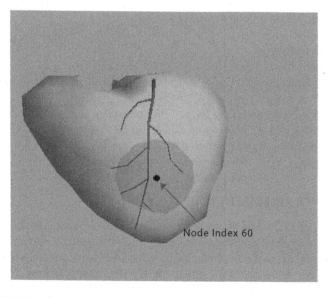

FIGURE 19.3 Node index 60 at left ventricular epicardium.

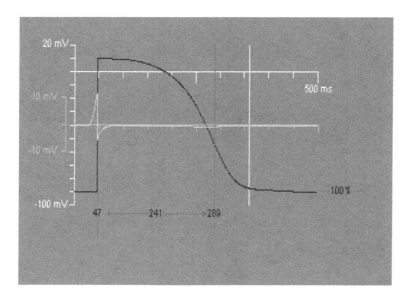

FIGURE 19.4   EGM at node index 60.

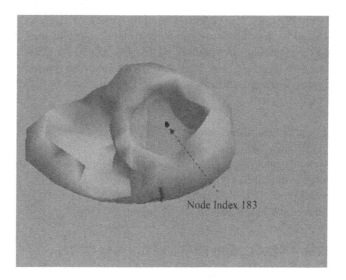

FIGURE 19.5   Node index 183 at left ventricular endocardium.

remote sensing and controlling of a patient's intracardiac signals and battery voltage, wireless medical telemetry is preferred [10]. In case of availability of plentiful power, low power, short-range RF devices with Bluetooth are used. The radio network has a great impact on a long-term monitoring and controlling system where a signal is sensed and transmitted at the required access node. In order to have long-term operation with the small, lightweight battery, the wireless transmission link must have low power consumption. Especially in an implantable pacemaker, the battery budget is very limited, and the telemetry unit placed and wireless network developed must consume less battery energy. Hence, an RF network other than Bluetooth is a better choice for a bio-telemetry unit.

An innovative wireless strategy, a low power wireless protocol like SimpliciTi, and a hardware–software codesign approach are used to develop a wireless network to test battery status. The hardware set up consists of a MSP430F2274 ultra-low power processor, transreceiver CC2500, chip antenna etc. IAR workbench is used for software realization.

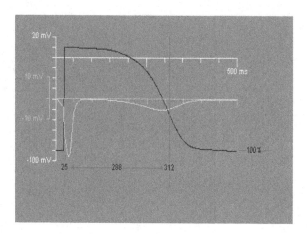

FIGURE 19.6   EGM at node index 183.

19.5   EXPERIMENTAL TARGET BOARD EZ430–2500

The eZ430-RF2500, shown in Figure 19.7, is a wireless development board that comprises an MSP430F2274 microcontroller, CC2500 2.4 GHz wireless transreceiver and chip antenna etc. This is a USB-based tool used to develop hardware–software codesign and uses the IAR embedded workbench integrated development environment (IDE). The eZ430-RF 2500 is a wireless target board with USB debugging interface. The MSP 430 UART interface is used to send and receive data by personal computer. External sensors can be interfaced with the board [16]. Special features of the target board are:

- USB debugging and programming interface.
- 18 development pins.
- MSP 430F2274 highly integrated ultra-low power microcontroller with 16 MHz.
- Two general purpose digital I/O pins connected to green and red LEDs.
- Interruptible push button for used feedback.
- Range up to 450 feet at 10 kbps and up to 300 feet at 250 kbps.

19.6   MSP430F2274 AND CC2500 FEATURES [9, 14, 15, 17]

MSP430F2274 is an ultra-low power microcontroller comprising five low power modes optimized for extended battery life in portable systems. It consists of a powerful 16-bit RISC central processing unit (CPU), 16-bit registers, and constant generators that contribute to maximum code efficiency. The digitally controlled Oscillator (DCO) allows wake up from low power modes to active mode in less than 1 μsec. It consists of a universal serial communication interface, two built-in 16-bit timers, a data transfer controller (DTC), a 10-bit A/D converter with integrated reference, two general purpose operational amplifiers and 32 I/O pines. An inbuilt sensor system accepts analog signals, converts them into digital signals, and transmits to the host system. Standalone RF sensor front ends can be used for system design [9, 15, 17].

Low-cost single chip 2.4 GHz transreceiver CC2500 is designed for very low power wireless application. This is suitable for industrial, scientific, and medical (ISM) as well as a short range device with a frequency band of 2400–2483.5 MHz and is integrated with a highly configurable baseband modem. The modem supports various modulation formats with a configurable data rate up to 500 kbps and provides extensive hardware support for data buffering, burst transmissions packet handling, link quality indication, clear channel assessment, and wake on radio. An SPI interface is used to handle operating parameters and 64-byte transmit/receive FIFOs of CC2500.

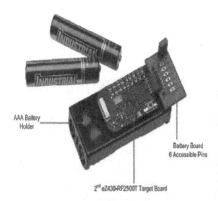

FIGURE 19.7   MSP430F2274 target board.

A microcontroller, CC2500, and some passive components will be used in specific applications [14]. Radio events of CC2500 are described in Figures 19.8 and 19.9. Basically, it consists of four sections, A, B, C, D, with a total duration of 4.70 msec., and the transmission execution pulse is obtained across 5 ohm resistors as given in [11].

Where,
A: XOSC startup = 300 μs
B: Ripple timer timeout =150 μs C-PLL calibration (idle) = 809 μs
D: (TX + RX) mode = 2.56 ms + 800 μs = 3.36 ms
Total interval = A + B + C + D = 4.619 ms = 4.70 ms (approx.)

19.7   BATTERY LIFE ESTIMATION ON THE BASIS OF INTERVAL OF TRANSMISSION

A sensor node transfers data to the access node at a programmable regular transmission interval. During the transmission period, the packet is transmitted. The transmission interval is inversely proportional to current consumption and directly proportional to battery longevity. Equations 1, 2, and 3 are used for battery life estimation. Interval of transmission decides average current consumption and battery life [11].

$$Iav = \frac{Imeas}{Pt} \tag{1}$$

$$Imeas = \frac{Vav}{R} \tag{2}$$

$$Blong = \frac{Brat}{Iav} \tag{3}$$

Where,
  Iav: average current,
  Imeas: measured current,
  Pt: period of transmission,
  Vav: Pulse average voltage,
  R: Resistance,
  Blong: Battery longevity,
  Brat: Battery ratings.

19.8   RESULT AND CONCLUSION

The interval of transmission is changed as shown in Figures 19.9 and 19.10 (i–x), in order to analyze current consumption for signal transmission. Figure 19.8 realizes the transmission pulse

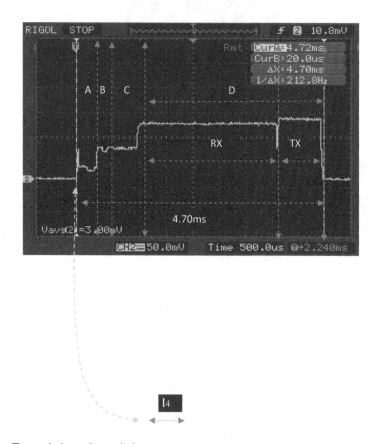

FIGURE 19.8   Transmission pulse period.

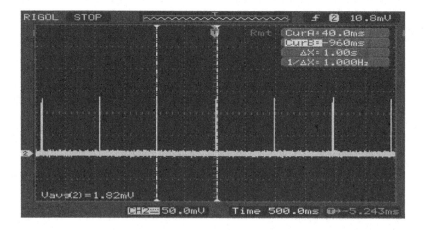

FIGURE 19.9   Transmission interval.

Radio events of CC2500 are described in the above figures. Basically, it consists of four sections, A, B, C, D, with total duration of 4.70 msec. and transmission execution pulse is obtained across 5 ohm resistors.

period. It is observed that current consumption decreases with increase in transmission period and battery life increases, as shown in Figures 19.11 and 19.12. Battery status detection is experimented with using an eZ430-CC2500 target board, and current values and battery life are estimated for various values of transmission periods as shown in Table 19.2 with battery rating of 0.85Ah. Especially to investigate implantable pacemaker parameters and battery status with optimized transmission control, such a WPAN telemetry unit, rather than IOT, will be an innovative approach. As continuous monitoring of pacemaker parameters consumes more power, the device can be programmed to indicate status at the desired interval. Similarly, the reed switch can be operated without placing a magnet close to the device to reduce complexity in device operation.

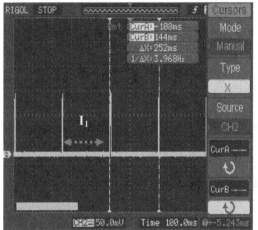

FIGURE 19.10(I)   Transmission period 0.25 sec.

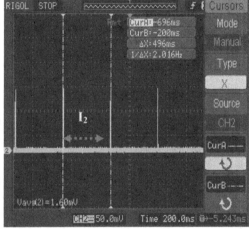

FIGURE 19.10(II)   Transmission period 0.49 sec.

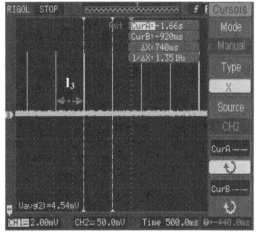

FIGURE 19.10(III)   Transmission period 0.74 sec.

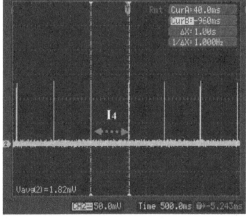

FIGURE 19.10(IV)   Transmission period 1.0 sec.

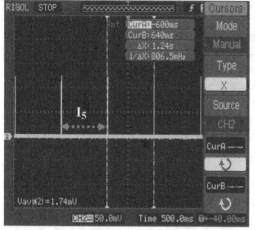

FIGURE 19.10(V) Transmission period 1.24 sec.

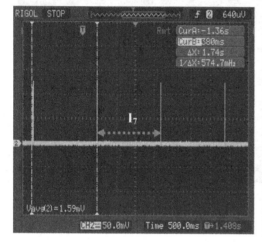

FIGURE 19.10(VII) Transmission period 1.74 sec.

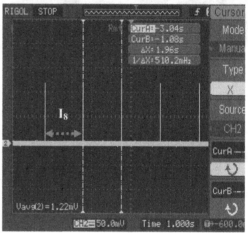

FIGURE 19.10(VIII) Transmission period 1.96 sec.

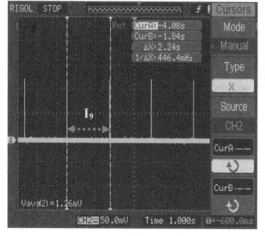

FIGURE 19.10(IX) Transmission period 2.24 sec.

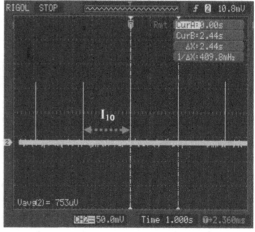

FIGURE 19.10(X) Transmission period 2.44 sec.

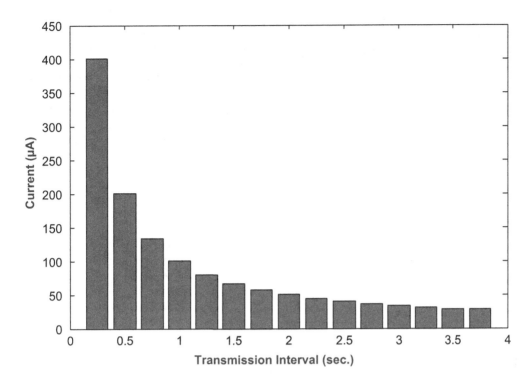

FIGURE 19.11   Transmission interval vs. current plot.

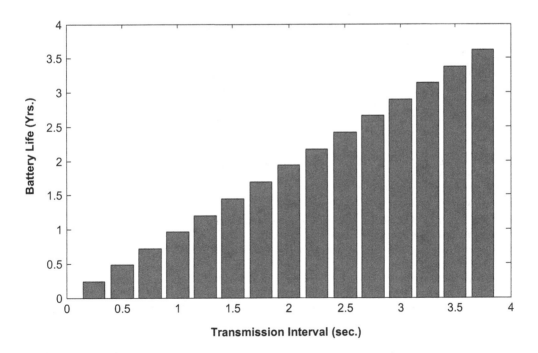

FIGURE 19.12   Transmission interval vs. battery life plot.

TABLE 19.2

Transmission Period and Battery Life Estimation

Period	Desired (Sec.)	Observed (Sec.)	Current (μA)	Battery Life (Yrs.)
I_1	0.25	0.25	401.12	0.24
I_2	0.50	0.49	200.56	0.48
I_3	0.75	0.74	133.70	0.72
I_4	1.00	1.00	100.28	0.96
I_5	1.25	1.25	80.22	1.20
I_6	1.50	1.50	66.85	1.45
I_7	1.75	1.74	57.30	1.69
I_8	2.00	1.96	50.14	1.93
I_9	2.25	2.24	44.56	2.17
I_{10}	2.50	2.44	40.11	2.41
I_{11}	2.75	2.72	36.46	2.66
I_{12}	3.00	2.96	33.42	2.90
I_{13}	3.25	3.24	30.85	3.14
I_{14}	3.50	3.44	28.65	3.38
I_{15}	3.75	3.76	26.74	3.62

REFERENCES

1. Emiliano Sisinni, Abusayeed Saifullah, Song Han, Ulf Jennehag, Mikael Gidlund, Industrial Internet of Things: Challenges, Opportunities, and Directions, *IEEE Transactions on Industrial Informatics*, Vol. 14, No. 11, November 2018, 4724–4734.
2. Osman Yakubu, Osei Adjei, Narendra Babu C., A Review of Prospects and Challenges of Internet of Things, *International Journal of Computer Applications*, Vol. 139, No. 10, April 2016, ISSN 0975–8887, 33–39.
3. B. Ananth Bhatt, Wireless Power Transmission for Internal Pacemaker IJSRD, *International Journal for Scientific Research & Development*, Vol. 2, No. 05, 2014, ISSN (online): 2321–0613.
4. W. Welkowitz S. Deutsch, M. Akay, *Biomedical Instruments-Theory and Design*, 2nd edition, Academic press, San Diego, CA, 1992.
5. Santosh Chede, Kishore Kulat, Design Overview of Processor Based Implantable Pacemaker, *International Journal of Computers (Academy publisher)*, Vol. 8, No. 8, 2008, 49–57.
6. Santosh Chede, Kishore Kulat, *Software Related Current/Energy Consumption in Implantable Pacemaker*, Proceedings of IEEE, ICIIS-2008, IIT Kharagpur, 8–10 December 2008.
7. Richard S. Sanders, Michel T. Lee, Implantable Pacemakers, *Proceedings of the IEEE*, Vol. 84, No. 3, March 1996, 480–486.
8. *Pacemaker Technical Notes, Patent Number 84—Non Manufacturer/Model Specific*, 20 September 2006.
9. BIOCRONIK CRM, *Implantable Medical Device Comprising Magnetic Field Detector*, Patent Number EP 1935450A1, 25/06/2008.
10. Mike Mitchel, *Choosing an Ultralow power MCU MSP 430*, Application Report, SLAA207, June 2004.
11. R.E. Geertsma, A.C.P. de Bruijn, E.S.M. Hilbers-Modderman, M.L. Hollestelle, G. Bakker, B. Roszek, *New and Emerging Medical Technologies*, Report, 2 February 2007.
12. Miquel Morales, *A Wireless Sensor Monitor Using eZ 430-RF2500*, Application Report, SLAA 378-November 2007.
13. Venkiateswara Samra, Mallela V. Ilankumaran, N. Srinivasa Rao, Trends in Cardiac Pacemaker Batteries, Indian Pacing and Electrophysiology Journal, *Technical Series*, Vol. 4, 2004, 201–202.
14. IEEE Std 802.15.4 TM -2003, Part 15.4: Wireless Medium Access Control (MAC) and Physical Layer (PHY) Specifications for Low Rate Wireless Personal Area Networks (LR-WPANs), *IEEE Computer Society*, 12 May 2003.
15. CC2500, *Single Chip Low Cost Power RF Transreceiver, Preliminary Data Sheet (Rev.1.2)*, SWRS040A, Texas Instruments.

16. MSP430x22x2, *MSP430x22x4 Mixed Signal Microcontroller*, SLAS504B, Texas Instruments, July 2007.https://fdocuments.in/document/msp430x22x2-msp430x22x4-mixed-signal-msp430x22x2-msp430x22x4-mixed-signal-microcontroller.html?page=1

17. Texas Instruments eZ430-RF2500 Development Tool, *User Guide.*

18. Texas Instruments MSP430x2xx Family User Guide, *SLAU144D.*

19. TEROS Series/Model SSI R603 Specifications, *Pacemaker Unit.*

20. CCC Medical Devices Patient's Guides.

21. www.ecgsim.org

22. www.meder.com

23. www.ti.com/wireless/simpliciTi

24. www.verywelth.com

20 Recent Advances in Drug Delivery Systems
MEMS Perspective

*H. T. Bhavana, M. Anantha Sunil, T. Sanjana,
and B. Harshitha*

CONTENTS

20.1 INTRODUCTION

Drug delivery systems are used to administer pharmaceutical compounds to patients considering the concluded disease; this helps to achieve a therapeutic effect. Conventional drug delivery systems release the drug by dissolution, diffusion, osmosis, or ion exchange processes. The patients are administered to orally, through tablet, tonic, or injections, but these mechanisms are not always appropriate since they possess many drawbacks [1,2]. Traditional mechanisms fail to attain targeted and controlled drug delivery to the specific tissues or pathological cells as they may degrade while passing several biological barriers [3]. Oral administration shows many limitations, such as enzymatic degradation, side effects, degradation of drug due to change in pH values, variation in time to reach target, and metabolism in primary levels [4]. Drug delivery through conventional injections is painful as a long needle pierces nerve endings and also leads to a burst release of the drug instead of sustained release. These traditional methods also suffer from unwanted release, reduced solubility, and non-specificity [5].

Controlled drug delivery aims at the release of a drug to a predetermined extent at a fixed time and at fixed rate at a specific pathological area by considering the potency of the drug [6]. These mechanisms are suitable for curative drugs since they progress administration, efficiency, and pharmacokinetics. A variety of controlled drug delivery mechanisms, such as microneedles, transdermal patches, nanoparticles, and micro reservoir implants have been designed and developed [7]. Figure 20.1 depicts the advantages of controlled drug delivery over traditional drug delivery methods.

Microelectromechanical systems (MEMS) is the well-established technology that aids in the miniaturization of mechanical systems, integrated with electrical circuits in order to implement the desired functionality. MEMS can overcome existing challenges in localized and controlled drug delivery; it allows microfabrication of novel devices that offer high therapeutic efficacy. Because of better performance, improved efficiency, and ease of implementation, it finds applications in a variety of sectors such as micro-medical, micro-manufacturing, and micro-assembly [8]. MEMS technology, material science, and batch production originated in the semiconductor industry and

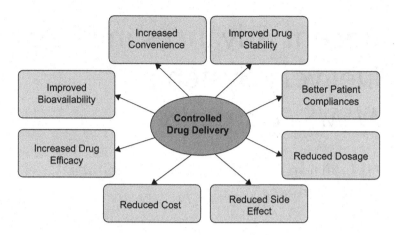

FIGURE 20.1   Advantages of controlled drug delivery.

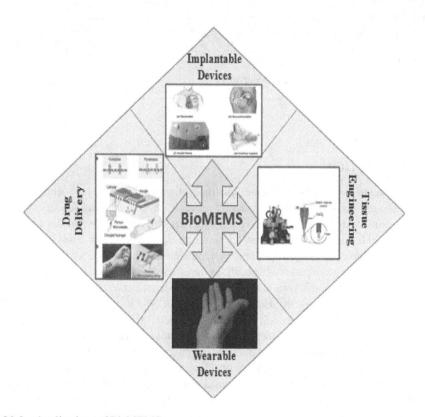

FIGURE 20.2   Applications of BioMEMS.

lead to the production of low cost, biocompatible, and integrated biomedical devices. BioMEMS finds application in different biomedical fields such as wearable and implantable MEMS devices, tissue engineering, and drug delivery, as shown in Figure 20.2.

In recent years, a variety of microfluidic devices, such as microgrippers, micropumps, microneedles, micromixers, and microvalves to micro–total analysis systems (μTAS), have been developed through MEMS technologies. The microfluidic devices fabricated from MEMS machinery find a wide range of applications in the field of lab on chip, controlled drug delivery, and chemical analysis

[9,10]. In this article, different MEMS-based microfluidic devices stated in literature are reviewed. The design considerations, challenges, and opportunities involved with brain infusion, oscular drug delivery, and gastrointestinal track drug delivery mechanisms are discussed. Different transdermal drug delivery systems for microneedle application have been summarized. Various biocompatible materials and MEMS-based wearable and implantable devices have been considered.

20.2 LITERATURE SURVEY

Microfluidic devices have been extensively used for implantable devices in controlled drug delivery; they can be implemented directly without carriers or with integration of carriers on a chip. Direct carrier-free delivery systems are of two types: highly integrated lab on chip [LOC] devices and simple micro reservoir-based systems [11,12]. Simple micro reservoir systems consist of one or multiple reservoirs for temporary storage of drugs; it gives accurate control over the rate of drug delivery. The physicians can start, change the flow, and stop the drug release at target locations in passive and active modes. Passive mode provides stable and prolonged drug release, whereas active mode flow rate of drug and time can be controlled. Barash et al. proposed a passive drug delivery system with a combination of hydrogels and gelatin for curative proteins [13]. In this method, proteins could be delivered with nominal invasive techniques and the fabrication process was easy. An MEMS-based in vitro implantable device for programmed delivery of doxorubin was proposed by Song et al. [14]. Zhuang et al. reported a controlled drug delivery device for alimentary canal; this was a piston-actuated system based on MEMS technology [15]. LOC for microfluids is a promising platform that manipulates a tiny amount of fluid with micro scale structures inside. Compared to micro reservoir systems, LOC consists of substrates, microchannels, microcapillaries, micro reservoirs, microvalves, and actuators integrated together. Sampling, synthesis, and testing within a small device are major functionalities of LOC, in sophisticated systems analysis of complex pathological fluids, or delivering therapeutic compounds is also available [16]. LOC devices are low cost, portable, and boast miniaturization and precise control; they have a variety of applications such, as detection of infectious diseases and cancer, tissue engineering, cellular analysis, drug and gene delivery, etc. [17,18]. N. M. Belliveau et al. fabricated a single device that can synthesize lipid nanoparticles for delivery of small interfering RNA [19]. LOC devices are also classified as active mode and passive mode devices. Lee et al. designed a subcutaneous LOC device that consists of microfluidic channels for sustained release of bupivacaine hydrochloride (BHCL) [20]. In this system, specific absorption of UV light was used to measure the amount of drug release, and drug release rate was determined by Fick's law. Pirmoradi et al. developed a MEMS-based self-controlled drug release device for release of docetaxel, which was controlled magnetically [21]. The drug solution released by applying a magnetic field through a magnetic membrane. Figure 20.3 depicts the carrier-free LOC consisting of nanochannels for controlled drug delivery system developed by Ferrati et al. [22].

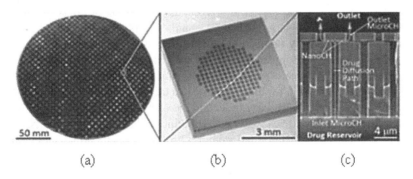

(a)   (b)   (c)

FIGURE 20.3 LOC nanochannel-controlled drug delivery system. (a) 700 nanochannel membrane in a single wafer; (b) single nanochannel membrane; (c) cross-section of vertical microchannels connected by horizontal nanochannels [22].

MEMS micropumps are trending devices in medical applications; an actuation mechanism invokes the drug by creating pressure in the chamber. Junwu et al. fabricated a piezoelectrically actuated micropump with a good flow rate and backpressure [23]. Gidde et al. designed a 3D valve-less micropump and performed numerical analysis to obtain optimum flow rate and back pressure at 50V [24]. Microneedle is most booming application of microtechnology for transdermal drug delivery. In the third generation of microneedle, development delivery for active control of RNA and vaccine are accommodated through smart triggering systems [25,26]. A large number of microneedles can be accurately fabricated in a single array for drug delivery. Intrusion of physical barriers poses the main challenge in targeting drug delivery to the brain and posterior eye segment. The control of dosage duration is most challenging in designing transdermal patches. This chapter reviews the recent works that address problems and challenges regarding targeting different areas of the body.

20.3   DESIGN CONSIDERATIONS, CHALLENGES, AND OPPORTUNITIES

In this section, design considerations, challenges, and opportunities associated with drug delivery to brain and ocular is discussed.

20.4   DIRECT BRAIN INFUSION

Direct brain infusion (DBI) or direct infusion (DI) is one of the invasive techniques that is commonly used in the field of neuroscience for treating the diseases related to the brain. The advantage of this technique is that controlled concentration of therapeutic drugs are infused to the desired area in the brain. For drug delivery to the human brain, there are three neurosurgical methods that are used [27]:

1. Intracerebral implantation
2. Intracerebroventricular infusion (ICV)
3. Convection-enhanced diffusion (CED)

Parameters such as required infusion area, the speed at which a drug is infused, drug delivery distribution, portion of tissue damage, and drug flux sensitivity help in choosing the correct neurosurgical method for treating the brain disease. The implantation and infusion neurosurgical methods use a concentrated source at the implanted sites, whereas the diffusion method uses external forces to diffuse the drug into the brain by cannula or needle by maintaining constant flow rate [28]. The advantages of the CED method are that maintaining a constant flow rate at the edge of the cannula helps to overcome the brain–blood barrier, homogenous distribution of drugs in the order of cm, and refluxed drugs are within the target volume. Cannula size plays a significant role in the diffusion of a drug, but it is limited by fabrication process used as well as flow rate at the desired site, which is proportional to the viscosity and density of the drug. The CED technique is the dominant neurosurgical method used to conduct trials on small animals. In mice, hypodermic needles with gauge numbers 30 and 31 are used for drug delivery to a target region of the brain. However, some portion of the mouse brain is of micro size order and thereby requires cannula size miniaturization. Hence, microneedles or neural probes integrated with microfluidic channel using MEMS technology is the desirable solution for DBI in small animals [29]. The first silicon-based microneedle using MEMS technology for brain infusion was fabricated in the year 1997, and the device dimensions are reported to be 58 μm wide and 15 μm thick [30]. To reduce the impairment in the brain tissue, scaling down the device dimensions can be carried out using various technologies such as buried channel and silicon [31,32].

The challenges that need to be addressed and resolved are clogging, reflux, and leakage. When a microneedle is inserted, bleeding takes place and thereby some of the neurons die, resulting in an astrogliotic reaction during the implantation process. Hence, a mismatch exists between the micromotion and implantation of the brain. To overcome these challenges, polymer-based materials such as SU-8 polymer and parylene are used as stretchy substrates for fabrication of the microneedles. Microneedles fabricated using polymer materials are denser compared to silicon-based microneedles. However, damage incurred during the infusion is still a concern and hence requires frequent removal and cleaning of microneedles.

The opportunities/challenges that can be resolved and implemented by MEMS technology are as follows [33]:

1. Complete control of releasing the single drug or multiple drug in situ
2. Prediction of accurate delivery of dosage to the intended site
3. In situ drug concentration through single implantation

20.5   OCULAR DRUG DELIVERY

The eye is a sensitive and complex sense organ of the human system for which drug delivery needs to be addressed. In case of the ocular (eyes) drug delivery system, the anterior section is accessed with the help of a thin layer of cornea, whereas the posterior segment is interfaced through the blood–retinal barriers. The possible channels where ocular drug delivery can be administered are topical, intravitreal, periocular, and systemic routes. The most common method of treating the ocular drug delivery systems is topical. In the topical systems, ointments and eye drops are used for treating ocular diseases. Five percent of the dose is absorbed by the eyes and can be cleared by using nasolacrimal ducts and low permeability of the corneal layer [34]. This leads to increase in drug dosage at the target size, and it also becomes difficult to transport the drug to the posterior segment of the eyes. The feasible solution to overcome this problem is 'implantable drug delivery systems'. Intraocular drug delivery systems penetrate into significant implantable sites such as vitreous space, intrascleral space, peribulbar, and pars plana. Implantable devices can treat various diseases such as cytomegalovirus (CMV) retinitis and proliferative vitreoretinopathy (PVR). These systems are suitable for age-related macular degeneration (AMD), macular edema, and retinitis pigmentosa. For testing purposes, animals have been used. In the early 1800s, polymeric implants were successfully developed and commercialized. Later, in 1900, it was observed that implantation surgeries resulted in complication and hence soft contact lenses have been used as an alternative non-invasive drug delivery system. Various non-invasive methods such as surface immobilization of drugs, soak and absorption, bandage contact lenses and molecular imprinting have been successfully implemented. However, diffusion of preservatives on the ocular surface, pharmacokinetics, drug stability, and cornea safety issues have been of severe concern for commercialization.

To provide drugs for longer duration, minimal complications, and maximal patient compliance, the feasible solution is the design of MEMS-based intraocular drug delivery systems. The design factors to be taken care of are implantation volume and size, biodegradable materials, sensing method, and reliability. The implantation size is smaller than millimeters so that patient comfort level and ease of surgery are enhanced. If the implantation size is less, then the volume of drug is reduced, and hence there is a tradeoff between implantation size and volume. Biodegradable materials have to be used in order to avoid after release effects of the drug at the implantation site. Hence, implantation size and volume are key factors to be taken care during the design of microneedle devices. Recent microneedles fabricated using the MEMS technology are shown in Table 20.1. The challenges to be addressed are fabrication of MEMS devices using biocompatible materials and developing self-powered devices.

TABLE 20.1

Minimally Invasive Microneedles Using MEMS Technology [35]

S. No	Type of Microneedles	Purpose
1.	Drug-coated and hollow needles	Intrascleral and suprachoroidal drug delivery.
2.	Multiplexed and switched	Delivery of multiple drugs.
3.	Dissolving polymeric needle	Surgery can be avoided for the dissolvable systems.

20.6 TRANSDERMAL DRUG DELIVERY AND MICRONEEDLES

Drug supervision via the skin is a striking alternative to oral administration and injections. It distributes drugs symmetrically through vascular network in the dermis. It utilizes biocompatible patches that help in long-term drug administration. Microneedles loaded with analgesia and nicotine patches require supervision for a long period of time. A number of transdermal drugs are approved by the USFDA, and a number of transdermal modes of drug delivery systems have reached the market [36,37].

Microneedles provide interference between the patient's skin and the drug for extracting or releasing fluids. The microneedle must be long enough to reach the epidermis and short enough not to penetrate the dermis so that the patient never experiences pain. Generally, the dimension of MEMS microneedles range will be of nano and micrometers. Microneedle design and fabrication depend basically on the structure; these structures are depicted in Figure 20.4. In-plane microneedle shafts and the substrate surface are parallel to each other; they have the advantage of accurate control over the length of needle during the fabrication process. There will be protrusion of microneedles out of the substrate surface in out-of-plane microneedles. The solid microneedles consist of more high strength than the hollow type because of strong lumens. There are two types of solid microneedles: dissolving and coated microneedles. Coated microneedles consist of coating the lumen surfaces and being injected into the patient's body. The microneedle is taken away once the coating becomes dissolute in the body. In the dissolving type, microneedles get dissolute and the non-dissolving base is taken away from surface of skin.

Selection of microneedle materials depends on the application; most researchers have used silicon for fabrication. Since silicon is harmful to health, polymeric materials have been used in later research works. Polymer materials are suitable for fabrication of microneedles as they have good mechanical and chemical properties. Some other materials, such as glass, metal, and alloys, are also reported in the literature [39,40].

Though numerous research activities have been carried out on microneedles, there are unresolved issues, challenges, and features that need innovation. Secure positioning of the microneedle on the surface of the skin is vital during drug supervision over a long period. Hence, continuous

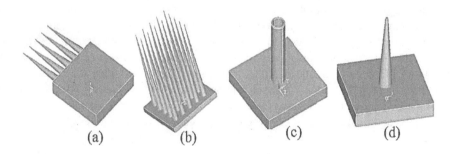

FIGURE 20.4 Structure of microneedles: (a) in-plane microneedles; (b) out-of-plane microneedles; (c) hollow microneedles; (d) solid microneedles [38].

optimization of tip shape, length, and spacing is required. Vaccine delivery demands completely dissolvable microneedles and polymer materials for fabrication. Biotechnology has led to delivery of a variety of drug candidates such as DNA and proteins [41]. Self-regulated or closed-loop drug delivery can be accomplished if drug discharge is activated through transformation in physiological signals such as pH, glucose, temperature, or enzyme concentrations [42]. Some design considerations of such systems are response rate of closed-loop systems, sensitivity and resolution of physiological signals, and a few biocompatible side effects. A similar closed-loop insulin injection system based on intravascular glucose level has been proposed by Hu et al., as shown in Figure 20.5 [43].

Closed-loop and on-demand drug delivery methods can be achieved through stimuli-responsive microneedles that work on either internal or external stimuli. Teodorescu et al. have designed a transdermal patch that triggers based on photo-thermal effect; it releases the drug loaded in microneedles when temperature is induced due to near infrared waves [44]. Chen et al. also developed a transdermal analgesia system that was also activated by near infrared waves, as is shown in Figure 20.6 [45]. Gulati et al. developed a switchable nicotine patch in which a carbon nanotube (CNT) membrane was used as a switching layer [46]. Di et al. designed a drug delivery system that

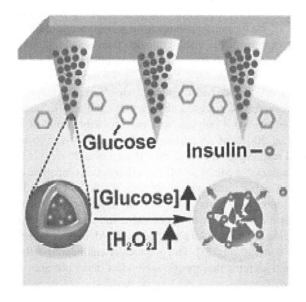

FIGURE 20.5   Intravascular network based closed loop system accordance with glucose level [43].

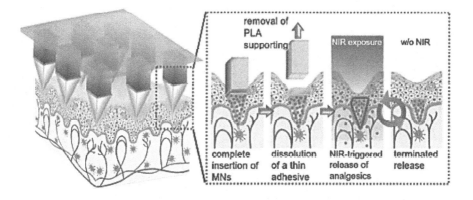

FIGURE 20.6   Closed-loop microneedles activated by near infrared light [45].

was made up of stretchable elastomer and microgel depots with nanoparticles loaded with the drug. This was a wearable device actuated by tensile strain [47].

20.7 IMPLANTABLE DEVICES

Subcutaneous implantable devices are persistent with low patient compliance and provide administration over years, though implantation under the skin depends on a patient's acceptance of drug delivery for cancer treatment, and insulin injections are needed over a long period of time through subcutaneous delivery mechanisms. The extended drug administration reduces requirements for regular injections and increases the comfort level and compliance of patients [48]. The design fabrication of a subcutaneous device largely depends on the size and volume of the implant; aside from this, the patient's compliance and comfort, surgery complexity, drug stacking capacity, and vacant space for circuit elements also should be considered. The loaded drug volume decides the maximum number of dosages and hence implant duration. The number of dosages can be increased, refilling reservoirs without causing infections and clogging. The active components can be minimized by introducing wireless technologies, and hence drug storage capacity can be increased. The drug activation can be carried through magnetic, electrothermal actuation, or piezoelectric pumping [49]. Robustness and biocompatibility over a long range of time are the foremost challenges for subcutaneous implants. Dijk et al. carried out a study on complications of implantable insulin infusion pumps and reported that 10–17% of people suffered from hematoma, pain, or other infections at the implanted sites. Of these, 5–17% of patients stetted the need for replacement because of technical failures and implantable pump failure [50].

Liu et al. reported a MEMS device based on electrodes for activation; they are refillable systems and hence consist of a reservoir to store the drug and a canula [51]. Silicon wafers were used to fabricate metal electrodes and SU-8 polymer was used for fabrication of the drug reservoir. This was tested with mice, and 50 μL of an adrenaline formulation was observed as blood pressure increased; the biological response of the implanted device over 28 days is shown in Figure 20.7(a). Chin et al. devised an implantable MEMS (iMEMS) that is biocompatible and reliable [52]. It consisted of hydrogel integrating reservoirs with singe gear, toothed rotors, and gate valves as shown in Figure 20.7(b). The development systems that can accommodate drugs such as vaccines, genes, and macromolecules with less bioavailability have been seen in recent years. Lathuiliere et al. designed a cellular implant for release of anti-amyloid antibodies for Alzheimer's disease in subcutaneous tissue, which is shown in Figure 20.7(c) [53]. The genetically engineered cells continuously produced monoclonal antibodies and secreted therapeutic antibodies in the plasma.

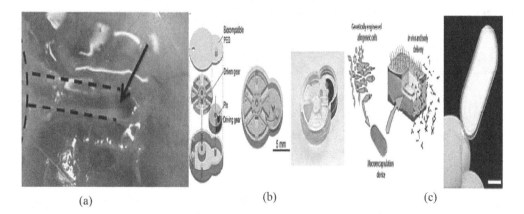

(a)   (b)   (c)

FIGURE 20.7   Drug delivery systems with implantable devices: (a) implanted device and biological response collected over 28 days [42]; (b) mechanical device components link gears and rotors fabricated with soft hydrogel for mems devices [53]; (c) an implantable device to deliver in vivo antibodies [54].

20.8 CONCLUSION

This chapter summarizes the different applications for BioMEMS, challenges involved in design and implementation, and some recent research activities carried on BioMEMS devices. MEMS technology aims at miniaturization, integration of multiple functionalities, and electromechanically actuated components to provide spatial, temporal, and dosage-controlled drug delivery. There are multiple challenges involved in the design of BioMEMS as different organs of the body possesses different anatomical and physiological changes. Thin neural probes are suitable for various parts of brain for localized drug delivery, whereas a microneedle array is well suited for transdermal and intraocular drug delivery. Self-regulated closed-loop systems can be designed that use the external or internal stimuli for drug delivery of gastrointestinal, intraocular, and subcutaneous devices. In implantable devices, maintaining efficacy of the system along with the patient's comfort is the major challenge. In subcutaneous drug delivery systems, reloading of the drug, storage of the drug, activation of the drug, power transfer, and selection of biocompatible material pose some other challenges. BioMEMS applications are only at the research stage and very few devices have been fabricated or are on the market for commercial usage. This is because of many issues and challenges involved, such as complicated microfluidic structures, biocompatibility, fabrication, investment, marketing, training of medical staff, lack of collaboration between medical research institutes and companies, awareness in public, and packaging.

REFERENCES

1. R. Lo, P.Y. Li, S. Saati, R. Agrawal, M.S. Humayun, E. Meng, A refillable microfabricated drug delivery device for treatment of ocular diseases, *Lab Chip* 8(7) (2008) 1027–1030.
2. H. Li, Y. Yu, S. Faraji Dana, B. Li, C.-Y. Lee, L. Kang, Novel engineered systems for oral, mucosal and transdermal drug delivery, *Journal of Drug Targeting* 21 (2013) 611–629.
3. E. Blanco, H. Shen, M. Ferrari, Principles of nanoparticle design for overcoming biological barriers to drug delivery, *Nature Biotechnology* 33 (2015) 941–951.
4. A. Muheem, F. Shakeel, M.A. Jahangir, M. Anwar, N. Mallick, G.K. Jain, M.H. Warsi, F.J. Ahmad, A review on the strategies for oral delivery of proteins and peptides and their clinical perspectives, *Saudi Pharmaceutical Journal* 24 (2016) 413–428.
5. K. Cheung, D.B. Das, Microneedles for drug delivery: trends and progress, *Drug Delivery*, (2014) 1–17.
6. K. Srinivasa Rao, Md. Hamza, P. Ashok Kumar, K. Girija Sravani, Design and optimization of MEMS based piezoelectric actuator for drug delivery systems, *Microsystem Technologies* 26 (2020) 1671–1679. https://doi.org/10.1007/s00542-019-04712-9
7. K. Yang, L. Feng, Z. Liu, Stimuli responsive drug delivery systems based on nanographene for cancer therapy, *Advanced Drug Delivery Reviews* 105 (2016) 228–241.
8. Marija Cauchi, Ivan Grech, Bertram Mallia, Pierluigi Mollicone, Nicholas Sammut, Analytical, numerical and experimental study of a horizontal electrothermal MEMS microgripper for the deformability characterisation of human red blood cells, *Micromachines* 9 (2018) 108. doi:10.3390/mi9030108
9. M. Staples, K. Daniel, M.J. Cima, R. Langer, Application of micro- and nano electromechanical devices to drug delivery, *Pharmaceutical Research* 23 (5) (2006) 847–863. https://doi.org/10.1007/s11095-006-9906-4
10. J.W. Judy, Biomedical applications of MEMS. In: *Measurement and Science Technology Conference*, University of California, Los Angeles, CA, 2000, pp. 403–414.
11. R. Riahi, A. Tamayol, S.A.M. Shaegh, A.M. Ghaemmaghami, M.R. Dokmeci, A. Khademhosseini, Microfluidics for advanced drug delivery systems, *Current Opinion in Chemical Engineering* 7 (2015) 101–112.
12. N.T. Nguyen, S.A.M. Shaegh, N. Kashaninejad, D.T. Phan, Design, fabrication and characterization of drug delivery systems based on lab-on-a-chip technology, *Advanced Drug Delivery Reviews* 65 (2013) 1403–1419.
13. H. Epstein-Barash, C.F. Stefanescu, D.S. Kohane, An in situ cross-linking hybrid hydrogel for controlled release of proteins, *Acta Biomater* 8 (2012) 1703–1709.
14. P.Y. Song, D. Jian, H. Tng, R. Hu, G.M. Lin, E. Meng, K.T. Yong, *An Electrochemically Actuated MEMS Device for Individualized Drug Delivery: An in Vitro Study, adv Healthc Mater* 2 (2013) 1170–1178; X.J. Li, Y. Zhou, *Microfluidic Devices for Biomedical Applications*, Elsevier, 2013.

15. Y. Zhuang, W. Hou, X. Zheng, Z. Wang, J. Zheng, X. Pi, J. Cui, Y. Jiang, S. Qian, C. Peng, A MEMS-based electronic capsule for time controlled drug delivery in the alimentary canal, *Sensors and Actuators A: Physical* 169 (2011) 211–216.

16. S. T Sanjay, M. Dou, G. Fu, F. Xu, X. Li, Controlled drug delivery using microdevices, *Current Pharmaceutical Biotechnology* 17 (2016) 772–787.

17. F. Shen, X. Li, P.C. Li, Study of flow behaviors on single-cell manipulation and shear stress reduction in microfluidic chips using computational fluid dynamics simulations, *Biomicrofluidics* 8 (2014) 014109.

18. M. Dou, S.T. Sanjay, D.C. Dominguez, S. Zhan, X. Li, A paper/polymer hybrid CDlike microfluidic SpinChip integrated with DNA-functionalized graphene oxide nanosensors for multiplex qLAMP detection, *Chemical Communications* 53 (2017) 10886–10889.

19. N.M. Belliveau, J. Huft, P.J. Lin, S. Chen, A.K. Leung, T.J. Leaver, A.W. Wild, J.B. Lee, R.J. Taylor, Y.K. Tam, Microfluidic synthesis of highly potent limit-size lipid nanoparticles for in vivo delivery of siRNA, *Molecular Therapy—Nucleic Acids* 1 (2012) e37.

20. K.J. Lee, S.Y. Yang, W. Ryu, Controlled release of bupivacaine HCl through microchannels of biodegradable drug delivery device, *Biomed Microdevices* 14 (2012) 583–593.

21. F.N. Pirmoradi, J.K. Jackson, H.M. Burt, M. Chiao, On-demand controlled release of docetaxel from a battery-less MEMS drug delivery device, *Lab Chip* 11 (2011).

22. S. Ferrati, D. Fine, J.P. You, E. De Rosa, L. Hudson, E. Zabre, S. Hosali, L. Zhang, C. Hickman, S.S. Bansal, A.M. Cordero-Reyes, T. Geninatti, J. Sih, R. Goodall, G. Palapattu, M. Kloc, R.M. Ghobrial, M. Ferrari, A. Grattoni, Leveraging nanochannels for universal, zero-order drug delivery in vivo, *Journal of Controlled Release* 172 (2013) 1011–1019.

23. K. Junwu, Y. Zhigang, P. Taijiang, C. Guangming, W. Boda, Design and test of a high-performance piezoelectric micropump for drug delivery. *Sens Actuators A* 121(2005) 156–161.

24. R.R. Gidde, P.M. Pawar, B.P. Ronge, V.P. Dhamgaye, Design optimization of an electromagnetic actuation based valveless micropump for drug delivery application. *Microsyst Technol* 25 (2019) 509–519. https://doi.org/10.1007/s00542-018-3987 01234

25. K. van der Maaden, W. Jiskoot, J. Bouwstra, Microneedle technologies for (trans) dermal drug and vaccine delivery, *Journal of Controlled Release* 161 (2012) 645–655.

26. K. Ita, Dermal/transdermal delivery of small interfering RNA and antisense oligonucleotides-advances and hurdles, *Biomedicine & Pharmacotherapy* 87 (2017) 311–320.

27. W.M. Pardridge, The blood-brain barrier: bottleneck in brain drug development, *NeuroRx* 2 (2005) 3–14.

28. M.S. Fiandaca, M.S. Berger, K.S. Bankiewicz, The use of convection-enhanced delivery with liposomal toxins in neurooncology, *Toxins* 3 (2011) 369–397.

29. H.J. Lee, Y. Son, J. Kim, C.J. Lee, E.-S. Yoon, I.-J. Cho, A multichannel neural probe with embedded microfluidic channels for simultaneous in vivo neural recording and drug delivery, *Lab on a Chip* 15 (2015) 1590–1597.

30. J. Chen, K.D. Wise, J.F. Hetke, S. Bledsoe, A multichannel neural probe for selective chemical delivery at the cellular level, *Biomedical Engineering, IEEE Transactions on* 44 (1997) 760–769.

31. M.J. de Boer, R.W. Tjerkstra, J. Berenschot, H.V. Jansen, G. Burger, J. Gardeniers, M. Elwenspoek, A. van den Berg, Micromachining of buried micro channels in silicon, *Journal of Microelectromechanical Systems* 9 (2000) 94–103.

32. H.J. Lee, Y. Son, D. Kim, Y.K. Kim, N. Choi, E.-S. Yoon, I.-J. Cho, A new thin silicon microneedle with an embedded microchannel for deep brain drug infusion, *Sensors and Actuators B: Chemical* 209 (2015) 413–422.

33. H. Shin, H.J. Lee, U. Chae, H. Kim, J. Kim, N. Choi, J. Woo, Y. Cho, C.J. Lee, E.-S. Yoon, Neural probes with multi-drug delivery capability, *Lab on a Chip* 15 (2015) 3730–3737.

34. E.M. Del Amo, A. Urtti, Current and future ophthalmic drug delivery systems: a shift to the posterior segment, *Drug Discovery Today* 13 (2008) 135–143.

35. T. Yasukawa, Y. Ogura, E. Sakurai, Y. Tabata, H. Kimura, Intraocular sustained drug delivery using implantable polymeric devices, *Advanced Drug Delivery Reviews* 57 (2005) 2033–2046

36. S.R. Patel, A.S. Lin, H.F. Edelhauser, M.R. Prausnitz, Suprachoroidal drug delivery to the back of the eye using hollow microneedles, *Pharmaceutical Research* 28 (2011) 166–176.

37. M.R. Prausnitz, R. Langer, Transdermal drug delivery, *Nature Biotechnology* 26 (2008) 1261–1268 [118].

38. S.M. Bal, Z. Ding, E. van Riet, W. Jiskoot, J.A. Bouwstra, Advances in transcutaneous vaccine delivery: do all ways lead to Rome?, *Journal of Controlled Release* 148 (2010) 266–282.

39. Muhammad Waseem Ashraf, Shahzadi Tayyaba and Nitin Afzulpurkar, Micro electromechanical systems (MEMS) based microfluidic devices for biomedical applications, *International Journal of Molecular Sciences* ISSN 1422–0067, *International Journal of Molecular Sciences 12* (2011) 3648–3704. doi:10.3390/ijms12063648

40. J.H. Park, M.G. Allen, M.R. Prausnitz, Biodegradable polymer microneedles: fabrication, mechanics and transdermal drug delivery. *Journal of Controlled Release* 104 (2005) 51–66.

41. S. Aoyagi, H. Izumi, M. Fukuda, Biodegradable polymer needle with various tip angles and consideration on insertion mechanism of mosquito's proboscis. *Sensors and Actuators A* 143 (2008) 20–28.

42. P.C. DeMuth, Y. Min, B. Huang, J.A. Kramer, A.D. Miller, D.H. Barouch, P.T. Hammond, D.J. Irvine, Polymer multilayer tattooing for enhanced DNA vaccination, *Nature Materials* 12 (2013) 367–376.

43. J. Yu, Y. Zhang, A.R. Kahkoska, Z. Gu, Bioresponsive transcutaneous patches, *Current Opinion in Biotechnology* 48 (2017) 28–32.

44. F. Teodorescu, G. Queniat, C. Foulon, M. Lecoeur, A. Barras, S. Boulahneche, M.S. Medjram, T. Hubert, A. Abderrahmani, R. Boukherroub, Transdermal skin patch based on reduced graphene oxide: A new approach for photothermal triggered permeation of ondansetron across porcine skin, *Journal of Controlled Release* 245 (2017) 137–146.

45. X. Hu, J. Yu, C. Qian, Y. Lu, A.R. Kahkoska, Z. Xie, X. Jing, J.B. Buse, Z. Gu, H2O2-responsive vesicles integrated with transcutaneous patches for glucose-mediated insulin delivery, *ACS Nano* 11 (1) (2017) 613–620.

46. M.-C. Chen, H.-A. Chan, M.-H. Ling, L.-C. Su, Implantable polymeric microneedles with phototriggerable properties as a patient-controlled transdermal analgesia system, *Journal of Materials Chemistry B* 5 (2017) 496–503.

47. G.K. Gulati, T. Chen, B.J. Hinds, Programmable carbon nanotube membrane-based transdermal nicotine delivery with microdialysis validation assay, *Nanomedicine: Nanotechnology, Biology and Medicine* 13 (2017) 1–9.

48. J. Di, S. Yao, Y. Ye, Z. Cui, J. Yu, T.K. Ghosh, Y. Zhu, Z. Gu, Stretch-triggered drug delivery from wearable elastomer films containing therapeutic depots, *ACS Nano* 9 (2015) 9407–9415.

49. J.T. Santini, M.J. Cima, R. Langer, A controlled-release microchip, *Nature* 397 (1999) 335–338.

50. M. Ochoa, C. Mousoulis, B. Ziaie, Polymeric microdevices for transdermal and subcutaneous drug delivery, *Advanced Drug Delivery Reviews* 64 (2012) 1603–1616.

51. P.R. van Dijk, S.J. Logtenberg, K.H. Groenier, J.W. Haveman, N. Kleefstra, H.J. Bilo, Complications of continuous intraperitoneal insulin infusion with an implantable pump, *World Journal of Diabetes* 3 (2012) 142.

52. Y. Liu, P. Song, J. Liu, D.J.H. Tng, R. Hu, H. Chen, Y. Hu, C.H. Tan, J. Wang, J. Liu, An in-vivo evaluation of a MEMS drug delivery device using Kunming mice model, *Biomedical Microdevices* 17 (2015) 6.

53. Y.C. Poh Chin, A.-C. Kohler, J.T. Compton, L.L. Hsu, K.M. Lau, S. Kim, B.W. Lee, F.Y. Lee, S.K. Sia, Additive manufacturing of hydrogel-based materials for next-generation implantable medical devices, *Science Robotics* 2 (2017) eaah6451.

54. V. Laversenne Lathuilière, A. Astolfo, E. Kopetzki, H. Jacobsen, M. Stampanoni, B. Bohrmann, B.L. Schneider, P. Aebischer, A subcutaneous cellular implant for passive immunization against amyloid-β reduces brain amyloid and taupathologies, *Brain* (2016) aww036.

21 Estimating the Blood-Vessel Response to Vaso-Active Agents by Microscope Video Image Processing

Rohit Nayak, Mikkel Brydegaard, and Ramesh R. Galigekere

CONTENTS

21.1 INTRODUCTION

Cardiovascular diseases contribute significantly to the morbidity and mortality of the human population. In particular, diseases affecting the coronary, cerebral, and renal blood vessels are the predominant age-related disorders [1]. Properties of the arterial tissues, in conjunction with those of the receptors, play an important role in the health of the cardiovascular system. It is well known that the arterial tissue undergoes dilation/relaxation or contraction, based on the type of the vaso-active agent administered, and also of the receptors present in a given segment [2]. It is this property of the vessel-tissue that allows neural control of the cardiovascular system through transmitters and their multiple receptors [3]. Any abnormality in the properties of the vessel-tissue would result in cardiovascular problems such as hypertension and vasospasm [3]. Thus, a study involving an assessment of the (physical) response of the blood vessels under the influence of vaso-active agents would be helpful in understanding cardiovascular receptor-physiology. Further, such a study may also pave the way for the development of newer drugs.

The traditional approach to estimating the physical response of a vessel to the administration of vaso-active agents involves the use of a tension transducer placed in an organ (perfusion) bath (e.g., [4–6]). However, such a method may not provide accurate results—elasticity of the vessel-tissue, physical restriction, and the application of the basal tension at two points of anchorage are factors that affect the accuracy of the results. Further, the vessel-slice can be so small (1 mm thick, and a few mm in diameter) that highly sensitive and expensive transducers would be required.

DOI: 10.1201/9781003272694-26

In this chapter, a novel method for estimating the physical response of an arterial cross-section to a vaso-active agent is described. The method involves capturing a video, i.e., a time-sequence of images of a thin slice of the artery, placed under an optical microscope, under the influence of a given vaso-active/bio-agent introduced on the specimen. The image sequence is stored for subsequent analysis by image processing techniques. The method is therefore not only flexible and sensitive but also inexpensive. Indeed, optical microscopes are widely used in laboratories around the world, and web-cameras are inexpensive. Initial results arising from the prototype that was built by the authors' team involved approximate segmentation based on gray-level images [7] were presented earlier than that of an apparently similar approach [8] in which a back-white video CCD camera and an edge-detection/tracking software are reported to have been used (further details are not available). The method developed by the authors' team was further improved [9] by using color-based segmentation using the hue-saturation-intensity (HSI) model. The latter approach allows not only more parameters (i.e., color-attributes) towards better segmentation, but also attributes that are independent of incident light intensity. The use of intensity-independent parameters provides robustness against possible fluctuations in light intensity.

The rest of the chapter is organized as follows. Section 21.2 describes the imaging apparatus set-up for the study. In Section 21.3, several segmentation-algorithms—both standard ones and those proposed by the authors specifically for the problem under consideration—are presented. Section 21.4 includes the results of validation of the methods, showing the one proposed to cater specifically to the situation under consideration to work well. The results of assessment, of the response of the cross-sections of the arteries of a frog (*Rana tigrina*), to various vaso-active agents with known properties, are presented. Section 21.5 is devoted to a discussion of the results and some other issues in the context. Section 21.6 concludes the chapter.

21.2 EXPERIMENTAL SET-UP AND IMAGING

The set-up involves an ordinary web-camera (Q-Tek 100K) that was mechanically hacked and mounted rigidly on the eyepiece of an optical (compound) microscope. The camera was connected to a personal computer (PC) through a USB port. The PC was loaded with the program implementing the algorithms described in the following, involving video-acquisition, display, and processing of the recorded data. The specimen (arterial cross-section) is placed under the microscope, within a modified perfusion chamber. The cross-section is illuminated from below. The experimental set-up is shown in Figure 21.1.

The protocol for data-acquisition—i.e., recording the video to capture the physical response of a vessel cross-section to a vaso-active agent—begins by placing the specimen on the modified perfusion chamber, so that the vessel-lumen lies well within the field of view (FOV). To truly demonstrate the action of the vaso-active agent, it is necessary to record the "control" signal, i.e., the response of the vessel in the absence of any vaso-active agent. Since the mechanical properties of an arterial cross-section can be affected on exposure to open environment and dry air, the vessel cross-section under study is placed in the perfusion chamber, along with the non–vaso-active (neutral) ringer solution (as per standard practice), and its video was captured for a duration of about 50 seconds. Subsequently, the vaso-active agent is introduced—carefully through a micropipette, minimizing possible movement of the vessel, although small movement is not an issue (since the proposed processing methodology is not sensitive to the same). The computer program allows one to select the frame-rate and the duration of capture. The captured-video sequences—in the presence of only ringer solution and subsequently after the administration of the vaso-active agents—are stored for the purposes of display and processing.

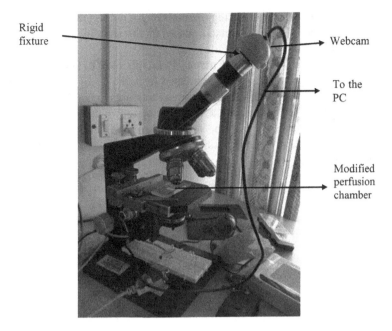

FIGURE 21.1 The experimental set-up.

The specimen (vessel cross-section) is placed in the modified perfusion chamber, kept under the microscope, and lit from underneath during the experiment.

21.3   IMAGE PROCESSING FOR LUMEN SEGMENTATION

Each of the frames of the video needs to be processed towards estimating the outline of the inner wall of the vessel, i.e., the vessel-lumen needs to be segmented from the background. An estimate of the number of pixels within the vessel-lumen is proportional to the area of the lumen. The response of the vessel, i.e., dilation or contraction, to a particular vaso-active agent may then be analyzed by plotting the lumen-area as a function of time.

Lumen segmentation can be achieved by working with the intensity-images (gray-level version of the color image frames) or by color-based segmentation. Gray-level segmentation can be achieved by a thresholding operation, based on the fact that the lumen appears brighter than the background. Color-based segmentation involves exploiting the difference between the color-parameters associated with the lumen and those of the background.

Several methods of estimating an optimum threshold-value have been proposed in the literature, each of which is useful in some specific context. In this chapter, two well-known/standard methods are reviewed, and a simpler but efficient method is proposed. Subsequently, the method based on color-segmentation is described, and its advantages are pointed out. The methods are validated against manual segmentation, towards selecting the best applicable to the scenario under consideration.

21.3.1   SEGMENTATION BASED ON THRESHOLDING

The first step in segmenting the vessel-lumen from the background involves outlining a region of interest (ROI) that includes the lumen-boundary in a manner that the boundary is circumscribed closely, while allowing sufficient space for expansion and possible (small) movement of the vessel.

Apart from the simple but quick step involving the marking of an ROI, the rest of segmentation is automatic. Two standard methods of segmentation based on thresholding, and another one specific to the current scenario, are described in the following.

Thresholding Based on the Maximum-Entropy Principle (MEP) [11]: The method is based on maximization of the entropy, which can be computed from the histogram of the ROI (specified in the preceding paragraph). Maximization of the entropy amounts to making least assumptions on the nature of the image. In the image (within the ROI), there are two main regions, one corresponding to the vessel-tissue (R_1) and the other to the vessel-lumen (R_2). Let the range of the gray-levels in the overall image be [A,B]. Let t be the possible threshold-value—a variable in the optimization problem. For a given value of t, the gray-levels in the regions R_1 and R_2 are in the range [min, t] and [$t + 1, max$], respectively. The optimum value T (of the threshold t), according to the MEP criterion, is given by [11]:

$$T = \arg \{\text{Max} \{\phi(t)\}\} \tag{1}$$

$$\text{where } \phi(t) = H(R_1) + H(R_2). \tag{2}$$

In Equation (2), $H(R_1)$ and $H(R_2)$ are the entropies associated with the regions R_1 and R_2:

$$H(R_1) = -\sum_{i=min}^{t} \frac{p_i}{P(t)} \log\left(\frac{p_i}{P(t)}\right) \tag{3}$$

$$H(R_2) = -\sum_{i=t+1}^{max} \frac{p_i}{1-P(t)} \log\left(\frac{p_i}{1-P(t)}\right). \tag{4}$$

The quantity $P(t) = \sum_{i=min}^{t} p_i$ is the cumulative probability distribution function, and p_i is the probability of occurrence of the gray-level i.

The significance of MEP lies in the fact that the threshold-value does not rely on prior knowledge about the input-image statistics; in other words, there is no assumption on the nature of data. While there are several variants of the method (e.g., [12]), for the simple situation under consideration, the method described in the preceding is known to be faster than some of them [11] and serves the purpose.

Thresholding Based on Uniformity Criterion (UC): Thresholding based on uniformity criterion [13,14] is equivalent to that proposed by Otsu [15] much earlier [16]. Let R_i, $i = 1,2$ be the two regions to be segmented, as indicated in the preceding (MEP) method—with mean and standard deviation μ_i and σ_i, respectively. In the problem of segmenting an image $f(m,n)$ into the two regions, the optimum value of the threshold "t" is one that maximizes the "uniformity-measure" defined as follows:

$$U(t) = 1 - \frac{\sigma_1^2 + \sigma_2^2}{K}, \tag{5}$$

where

$$\sigma_i^2 = \frac{1}{N_i} \sum_{(m,n) \in R_i} (f(m,n) - \mu_i)^2, i = 1,2 \tag{6}$$

$$\mu_i = \frac{1}{N_i} \sum_{(m,n) \in R_i} f(m,n), i = 1,2, \tag{7}$$

and N_i is the number of pixels in the region R_i. Note that the values of μ_i and σ_i pertaining to the two regions can be computed from the respective histogram. The constant $K = \dfrac{(f_{max} - f_{min})}{2}$ is a normalizing factor [13,14].

21.3.2 SEGMENTATION BASED ON THE HSI COLOR MODEL

The motivation behind considering color is two-fold: it allows one to include more parameters (i.e., color-attributes) towards improved-detection; further, as in the case of *hue* (*H*), *saturation* (*S*), and *intensity* (*I*) i.e., the *HSI* model [10], the attributes representing chromatic information are decoupled from that representing intensity. Consequently, the *HSI* model is proposed for segmentation. Hue is an attribute that describes a pure color, while saturation refers to the "degree of dilution from purity" by white light, and intensity is similar to that associated with gray-level pictures. A color-image in (the normalized) *RGB* format can be converted to its *HSI* version by the following formulae [10]:

$$H = \begin{cases} \theta, & B \le G \\ 360 - \theta, & B > G \end{cases} \tag{8}$$

$$\text{where, } \theta = \cos^{-1}\left\{ \frac{\frac{1}{2}[(R-G)+(R-B)]}{\sqrt{(R-G)^2 + (R-B)(G-B)}} \right\}$$

$$S = 1 - \frac{3}{(R+G+B)} Min\{R,G,B\} \tag{9}$$

$$I = \frac{1}{3}(R+G+B) \tag{10}$$

The values of S and I are in the range $[0,1]$; H, the angle measured from the red-axis in the *HSI* space, can also be normalized to $[0,1]$.

Color-based segmentation involves building clusters in the color-space associated with pixels belonging to the lumen and of the background, respectively. Subsequently, images are segmented by mapping each pixel based on the minimum-distance criterion—to the lumen or the background—in a manner similar to that described in [17]. Note that all three color-parameters may not be required for segmentation (as in the present case).

21.3.3 SEGMENTATION BASED ON HISTOGRAM-PEAK LOCATION (HPM)

When bright white light is used to illuminate the vessel-lumen from below, the lumen, though filled with the vaso-active agent, passes the light nearly completely. On the other hand, the vessel cross-section (annular ring) would attenuate the same, by a higher margin. An ROI is selected by cropping the image to a polygon such that the cropped image consists of the lumen and only a thin strip of the vessel-tissue. The histogram of the image within the ROI so selected consists of a large peak due to the highly illuminated pixels. Clearly, summation of the values of the samples in the histogram over a small neighborhood of the peak (also called the mode—which may also be approximated robustly by the median value) would yield a good approximation to the number of pixels within the lumen.

The method just described, although specific to the experimental set-up under consideration, is very simple, fast, and seen to be accurate from the subsequent results. It can be used on the gray-scale image, or even the saturation-image.

21.3.4   PROCEDURE FOR ESTIMATING THE RESPONSE

The algorithm for estimating the vessel-response consists of the following steps:

1. The specimen (with the ringer solution) is placed under within the modified perfusion chamber, which is in turn placed under the microscope.
   (a) In the context of control, video of the same is immediately recorded over a pre-specified period of time.
   (b) The specified agent is introduced carefully into the modified perfusion chamber containing the specimen. Quickly, the video-capture of the specimen under the influence of the vaso-active agent is begun and recorded for a specified duration of time.
2. The video is previewed, to identify whether the vessel is relaxing or contracting.
3. The ROI is marked on the first frame in the recorded sequence; the ROI should give room for expansion (if relevant) and possible vessel-movement while introducing the vaso-active agent.
4. The lumen-area is estimated after segmentation—by any of the methods described in the preceding, automatically, over the rest of the frames in the video.
5. The lumen-area is plotted as a function of time.

The plot of the area of the lumen gives an assessment of the physical response of the vessel as a function of time.

21.4   EXPERIMENTAL RESULTS

Several experiments have been conducted with the set-up described in the previous section, on the arterial cross-sections of the frog *Rana tigrina*. The vessel-segments—whose cross-sections were used—were available as a disposable by-product of dissection-experiments at the physiology laboratory, Kasturba Medical College, Manipal Academy of Higher Education, Manipal 576104, for a different purpose; it may be noted that the frogs were not sacrificed for the experiments considered in this work. A snapshot of a typical vessel (arterial) cross-section is shown in Figure 21.2. Each of the experiments began with the recording of the video of vessel cross-section, under control. Subsequently, the video of the cross-section after the administration of the vaso-active agent of interest was recorded. The recorded videos have been analyzed with two goals: (i) validation of segmentation-algorithms, and (ii) estimation of the vessel-response using the best algorithm (as determined by the validation-step). The vaso-active agents considered in the experiments are:

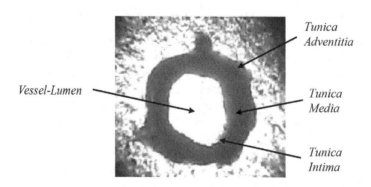

FIGURE 21.2   A view of a thin cross-section of an arterial vessel of a frog *Rana tigrina*.

adrenaline, KCl, and caffeine. Justification for the use of these agents includes the fact that the type of the response of the arteries to these agents are known, and such a prior knowledge allows validation of the methods.

21.4.1 VALIDATION OF THE SEGMENTATION-ALGORITHMS

Extensive experiments were conducted with the *HSI* model and gray-level (intensity) based methods of segmentation.

In the case of color-segmentation, the *HSI* values associated with each pixel in the image were extracted from the *RGB* values. For the light-source used, the *S* and *I* components were found to be sufficient to provide good discrimination between the two regions. The lumen-area based on *I* alone was found to over-estimate the area by ~5%, as it was brighter also over the borders (due to bright illumination). On the other hand, *S* yielded a sharp change and remained more uniform within the lumen, indicating that the results based on *S* should be more accurate (than that based on *I*). Further, using *S* and *I* together yielded a result very close to that obtained using *S* alone. Finally, note that *S*-values are invariant to possible fluctuations in ambient light. Thus, it was decided to use the *S*-image in conjunction with an automatic thresholding algorithm.

A set of 50 images (five image frames per capture, associated with each of three agents), selected arbitrarily, were considered for the purpose of validation. Each of the images in the set was segmented manually, and also by the three methods discussed. The results of computer-based segmentation were validated in terms of the area within the segmented lumen, i.e., A_{comput}, the number of pixels in the segmented lumen (this being the main parameter of interest). The measure of comparison in the case of the latter is the normalized error with respect to the result A_{manual} obtained by manual segmentation:

$$E_{norm} = \left| \frac{A_{comput} - A_{manual}}{A_{manual}} \right| 100. \tag{11}$$

The measure is plotted as a function of the number of experiments/trials in Figure 21.3. It is clear from the figure that the method based on the MEP performs the best. Interestingly, the simple,

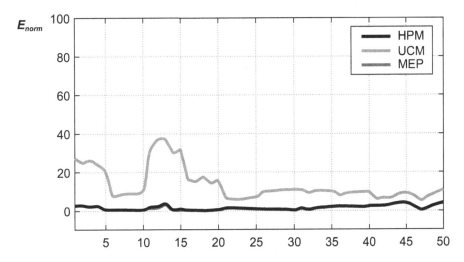

FIGURE 21.3 Normalized error pertaining to the estimated lumen-area. Note the simple HPM to be performing very well (as good as the more sophisticated MEP-based method).

fast method based on histogram-peak location—custom-devised for this equipment—has been found to perform very closely. This should not be surprising, as the relatively high brightness (of white light) of the lumen with respect to that of the background renders the latter method a natural choice.

21.4.2   RESPONSE TO VASO-ACTIVE AGENTS

Prior to recording the response to vaso-active agent, the response under "control" conditions, i.e., in the absence of any vaso-active agent, was recorded. To avoid the vessel from getting exposed to dry air, the thin cross-section of the artery under consideration was dissected and placed immediately under the microscope and submerged in the neutral ringer solution. Under this (neutral) condition, its video was captured and stored. Subsequently, the vaso-active agent was introduced slowly, just before the video-capture began. Experiments with all the agents were performed in the same fashion. The stored videos were subject to segmentation and processing as described in the previous section, to calculate the response.

The responses—in terms of percent area of the vessel-lumen with respect to the initial area—under control condition (prior to administration of the agent) are plotted in Figure 21.4 (a)–(c). These plots correspond to the lumen-area associated with the three trials per agent, prior to the administration of adrenaline, caffeine, and KCl, respectively. Note that the areas do not exhibit significant change, i.e., maximum deviation from the initial area is about 0.8% in the first two cases, while it is about 2% in the last case. These numbers are relatively much smaller—as may be observed in the sequel—compared to the respective areas under the influence of vaso-active agents.

The response to the administration of adrenaline, in terms of percent area of the vessel-lumen normalized with respect to the initial area, is shown in Figure 21.5 (a). Normalization with respect to the initial area is performed to account for the fact that the vessel-diameters may be different, and minor changes may occur during the time that lapses between the end of control and the recording that starts subsequent to the administration of the agent (a minor, possible artifact due to limitations in the experimentation using the simple prototype developed). It may be inferred that the vessel contracts under the influence of adrenaline, as indicated by the reduction in lumen-area. The response to the administration of caffeine is shown in Figure 21.5 (b). One can infer that the vessel expands, as indicated by the increase in the area upon the administration of caffeine. In both cases, the change of about 4% to 8% is significant with respect to that under control. Figure 21.5 (c) shows the response under the influence of KCL. The vessel contracts, but the rate of contraction is different from that associated with adrenaline. Further, the change of about 12% to 22% is significant with respect to that under control. It may be noted that the results are in agreement with the well-known properties of adrenaline [2], KCl (used for "pre-contracting the vessel" [4,5]), and caffeine (known to relax the vessel-tissue, e.g., see [6]).

The goal of this chapter has been to describe the device developed with a simple web-camera and a simple microscope and to validate its working with a few of the known vaso-active agents. The actual (deeper) study of the response of the vessel under the administration of many different vaso-active agents would be a separate topic. Nevertheless, the results in response to the administration of vaso-active agents considered so far (Figure 21.5) are interesting. In an attempt to explain the dynamics of the curves, or to try modeling or parametrizing them—in the experiments under consideration, one may observe that the dynamics of the lumen-area pertaining to adrenaline and

KCl seem to follow a first order system with one state, of the form $A_{adr} = 100 \times \left(1 - A_{\infty}\right) e^{-\frac{t}{\tau}}$, where the time-constant $\tau_{KCl} \gg \tau_{Adr}$. Note that one may not expect A_{∞} to return to the initial area, as the vessel is exposed to the external environment and may lose its elasticity with time. This is a

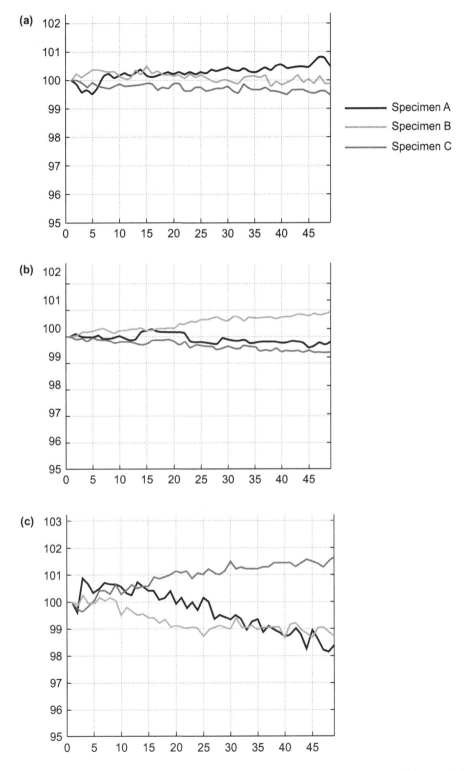

FIGURE 21.4 Control: percent area before the administration of: (a) adrenaline, (b) caffeine, and (c) KCl. Note that the deviation from the original area is very small.

limitation of the *in vitro* experiment itself, and not of the equipment or the technique. As far as caffeine is concerned, the large delay may imply some kind of transport, possibly a diffusion through the tissue membranes or something similar. These curves would at least require three dynamical states, of which one is probably hidden.

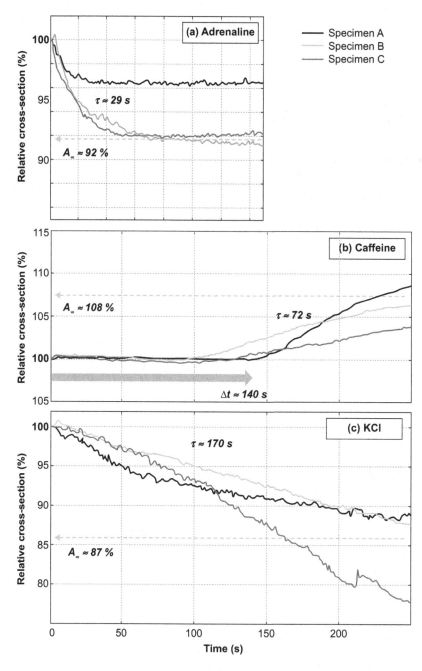

FIGURE 21.5 Response of the vessel-slice (cross-section), in terms of percentage of the initial area of the lumen (A) as a function of time, to: (a) adrenaline, (b) caffeine, and (c) KCl. Different colors represent different experiments.

21.5   DISCUSSION

This chapter describes the construction of a novel apparatus assisted by a suitable algorithm developed for segmentation, to estimate the physical response of blood vessels to vaso-active agents, by image processing. This is in contrast to the traditional approach (at the time the device was developed) based on tension transducers. The proposed method is inexpensive and can be used in any laboratories wherein optical microscopes are available. Indeed, the results have been demonstrated by experimenting with a very old simple laboratory microscope and a cheap webcam. The method is flexible, because, after recording the video, processing schemes to assess other parameters, e.g., vessel-lumen-area (with suitable calibration), and the characterization of the behavior of the vessel under different vaso-active agents, can be devised. Since the object under study is not physically bound, the results are expected to be more accurate than that based on tension transducers, which apply physical restriction on the vessels at the points of anchorage. In fact, tension transducers may not even be feasible when the vessel is extremely small. Note that the results presented are qualitative—they provide information about contraction/expansion, and perhaps, to some extent, about the shape of the curve representing the change. With this proof of concept, one can think of further work, e.g., to improve the apparatus by the use of infusion pump, calibration towards the measurement of the physical area of the vessel, etc.

In the context color-segmentation, although S was found to be sufficient with the present white light-source, one may aim at improving accuracy by a different light-source and allowing the use of all the color-parameters.

It would be useful to make the complete lumen-area estimation procedure fully automatic—by avoiding the necessity for pre-viewing. One approach is to ensure that the vessel does not move beyond the FOV—perhaps by the use of an infusion pump, in conjunction with a magnification to ensure that the exterior of the vessel-ring is just excluded from the FOV. A better approach would be to automate the segmentation algorithm to identify the vessel-lumen from the region outside it. Different methods of region-segmentation may also be applied towards possible improvement. Finally, a stand-alone plug-in device (that can be fixed on any microscope-eyepiece) with embedded software is possible. The aim of the work presented in this chapter, however, was to present the proof of concept with a prototype device developed and described [18].

Thus, the emphasis in this chapter is on the application of video/image processing methods involving simple algorithms and inexpensive equipment, which may often by used to replace expensive gadgets for certain purposes. Such an apparatus, today, can be replaced by USB microscopes, instead of hacking an existing microscope. Further, the algorithms for lumen segmentation may be performed by using statistical moments rather than thresholding or by many of the other methods that may be more robust.

21.6   CONCLUSION

A novel and inexpensive method of assessing the physical response of blood vessels under the influence of vaso-active agents has been described. The method involves capturing a video of the vessel-segment kept under an ordinary microscope and analyzing the same using simple methods. The image processing step involved segmentation of the saturation-image pertaining to each of the frames in the video. The saturation-image was found to be sufficiently robust to mild fluctuations in intensity. The proposed method of segmentation has been justified by validating against two standard methods and also manual segmentation. The system developed should produce accurate results as the specimen is not physically restricted to the extent that happens in the case of traditional tension transducer–based method. The method is flexible, as the recorded image sequence can be analyzed for various aspects. The apparatus allows any vessel—however tiny—to be studied. The results of experiments involving several vaso-active agents are in conformity with the known properties. This is an excellent example to illustrate the potential of video processing techniques to solving problems—other solutions to which may be very expensive.

ACKNOWLEDGMENTS

The authors dedicate this chapter to the memory of Dr. Prakasa Rao, formerly a professor, Dept. of Physiology, Kasturba Medical College, Manipal Academy of Higher Education, Manipal—576 104. His untimely demise has left us all shocked. He had been involved with this project since its very inception, as the physiologist driving it.

REFERENCES

[1] N.A. Boon *et al.*, "Cardiovascular Diseases", Ch. 12, in *Davidsons's Principles and Practice of Medicine*, 19th Edition, Harlett C. Churchill Livingston, Edinburgh, 2002.

[2] W.F. Ganong, subsection "Responses of Effector Organs to Autonomic Nerve Impulses" of Ch. 13: "Autonomic Nervous System", in *Review of Medical Physiology*, McGraw Hill, New Delhi, 2005.

[3] T. Michel, "Treatment of Myocardial Ischemia", Ch. 31 in Goodman and Gilman's *The Pharmacological Basis of Therapeutics*, L.L. Brunton, J.S. Lazo, and K.L. Parker (Editors), 11th Edition, McGraw Hill, New Delhi, pp. 823–844, 2006.

[4] A. Brezzolara-Gourdie and J.G. Webb, "Angiotensin II Potentiates Vasodilation of Rat Aorta by cAMP Elevating Agonists", *Journal of Pharmacology and Experimental Therapeutics*, Vol. 281, No. 1, pp. 354–359, 1997.

[5] M. Tosun *et al.*, "Sarcoplasmic-Endoplasmic Reticulum Ca^{2+}—ATPase Inhibition Prevents Endothelin A Receptor Antagonism in Rat Aorta", *American Journal of Physiology-Heart and Circulatory Physiology*, Vol. 292, pp. H1961–H1966, 2007.

[6] F.R. Montes *et al.*, "The Role of Potassium Channels in the Vasodilatory Effect of Caffeine in Human Internal Mammary Arteries", *Vascular Pharmacology*, Vol. 50, No. 3–4, pp. 132–136, Mar.–Apr. 2009.

[7] Mikkel B. Sorenson, T. Christopher, J. Prakasa Rao, Ramesh R. Galigekere, "In vitro Analysis of the Physical Response of the Blood Vessels to Adrenaline: An Image Processing Approach", *International Conference Cardio-pulmonary Regulation in Health and Disease: Molecular and Systemic Integration*, University of Delhi, Delhi, Feb. 22–24, 2007.

[8] J. Park *et al.*, "Differences in Sympathetic Neuroeffector Transmission to Rat Mesenteric Arteries and Veins as Probed by *In vitro* Continuous Amperometry and Video Imaging", *Physiol*, Vol. 584, No.3, pp. 819–834, Aug. 2007.

[9] Rohit Nayak, Nikhil Prabhu, J. Prakasa Rao, and Ramesh R. Galigekere, "*In Vitro* Analysis of the Physical Response of the Blood-Vessels to Vaso-active Agents by Color-Image Processing", *Proc. 2nd Cardiovascular Control Conference*, Mahabalipuram, India, p. 20, Dec. 9–12, 2008.

[10] R.C. Gonzalez and R.E. Woods, *Digital Image Processing*, Second Edition, Pearson Education, Singapore. Eighth Indian Reprint, 2004.

[11] B. Liu *et al.*, "Automatic Extraction of Positive Cells in Tumor Immunohistochemical Pathology Image Based on YCbCr", *Proceedings 6th World Congress on Intelligent Control and Automation*, pp. 9708–9712, China, 2006.

[12] P.K. Sahoo and G. Arora, "A Thresholding Method Based on Two-Dimensional Renyi's Entropy", *Pattern Recognition*, Vol. 37, pp. 1149–1161, 2004.

[13] M.D. Levine and A.M. Nazif, "Dynamic Measurement of Computer Generated Image Segmentation", *IEEE Transactions on Pattern Analysis and Machine Intelligence*, Vol. 7, pp. 155–164, 1985.

[14] A.K.C. Wong and P.K. Sahoo, "A Gray-Level Threshold Selection Method Based on Maximum Entropy Principle", *IEEE Transactions on Systems, Man, and Cybernetics*, Vol. 19, No. 4, pp. 866–871, July–Aug. 1989.

[15] W.S. Ng and C.K. Lee, "Comment on Using the Uniformity Measure for Performance Measure in Image Segmentation", *IEEE Transactions on Pattern Analysis and Machine Intelligence*, Vol. 18, No. 9, pp. 933–934, 1996.

[16] N. Otsu, "A Threshold Selection Method from Gray-level Histogram", *IEEE Transactions on Systems, Man, and Cybernetics*, Vol. 9, pp. 62–66, 1979.

[17] Rohit Nayak, Vishnu Prasad S. and Ramesh R. Galigekere, "A New Algorithm for Automatic Assessment of the Degree of TB-infection Using Images of ZN-stained Sputum Smear", *Proc. International Conference of the IEEE Engineering in Medicine & Biology*, (ICSMB '10), Dept. of Elec. Engg. & the School of Medical Science & Tech., IIT Kharagpur, Kharagpur, India, pp. 308–314, 16–18 Dec. 2010.

[18] Ramesh R. Galigekere, Mikkel Brydegaard Sorensen, Rohit Nayak, J. Prakasa Rao, "Method and Apparatus for *In vitro* Analysis of the Physical Response of Blood-vessels to Vaso-active Agents", US Patent US8929622B2, Jan. 6, 2015.

22 Organ Donation and Transplantation Challenges, Opportunities, and the Role of Blockchain

Rachana Y. Patil, Yogesh H. Patil,
Sujeet Kumar Gupta, and Aparna Bannore

CONTENTS

22.1 INTRODUCTION

According to the World Health Organization (WHO), in a year there are nearly 70,000 patients waiting for a kidney transplant, while the availability of kidneys from live donors is around 20,000, out of which at least 10,000 are trafficked [1]. Kidneys available from living donors are healthier and have a longer life (15–20 years) than kidneys from the deceased (10–15 years).

AnGlobal Observatory Committee on Donations and Transplants (GOCDT), formed by the Spanish government's National Transplant Organization in association with the WHO, which works globally [2]. GOCDT takes care of organ donations and their transplants with the necessary documents related to organ distribution, and transplantation programs in the nation report their records to the GOCDT to analyze access of organ transplantation programs worldwide. Figure 22.1 shows the general statics of organ donation and transplantation globally.

Apart from these, healthy and young people who lost their lives due to accident or any unfortunate reasons have healthy organs available compared with donors with age and illness.

The scarcity of donors decreases patients' hopes of recovery, and sometimes they look for illegal options to obtain organs by any means necessary, and this promotes the organ trafficking black market. The tracking of the black market is difficult as there is no official network to trace and it is run by unauthorized persons who carefully maintain their secrecy.

A few nations are trying to curb such black markets through strict bans or by making it open like trade. In 1988, Iran permitted selling and purchasing of organs irrespective of trained healthcare facilities and lack of organ availability, but it has had a positive impact, showing Iran as one of the few countries to have sufficient organ availability [4].

Only 10% of organ needs at a global level can be fulfilled by legal donors; most patients die due to organ unavailability, while a large number of patients become sicker due to the longer waiting period and finally lose their lives [5].

Figure 22.2 shows the black-market values of various body organs, for instance that kidneys are the most sold organ due to its dual availability in humans. This eases the demand–supply gap for kidneys especially and interested donors can trade as per particular situations.

Organ transplants have become a vital method to save valuable human lives with the assistance of fast increasing healthcare technologies. We live in an era where a healthy human organ can be

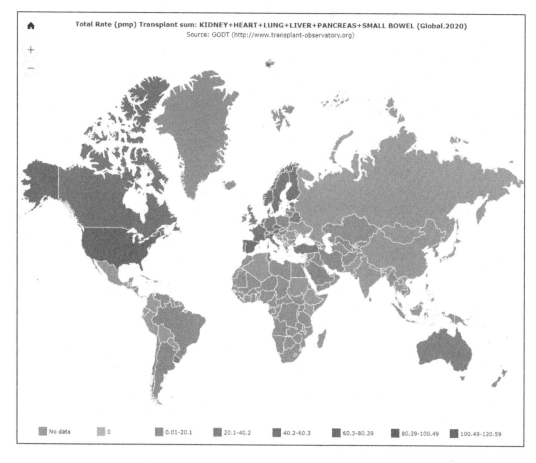

FIGURE 22.1 Global organ transplantation rate [3].

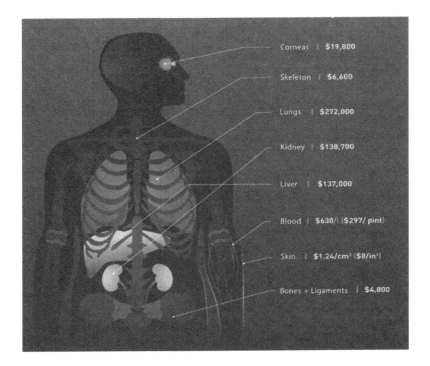

Corneas | $19,800
Skeleton | $6,600
Lungs | $272,000
Kidney | $138,700
Liver | $137,000
Blood | $630/L ($297/ pint)
Skin | $1.24/cm² ($8/in²)
Bones + Ligaments | $4,800

FIGURE 22.2   Black market value of various body parts [6].

readily available to a patient in need (recipient). Though the transplantation success rate is daily improving, the whole organ transplantation process is extremely difficult. As there are numerous unethical, ineffective, and corruptive practices in organ transplantation [7], the absence of adoption of suitable organ transplantation guidelines is a cause of concern. Several such observations are:

- Corrupt practice of organ donations and its trading
- Unorganized integrated planning and poor management for prioritized organ waiting list
- Incompetent organ conservation facilities
- Retailing of organ for financial gains without verifying donor health ailments
- Absence of government-authorized organ distribution network
- Lack of organ donation awareness and its importance in society

In nations like India, the present process for detection of organ recipients mostly relies on the organ waiting list issued by the organ transplantation facilities involved. No system exists to determine if an organ is available to the most necessary common individual. This leads to poor patients being unable to receive organs in time while the rich and powerful can avail themselves of organs as required.

Different barriers to effective lifesaving therapy for certain patients have improved over the last few years. Among these was the refining of surgical procedures and the convenience of effective immuno-suppressive rejection regimes. Nevertheless, the only way organ transplantation was developed around the globe for patients with organ failure was through the availability of deceased organ donations (DD).

It is hard to conceive how many lives could have been saved without the "gift of life" from the departed donors. The dearth of organs currently constitutes the biggest impediment for a bigger number of contenders making organ transplantation more accessible. In the United States in 2015, only 30,973 transplants of 15,064 donors were carried out, with over 121,000 waiting for a transplant.

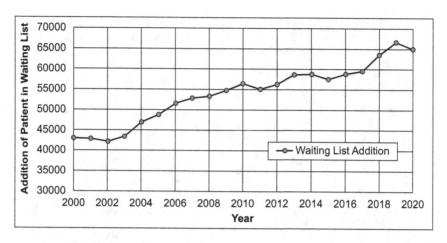

FIGURE 22.3   Patients waiting list addition per year.

Moreover, the gap has continued to increase between the number of patients on the waiting list and the restricted quantity of accessible organs. As a result, about 6,000 individuals die each year in the transplant waiting period [8]. Figure 3.3 describes the patient waiting list addition per year for organ transplantation.

22.2   CHALLENGES IN ORGAN DONATION AND TRANSPLANTATION

Organ donation and transplantation are troubled with many challenges like expenses of treatment, lack of infrastructure and supporting facilities, availability of highly trained healthcare expertise, and shortage of well-connected ethico-legal framework and strategies [9,10]. Figure 22.4 lists the challenges in organ donation.

22.2.1   SCARCITY OF ORGAN

Scarcity of organs is one of the world's biggest problems. There is a huge gap between organ donors and needy patients constantly being added to the waiting list for transplantation. In circumstances that we would not consider were a decade past, the advancement in medical and surgical skills that allow transplantation was not accompanied by comparable growth in the availability of transplant organs. According to [11], the demand supply statistics of life supporting organs shown in Figure 22.5 implies a huge requirement for donors, especially for kidney and liver donors.

There is a multifold scarcity of donors. The number of possible donors is fewer in numbers than donors fulfilling the brain-dead diagnosis conditions that are used for the transplant [12]. The distinction is based on medical and logistical considerations, the capability to establish brain death, and social and spiritual issues that affect people's desire to offer organs. This significantly affects the organ donation rates in countries and, consequently, varies the wait times for transplantation. Organ shortages for living donors and dead donors should be examined.

A strong national or regional transplant program that fulfills international criteria is the most significant factor for donor programs apart from localized social awareness on organ donations. Such a program, per WHO guidelines, needs to be independent regarding its population and the need of organs in the long run that exists in each nation. Cultural conformity and broad agreement of society regarding organ donations is significant. The ethical and religious problems of organ donation are diverse and varied. Although donating organs in all major religions is recommended to save lives, the practical reality may be different among various sections of it.

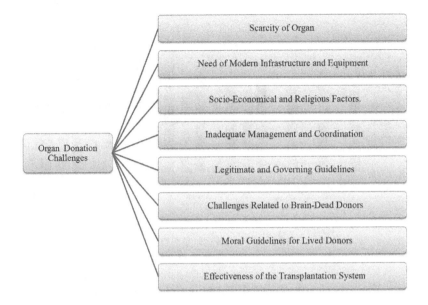

FIGURE 22.4 Organ donation challenges.

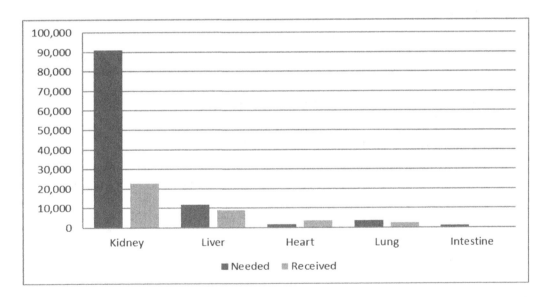

FIGURE 22.5 Scarcity of organs.

22.2.2 Need of Modern Infrastructure and Equipment

Assessing the immunological compatibility of tissues from independent sources, cross-cutting and some virus investigations are conducted overseas, which are important components of patient preparation. The process tends to be delayed and results in an increase in transplantation costs. An appropriate histological assessment of biopsy materials is largely unavailable, which makes it difficult to handle refusals and infections without delay [13].

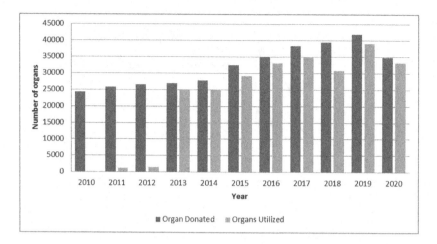

FIGURE 22.6   Effect of modern healthcare infrastructure on organ transplantation.

From Figure 22.6 it is clearly observed that utility of donated organs over recent years has improved drastically compared to 2012. This effect is because of improvements in high-end technology in surgical practices and organ preservation and transportation facilities.

22.2.3   Socio-Economical and Religious Factors

The predominant beliefs of dominant religions in individual nations and their relationship between belief, religion, and social mindsets and their perspectives on organ donation can make things difficult. Responding to disease as the will of a deity denies the donation or receipt of organs. Belief in rebirth prevents the donation of organs, while the sanctity of the corpse is also factor that prohibits the donation of body parts by the family members of their departed relatives [14].

22.2.4   Inadequate Management and Coordination

There is a limited functional organizational system for organ transplantation programs, which consist of a transplantation services license, ethical committees, regulations, and protocol. Furthermore, transplantation in national health services is not fully integrated due to inefficient work of functional and reliable registries that causes insufficient data collection [15]. The national health information schemes of most of nations do not incorporate performance measures and its analysis of organ donation and transplantation. Moreover, multisectoral participation in transplantation schemes (schools, transport departments, NGOs, CSOs) is unsatisfactory.

22.2.5   Legitimate and Governing Guidelines

Most of the nations have their individual laws on organ donation and transplant; some nations are in different phases of development. In many nations, the poor legal frameworks noted are often not enough to ensure that the quality criteria for organ transplantation are effectively monitored.

22.2.6   Challenges Related to Brain-Dead Donors

Death of Brain Declaration: There is no official training in the hospital for brain-death conditions. It is addressed by everyone based on their past education in nursing schools or medical colleges. Brain-dead statement timing is an important component in protecting a brain-dead person's organs. Healthcare personnel frequently experience indifference, however, leading to a lack of compliance with the second brain-dead statement after six hours, and/or laboratory data connected to the brain mortality statement [16]. Laboratories often delay test findings or air crews that are required to do brain death tests are not on time

The brain-dead statement can be delayed owing to lack of knowledge regarding confirmatory brain death tests because specialists occasionally produce misleading results, like the "maybe alive" that brings back their statement.

Management and Maintenance of the Donor: Lethargy can occur with regard to brain-dead patients when other living patients in need of ICU care are waiting for their beds, or if they refuse to keep brain-dead until their agreement is commonly achieved, organ viability will deteriorate. Donor administration demands a global strategy. Upkeep of donors and their management is the crucial task; most hospital have lost donors because of the maladministration of the donor at the time of permission.

Figure 22.7 shows the data of organ donation from brain-dead patients. A total of 137 brain-dead patients donated organs, out of whom around 70.07% organs are utilized for transplantation on needy patients and 30% were declined due to various compatibility issues [17].

22.2.7 Moral Guidelines for Live Donors

Worldwide usage of live donor donations is widespread, and the number continues to increase steadily. Globally, a total of 27,000 live donors for renal and 2,000 live donors for liver transplants are made yearly, corresponding to the latest publications [18]. The lack of dead donor organs in recent years has shifted to a continuous growth in living donors.

The moral guidelines for living donations are different from those for departed donors, but both commonly apply to the fact that morals, faith, and medical groups pay close attention to the act of organ donations. Most live organ donations include renal transplants and partial liver and lung transplants. In live donations, the key ethical criterion is that donors suffer little or no injury. Organs are accepted and appreciated by society among family members.

22.2.8 Effectiveness of the Transplantation System

The productivity of a national or regional program depends on their capability to track possible donors, speak to the patient's family, monitor closely all testing and actions necessary for the diagnosis of brain death, and offer an exact mechanism for the coordinating and assignment of organisms.

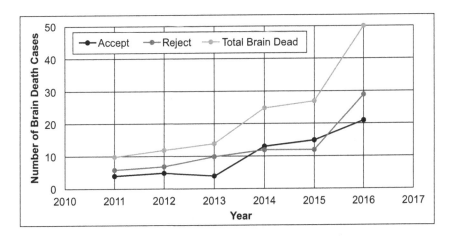

FIGURE 22.7 Acceptance rate in brain-dead donors.

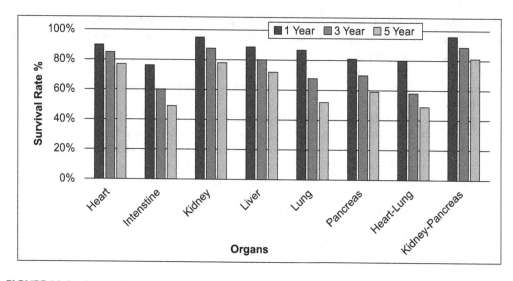

FIGURE 22.8   Survival statistics of organ transplantation.

The WHO has established standards and systems for tracking the effectiveness of the various processes in the organ donation process [19]. Organ donation and transplantation are considered major surgical procedures and involve many physiological parameters that decide the success rate of organ transplantation. From Figure 22.8, it is observed that most organ transplants are successful up to one year, followed by decreasing health and its failure. Consequently, maintaining the effectiveness of the transplantation system is a major challenge.

22.3   OPPORTUNITIES IN ORGAN DONATION AND TRANSPLANT

Transplantation carries loads of prospects that, if perfectly channeled, can improve the healthcare of the overall nation. Figure 22.9 describes opportunities in organ donation and transplantation.

22.3.1   READINESS OF ORGANS FOR TRANSPLANTATION

Individual and government engagement and their alliance are necessary for sustained transplantation programs. Increased public information efforts focusing on preventive medicine and changes in organ perceptions can enhance the availability of organs through associating with religious entities; personal, family, and public education; transplant and donation inclusion into school curricula; social awareness programs etc.

22.3.2   COMPLETE REGULATION AND LEGISLATION

Transplantation requires a comprehensive legal framework with substantial medico-legal ramifications. This should include the legitimacy of organ donations, regulatory agencies, accreditation, certification, and standardized criteria and processes in transplant centers [20]. Transplantation programs provide the opportunity to learn from other regions and adjust legislation. Laws are defined with the priority of enrolled donors, donor compensation, and life coverage for ethical, lawful, and administrative aspects relating to organ donation, distribution, and transplants, with the end of unlawful transplant and compensation substantially.

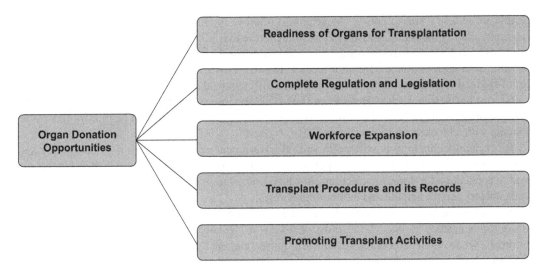

FIGURE 22.9   Opportunities in organ donation and transplantation.

22.3.3   WORKFORCE EXPANSION

In many different sections of individual countries, the multidisciplinary nature of transplantation requires a highly skilled staff and consequently must cooperate with modern transplantation centers. Such a collaboration enables specialist personnel, serving local and sister institutions, to build and train their capacity.

22.3.4   TRANSPLANT PROCEDURES AND ITS RECORDS

Successful transplantation involves receiver and donor care regimens. Advanced transplantation centers, such as the United Network for Organ Sharing, Donation, and Transplantation institutions, etc., can establish or update procedures for regional transplant centers. National organ transplantation registers and results are critical for documenting and reporting transplant activities, and planning and budgeting for short- and long-term outcomes.

22.3.5   PROMOTING TRANSPLANT ACTIVITIES

Individual nations need to develop viable transplant programs. Expansion of similar facilities will curtail organ smuggling and troubled transplant [21]. A precise means of financing that comprises transplantation in national health insurance reporting certifies the nourishment of the program. Transplantation programs can be organized in a dramatic trend: legislating transplantation-linked by-laws and guidelines, capability formations, comprehensive public insight drives and transplant commencing with live donor and, consequently, decedent-donor.

22.4   BLOCKCHAIN'S APPLICATION IN DIFFERENT SERVICES

Significant advantages of efficiency, transparency, integrity, and security promote the applicability of blockchain technology being adopted by a variety of industries like healthcare, finance, manufacturing, business, government, and education. Numerous applications and existing systems in the healthcare industry are accepting blockchain to improve medical record administration, improve insurance claim processing, and accelerate clinical research [22].

Patients will be able to restrict access to their healthcare data if blockchain is used to store patient health record information and monitor medical records. This will eliminate the need to obtain copies of medical records or submit information to a different healthcare practitioner.

Several businesses, such as Healthcare Data Gateways, are experimenting with blockchain technology. Guard time, another well-known organization, is securing 1 million healthcare records in Estonia with a blockchain-based system [23].

Blockchain technology is utilized in several government activities due to its transparency and immutability. For example, a Danish political party has implemented the world's first blockchain voting application for domestic elections, in which every vote is captured in a safe environment and stakeholders can participate and monitor other votes.

Several applications utilizing blockchain technology have been developed in the financial industry. Cryptocurrency is one of the most well-known blockchain-based financial applications. It ensures a secure environment for virtual cash transactions such as Bitcoin, Ripple, and many more. Securities exchange, smart contracts, trading and settlement, and payments and remittance are only a few of the blockchain applications connected to stock market services. In general, these applications are designed to make traditional procedures easier and faster.

Even in the educational field, blockchain technology is employed in a variety of ways. Several educational institutions have used blockchain to solve a number of issues. The National University of La Plata (UNLP), for example, has established a blockchain-based system that certifies students' educational achievement and awards diplomas accordingly. In 2015, a school in San Francisco began experimenting using blockchain to help companies verify academic credentials.

Everything in today's modern society revolves around internet communication. The security of data associated with applications is extremely important, and any neglect on the part of programmers can have disastrous consequences.

22.5 ROLE OF BLOCKCHAIN IN HEALTHCARE

Today's healthcare sector is extremely complex, including a wide variety of players, including insurance companies, pharmaceutical manufacturers, and end users of these medical items [24]. However, in the actual world, several data handling and communication issues must be fixed with suitable information flow and process audits, which are incredibly costly and ultimately result in the slowing down of healthcare services. Governments and health insurance corporations are key players who collaborate with paramedics to design and implement healthcare policy.

Using blockchain technology, scientists, research organizations, universities, and even pharmaceutical corporations can gain better access to data without worry of compromising data security or patient privacy, which will ultimately benefit research. Paramedics, doctors, and other medical personnel can also benefit from blockchain-based systems in executing their daily responsibilities with greater efficiency. By accessing the universal patient record ledger, uncertainties about the recovery or reactivity of any medicine on any specific patient or group of patients in a specific situation would be reduced [25, 26].

Many contemporary advances in the healthcare field are based on blockchain technology. Figure 22.10 describes the different applications of healthcare that can securely access the data from blockchain-based systems. The conceptual organization of emerging blockchain-based healthcare technologies includes data sources, blockchain technology, healthcare applications, and stakeholders. Securing data, preservation, transactions, and maintaining their seamless integration are crucial to any data-driven company, particularly in healthcare, where blockchain technology has the ability to address these critical concerns in a comprehensive and efficient manner.

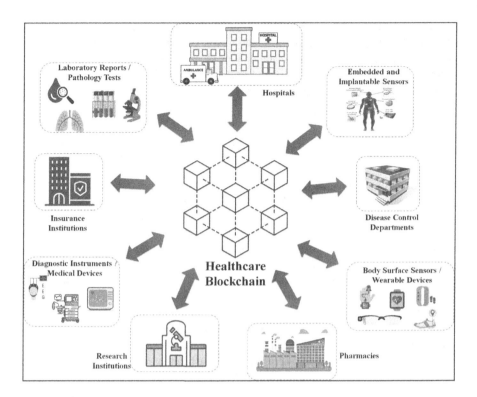

FIGURE 22.10 Role of blockchain in healthcare.

22.5.1 Benefits of Using Blockchain Technology

Traceability: The proposed blockchain based in the healthcare industry ensures the privacy and security of the patient's health records. The traceability features help to track the origin of organ from donor to genuine recipient, and it will put a cap on illegal activities like organ trafficking.

Data Security: As observed in the last decade, around 176 million data violations have been reported specifically in the healthcare sector. Here blockchain plays important role for data security by treating individual patients as private keys that will maintain health records unchanged until accessed by authorized person.

Transparency: Faithful transactions of unchanged health records are an added advantage of blockchain technique. It is applicable for the network where lack of trust issues exists among participants and data block size is limited, like the health industry.

22.6 ROLE OF BLOCKCHAIN IN ORGAN DONATION AND TRANSPLANTATION

The problem with organ donation systems around the world is that there are more people on the waiting list than real donors, and the gap is growing. Due to the length of the waiting list, patients may die before their organs are transplanted. The current organ donation and transplantation system also lacks in transparency [27]. These systems are typically slow, which is unbearable in a situation that is so critical and life threatening. These systems are hardly up to date with the very minimum of security and safety options. Modern systems use typical databases to handle and organize data, but most hospitals and other medical facilities lack a consistent data communication system [28, 29]. The existing organ recipient identification method in countries like India is heavily reliant on the organ waiting list supplied by the participating organ transplantation facility. There is no way to tell if the organ is reaching the person who needs it the most. As a result, poor patients do not receive organs on time, whereas the wealthy and influential have easy access to organs.

The goal of this scheme is multidimensional. This chapter discusses a blockchain-based system that can provide a corruption-free and efficient organ allocation process. The following objectives are taken into account by the blockchain-based system.

- A waiting list for organs and donors is recorded, which will be transparent to all parties involved.
- Organ matching of donors and recipients will take place on a blockchain-based decentralized network.
- Every transaction among any two network elements will be reviewed and verified.
- Any modifications to the priority list may be monitored, and the reasoning behind them can be investigated.

There has been a huge surge in the usage of blockchain technology in healthcare due to its practical benefits, trust in results, integrity, and nearly impregnable security [30]. The process of organ donation must be efficient, secure, distributed, trackable, and immutable, which can only be achieved through the proper application of blockchain technology. The potential for a blockchain-based approach to improve and streamline organ donation, transplantation, procurement, correct recipient identification, and decrease processing and transit delays is enormous.

The proposed organ donation system based on blockchain involves two phases. In the first phase, described in Figure 22.11, the organ donors register with the healthcare systems, and the patient in need

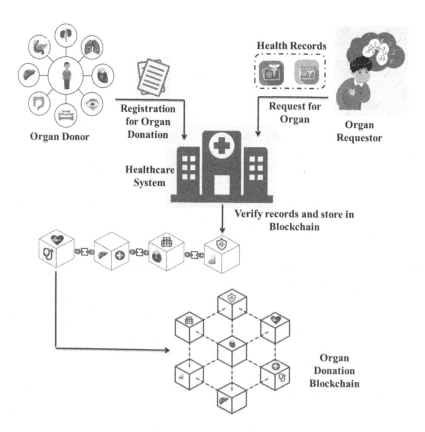

FIGURE 22.11 Blockchain-based registry of donors–patients.

of organs also registers with the healthcare system along with their healthcare records. The responsibility of the healthcare system is to verify the records of donors and requestors and generate the waiting list of patients for the organs. To achieve transparency in the system, the database of donors and requestors is stored in the blockchain so that the available organs reach to the right person on the waiting list.

The second phase depicts a typical use-case for the organ donation process when an organ becomes available in the system, as shown in Figure 22.12. The organ donor and the patient on the waiting list record can be thought of as a worldwide database built on blockchain technology and protected by cryptographic techniques. The process of matching available organs the patient healthcare records on the waiting list is done, which will improve the possibilities of quickly finding an appropriate match while remaining entirely safe. Encryption methods and procedures can be used to achieve confidentiality and privacy. Additionally, recognized digital certificates issued by authorized healthcare entities can be used to verify validity. The detailed description of the steps in Figure 21.12 are as follows:

1. The living donor who decides to donate an organ needs to undergo the medical tests; after that, the compatibility testing of the donor is fulfilled and the organ is surgically extracted from the donor's body. In case of a deceased or brain-dead donor, the organ is extracted after getting consent from the donor's family. In either case, when the organ becomes available in the healthcare system, the process of organ transplantation starts.
2. The organ allocation process is initiated when the organ becomes available for transplant. The common pool of the patient waiting list is available to all healthcare systems. The patient on the waiting list is identified and the healthcare records of that patient are matched with available organs.

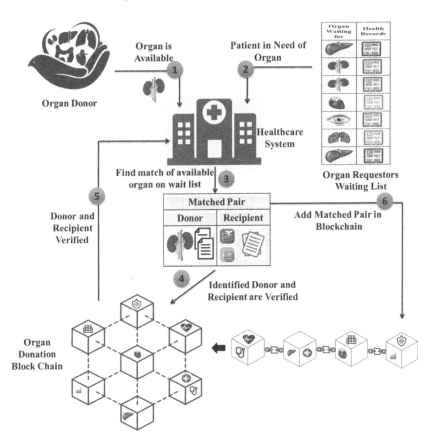

FIGURE 22.12 Blockchain-based organ donation process.

3. If the available organ is compatible in all respects with the recipient from the waiting list, the organ is allocated to that patient. The match pair of donor and organ is formed.
4. The identified pair of organ donor and recipient is broadcasted in the blockchain to verify the donors' and patients' records.
5. If the records are verified, then the approval is sent from the organ donation blockchain to the healthcare system.
6. After seeking approval, the organ transplantation procedure can be initiated, and the pair of organ donor and recipient patient is added into blockchain. The recorded pair of donor and recipient is now immutable and available for any future reference.

CONCLUSION

The difference in number of available organs and the number of needy patients for transplants on the waiting list is extending globally. The urgent need for organs promotes illegal transplants and organ trafficking. In this chapter, we focused on distinctive challenges in successful implementation of an organ donation and transplantation system globally that comprises legal, regulatory guidelines, shortcomings in infrastructure and healthcare machinery, weakness in management, and coordination among authorities and medico-legal teams. However, there is sufficient scope for directing and implementing the healthcare facilities to enhance effectiveness of overall organ donation and transplantation program. The chapter also elaborates possible blockchain-based cases and its applicability in healthcare. Blockchain's transparency, classified nature, and immutable record storage throughout all contributing users can support the minimizing of these operational costs. The chapter ends with the conclusion that emphasis should be on the adoptability of blockchain technology in organ donation and transplantation systems. This can safely coordinate and collect data from several providers, offer better patient commitment, and assist with assured availability of organ data, direct access, and secured communication between patients and doners. Appropriate use of technology to curb malpractice in the organ demand–supply system and to serve society for socio-economic harmony contributes indirectly to nations' growth.

REFERENCES

1. Ambagtsheer, Frederike. "Understanding the challenges to investigating and prosecuting organ trafficking: a comparative analysis of two cases." *Trends in Organized Crime* (2021): 1–28.
2. Cappadona, R., A. De Giorgi, E. Di Simone, M. Di Muzio, F. Di Muzio, N. Lamberti, F. Manfredini, A. Storari, R. Manfredini, and F. Fabbian. "Infodemiology of solid organ transplantation: relationship to the global observatory on donation and transplantation data." *European Review for Medical and Pharmacological Sciences* 24 (2020): 12630–12637.
3. www.transplant-observatory.org/
4. Mashadi, Ali. "Combating illegal organ transplantation under international human rights law." (2020): 27–49.
5. Haddiya, Intissar, Hicham El Meghraoui, Yassamine Bentata, and Mohammed Guedira. "Attitudes, knowledge, and social perceptions toward organ donation and transplantation in eastern Morocco." *Saudi Journal of Kidney Diseases and Transplantation* 31, no. 4 (2020): 821.
6. This is how much your body is worth. www.sciencealert.com (2015).
7. Edgar, Leith B., and Walter E. Block. "Toward the legalization of markets in used human body parts." *DialogiPolityczne* 30 (2021): 229–242.
8. Organ procurement and transplantation network. *U.S. Department of Health & Human Services.* https://optn.transplant.hrsa.gov/
9. I. Ulasi, C. Ijoma, N. Ifebunandu, E. Arodiwe, U. Ijoma, J. Okoye, U. Onu, C. Okwuonu, S. Alhassan, and O. Onodugo, "Organ Donation and Transplantation in Sub-Saharan Africa: Opportunities and Challenges", in *Organ Donation and Transplantation*. London, United Kingdom: IntechOpen, 2020 [Online]. Available: https://www.intechopen.com/chapters/74329 doi: 10.5772/intechopen.94986.
10. Loua, André, Margot Feroleto, Aissatou Sougou, Ossy Muganga Julius Kasilo, Jean Baptiste Nikiema, Walter Fuller, Stanislav Kniazkov, and Prosper Tumusiime. "A review of policies and programs for human

organ and tissue donations and transplantations, WHO African Region." *Bulletin of the World Health Organization* 98, no. 6 (2020): 420.

11. www.organdonor.gov/learn/organ-donation-statistics

12. Lewis, Amy, Angeliki Koukoura, Georgios-Ioannis Tsianos, Athanasios Apostolos Gargavanis, Anne Ahlmann Nielsen, and Efstathios Vassiliadis. "Organ donation in the US and Europe: the supply vs demand imbalance." *Transplantation Reviews* (2020): 100585.

13. Cole, Harrison. "The organ supply chain: geography and the inequalities of transplant logistics." *Transactions of the Institute of British Geographers* 4 (2021): 1008–1021.

14. Ali, Abeera, Tibyan Ahmed, Ali Ayub, Sumaya Dano, Maroof Khalid, Noor El-Dassouki, Ani Orchanian-Cheff, Shabbir Alibhai, and Istvan Mucsi. "Organ donation and transplant: the Islamic perspective." *Clinical transplantation* 34, no. 4 (2020): e13832.

15. Loua, André, Margot Feroleto, Aissatou Sougou, Ossy Muganga Julius Kasilo, Jean Baptiste Nikiema, Walter Fuller, Stanislav Etheredge, and Harriet Rosanne. "Assessing global organ donation policies: opt-in vs opt-out." *Risk Management and Healthcare Policy* 14 (2021): 1985.

16. Yazdi Moghaddam, H., Z. S. Manzari, A. Heydari, and E. Mohammadi. "Challenges in the management of care of brain-dead patients in the donation process: A qualitative content analysis." *International Journal of Organ Transplantation Medicine* 11, no. 3 (2020): 129.

17. Yılmaz Ferhatoglu, S., and N. Yapici. Brain Death and Organ Donation Rates in a City Hospital: A Retrospective Study. *Cureus* 11, no. 2 (February 04, 2019): e4006. doi:10.7759/cureus.4006

18. Lederer, Susan E. "Living donors and the issue of 'informed consent'." *Hastings Center Report* 50, no. 6 (2020): 8–9.

19. Iske, Jasper, Midas Seyda, Timm Heinbokel, Ryoichi Maenosono, Koichiro Minami, Yeqi Nian, Markus Quante et al. "Senolytics prevent mt-DNA-induced inflammation and promote the survival of aged organs following transplantation." *Nature Communications* 11, no. 1 (2020): 1–13.

20. Shroff, Sunil. "Legal and ethical aspects of organ donation and transplantation." *Indian Journal of Urology: IJU: Journal of the Urological Society of India* 25, no. 3 (2009): 348.

21. Deliva, Robin D., Catherine Patterson, Stephanie So, Vanessa Pellow, Stephanie Miske, Carol McLister, Cedric Manlhiot, Stacey Pollock-BarZiv, Alison Drabble, and Anne I. Dipchand. "The world transplant games: an incentive to improve physical fitness and habitual activity in pediatric solid organ transplant recipients." *Pediatric Transplantation* 18, no. 8 (2014): 889–895.

22. Ivan, Drew. "Moving toward a blockchain-based method for the secure storage of patient records." In *ONC/NIST Use of Blockchain for Healthcare and Research Workshop*. Gaithersburg, Maryland, United States: ONC/NIST, pp. 1–11, sn (2016).

23. Dettling, Walter. "How to teach blockchain in a business school." In *Business Information Systems and Technology 4.0*, pp. 213–225. Springer, Cham (2018).

24. Deore, Siddhesh, Ruturaj Bachche, Aditya Bichave, and Rachana Patil. "Review on applications of blockchain for electronic health records systems." In *International Conference on Image Processing and Capsule Networks*, pp. 609–616. Springer, Cham (2021).

25. Guo, Rui, Huixian Shi, Qinglan Zhao, and Dong Zheng. "Secure attribute-based signature scheme with multiple authorities for blockchain in electronic health records systems." *IEEE Access* 6 (2018): 11676–11686.

26. Attaran, Mohsen. "Blockchain technology in healthcare: challenges and opportunities." *International Journal of Healthcare Management* (2020): 1–14.

27. Dajim, Lama Abdulwahab, Sara Ahmed Al-Farras, Bushra Safar Al-Shahrani, Atheer Abdullah Al-Zuraib, and Rincy Merlin Mathew. "Organ donation decentralized application using blockchain technology." In *2019 2nd International Conference on Computer Applications & Information Security (ICCAIS)*, pp. 1–4, IEEE (2019). doi:10.1109/CAIS.2019.8769459

28. Niyigena, Clemence, Soonuk Seol, and Artem Lenskiy. "Survey on organ allocation algorithms and blockchain-based systems for organ donation and transplantation." In *2020 International Conference on Information and Communication Technology Convergence (ICTC)*, pp. 173–178, IEEE (2020). **doi:** 10.1109/ICTC49870.2020.9289421

29. Avdoshin, Sergey, and Elena Pesotskaya. "Blockchain in charity: platform for tracking donations." In *Proceedings of the Future Technologies Conference*, pp. 689–701. Springer, Cham (2020).

30. Chavez, Nicanor, Stefan Kendzierskyj, Hamid Jahankhani, and Amin Hosseinian. "Securing transparency and governance of organ supply chain through blockchain." In *Policing in the Era of AI and Smart Societies*, pp. 97–118. Springer, Cham (2020).

Index

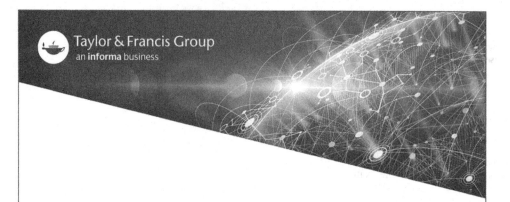

Printed in the United States
by Baker & Taylor Publisher Services